VOYAGE
OF THE
DAMNED

BY

GORDON THOMAS
AND
MAX MORGAN-WITTS

"VOYAGE OF THE DAMNED"
Second Edition published in 1994:-

in Great Britain by:
Dalton Watson Fine Books
P. O. Box 2, Belton, Loughborough LE12 9UW, England

ISBN 1-85443-123-4
British Library Cataloguing in Publication Data
A catalogue record for this book is available from the British Library

in the United States of America and Canada by:
Motorbooks International Inc.,
275 South Third Street, Stillwater, MN55802

ISBN 0-87938-909-5
Library of Congress Card Number available from the Library of Congress

© Copyright 1974 and 1994 – Gordon Thomas and Max Morgan-Witts

All rights reserved. Apart from any fair dealing for the purpose of private study, research, criticism or review, as permitted under relevant copyright legislation worldwide, no part of this book may be reproduced or transmitted in any form or by any means, electronic, electrical, chemical, mechanical, optical including photocopying, recording or by any other means placed in any information storage or retrieval system, without the specific written permission of the publishers.

Designed by: David G. Styles
Pageset by: Wordcrafts, 186 London Road, Leicester LE2 1ND, England.
Printed by: Budapest, Hungary,

Limited Leatherbound Library Edition (numbered 1-500) produced exclusively by Dalton Watson Fine Books
ISBN 1-85443-124-2.

VOYAGE
OF
THE
DAMNED

Give me your tired, your poor,
Your huddled masses yearning to breathe free,
The wretched refuse of your teeming shore.
Send those, the homeless, tempest-tost to me.
I lift my lamp beside the golden door.

INSCRIPTION BY EMMA LAZARUS

Statue of Liberty, New York Harbour

Yet there comes a time for forgetting,
for who could live and not forget?
Now and then, however, there must
also be one who remembers.

ALBRECHT GOES,
Das Brandopfer

PUBLISHER'S ACKNOWLEDGEMENTS

For their kind assistance in providing illustrations, guidance and sources of illustrations for this new edition, we are especially indebted to the Wiener Library in London, Dvora ben David and her colleagues at the Israeli Embassy in London, Rabbi Albert Friedlander at the Westminster Synagogue in London, the Senat der Freien und Handsestadt in Hamburg, the Hapag-Lloyd shipping line in Hamburg, Genya Markon and her colleagues at the United States Holocaust Memorial Museum in Washington DC, Shari Segal at the Museum of Jewish Heritage in New York, the Franklin D Roosevelt Library in New York and the following individuals:-

Mr & Mrs Alfred Aron
Reuben Babich
Mrs Renate Breslow
Philip Freund
Heinz Goldstein
Gerald Granston
Edgar Glucksman
Harry Goodman
Mrs Ruth Holman
Mrs Ruth Isner-Kissinger
Mrs Gerda Jockl
Herbert Karliner
Mrs Jane Keibel
Rabbi Barry J Konovitch

Dr Liane Reif-Lehrer
Mrs Liesl Joseph-Loeb
Mrs Vera Mahler
Mrs Gertrud Mendels
Dr Sol Messinger
Frank Metis
Gene Moser
Mrs Alice Oster
Stephen Rosenbach
Mrs Hella Roubicek
Rolf Schröder
Jules Wallerstein
John H Wolff

Every effort has been made to trace and record the source and copyright of illustrations used in this book, but if any material has been used which has not been properly acknowledged, we sincerely apologise and undertake to rectify the situation in future editions.

"VOYAGE OF THE DAMNED"

CONTENTS:

PUBLISHER'S PREFACE TO "VOYAGE OF THE DAMNED"

"Voyage of the Damned" is a story which could never have been told without the survivors. It is to them and their relatives that we are enormously indebted for the help given in our research for illustrations to expand the book into an even more notable document of history, for with illustrations, it truly comes alive.

There are pictures here of pre-war Germany, pre-war Hamburg in particular. There are picture "cameos" of families in Germany before World War Two – indeed, even some before the Great War of 1914-1918. This book will show you German citizens, Jewish by faith but German by nationality, who served their country in the Great War with pride and dignity. Some lost their lives in the service of their country and their families mourned them as German patriots. Many thousands of Jewish families had been in Germany for hundreds of years and were firmly established as part of the community, just as Catholic and Protestant Christians were part of that community.

Some of the illustrations in this book are quite chilling. For example, the passports which carried the red letter "J" to denote their Jewish bearers, the documents essential to departure from Germany in 1939, when that country was in the grip of one of the most horrifying reigns of terror in history. There are pictures of the key personalities involved, also the shipping documents, the pictures on the ship of passengers who earnestly thought they were bound for a new freedom – and more pictures taken after they realised that they were not. Among the most significant of these illustrations are those which form the Appendix to this book – the Passenger Manifest, listing the name of every passenger on board that fateful voyage which began on Saturday 13th May 1939 and which set the stage for Adolf Hitler's "Final Solution" – the Holocaust.

This magnificent book was first published in London in 1974 and has been the subject of the most glowing critical acclaim. It has been published in 22 editions worldwide in seven languages, but never with the illustrations which are before you in this edition. Most of these are hitherto unpublished private pictures and personal documents. As much as is possible for one who has never been through what these people went through, these illustrations, in company with the vibrant text, help to put you, the reader, "right there", sharing the passengers' experiences as they went from an environment of fear and suspicion to the peaks of elation and thence to the troughs of despair, relieved only at the eleventh hour by four relenting governments.

Universal Critical Acclaim for
VOYAGE OF THE DAMNED
by Gordon Thomas and Max Morgan-Witts

"Suspense, love, despair, unexpected acts of kindness mixed with treachery, Voyage of the Damned tells one of the most poignant stories in the long death march to the furnaces of Hitler's Holocaust . . . an extraordinary human document and a suspense story that is hard to put down. But it is more than that. It is a modern allegory, in which the St. Louis becomes a symbol of the SS Planet Earth. In this larger sense the book sense serves a greater purpose than mere drama."   New York Times

"A deeply moving and gripping account that poses moral questions as relevant now as they were then. It deserves a wide audience because this is the re-telling of a tragedy that holds lessons for us all.
"   Philadelphia Enquirer

"Probably the last great untold spy story to come out of the eve of World War II . . . a classic example of how propaganda can be used to dupe the whole world."   San Francisco Examiner

"The drama of the voyage, the fears, the mounting tension, the final corruption, all are told in skillful reportage that grips the interest throughout."   Nottingham Evening Post

"A shocking chronicle of a voyage of betrayal, fraud, corruption and broken promises. Yet the calm, meticulous documentary style is the perfect way for capturing the Kafkaesque atmosphere of the time."
                                                                      Present Tense, USA

"Riveting, written with passion, it should be widely read."   Publishers Weekly

"Chroniclers. They have written a book that will survive for many generations to come."   Forth Worth Press

"High level suspense and political chicanery – a combination guaranteed to keep you reading on and on."
                                                                      Chicago Tribune

"This book will wring your heart."   Dallas Morning News

"Evocative and shocking, it is both a triumph and a testament that will stand the test of time."
                                                                      Milwaukee Journal

"What make Voyage of the Damned so important is that it stands as a monument to mankind's ability to survive. Written with great skill and controlled passion, it is a monumental work which takes non-fiction on a new course."   Oakland Tribune, USA

"A moving story which should be read in some countries with shame."   Daily Mirror

"Everything about Voyage of the Damned has been touched with greatness."   New York Post

"Rich in detail . . . powerful in the writing."   El Pais, Spain

"Challenges the emotions, fires the spirit and seizes the heart."   Variety

"Perceptive, eloquent and enduring."   New York Sunday Post

"Poignant and moving."   McCalls Magazine

"Gripping and compulsively readable."   Sunday Express, UK

"There have been 10,000 books, and more, written on the Holocaust. Few can match this dramatic saga – all the more powerful for being told in a cool and swiftly moving way."   Yorkshire Post

"Adrift and alone, they were pawns in a plan that foretold the Nazi horrors to come. History with the power of a well-wrought suspense novel, will hold the reader gripped."   Literary Guild Journal, USA

"Detailed and meticulous, this admirable work is both an indictment and a thriller. One reads it with a mixture of excitement and anger."   Jewish Chronicle, USA

"Stark and shocking, few governments emerge from this deeply tragic affair with honour."
                                                                                      Yorkshire Evening News

"A poignant and powerful saga of deception and deceit – and courage beyond belief."   Morning Star, UK

"Fascinating, absorbing, anger-inducing – yet in the end a tribute to mankind's ability to rise above a chilling nightmare."   American Examiner

"Journalism at its best."   Philadelphia Bulletin

"Voyage of the Damned is one of the few books that are so powerful and so moving as to leave a lasting impression."   CBS News

"A gripping account that must be especially recommended to those who are too young to remember the Holocaust and the unspeakable actions man inflicted upon his fellow man. To read this book will, in a small way, help to atone for the sins of discrimination."   San Antonio Light, USA

"A real human drama with complex motivations and reactions. The sheer treachery and suspense and folly are told with acute sensitivity."   San Francisco Chronicle

"A brilliant book by two of the great masters of the 'you-are-there' genre of reportage."
                                                                                      Sunday Independent, Ireland

"A ship of ill-omen on a voyage with a powerful ending."   Sunday Times

"A spine-tingling, heart-rending book, you will weep and be humbled by this blot on the world's humanity. And yet it is also a story of unexpected triumph."   The Trintonian, USA

"Factual, objective, a detailed account of a voyage that should haunt everyone to this day."   Miami Herald

"A gripping narrative that has its parallel in the world today."   Jewish Chronicle, UK

"Voyage of the Damned is the Holocaust in miniature. An unforgettable account of racism, greed and isolationist world politics."   Jewish Times, USA

"Harrowing, evocative, unforgettable."   Detroit Free Press

"A truly meaningful book about the events leading up to World War II. Painstaking research has been set out in incisive reportage."   Times, Israel

"An epic account of pawns in a struggle for power."   Associated Press of America

"It lasted forty days . . . you will remember it until you die."   NBC Network Radio News

INTRODUCTION TO THE SECOND EDITION OF "VOYAGE OF THE DAMNED"

The historian William Manchester has said that research can be no substitute for wisdom; that the sum of a million facts is not the truth. To this he also wisely added the rider, an equal truth, that from time to time "the images and lost notes which drift down from the past" provide unexpected insights into the accumulation of data. So it is with this illustrated edition of "Voyage of the Damned".

It contains a great deal of new material which has surfaced – much donated by those who were directly involved in that epic voyage. The reason they have made their material available now, some twenty years after the original edition of this book was first published, is a very simple and moving one. The survivors hope their data will help to stem the growing world trends in anti-semitism. The word itself no longer applies exclusively to the racial persecution of Jews, but to an already large, and still growing, number of ethnic groups.

Through allowing us originally to share their experiences for this book, many of the survivors of the voyage of the Damned have remained friends. How could it be otherwise? There is something en-nobling in knowing these people: there is a dignity and simple honesty about them that is both fulfilling and a powerful reminder. To spend an hour in their company, or to read their letters is, we have found, an incentive to go on believing that all is not yet lost in our world.

Their faded photographs, yellowed documents and private correspondence provides an added poignancy to what they endured. Many said they could still, fifty-five years after the events described, only look at their own memorabilia with primaeval emotions they had thought excised.

What these images and "lost notes" provide is a context in which to understand that their own agony was played out against a world yearning to simple solutions. In many ways, there is an echo to this today in East and Western Europe, Africa and Asia – indeed in all those places wherein Man's inhumanity to Man is still in daily evidence.

GORDON THOMAS
ASHFORD, COUNTY WICKLOW
MAX MORGAN-WITTS
LONDON

1994

Dedication

This book is dedicated to those who were the damned, on the St. Louis, not only the passengers who are alive today and told their story to us, but all on board the ship, who were caught up in events they did not understand and could not control.

Those who survived the voyage and aftermath are today scattered throughout the world—North and South America, Great Britain, Australia, Europe, and, of course, Israel. And also Germany. Some are now wealthy, a few poor. Some still live in fear.

Almost everyone we approached was willing to meet us. One or two found that when the time came they could not bring themselves to recall and relive the experience. The minds of a few, in particular those who were young and impressionable in 1939, are now so cruelly scarred by what happened to them that their mental state led us, regretfully, to conclude their testimony was untrustworthy.

A few agreed to talk to us on condition that they not be quoted. We have respected this wish, understanding their desire for anonymity; what they told us was useful as background information and corroborative evidence. But they, and those unwilling or unable to meet us, were in the minority. For most, telling a stranger things they could hardly bring themselves to discuss with their closest friends seemed therapeutic, almost as if the experience was exorcised by the telling.

Inevitably, the passage of time, the insidious influence of propaganda, a confusion between what they have read and what actually happened, led some we interviewed to mix fiction with fact. We have tried to get around this by relying on interviews with survivors, crew members, and others directly involved with the voyage of the St. Louis, and consulting official archives, diaries, letters, and other eyewitness accounts written at the time.

Our responsibility to those living and dead was to tell the story as impartially and truthfully as the available sources and our combined talents allowed. Voyage of the Damned is not meant to be a crusading book, but it is, we hope, an honest and revealing one.

We thank especially those passengers whose names are listed below. Their experience has taught most of them to revere life, and to respect time. They told us something of the first, and granted us a precious proportion of the second. Without both, this book could not have been written.

Max S. Aber	Lilly Kamin (formerly Joseph)
Otto Bergmann	Carl Lenneberg
Rosemarie Bergmann	George Lenneberg
Hildie Bockow (formerly Reading)	Gisela Lenneberg
Liesl Loeb (nee Joseph)	Meta Bonne
Fritz Loewe	Richard Dresel
Gertrud Mendels (nee Scheuer)	Ruth Dresel
Werner Feig	Pessla Messinger
Alice Feilchenfeld	Frank Metis
Hans Fisher	George Moss
Herbert Glass	Thea Moss
Herta Glass	Renatta Rippe (nee Aber)
Rita Goldstein	Babette Spanier
Frank Gotthelf	Marianne Vargish(nee Bardeleben)
Herman Gronowetter	

Prologue

On January 30, 1933, Franklin Delano Roosevelt celebrated his fifty-first birthday; in little more than a month he would be president of the United States.

That same day, Adolf Hitler became chancellor of Germany; in a little less than two months, the Reichstag would make him absolute master of his country.

On taking office, the two men faced similar problems, but they chose opposite paths to a solution. Their policies would force them inexorably onto a collision course.

In Germany, the Fuehrer took over a country suffering from self-doubt and in the grip of an economic collapse so serious it seemed insoluble. His solution was to make the Jews scapegoat for all the nation's ills. Get rid of them, he maintained, and the patient would recover. Hitler never wavered from this prescription, never concealed it, and by May 1939, thousands had fled, thousands were in hiding, thousands in concentration camps. Though the gas ovens were not yet in operation, many people died daily of malnutrition and maltreatment, and what was happening in Dachau and Buchenwald was already known to the governments of the major powers.

In America, in 1933, Roosevelt had also been confronted by a critical situation. The worst economic crisis in history left banking in chaos: there were some twelve million unemployed; the nation was suffering from an acute loss of self-confidence.

In 1935, America's isolationism was strengthened with the passing of the Neutrality Act: the United States was not yet willing to take sides.

The Jews in Germany—there were some 500,000 of them when Hitler took power—were of two minds. Some viewed Hitler as a temporary aberration and waited, alas in vain, for things to change. Other Jews sought to escape. They illegally crossed the borders of Switzerland, Holland, Belgium, and France; they sometimes intentionally broke laws in order to be put into prison, a safer course than being returned to Germany. A small percentage made it to America or England. But for most of those trapped in the German concentration camps, or those about to be put to death, escape could come only if they could convince the Nazis that they could book passage on a ship that would take them away from the Fatherland. There were few ships available, and precious few countries willing to accept them as passengers.

By 1939, Britain, faced with an Arab revolt in the Middle East, was about to drastically curtail the number of immigrants it would allow into Palestine. At home, there were 25,000 refugees. Britain may have been more charitable than many other nations, but His Majesty's Government was preparing for all-out war, and there was no great enthusiasm for accepting more refugees from the country Britain was about to fight.

France, overflowing with some 250,000 refugees, many from Spain's Civil War, stated that it had reached the saturation point. A trickle of German refugees was allowed into certain South American, African, and Commonwealth countries, but not nearly as many as needed a haven. Shanghai was the end of the road; 15,000 found refuge there in two years. But even Shanghai's open door was soon to be shut when the Japanese occupied the port.

President Roosevelt appealed to the world for a suitable area "to which refugees could be admitted in almost unlimited numbers." Hitler suggested Madagascar. Roosevelt wrote to Rome about Ethiopia. Mussolini replied in favour of "the open areas of Russia." The Soviet Union considered Alaska appropriate. America suggested Angola; Portugal thought other places in Africa had more to commend them. The United States then favoured the Central African highlands for the German Jews, most of whom were middle-class professionals, shopkeepers, and businessmen now softened by centuries of European civilisation.

The Orinoco River valley in Venezuela, Mexico, the plateaus of south-western Africa, Tanganyika, Kenya, Northern Rhodesia, Nyasaland—the entire confusing collection of suggested sites was discussed, investigated, and dismissed, either by Jewish organizations or by national governments. Understandably, most of the refugees wanted to go to the legendary land of opportunity, America.

Throughout the thirties, America stuck rigidly to its old immigration laws. Her early settlers were mainly British, Irish, and other northern European whites. When the quota system was introduced, it had the effect of maintaining America's status quo: the number of immigrants allowed in from any one country depended on the proportion of settlers who were already in America from that country around the turn of the century. Thus a system originally introduced to stop the wholesale entry of "undesirables" of the nineteenth century was, by 1939, acting as a deterrent in a quite different situation.

The United States was prepared to accept 25,957 immigrants from Germany per year, in normal times a relatively large number, but in the critical situation of German Jews, all too few. In any case, since the Jews in Germany were hardly treated as ordinary Germans, the question remained: of the 25,957 Germans allowed into America per year, how many should be German Jews? The answer often depended on the personal inclinations of American consular officials in Germany.

Any applicants "likely to become a public charge" were refused. The ten Reichsmarks—about four dollars—Germany allowed refugees to take with them was insufficient, according to many consular officials. Nor did the officials always understand it was not possible for the refugees to acquire from the Nazi government the character references required for admission to the United States.

Eleanor Roosevelt, wife of the President, was sympathetic to the plight of the refugees; she favoured every move in support of refugee aid. But her husband Franklin Roosevelt was a politician who knew it was hazardous to ignore public opinion. The majority of the American electorate, then as now, wished not to be involved in the affairs of others. A large part of the populace, "middle America," the blue-collar class, was openly anti-Semitic. Many were themselves earlier emigrants from central and eastern European countries where anti-Semitism was endemic. In America, they were further influenced by men like Father Charles E. Coughlin, the Detroit priest who used his Sunday-afternoon radio broadcasts to preach Nazi principles to an audience of fifteen million. In Yorkville, American heart of Nazism, the Fuehrer of the German-American Bund, Fritz Kuhn, found especially receptive audiences for his views; large crowds thronged to Madison Square Garden for Nazi rallies.

Roosevelt's cabinet was not generally composed of men inclined to confront the issue. Some senior members, such as Secretary of State Cordell Hull, seemed to have been chosen more for their usefulness as a bridge between the President and the conservative senators than for their energy or diplomatic and intellectual abilities. And most congressmen were rigidly isolationist.

In 1939, with an election pending, an opinion poll showed that 83 per cent of the electorate was against increasing the number of refugees allowed into the country. The message was clear: any president would change the American immigration laws at his peril.

Refugees from Germany, who wished to enter the United States, if they were able to satisfy all the requirements, were put on the quota. This gave them a place on the increasingly long waiting list; when their number came up in the queue, they would be allowed in. In 1939, many on the quota were told the waiting time for them would be years. They knew they would not survive the delay; they had to find somewhere outside Germany where they could wait safely until their numbers came up and they could then enter America. There were few friendly countries who offered this essential temporary refuge.

Cuba was the only country close to the United States willing to accept refugees in large numbers—for a price. But the question was, Which Cuban politicians would get the money?

By early May 1939, the cast for the drama was beginning to assemble. They were 937 men, women, and children. Some had been on the run, some in concentration camps, some had been waiting to be imprisoned; all were seeking an opportunity to escape.

The decision that they would be allowed to leave Germany was approved during a working luncheon in a private dining room of the Hotel Adlon in Berlin, in April 1939.

For Reichsmarschal Hermann Goering the decision was a practical temporary solution. He accepted the Fuehrer's directive that there must be a final solution to the Jewish Problem, but until it could be implemented, he was in favour of letting Jews go. Naturally the Reich would extract as high a price as possible:

confiscation of all goods and property except personal clothing, or the imposition of prohibitively high taxes—payable preferably in the foreign currency needed to boost Germany's faltering economy and to purchase raw materials for a war to come.

What most interested the Nazis was the use that could be made of the ship and its passengers once it had left Germany. Dr. Joseph Goebbels, Minister of Propaganda, spoke openly at the luncheon. The voyage could be exploited to the full for propaganda purposes: the German nation could be told that it was part of the general "housecleaning" operation; the world at large could be told that here was clear evidence that Germany was allowing Jews to leave unharmed and unimpeded. The host, Admiral Wilhelm Canaris, head of German Military Intelligence —the Abwehr—laid his plans quietly. By the time he returned to his second-floor office at 72-76 Tirpitz Ufer, he had begun to work out a scheme. The ship would be used for an important espionage mission. And so it was that in May 1939, the S.S. St. Louis sailed into a sea of uncertainty, one of the last ships to leave Nazi Germany before Europe was engulfed in war.

PICTURE PROLOGUE:

Even before the turn of the Century, Isidore Karliner ran this small general store on Tasterstrasse in Peiskretscham, Silesia. The lady in the doorway is Herbert Karliner's grandmother with some of her children. The picture was taken in 1909. (Herbert Karliner)

When war came in 1914, many thousands of Germans loyal to the Kaiser and the Fatherland joined the armed forces to fight for their country. The man marked out is Alfred Moses, shown here in a platoon picture taken in 1914, before the real battles began. (Gene A Moser)

Below: Hermann Goldstein had a studio photo taken for his family at home, before entering the fray of the 1914-1918 War ......

..... But then, a photo "in the field" shows Cavalryman Goldstein on horseback. The caption on the back, addressed to his wife, read: "So that my dear Rita may see that I know how to handle a war horse, I enclose this important document". (The collection of Henry Gallant, now in the US Holocaust Memorial Museum)

Schnellzugbenutzung gestattet.
Immob.-Bhfs-Kdtr. I Breslau

Urlaubs-Schein.

OFFENBURG
23. JUL 1916

Der *Kanonier Alfred Moses*

von der __2.__ Kompagnie 1. Garnison-Bataillon VI. A. K. wird hiermit

vom __24. Mai__ bis einschl. __20. Juni__ 1916

nach *Haslach im Kinzigtale (Baden)* beurlaubt.

Alle Behörden werden ersucht, ihn ungehindert reisen zu lassen und ihm
nötigenfalls Schutz und Hilfe zu gewähren.

Neustadt O.-S., den __23. Mai__ 1916.

OFFENBURG
B.E. AUG 16

Darf den _____ fahren

HASLACH
23. JUL 16

OFFENBURG

This leave pass issued to Alfred Moses was originally for one month, but was extended from the expiry date of June to August, before he returned to the lines. (Gene A Moser)

Even in the thick of battle, there was the odd occasion for a photo and this one shows Hermann Goldstein (third from right on the second row) with his cavalry platoon. (The collection of Henry Gallant, now in the US Holocaust Memorial Museum)

This was Gerschon Reif's mobilisation document with which he was enlisted into the infantry. (Dr Liane Reif-Lehrer)

In Austria too, Jews were accepted as part of the community – citizens, not a race apart. A certificate similar to this magnificent example was presented to all who served the Fatherland in the Great War. This one was presented to Dr Gerschon Reif, who later became a dentist in Vienna. The translation on the right explains the document fully. (Dr Liane Reif-Lehrer)

Dr. Gerson Reif

One-year volunteer Corporal in the 18th k.k. [kaiserlich-königlich] rifle-regiment

Enlisted in the k.k. infantry regiment 18 in 1915 and went into battle against Russia with them. Deployed in the area of Luck, he joined in all the battles of his regiment, and during the Brussilov Offensive near Luck he was taken prisoner and put in the camp in Kiev, where he remained until the treaty of Bresk-Litovsk, and was thereafter released home. He was granted a study-leave, studied medicine, and then returned to the regiment, until the collapse [of the Austro-Hungarian empire] shortly thereafter. In November of 1918 he finally disarmed [left the military for good] and in 1924 took his degree as a general practitioner of medicine.

As peace returned to Europe, so Berlin put out the banners and the Kaiser went to visit wounded German soldiers, Jews and Gentiles, as well as being seen in the celebrations marking the end of war. (Edgar Glucksman)

In peacetime, Jewish youths were as much a part of sporting achievements as any others in the community. This German Sports Club award booklet tells us that Heinrich Glucksmann achieved his bronze medal for swimming in 1928, when just 17 years old. (Edgar Glucksman)

Unterschrift des Bewerbers:

Heinrich Glücksmann

Das Lichtbild und die eigenhändige Unterschrift des Bewerbers wird hiermit beglaubigt.

Der Bewerber hat sich durch Vorlage des (Name, Nr. und Datum) amtlichen Ausweises _____ genügend ausgewiesen.
(Nicht Zutreffendes ist zu streichen.)

Stempel und Unterschrift des Verbandes bzw. Vereins, der Ortsgruppe oder des Truppenteils

Schwimmklub „Wasserfreunde"
OPPELN
Krakauer Strasse Nr. 22
(Geschäftsstelle u. Kasse)

2

B.R.A.f.L.
Eing. 19 SEP. 1928

Deutsches Turn-
~~nd~~ Sportabzeichen
für Männer

...ng des Deutschen Reichsausschusses für Leibesübungen

Vor- und Zuname des Bewerbers:

...einrich Glücksmann

Geboren am *25. November 1909*

...einsangehörigkeit des Bewerbers:

Schwimmklub Wasserfreunde Oppeln

Name des Verbandes: *Deutscher Schwimmverband*

Wohnort (Ort) des Bewerbers: *Oppeln O/Schlesien*

(Straße, Hausnummer) *Karlstraße 3 I*

Bewerbung um das Sportabzeichen in: ~~Gold~~ - ~~Silber~~ - Bronze
(Nichtzutreffendes ist zu streichen)

Generalsekretariat des Deutschen Reichsausschusses für Leibesübungen
BERLIN W 35, Kurfürstenstraße 48. Fernruf: Kurfürst 4192

6. 23. 10 000. 83.

3

By the early 1930s, scenes like this in Hamburg were becoming commonplace. (Senat der Freien und Handsestadt, Hamburg)

Austria, on the other hand, was not yet blighted by the Third Reich and so there were still carefree family pictures being taken like this one of young Fred Reif, giving a violin recital in his home town of Vienna in March 1933. (Dr Liane Reif-Lehrer)

After the recital came this portrait of Fred with his mother. The dread was yet to come. (Dr Liane Reif-Lehrer)

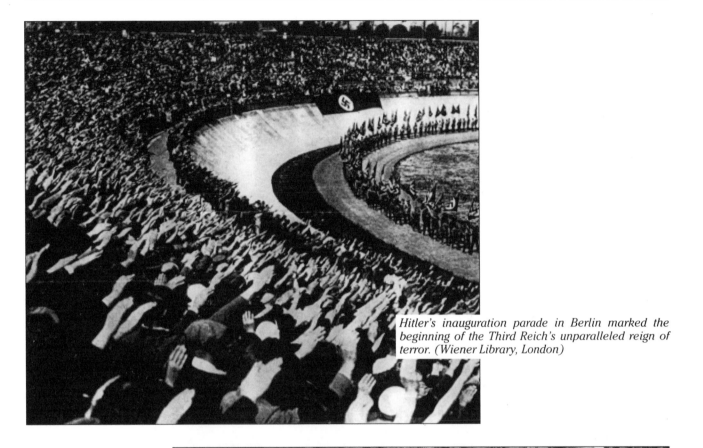

Hitler's inauguration parade in Berlin marked the beginning of the Third Reich's unparalleled reign of terror. (Wiener Library, London)

By the mid-1930s, Hamburg had taken on the appearance of a flourishing modern harbour city. (Senat der Freien und Handsestadt, Hamburg)

The centre of Hamburg in the late 1930s gives and
air of peaceful prosperity – the "Star of Northern
Germany" as someone described it. (Senat der
Freien und Handsestadt, Hamburg)

By the end of the Thirties, Hamburg's waterways were flourishing and prosperous, the base for the prestigious Hamburg-Amerika Line, HAPAG. (Senat der Freien und Handsestadt, Hamburg)

November 9th, 1938 brought "Kristallnacht" (the
night of broken glass) and with it the true scale of
the potential horror facing Jewish families and
businesses, when shops, houses and synagogues
were smashed and many people arrested and taken
to labour camps. (Wiener Library, London)

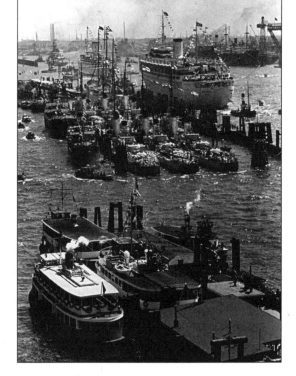

By early 1939, Hamburg was taking on a new aura,
too, as the scene here shows, with six Kriegsmarine
frigates nestling alongside each other amidst the
commercial bustle of liners and freighters plying
their way into and out of the harbour. (Senat der
Freien und Handsestadt, Hamburg)

As events developed in early 1939, so the Motor Ship "St Louis" was to become a significant player in a new and sinister drama. Here, the vessel is shown just after its launch in 1928, during fitting-out, and sitting fully be-decked in Hamburg Harbour shortly before its momentous journey in May 1939. (Hapag-Lloyd, Hamburg)

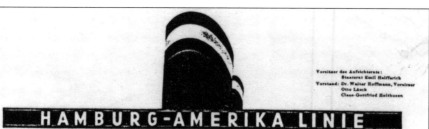

Vorsitzer des Aufsichtsrats:
Staatsrat Emil Helfferich
Vorstand: Dr. Walter Hoffmann, Vorsitzer
Otto Lösch
Claus-Gottfried Holthusen

HAMBURG-AMERIKA LINIE

Reisebüro am Hauptbahnhof Hamburg

FERNSPRECHER: 345625, 221001, NEBENANSCHLUSS 904, FÜR FERNGESPRÄCHE 225027
DRAHTWORT: HALREISE HAMBURG / POSTSCHECK: HAMBURG 4300
BANKKONTO: DEUTSCHE BANK FILIALE HAMBURG
UNTER: HAPAG-REISEBÜRO AM HAUPTBAHNHOF HAMBURG

Ihr Zeichen: Unser Zeichen: HAMBURG-HAUPTBAHNHOF
_____ / Kü./Sch.   (Hapaggebäude)

den 2.Mai 1939

Frau
Edith Sara L ö w i n s o h n ,
Berlin-Charlottenburg 4,
Mommsenstrasse 20.

Betr.: Sonderfahrt nach Habana M-S."St.Louis" am 13.Mai ab Hamburg.

    Wir bestätigen Ihren telephonischen Anruf und teilen I[hnen]
höflichst mit, dass wir die Originalschiffskarten, wie bereits in un[serem]
Schreiben vom 29.April erwähnt, erst in Hamburg aushändigen können.
Unsere Empfangsscheine werden jedoch von der Polizeibehörde anerkann[t],
wenn Sie diese vorlegen.

    Wir überreichen Ihnen jedoch der Sicherheit halber noc[h]
eine besondere Bescheinigung für die Polizeibehörde, die Sie mit uns[erem]
Empfangsschein zusammen vorlegen wollen.

    Stets gern für Sie beschäftigt, zeichnen wir inzwische[n]

        mit bester Empfehlung

        Hamburg-Amerika Linie
        Reisebüro am Hauptbahnhof

Anlage.

BÄDERAUSKUNFTSTELLE DER WELTKURORTE KARLSBAD, MARIENBAD, FRANZENSBAD, TEPLITZ-SCHÖNAU

Schiffspassagen nach allen Welthäfen / Vergnügungs- und Erholungsreisen zur See. Hapag-Nord- und Teilfahrten. Hapag-Mittelmeerfahrten.
Atlantische Inselfahrten. Hapag-Reisen um die Welt. Hapag-Westindienfahrten / Hapag Seebäderdienst G. m. b. H. / Reisebüro / Eisenbahnfahrkarten,
Bett- und Platzkarten / Ihrer-Fahrscheinhefte in beliebiger Zusammenstellung für In- und Ausland / Pauschal- und Gesellschaftsreisen
Hotelgutscheine / Geldwechsel / Reisekreditbriefe / Passvisa / Reisegepäckversicherung / Buchungsstelle für Zeppelinfahrten / Luftverkehr.

Geöffnet: Werktags von 9 bis 18 Uhr, Sonntags von 10 bis 12 Uhr.
Sonnabends bis 15 Uhr.

As the "voyage of the Damned" drew near, so intending passengers were notified by letters like this of the vessel's sailing. (Mrs Hella Roubicek)

I

A Chance

To Live

WEDNESDAY, MAY 3, 1939

The captain of the Hamburg-America Line passenger ship St. Louis did not look forward to the meeting that cool Wednesday morning of May 3, 1939. For the first time in his thirty-seven years at sea Gustav Schröder was uncertain and uneasy about a voyage.

The newly pressed blue serge trousers and high-buttoning jacket were, for him, a reminder that his meeting with line director Claus-Gottfried Holthusen was to be an important one; usually Schröder slipped into his favourite gray suit to go ashore for his end-of-voyage report to the marine superintendent in Hapag House, a few blocks away from shed 76, where the St. Louis was now tied up on the Hamburg waterfront.

But this morning, when the liner berthed after another voyage from New York, Schröder had been ordered to report personally to Holthusen.

After he dressed, slowly and carefully, Schröder once more opened the wall safe in his day cabin to read the cable again to seek a clue in its content.

The message had come during dinner some eight hundred miles out of New York when his steward discreetly handed him the radiogram. It gave him an excuse to leave the tedious table talk about Hitler and Nazi dreams of expansion in the half-empty first-class dining room.

The absence of passengers—the liner was less than a third full—was depressing evidence of the deepening world crisis. The majority on board were Germans returning from the United States. Some of them wore party badges and were pleased to see that many of the crew also displayed the Nazi emblem on their uniforms. The fact that the captain did not caused much comment, but no one dared raise the matter with him.

He was reputed to be precise, studious, and correct in all details. To his deck officers he seemed to be of the courtly nineteenth century, not of the twentieth. But when Schröder was roused by something that displeased him, his language was so forceful and salty that it stunned those he addressed. He was also said to be "the smallest officer in the German merchant navy," and "the Graf on the bridge." Captain Schröder was only five feet, four

inches tall, but although he was small, it seemed immaterial. His body had hardly an ounce of surplus fat; he practised callisthenics for twenty minutes each day without fail. The only wrinkles on his face were tiny crow's feet fencing his clear, blue eyes; he had the look of a man who had measured distant horizons all his life. His hair was gray, clipped short at the temples. He had it trimmed once a week by his steward. His skin was tanned from almost a lifetime at sea. Gustav Schröder looked what he was—an energetic, experienced, and capable captain.

After the cable came, Schröder had deciphered the apparently meaningless numbers. The code had been introduced by the line to communicate confidential information to its captains at sea. In the four months he had commanded the 16,732-ton liner, Schröder had never before received a coded message.

The coded cable was typical of the nagging pressures now intruding on his orderly life. Recently such pressures had exceeded the bounds of what Schröder believed were proper company demands. He was increasingly aware of the intrusion of Nazi influence on his ship, and did not like it. There had been the compulsory signing on of six Gestapo agents as firemen officially on board to check sabotage attempts. A few voyages before, in New York, a bomb threat had been made against the St. Louis. No bomb was found, but the rumour made it difficult for Schröder to argue that the firemen were not needed. The Gestapo agents had tightened security precautions and made attempts to spread party doctrines to all sections of the crew. Schröder ordered them to stop such blatant propaganda, but he knew it was impossible to enforce such an order. He personally loathed the Nazi ideology; he had steadfastly maintained to his few close friends that as long as he believed in Germany's future as he did in the company's destiny, he would continue to oppose Hitler's doctrines. But he must do so circumspectly.

The most serious interference with the captain's command was the presence of a second-class steward he had inherited when he took command of the St. Louis in February 1939. Otto Schiendick had established himself as the ship's Ortsgruppenleiter, but his powers went beyond those of mere party political shop steward. He had arranged for at least two members of the crew to be forcibly removed from the ship for expressing attitudes not in keeping with Nazi policy. His greatest coup had been the dismissal of Captain Friedrich Buch, master of the St. Louis since its maiden voyage in 1929; Buch had been escorted from the ship by Gestapo agents under Schiendick's guidance.

Captain Schröder took over from Buch, and during the short time he had been in command, tension had grown between him and Schiendick. Each man tested the other's strengths and weaknesses, waiting for a chance to make one swift, decisive thrust that would resolve the conflict. By simply not wearing the party badge Captain Schröder knew he had made himself vulnerable; in the end, either he or Schiendick and the Gestapo "firemen" would have to go.

For six years Schröder had resisted requests to join the Nazi party. Before the last voyage, a line official called on him as the ship was about to sail and warned him that refusal to join the party might mean loss of command. Schröder was shaken, but he ordered the man off the ship.

Perhaps the radiogram was retribution for that action. The message he found was simple but mysterious: his next voyage was to be an unscheduled, "special" trip. He was filled with apprehension.

Schröder knew his meeting with Holthusen was linked with that message; he had remembered that the director had responsibility within the company for all "special" ventures. Claus Gottfried Holthusen was one of the most powerful men in German shipping. Schröder had met him only once, some four months earlier, shortly after taking command of the St. Louis. At a lunch given by the company for its captains, Schröder had sat opposite Holthusen. The director was expansive, suave, and charming; Schröder was shocked that he so easily accepted Nazi domination of the line. Holthusen's optimistic predictions at that luncheon had not come true: Hamburg-America, Hapag, was in deeper financial difficulties. Schröder hoped Holthusen would reassure him that the line was in good health; he trusted the line would return "to the old ways."

In 1934, the Reich had become the majority shareholder, and the company had lost the independence it had successfully defended for ninety years. The swastika flying over the portal of the sombre Hapag House represented a major upheaval involving both the Gestapo and German Military Intelligence, the Abwehr. Many of the line's ships now carried espionage couriers as crew members; the Gestapo had a number of agents constantly watching the staff.

Schröder walked into Hapag House, a place that seemed to him to have little to do with the sea, filled with its clerks perched on high stools, concerned with profits and apparently little else. As he reached Holthusen's office he wondered whether the time had come for him to present his resignation; if not immediately, then he would do so soon.

Holthusen was in no hurry to come to the point. He discussed the last voyage. Had there been any problems? It was the opening Gustav Schröder wanted. He told him bluntly that there were "disruptive elements" on board. He described "the intrusion of politically motivated persons."

Holthusen was silent.

Then, in the loud, confident voice Schröder remembered and disliked, Holthusen said: "There are some things which are better left alone. For your own good, and the good of the company."

Schröder was too disappointed to speak. He could expect no support to rid the St. Louis of its Nazi elements.

Holthusen was speaking again, this time about the "special" voyage. The St. Louis was to carry nearly 1000 refugees from Germany to Cuba. The trip would require "the greatest tact" on Schröder's part. Though he was new to command, it had been decided that only Schröder had the necessary qualities for such a voyage.

"Most important of all, Captain," the director continued, "this trip will ensure that your ship is fully booked at a time when our financial resources are at a low ebb."

Captain Schröder responded to this appeal to his company loyalty. He had one question: Who were the refugees?

"Jews. But nothing out of the ordinary. Only people wanting to leave Germany," Holthusen replied.

Schröder knew now that he must not resign

Born and raised in the
atmosphere of an aca-
demic German family, the
sea had always held a
strong appeal for young
Gustav Schröder. Even at
the time these photo-
graphs were taken, his
longing for a life which, as
he would later write: "...is
far and away, homeless
on the high sea" was
strong. In the top photo-
graph, he is seen in sea
cadet's uniform, whilst the
lower shows him in a
more formal family
portrait, standing at the
back between his father
and mother. (Rolf
Schröder)

Sea Cadet Schröder (left) first went to sea on sailing ships. Today, we have no record of the name of the vessel, but on the right is the ship upon which he learned seamanship and below is Schröder at the helm. (Rolf Schröder)

Sport and fitness were always a passion of Gustav Schröder, seen on the left at a sports meeting. On the right is Schröder as a young Seaman Officer aboard the "SS Titania" in 1914. (Rolf Schröder)

Above is Gustav Schröder (sitting), with his brother, Ernst, who became a journalist and author. To the right is Gustav on a home leave shortly before assuming command of the "Oceana". (Rolf Schröder)

These two pictures are of the idyllic countryside around the Schröder family home in Prussia. They travelled with Gustav Schröder wherever he went, finding pride of place in his cabin. (Rolf Schröder)

Above left is Schröder (second from left) with other members of the crew of the "Titania", and right is the newly-promoted Captain Gustav Schröder upon his appointment as Master of the "MS Oceana". Below is the ship of his first command – the "Oceana". (Rolf Schröder)

Left: Captain Schröder moves among his passengers on board the "Oceana" (Rolf Schröder) and below right: Schröder's second and last sea command, the "St Louis", from a shipping line brochure. (Hapag-Lloyd, Hamburg)

Captain Schröder's official portrait upon appointment as Master of the "St Louis". (Rolf Schröder)

Neither Schiendick, the Gestapo agents, nor anyone else said a word. Gustav Schröder returned to his cabin aware that he would have to take with him to Cuba members of a crew who actively hated the passengers for whom he would be responsible.

The first of those passengers—the Spanier family—arrived in Hamburg late that same evening of May 3, ten days before the St. Louis was due to sail. They came in a car flying a swastika and driven by a young S.S. officer.

On the long drive from Berlin, Dr. Fritz Spanier repeatedly whispered to his wife that this was the most bizarre twist of fate they had experienced in six years of increasing persecution; the memory of his remark remains with Babette Spanier to this day.

In April 1933, a Nazi decree barred Jews from

Otto Schiendick, second class steward on board the "St Louis" and the Nazi Party's "Orstgruppenleiter". (Gordon Thomas collection)

until he had delivered the refugees to Cuba. But as he was driven back to the ship, he felt deeply perturbed by a conviction that the director had not been totally frank about the voyage.

His first action aboard was to muster the entire ship's complement in the first-class social hall. He briefed them on the forthcoming voyage and its passengers, then took the first deliberate step toward a confrontation with Otto Schiendick and the Gestapo "firemen," as he announced: "Any of you who do not want to accompany these people to Cuba can sign off now."

working in state hospitals or clinics. Within a year, Dr. Spanier had to move his wife and seven-year-old twin daughters, Renee and Ines, from his comfortable home in the fashionable Berlin suburb of Dahlem, to a more predominantly Jewish quarter of the city. He found work in private practice, Babette Spanier was still able to dress fashionably in the Paris models offered by the Kurfuerstendamm shops. The family continued to go sailing at weekends on the Wansee; they could still buy lox and matzo. Dr. Spanier avoided those who said there were only two alternatives to the worsening situation: arm and fight, or leave Germany. The majority of his friends and relatives, anchored by their possessions and inured to the prospect of suffering, also stayed on.

Once, out of curiosity, he had attended a meeting of an underground Zionist organisation. The twenty present had listened to a young man arguing that if each Jew in Germany was prepared to kill one Nazi before being taken to the camps, the wave of arrests would end. Hitler would realise he could not continue such persecution. It might take hundreds, even thousands, of lives, but it would happen.

Dr. Spanier had been shocked by the crudity of the plan. He could not accept that argument that those who had already gone so meekly to the concentration camps had doomed the rest. He had never attended another meeting. He ignored all the signs until July 25, 1939, when a decree drove Jewish doctors even from private practice. A few were authorised to serve their own community; Dr. Spanier was one of them.

Four months later had come the Kristallnacht. On that "night of broken glass," November 9/10, 1938, the Nazis committed a national act of vengeance against all German Jews in the Third Reich: 191 synagogues were desecrated, 171 Jewish-owned apartment houses set on fire, 7500 Jewish shops looted; 20,000 Jews were taken into "protective custody," half of them being shipped to Buchenwald camp. The police made only 117 arrests of non-Jewish Germans; not one was ever brought to trial.

The Spaniers escaped unhurt, but soon afterward they were forced to escape from their rented apartment to a garret owned by a widow. Her son was a medical student, and Dr. Spanier befriended and helped tutor him, not knowing the youth was a member of the S.S. When the student heard that the Spaniers were due to be arrested in the next roundup of Jews, he offered to drive the family to Hamburg.

Some time before that Dr. Spanier had spent 3000 Reichsmarks on permits for the family to enter Cuba and later, hopefully, the United States; he had kept to himself the knowledge that the permits were worthless unless the family obtained passage to Cuba. For weeks he had haunted the Berlin travel agencies that specialised—and grew fat—on "facilitating" the departure of refugees.

When he was informed of the impending arrest, he tried again, and fortunately, found one agency that was selling tickets for the St. Louis. He bought four first-class berths for 3200 Reichsmarks.

He paid an extra 1000 Reichsmarks for permission to take his surgical instruments out of the country. All the money had come from a relative in Canada. The family were assigned to cabins 111 and 113 on B Deck. By mid afternoon of May 3, they held the papers that could keep them from Dachau, or Sachsenhausen, or Buchenwald.

Babette Spanier had spent a busy morning selling off what remained of her household goods to buy more clothes for the twins; Renee and Ines now had enough dresses to last them for the next five years. She bought a topcoat for her husband and a fur wrap for herself, and packed the family's remaining possessions into trunks.

Babette Spanier had been reluctant to leave Berlin. In spite of the insults, the taunts, the jostling on the pavements, the shops, theatres, and cinemas proscribed to her and her family, she wished to stay, because, as she explained later, she was a Seidemann, and there had been Seidemanns in the Ruhr for more than four hundred years: "We regarded ourselves as German through and through. We spoke German, we thought in German, we were German. The very idea of leaving the country where our roots were was heartbreaking."

There was another, and more personal, reason why Babette Spanier did not wish to emigrate. Her marriage was in difficulty; she feared that it could not survive a move halfway across the world, that her handsome husband might divorce her once they reached his ultimate goal, America. But, faced with the sailing tickets, the spectre of the Gestapo, and her husband's promise of a "wonderful new life ahead," she, with the children, left Berlin; she was comforted by her husband's hand in hers throughout the journey.

That evening, in Hamburg, near the railway station, their car was forced to a halt by men and youths from a big Nazi rally who surrounded it. Many carried party banners on their shoulders, like rifles, rolled tight around the staves. Suddenly a squad of storm troopers surged toward a man coming out of the railway station, carrying a cheap suitcase. He tried to flee, but the soldiers were too quick. They rammed him against the wall, kicking and jabbing him with their staves. In moments the storm troopers stepped back, leaving him crumpled on the sidewalk.

In the back of the car the twins whimpered; their mother calmed them with a lullaby. Only later did she realise she had crooned a Jewish lament her mother had sung to her. As the car drove on, protected by its swastika flag and uniformed S.S. driver, Dr. Spanier noticed dozens of people staring at the figure on the ground. Not fifty yards away a squad of armed policemen ignored the whole incident. The Spaniers saw the man crawling away, shaking his shaved head, dragging his suitcase behind him. Though they did not know it, he had also come to Hamburg to board the St. Louis.

That night the young S.S. officer drove them to a small hotel in the old quarter of Hamburg. Inside, a sign over the desk stated: "Jews forbidden." Dr. Spanier booked two adjoining rooms, and then the family shook hands with the benefactor who gave each of the children ten Reichsmarks and wished them all a safe journey.

Shortly afterward two Gestapo officers arrived at the hotel.

About a mile from the hotel, Aaron Pozner, the man who had been beaten, finally found a hiding place that even the Gestapo would have little stomach to stand. He had dragged himself down to the waterfront and there, a few cable lengths from the St. Louis, he discovered a yard stacked with animal hides from an adjoining slaughterhouse. Born and raised in a farming community, he knew the skins would be left undisturbed for weeks to cure. So, tying a handkerchief across his nose and mouth, he burrowed into the pile of skins, ignoring the dried blood and pieces of flesh, the flies, and the stench. For a man who had survived Dachau, it was not hard

to bear.

On Kristallnacht, 178 days ago, Pozner, a Hebrew teacher, had been dragged from his home by the Gestapo and shipped to Dachau, one of some 8000 Jews brought to the camp during that November night. His head had been shaved, and his clothes exchanged for a coarse linen suit with a yellow star

This sketch of Aaron Pozner was drawn in 1946 by the ship's hairdresser, Irene Benowski. Mrs Bendowski produced the sketch as part of the effort of the crew and passengers to find survivors of the voyage who would tell the world what happened. In the case of Aaron Pozner, it helped to establish what became of him. (Authors' collection)

stamped on it; it became his badge of shame, an excuse for the guards to beat him at every opportunity. His only link with the outside world—a snapshot of his wife, Rachel, and his small children, Simon and Ruth—was snatched from him by a guard, who urinated over it.

He wrote in his diary of the public hangings after morning roll call which he was forced to witness, the public floggings before afternoon roll call, and the drownings in vats after the evening count. In between there were crucifixions, garrottings, and, the speciality of one guard, castration by bayonet. Men died and their bodies were barrowed away by their brothers to quicklime pits; across on the far side of the vast Dachau complex the foundations were being laid for what would become the crematoria.

Then, suddenly, incredibly, he and a group of other men were released on condition they all leave

Germany within fourteen days. They were driven out of the camp and dumped at Nuremberg's station. There, waiting for him, aged and drawn but smiling was Rachel, with the children. She held a shabby suitcase filled with his clothes. She explained that her family had raised the money to buy him a Cuban visa and tourist-class ticket on the St. Louis; he wept as she said that she and the children would follow, later, on another boat.

"The important thing, Aaron," Rachel insisted, "is for you to go and prepare a new life for us."

Moments later he had boarded the train to Hamburg. Aaron Pozner knew his wife's parents would never be able to raise the money to send his family after him; that unless he was able to do so, he would never see any of them again.

As the train had steamed northward, despair over leaving his family so overwhelmed him that he decided to return to them, but as he tried to leave his compartment with its "J" labels plastered on the window and door, at the Cologne station, a Gestapo official drove him back with a flurry of blows. In Hamburg had come that second beating outside the railway station.

Others, too, ran the gauntlet of storm troopers at the station. But the Loewe family were lucky; they had arrived in Hamburg at an hour when the Nazis' bullyboys were diverting themselves by hounding Jews out of the city parks. Max Loewe, with a cunning that surprised his family, swiftly ushered them out of the station to wait in a safe place for the moment they could board the ship.

For the past three weeks, waiting, hiding, and running had become second nature. He knew that neither his wife, Elise, nor Ruth, seventeen, or Fritz, twelve, would ever really understand his fear. Unlike him, they had not been on the Gestapo's wanted list, prepared at a moment's notice to move from one place to another to avoid being caught and sent to a concentration camp.

Max Loewe had been a successful attorney until a Reich act removed him from practice in September 1938. He had wanted to leave then and obtained visas to take the family to England. But war was coming, and even Britain had not seemed safe.

He bought permits for Cuba.

Still, Elise Loewe had not wanted to leave Germany, and they waited. Max Loewe made a living as an "economic adviser," discreetly preparing briefs for trials, and then handing them over to a friendly German lawyer to present in court. It was unsatisfying, and it was illegal. In April 1939, he learned the Gestapo had discovered his ruse. He was forced into hiding.

In these past weeks he had been pushed almost beyond terror as he waited for the day when he could surface long enough to join his family and make a train dash to Hamburg and board the St. Louis before the Gestapo were aware he had slipped through their net.

When he had reappeared, Ruth and Fritz were shocked by the change. He was older, more nervous, irritable. His world had crumbled; he stood outside himself and could never return to his past life. His wife and children had tried to cheer him up on the journey to Hamburg. He had not responded, sitting in the train, smaller, shrunken, huddled in his clothes, looking much older than his forty-eight years.

But when he arrived in Hamburg, he guided his family on a dangerous and deadly game of hide and seek, now alert and watchful, darting out of the way of any uniformed official, convinced each was a Gestapo officer waiting to take him.

That same night, Otto Schiendick, the acknowledged ringleader of the Nazi cabal on board the St. Louis, hurried ashore with the Gestapo "firemen." Like other members of the crew, they had been granted shore leave. But Schiendick and the Gestapo men did not follow their custom of spending time around the bars and brothels of Hamburg's Reeperbahn. Instead they made their way to Gestapo headquarters. Afterward Schiendick went to the local office of the Abwehr. The crewmen who saw him enter the building did not realise until years later that this was a further indication that Schiendick was what nobody on the St. Louis except the Gestapo "firemen" knew at the time—a courier of the German Secret Service. His position as party Leiter on the ship provided the perfect cover for this far more important role.

Schiendick had been recruited by the Abwehr in 1935, and within months shown himself highly adept at smuggling out classified material from German spy rings operating within the United States. By 1937 his name and reputation had even reached the ears of Admiral Canaris, head of the Abwehr; he looked on Schiendick as one of his important links in the Nazi espionage chain extending across America.

By 1939, the Abwehr had more spies in the United States than almost anywhere else in the world. The agents channelled their information to New York, to the Times Square area, close to the piers of the German shipping lines on the Hudson River.

Before almost every voyage out of New York for many months past, Schiendick attended a Treff—a secret meeting—in one or more of the cafes or beer cellars on East Eighty-sixth Street, the stronghold of German, and often Nazi, sympathies in New York. There he received documents and blueprints, exchanging them for equally secret orders he brought from Hamburg.

For star runners in its stable of couriers, the Abwehr was generous with expenses, and Schiendick, a dumpy, unattractive man, found that the money bought him female company of a kind in both New York and Hamburg. Then, in the spring of 1939, in one swoop after another, the F.B.I. broke link after link in the Abwehr spy chain; stewards from a number of German ships were arrested, spies were picked up in many American cities and indicted before grand juries. Before this last voyage out of New York, the Hapag pier had teemed with F.B.I. agents, police, and customs men, who subjected the crew to a thorough search. They failed to find the hiding place Otto Schiendick used to carry his information—almost certainly a sealed tube inserted in his anus, a means long favoured by Abwehr agents.

Now, in the Abwehr office in midtown Hamburg, Schiendick gave the information to his debriefing officer. Exactly what followed cannot be known in precise detail, but enough clues exist in surviving German intelligence records and the recall of crewmen to confirm that the meeting Schiendick had with Commander Udo von Bonin, head of the Abwehr section responsible for all espionage activities in America, was to affect, in varying degrees, the refugees on the St. Louis, the ship's captain, his crew, and the intelligence services of the United States.

Although German intelligence had suffered severe blows in America, the need for updated information was greater than ever; with war drawing closer it was vital for Germany to know the hidden strengths and weaknesses of the United States. The Abwehr had forged a new and elaborate chain to get secret information out of America to Havana, Cuba. There they maintained a highly organised espionage ring which had stockpiled American secrets, awaiting a safe means of bringing them to Germany. The material included blueprints of several American destroyers, and specifications for an underwater sound detector which could be used against submarines.

Otto Schiendick and the St. Louis had been selected by von Bonin as the safest and fastest method of bringing those secrets to Germany. The plan, code-named Operation Sunshine, was bold and simple: Schiendick would go ashore in Havana, pick up the material, and return to the ship, which was scheduled to sail for Europe after only a day's stopover.

Schiendick was given $500, which he could use to bribe any inquisitive Cuban official. His contact was to be Robert Hoffman, assistant manager of the local Hapag office in Havana—the very office Captain Schröder would have to rely on for help should he run into difficulties in Cuba.

THURSDAY, MAY 4, 1939

In Havana, Robert Hoffman was already being watched by members of four separate American intelligence agencies—the secret service of the U.S. Immigration Department, the F.B.I., and Naval and Military Intelligence. The most active of these was Colonel Ross E. Powell, of Naval Intelligence, who had been in Cuba for only a month, but whose secret reports to Washington were already being studied with special interest.

Now, on May 4, he returned to his small office in the American Embassy on the Avenida de Mislones to draft another communiqué; its subject was a known Nazi woman courier who had arrived from the Panama Canal Zone to keep a Treff with Hoffman.

Neither Powell nor any of the other American intelligence officers in Cuba had authority to search or arrest a suspect. There was little point in enlisting the help of the indolent Cuban police. Bribery and persuasion allowed the Abwehr an almost free hand to use Havana as the centre of their activities throughout North and South America.

Virtually all Powell could do was watch, listen, and report, but his reports left no doubts about the power of the Nazi spy ring on the island. Report S/N R-233-39 identified the Abwehr strength in Havana as "about sixty agents." Report R-304-39, prefaced, "Source of information: semi-reliable: Subject: Germany, intelligence ashore," contained an insight into Hoffman and his methods. The Nazi spy emerged as a cold man, well versed in bribery and blackmail. Report R-236-39, "reliable," identified a key Abwehr agent as:

"Julius Otto Ott, owner of the Swiss Home Restaurant in Havana. It is not known whether he is a Swiss or a German. He resides at Edificio Carreno, Apartment 39. Ott is between 35 and 40 years of age and is a hump-backed dwarf, being not more than four feet five inches in height. He has a sandy complexion, is freckled, and sometimes wears glasses."

Powell knew that the woman courier who had delivered a packet to Hoffman was staying in Ott's apartment. She posed as a tourist and, as such, could move about freely without restriction. On previous visits to Havana, Powell had tailed her to Ott's restaurant, a meeting place for European immigrants.

He had identified, in the words of his Report R-237-39, again "reliable," many of the diners as "high-powered Nazi agents, camouflaged under the guise of Jewish refugees."

He had also unearthed a nest of such spies living nearby in the Hotel Nacional and the Hotel Sevilla. Powell had tapped their mail. Among other things, he discovered an Abwehr plot to buy 100 tons of glycerine in New York for sabotaging key American plants in the event of war. His tip resulted in the Abwehr men in New York being arrested.

But the agents living in the Nacional and the Sevilla were immune from arrest, living out their cover as refugees—even to the point of seeking welfare aid from the local Joint Relief Committee. Powell had cultivated the organisation to build up a file on each bogus refugee waiting for his American quota number to come through; once they entered the United States they would be arrested.

What Powell did not know on this humid May evening as he drafted his latest report to Washington was what the package the woman delivered to Hoffman contained. Years later, an Abwehr source claimed the package held detailed drawings of the dams at Lakes Gatun and Pedro Miguel, source of all the water from the Panama Canal locks, plus a wealth of information about secret military installations that rendered them vulnerable to sabotage; that package the source claimed, represented the most telling single blow the Abwehr had yet struck against the United States. The documents were to get to Germany by courier on the next Hapag ship, the St. Louis.

In Hamburg, on the afternoon of May 4, Claus-Gottfried Holthusen waited with some anticipation for the telephone connection to Paris. He would have to choose his words carefully, for as a result of the call, the voyage of the St. Louis would become public knowledge. How much of the background to the trip would it be wise to divulge?

Holthusen had received permission for the St. Louis "special voyage" from the Reichssicherheitshauptamt, R.S.H.A., a powerful government division destined to spawn the notorious Department IVB4, which, under the leadership of a thirty-three-year-old up-and-coming bureaucrat, Adolf Eichmann, would soon be responsible for the concentration, deportation, and extermination of Jews within the Reich and its occupied countries.

Since early 1938, four Hapag ships had regularly carried to Shanghai and South American ports those allowed or forced out of Germany. The profits were considerable; passengers had to pay for a return ticket to cover unforeseen "eventualities." Once ashore in Chile or China, if they were lucky, they received a credit note stating that the return portion of their fares was lodged in a "special" account in Germany which could be redeemed if they ever returned to the Fatherland. Hapag did not expect to be required to repay the money.

As his telephone rang to connect him with Paris, Holthusen decided to say as little as necessary to the man at the other end, Morris Troper, the European director of the American Jewish Joint Distribution Committee–the Joint–one of the organisations responsible for helping the victims of Nazism. Holthusen was wary of the American, whom he had never met but knew to have considerable connections in the United States, and listening posts in a dozen European countries. More than anyone else Holthusen knew, Troper was exceptionally well informed on events in Germany, and that, above all, made Holthusen uneasy in his dealings with him.

Holthusen explained the "special voyage" to

Cuba, adding that the St. Louis had been chosen simply because of her availability. She would carry, he continued, nearly 400 first-class passengers at 800 Reichsmarks a head, and more than 500 tourist-class at 600 Reichsmarks. All would be required to pay the "customary contingency fee" of 230 Reichsmarks for the return voyage in case of "circumstances beyond Hapag's control." Tickets were being issued on a first-come, first-served basis.

Troper had only one question for Holthusen: Was the line sure Cuba would accept such a large single consignment?

The question alarmed Holthusen: Had Troper heard something?

He had not. The remark simply stemmed from the fact that nearly 1000 emigrants on the St. Louis would be the largest number ever of refugees to land in Cuba at one time.

Holthusen insisted there was no cause for alarm, provided the "usual precautions" were enforced: no publicity, no violation of any Third Reich decree applying to emigrants. In practice that meant each passenger would be allowed to leave Germany with only ten Reichsmarks in cash—about four dollars—plus "shipboard money," which they could purchase from Hapag up to the value of 230 Reichsmarks. This money could be spent only at sea and could not be converted back into Reichsmarks.

Troper realized Holthusen had side-stepped his question, but he decided not to press the matter. Theirs was a strictly working relationship, born out of the need of one of them to advance company profits and the desire of the other to save lives.

Holthusen ended the conversation with the words, "You know our motto: 'You travel well with the Hamburg-America Line.' "

Morris Troper was both elated and depressed by news of the voyage. There would be no problem in filling the St. Louis with those who were financed by hidden money, contributions sent from relatives outside Germany, and even help from ordinary Germans. But it would require Hapag's entire fleet to satisfy the demands of all those desperate to get out of Germany. Yet the majority would be prevented from leaving by the simple need of money. After six years of being crowded into ghettos and charged exorbitant rents, their profits confiscated by the state, their professional services rejected, the

resources of most were exhausted. They could not even raise the basic passage money, let alone the cash for all the other "dues."

Morris Carlton Troper was European Director of the American Jewish Joint Distribution Committee ("The Joint"). He made it his business to know more than most about current affairs in Germany and worked hard in the cause of the "St Louis" passengers. (Mrs Betty Troper Yeager)

Morris Troper cabled the head office of the American Jewish Joint Distribution Committee in New York. The Joint would undoubtedly help the emigrants find their way in the New World. News of the forthcoming voyage was received with satisfac-.tion, and the Joint immediately made it known to a number of interested American organisations, among them the President's Advisory Committee on

Refugees. It would ensure that the voyage did not come as a surprise to President Franklin Roosevelt.

In London, Sir Herbert Emerson, newly appointed director of the International Committee on Political Refugees, also learned of the voyage from Morris Troper.

Emerson's committee was virtually the only positive outcome of the much-mooted Evian Conference of almost a year earlier. The initiative for the conference had come from President Roosevelt himself. Its purpose was to co-ordinate emigration from Europe. The hope was that the thirty-two countries attending would be willing to relax their immigration policies, but the United States, to whom the world looked for leadership, had shown itself unwilling to put into practice the principles which had led Roosevelt to suggest the conference in the first place. America would allow all the places on its German quota to be used; the "concession," which required no change in existing United States laws, meant that the entire German quota of 25,957 could be made use of each year, but that still did not mean they would all be German Jews.

The Intergovernmental Committee had first established its offices in London under an elderly American director, with a mandate to negotiate with Germany. In late 1938, the president of the Reichsbank, Germany's "financial wizard," visited London with a plan: during three years, 150,000 refugees would be allowed to emigrate in return for a loan of one and a half billion Reichsmarks, to be provided in foreign currency by a corporation financed by "international Jewry."

Negotiations were prolonged. Hitler became disenchanted with the Reichsbank president and dismissed him. Goering appointed his own nominee to negotiate. In February 1939, the American director of the Intergovernmental Committee tendered his resignation, and in April Sir Herbert Emerson had taken his place.

One of the first delegations with whom Emerson had to deal came from Germany with a message from the Gestapo: "Unless a settlement for the proposed 150,000 was established quickly, German authorities would return to the 'shock' tactics so successful in ridding Germany of Jews in the past." Emerson replied that he would not allow the Gestapo to "dictate what my committee will, or

will not, do." The delegation returned to Germany empty-handed.

Now, as Emerson considered the news of the St. Louis voyage, he came to the conclusion that it could do little but complicate the delicate negotiations he was conducting. While the trip would provide respite for a few, it might well boomerang against the many remaining in Germany.

This view was confirmed when Emerson took a phone call from the principal private secretary to the British Foreign Secretary. The secretary read to the director a message recently received from the British consul in Havana. If the contents were correct, the St. Louis and its passengers would become the excuse for a Nazi propaganda campaign.

Sir Herbert Emerson decided the matter could not be left to run its course.

FRIDAY, MAY 5, 1939

Captain Schröder had learned of the allegations Schiendick had made against him at police headquarters when a Gestapo officer arrived on board to question him about his offer to crew members to sign off instead of accompanying the refugees to Cuba. Schröder had explained that, for "this delicate trip," he had made the suggestion for the good of the crew, the line, and the passengers. Over schnapps, he convinced the officer there was no need to probe further.

Afterward, the captain prepared his ground meticulously for a showdown with the steward. First he studied Schiendick's personal file, then he consulted a manual on marine law, and finally he created a "trial atmosphere" in his day cabin by removing all personal effects and clearing his desktop of everything apart from the law book. The final touch was to flank himself at one end of the desk with the ship's first officer, Klaus Ostermeyer, and with the purser, Ferdinand Mueller, at the other. He liked and trusted both men. At nine o'clock sharp, his traditional hour for dealing with defaulters, Captain Schröder ordered Schiendick to be marched in to stand before the desk.

If the steward was nervous, he managed to conceal it until the captain began to speak. He was reminded of his legal right to remain silent. If he did, however, the case would be referred to a higher authority. The steward stirred uneasily and then began to bluster that he had no idea why he had been marched before the captain.

Schröder cut him short: "You are here to explain why you have tried to create a mutinous atmosphere on my ship. I must further tell you that under the penal code you could be sentenced to death by a court if found guilty of such a charge."

For the first time, the captain saw fear in Schiendick's eyes. Quietly and incisively, he hammered away at the charge of "mutinous behaviour"; that the Gestapo had found the steward's accusations to be baseless; that his record of service was peppered with complaints from passengers; that, in short, he owed his seaman's ticket solely to his position as party Leiter—and even that would not save him from punishment in a court of law.

The silence in the cabin stretched between the two men. Schröder waited, wondering if he had pressed his luck too far, wondering whether Schiendick would realise that much of what he had said was little more than bluff; that, if pressed, it was very likely the party would back the steward.

But still Otto Schiendick made no reply.

The captain seized his advantage. He told the steward his behaviour was enough to have him dismissed from the ship at the very least. The steward began to plead it had all been a misunderstanding and that such behaviour would not happen again. He talked on and on.

"Enough!"

Schröder pronounced "sentence" in a cold and distinct voice.

"One more 'misunderstanding,' and I will personally see that you will regret it all your life. Now get out of here, and get back to your real job of trying to be a credit to this ship!"

Afterward the captain, first officer, and purser debated why the steward had appeared so fearful of being put ashore, and finally agreed that it was probably the reaction of a man desperate to cling to his iota of power. Schröder believed that the steward would now subside.

The captain was wrong.

Schiendick feared being put ashore because if he was his Abwehr mission would be aborted. Now he summoned the Gestapo "firemen," told them what had happened, and vowed revenge on the captain. As

soon as the Jews boarded, they would have a chance to retaliate.

The Spaniers had already witnessed how harsh Gestapo methods could be. After they had checked into their hotel room, two Gestapo men had dragged a terrified man out of a nearby bedroom. Dr. Spanier had inched open his own bedroom door in time to see the Gestapo officers kicking the man down the stairs, while the desk clerk hovered in the background, pleading that he had no idea the guest was on a "wanted list."

Babette Spanier urged that they check out before the Gestapo went further. They might not be able to find another hotel easily, her husband said; besides, the fact that they had arrived in the company of their S.S. benefactor would protect them.

"You are always saying we are German to the core," he chided gently. "So we shall behave like ordinary Germans."

All the same it seemed prudent to avoid the hotel as much as possible, and they spent long hours trudging Hamburg's streets. The city was decorated for the city's 750th anniversary celebrations with bunting and gay lanterns, yet an air of menace, of violence, was everywhere. Serried rows of swastikas lined the main streets; the streets were filled with military traffic, S.S. men, police, and troops.

The twins were frightened and their mother did her best to soothe them. Once they were caught up in a mob of banner waving youths. Only Dr. Spanier's explanation that they had left their party badges back at their hotel averted the gang's suspicions, and they were allowed to pass.

"You see," Fritz Spanier told his wife, "we look so German."

Babette replied that for the first time in her life she hated the thought that she was German.

SUNDAY, MAY 7, 1939

By May 7, the last of the tickets for the voyage were sold. Many of the passengers, too frightened to remain in their home or in hiding, had made the trip to Hamburg well in advance of sailing. Many found the delay bearable; they were nearer their destination, and somehow safer.

A few of the passengers, those who had managed to retain some wealth, came to Hamburg by plane. They were so sure of their position that they did not mind rubbing shoulders with Nazi officers. But most travelled third-class on trains, terrified that they would be recognised.

Leo Jockl had buried his face in a newspaper ever since leaving Berlin. He spoke to no one, but from time to time glanced up at other passengers on the train, wondering if they too were heading for the St. Louis. Once, after a Gestapo officer passed, he went to the washroom and examined his face in the mirror. The tiredness showed in his eyes: they had an expression of almost perpetual sadness, as if he were close to tears. But Jockl was concerned about one disturbing feature; his nose was slightly large. He had come to fear it was enough to give away the fact that he was half Jewish.

For six difficult years he had successfully concealed the knowledge from all but a few trusted friends. Until 1933, Jockl had been only vaguely aware of the anti-Semitism in the Vienna of his childhood. Even later, he was cosseted by living in a pre-dominantly Protestant area. Before the Anschluss of 1938, when 45,000 Jews were forced to leave Austria within eight months and suicides rose to two hundred a day, Leo Jockl, then twenty-four, had slipped into Germany and assumed a new background. Since then he had lived in terror of discovery.

He stayed in the train's washroom as long as he dared. When he returned to his seat, as the train neared Hamburg, he, like the other Jews on the train, believed everyone was looking at him. Leo Jockl was the captain's steward on the ship. And that night of May 7, when he boarded the St. Louis, returning from shore leave, Schiendick sought him out. Schiendick had chosen Leo deliberately as a means of revenge against the captain, not only because Jockl was in a position to observe the captain closely, but because it gave him keen pleasure to pit the steward against the captain. He was jealous of Jockl's good manners, his general popularity on board, and his coveted place in the captain's life.

If Schiendick had suspected how close the relationship between Jockl and Schröder really was, he would likely have made sure the senior steward was dispatched to a concentration camp. If he had known he was half a Jew, Jockl would have been in grave danger. So would the captain, for knowingly concealing a person of Jewish blood was enough to

destroy Gustav Schröder.

The captain had inherited Jockl when he assumed command of the St. Louis, and he liked him immediately. Over many voyages, they had come to know each other better, and a mutual affection, something not unlike the relationship between a stern but just father and a happy-go-lucky son, had developed. The natural barrier of rank and background which kept them apart ashore did not matter in the privacy of the captain's day cabin. Both men realised that such a close relationship must remain unknown to the rest of the crew; it could only give rise to speculation and jealousy.

Jockl had confided that he was half Jewish. Schröder had listened attentively and given a firm promise that his steward's secret was safe with him.

The matter was never referred to again.

Now, as Jockl listened to Schiendick's demands that he should spy on the captain, he felt almost ill. For a moment he considered striking out at Schiendick, but assaulting the party Leiter was bound to be a punishable crime; it would achieve nothing except to bring unwelcome attention.

Instead, he nodded. His instinct told him that apparent agreement was the safest strategy for himself and Captain Schröder. Later, alone in his cabin, he decided that, if necessary, he would feed Schiendick trivia, even lies. Jockl failed to take into account the fact that Schiendick could confirm his reports through other spies, and that he would then be in greater danger than before.

Aaron Pozner had made a discovery which filled him with anxiety. Since crawling into his hiding place, he had followed a routine. Each day he slept among the animal hides, fitfully, in the middle of the busy and noisy harbour. Each night and into the early morning, when the waterfront was mostly quiet and the pier deserted except for its guards, he crept out of his hiding place to scavenge for food. There was always the odd crate of fruit from which a banana or orange could be prized; one night he had even found a half-full bottle of milk left over from a workman's lunch. After his diet at Dachau of bread and water, with only rainwater for washing, these were treasures.

On the night of Sunday, May 7, he noticed the warships in the harbour were lit up very late. He could hear the sound of voices coming from them. Peering through the hides, he saw civilians, women, walking the decks with young officers. Sunday he thought, must be the time for cocktail parties, for showing off the new-found strength of the German navy. He could see at least a dozen such warships, each with its swastika flying at the stern. There was also a passenger ship. He crawled out of his hole, crossed behind a building, and read its name. It was the St. Louis. He then made the discovery that sent him scurrying back to his hiding place; the St. Louis, like the warships in Hamburg harbour, and like the Gestapo guard's towers ringing Dachau, was flying the Nazi swastika.

The swastika symbolised the party's control over the St. Louis. He understood by instinct what the captain disbelieved, that the ship was a pawn of the Nazis.

The German Minister of Propaganda, Joseph Goebbels, had, a month before, laid the foundations for a part of his plan for the St. Louis. He authorised fourteen Nazi propaganda agents to infiltrate Cuba, and within the month they had succeeded in stirring up anti-Semitism on the island. They arranged that an intensive, inflammatory campaign be waged on the radio and in three Havana newspapers, directed against German refugees and Jews long established in Cuba. Cuban President Frederico Bru could not ignore the growing anti-Semitism.

It was just what Goebbels wanted. The Munich Agreement of September 29, 1938, had provided, for more fortunate Jews, a delay of war and time to get out of Germany, but since 1939, the repression of the Nazis, the restrictions imposed by countries of refuge, and the success of Goebbels' propaganda machine had dammed the flow. Goebbels had told his followers: "The poorer and therefore the more burdensome the immigrant to the country absorbing them, the stronger that country will react, and the more favourable will be the effect in the interests of German propaganda." He was therefore pleased at the effect of the anti-Semitic campaign in Cuba.

From the moment the St. Louis passengers boarded, Goebbels intended his ministry to capitalise on the ship's journey. Passengers like Pozner—shabby, dirty, "undesirable"—would be much more than anonymous refugees. Goebbels would ensure that they, and the St. Louis, appeared as an example to the entire world of the Jewish situation in microcosm.

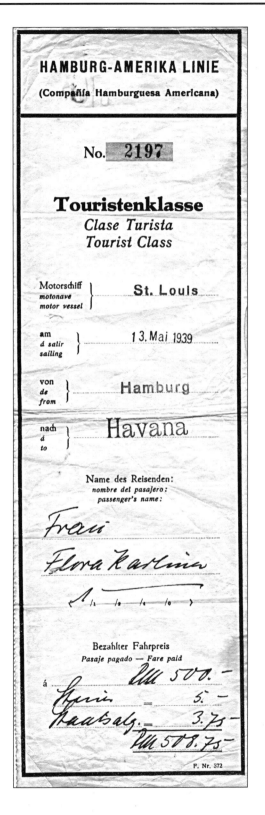

Left: Passenger tickets like this one on the left were issued to individuals of families for their voyage to Cuba from Hamburg. First Class passengers were allowed to take ten pieces of luggage, whilst those travelling tourist Class were allowed seven – all rather academic if, like Aaron Pozner, you had been released from a labour camp such as Buchenwald or Dachau, so were travelling with only one small suitcase, far from full, but containing your most precious memories. On the other hand, many took their maximum allowance, for they were trying to take a lifetime's possessions. Gertrud Scheuer remembered: "It was still pitifully small... Women carried their jewellery and treasured possessions in small tin boxes... they hoped to use the jewels to pay their way in America... they believed you could sell anything in America... I had seven pieces of baggage, clothes mostly, but at the count, there were only six... I challenged the port official about this, not an easy thing to do, given his position. But before he could do anything, one of the ship's crew found the other piece and the Nazi official changed my baggage coupon. (Passenger coupon of Flora Karliner from Edgar Glucksman)

Overleaf: Passengers were issued with transit cards and vaccination certificates for the journey from Hamburg. Equipped with such documentation, they believed, in the words of Gertrud Scheuer: "...we were safe. How could we believe otherwise? In Nazi Germany, we had learned the meaning of documents and the letter "J" that we wore like the Mark of Cain... the documents that the Third Reich made us carry so we could easily be singled out when the time came to transport us... we knew, alright about documents. So, when we received those for Cuba, we were overjoyed. It did not matter that they were only intended for us to be 'in transit' – the very word 'transit' gave us further hope... the fact that they were in languages with which we were not familiar gave us further hope.... (Mrs Gertrud Mendels)

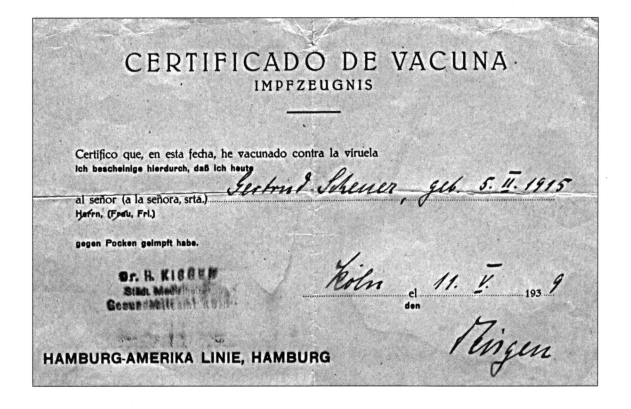

MONDAY, MAY 8, 1939

By the morning of May 8, preparations for the voyage aboard the St. Louis had developed a steady momentum. The liner was held to the shore fore and aft by hawsers as thick as a man's leg; 575 feet long, it was streamlined with a tapering stern and raked bow, black hull and white superstructure topped with twin black, red, and white smokestacks. Five of her decks reared above the water line; three, filled with machinery, storage tanks, and compartments, plunged deep below the surface. The crew of 231 prepared to cook, scrub, clean, polish, entertain, fetch and carry, and meet the whims of both ship and passengers.

On that Monday morning, the crew had been assembled once more in the social hall to be addressed by the captain, standing on the dance-band podium. Gustav Schröder was brief: the slightest lapse in standards, any hint of discrimination, the briefest sign of resentment toward the refugees, would be swiftly punished.

"You will all never forget for a moment that these passengers are to be treated no differently from any others we have carried," he concluded.

Schröder walked briskly from the room, followed by Ostermeyer, the first officer, and Mueller, the purser, aware of the silence, sensing the hostility on some faces. When the trio reached the captain's day cabin Schröder gave way to his own feelings; in spite of his warning to the crew he knew that, as far as Hapag head office was concerned, the refugees were not to be treated as other voyagers.

That morning Hapag House informed him that there would be cheaper cuts of meat, that the ship's shop must lock away its usual range of expensive cameras, binoculars, and perfumes, replacing them with shoddier goods. The economies extended everywhere: the ship's hairdressing salon was to remove its excellent range of cosmetics, the bars were to lock away a variety of drinks. There were not even to be writing pads, pencils, and free postcards in the public rooms.

After reading out the long list of banned goods and their replacements– it extended even to the quality of toilet paper– Gustav Schröder made a major decision: wherever possible the orders were to be ignored. The purser was told to ensure that the ship was adequately and properly supplied. Schröder did not care how it was done: "Just do it, and do it well."

Ferdinand Mueller, the ship's equivalent of a hotel manager, was a kind man, devoted to the job of keeping passengers happy. His secret, which he constantly impressed upon stewards and cabin staff, was to take pains over those they served. He himself set an excellent example in his attentiveness, respect, and keeping a proper distance. After twenty-five years at sea, he believed he had refined it to an art. Now Gustav Schröder had given Mueller the opportunity to show another of his qualities—the ability to scrounge and juggle with way bills. The purser set off to show that when it came to such things, there was none better on the Hapag payroll.

Alone with Ostermeyer, Schröder confided his private feelings about the voyage. It was not only the crew's attitude that concerned him, but the attitude of the passengers as well: they had been subjected to years of tyranny, and now would find themselves in a position in which they could give the orders. When the initial shock of that wore off, if they then went too far in their demands—and they both knew, Schröder added, how demanding passengers could be—there were bound to be repercussions.

"And then," Schroder remarked, "we will be a floating time bomb."

For the rest of the morning the two senior officers on board discussed ways and means of avoiding that crisis.

Their relationship was a close and cordial one, despite their age difference—the captain was twenty years the senior of his first officer—and their outward dissimilarity. Ostermeyer towered over Schröder by many inches and was close to eighty pounds heavier. He had an urge for social life that the captain had no desire to match; Schröder was more interested in the collection of books on ornithology that he kept in his cabin and in his campaign for bodily fitness; it had become a running joke between them that Ostermeyer's physical exertions did not go much beyond uncorking a wine bottle. Their friendship drew its strength not from habits shared but from a common interest in seamanship and serving passengers.

By the end of the morning Gustav Schröder had decided how best to serve the refugees. He would, he told Ostermeyer, remain aloof from the passengers, taking, as he put it, "the view from the bridge on how the voyage develops." The effective day-to-day running of the St. Louis would now be in the hands of the first officer.

It was the captain's first mistake—not because Ostermeyer was incapable of such responsibility, but because he had miscalculated that the view from the bridge would provide access into every corner of the St. Louis. He thought he could spot trouble from above. He was wrong.

In London, the director of the Intergovernmental Committee on Political Refugees, Sir Herbert Emerson, carefully prepared the ground for a move which he hoped would halt the voyage. He had studied the reports from Cuba and elsewhere, analysing them with the calm, unemotional mind which made some refugee organisations feel Emerson was a hard, inflexible man who would never let sentiment sway him. Then he acted. Emerson's telegram was delivered the afternoon of May 8 to Claus-Gottfried Holthusen, the Hapag director, who had previously briefed Schröder. It read:

I AM INFORMED THAT IT IS CONTEMPLATED TO SEND 900 REFUGEES TO CUBA BY YOUR STEAMER ST. LOUIS SAILING ON MAY 13. I UNDERSTAND THAT GREAT DIFFICULTIES ARE LIKELY TO ARISE IN REGARD TO THEIR ENTRY INTO CUBA AND I STRONGLY ADVISE THAT THE REFUGEES SHOULD NOT BE SENT THERE.

Holthusen was disturbed by the telegram. Although he had never met Emerson, he knew the Englishman was in a position to make his views known even to the Fuehrer himself. The shipping director had immediately sent a priority cable to the Hapag office in Havana asking for clarification of the situation. There, Robert

Hoffman, the Abwehr agent who doubled as assistant manager, and with whom Schiendick planned to rendezvous, discussed it with his immediate superior, Luis Clasing.

Holthusen received the reply the next morning. It stated that Hapag, Havana, had the "personal guarantee" of the Cuban director of immigration that the St. Louis faced no difficulties. Holthusen, reassured, decided it was unnecessary to reply to Emerson's cable or to inform the one man who should have known of the incident—Captain Gustav Schröder.

FRIDAY, MAY 12, 1939

For nearly an hour on the afternoon of Friday, May 12, Captain Schroeder stood alone on the starboard wing of the bridge watching passengers emerge from shed 76 to climb one of the gangways. They were Orthodox Jews, anxious to board before the onset of their Sabbath at sunset; their beliefs forbade them to begin any journey during the period from Friday evening until dusk on Saturday.

The captain had visited the customs area in the cavernous shed and had been outraged at the way these early arrivals were treated. Uniformed officials jostled them, subjected them to rough body searches, and ransacked their cases and trunks.

Schröder had remonstrated with the senior Gestapo officer present, and so forceful was the captain's language and his threat to "raise all hell" at police headquarters that the Gestapo man had reluctantly given an order for the refugees to be treated more gently. The captain despatched Ostermeyer and Mueller to make sure that this promise was honoured, and then returned to keep his own station on the bridge wing.

The appearance of the passengers distressed him. They were cowed and frightened and made him all the more determined that once on his ship their faith in the "old Germany" would be restored. Now, in the fading light of Friday evening, he was gratified to see two stewards hurrying down the gangway to assist an elderly couple weighed down with baggage.

Professor Moritz Weiler and his wife, Recha, were stunned by the stewards' offer of help; it was the first act of kindness they had experienced on the long journey from Dusseldorf. Before that, there had been another, longer, train journey, a five-hundred-mile round trip to Stuttgart, to an office block on the Koenigstrasse, to obtain their visas through OBERRAT, an old and respected Jewish administrative organisation.

The journey to Stuttgart had exhausted the professor, for he was in poor health, and he had been shocked at the way they were treated by railway officials and their fellow travellers, who alternately ignored and insulted them. Recha Weiler, long accustomed to such ostracism, bore the behaviour stoically.

Both had been bewildered to find at

OBERRAT's offices Gestapo officers working alongside Jews. The Weilers could not comprehend that they owed their visas to an extraordinary alliance between OBERRAT and the Gestapo. OBERRAT held records dating back to the seventeenth century. They contained a mass of detailed personal information on hundreds of thousands of German Jews, information of continuing interest to the Gestapo. Since 1933 the Nazis had allowed the agency to become a "servicing organisation" for emigrants, and Gestapo officers were attached to OBERRAT not only to facilitate their exodus, but to consult the records when required.

OBERRAT had found the Cuban consul in Frankfurt-am-Main most willing to sell visas for the right money, and two of those permits had been obtained for Moritz and Recha Weiler. They had spent the last of their savings on tickets for a twin-bedded first-class cabin on the St. Louis. Then they had packed what they could, Recha taking care to include her husband's books on religion and philosophy, dressed carefully in their best clothes, taken a train to Hamburg, and finally made their way to the ship.

Now, as they climbed the gangway, Recha Weiler wondered if they had left it until too late to leave Germany, whether her ailing husband would ever recover from the terrible blows to his pride and health. For many months she had realised that his intellectual assessment of the situation had not taken into account the emotional strain it placed him under. When the Nazis took office, Moritz Weiler had told his friends it was important to view the situation coolly. He had argued that the wave of hatred rolling across Germany was a passing phenomenon that would peak and die away. He had even predicted that the climax would come in 1936, and that afterward life would revert to normal.

In that year he lost his teaching post at the university, he was first spat upon in public, a youth threw dung at him, and this gentle and courteous old man was called a dirty Jew.

Now, alone in their cabin, B-108, Moritz Weiler clung to his wife, happy that there still seemed a Germany where people were human.

Ever since he had noticed the swastika on the St. Louis, Aaron Pozner had spent his waking hours watching the ship, looking for any sign of something untoward. There had been none. Even so, the St.

Louis, flying that flag, had come to him to look like a floating prison On Friday evening, as he observed a number of passengers going aboard, he decided to leave his hiding place and chance boarding himself.

Pozner eased his way past the animal hides, pushing his suitcase in front of him, and went to a public lavatory outside shed 76. He splashed water over the stubble on his bruised face and shaven head, and washed his hands. He and his clothes reeked with the smell of stale perspiration, but he was unaware of it. He got out his papers from his suitcase, and then strode hesitantly, but as confidently as possible, into shed 76.

Inside the customs area, he was promptly surrounded by uniformed officials. They looked carefully at him, at his papers, and cursorily into his suitcase, then stood back, and motioned him toward the ship.

From a vantage point on the promenade deck, Otto Schiendick watched Pozner slowly climbing the tourist gangway. To him, as to others, the man looked a vagrant, not like the teacher of Hebrew he was. But to Leo Jockl, also watching, the suffering and courage were clear. He was filled with pity for the figure who hesitated at the top of the gangway.

A steward stepped forward and offered to take his case. Pozner instinctively drew back, pulling the case closer to him. Another steward told him an evening meal was available. He could hardly believe his ears; it had been years since a German had spoken to him politely. A third steward asked to see his boarding card and offered to direct him to his cabin. Confused, but determined to maintain some independence, he shook his head and walked away down the deck.

Otto Schiendick had viewed the scene with contempt, confirmed in his belief that all Jews were ill-mannered. As the shabby figure approached him, he placed himself in his way so that Pozner had to walk around him. Schiendick reported to the small group of stewards nearby that there went positive proof that Der Stuermer, the party's scandal sheet, was right—"Jews give off a peculiar aroma."

Pozner eventually found his way down to cabin 373 on D deck, and closed the door behind him. Everything was so different from what he had expected: a young cabin steward had called him Herr

Pozner, an officer had actually wished him a pleasant voyage. His cabin surprised him further. Though small, it was comfortable and spotlessly clean. The pillowcase and bed linen were crisply laundered; even the hand towels were pressed and neatly folded.

Some German had taken the trouble to do all this for him. As he looked at his face in the mirror, he could not believe he was seeing the same person who, for the past nine days and nights, had spent his time in a hideout reeking of animal hides.

THE MOTOR SHIP "ST LOUIS":

The Motor Ship "St Louis" was one of two vessels to the same design laid down at Bremerhaven in the 1920s for the prestigious Hamburg-Amerika line. They were built specifically for the trans-Atlantic cruise route, so were given American-sounding names ("St Louis" after the Missouri capital) and were intended to be large revenue earners for Germany in those heady days before the Wall Street Crash. Despite the crash, they plied their route with good passenger complements and kept the line's name on the lips of those still able to afford to travel (Hapag-Lloyd, Hamburg)

The "St Louis" was built to give passengers a sense of confidence and security as they boarded – a magnificent ship, fitted out to the highest standards of comfort and safety. The upper decks were bright and airy, as these views show, and whilst many ships being built at the time used painted steel decking, the "St Louis" was fitted with wooden decking wherever people were expected to walk. (Hapag-Lloyd, Hamburg)

Unlike the main Promenade deck in the previous picture, the Tourist Class Promenade Deck was not covered and doubled as a sports deck and sun-deck, but because it was "Tourist" did not mean it was not of a very high standard. (From the collection of Gerald Granston, currently on permanent loan to the Museum of Jewish Heritage, NY)

The swimming pool was to be a main focus of attention for the passengers on this fateful voyage. It was intended to be a focus of attention anyway, laid out as it was, with galleried decks above, so that swimming contests could be watched in comfort. The screening was not for modesty, rather to protect the swimmers from the Atlantic's cross winds. Those on board, like First Class passenger Margot Luft, found themselves "...back in the land of the living. The pool was opened once we were clear of the North Atlantic. At first, many of us were to amazed to actually enter the water. We felt this might be some sort of trick: that we would actually be punished for swimming! After all, we had not been allowed to share swimming pools in Nazi Germany. It was the children who went in first. Then, as each day passed, under the encouragement of the crew we became more and more bold. Soon, the pool was almost filled. It became the centre of attraction for many of us. We would spend hours on the deck overlooking the pool, watching people playing. It was another way of reminding ourselves that we were human beings again". (From the collection of Gerald Granston, currently on loan to the Museum of Jewish Heritage, NY)

In the library-like atmosphere of the ship's Games Room, many of the elderly passengers enjoyed card games, or contemplating their new life. In the words of one First Class passenger: "Simply going into this room was a reminder of old times. There was a timelessness about it... old books in glass-fronted cases... soft lights... even the photos on the wall were from another time, when we were simply people, not Jews. (From the collection of Gerald Granston, currently on loan to the Museum of Jewish Heritage, NY)

The First Class Lounge of the "St Louis". After the Passenger Committee was formed, it was in this room that they regularly met and planned their strategies, wrote their messages for transmission around the world and discussed the problems facing the whole group. (From the collection of Gerald Granston, currently on loan to the Museum of Jewish Heritage, NY)

The main Dining Room carries through the theme of comfort and passenger care typical of this ship. (Hapag-Lloyd, Hamburg)

Right: Even the Ship's Hospital was appointed to a superb standard of comfort and care. (Hapag-Lloyd, Hamburg)

The "St Louis" Smoking Room. Alice Kochmann recalled that her husband, Friedrich, would join other men there after dinner. "Life on board ship was very traditional," she wrote on a postcard sent home to friends. (From the collection of Gerald Granston, currently on loan to the Museum of Jewish Heritage, NY)

A corner of the Tourist Class Salon. Even at this lower level of luxury, the quality of fittings and decor was of a very high standard. Attention to atmosphere and detail is demonstrated here by the floral display at the foot of the stage, as well as by the general aura of the room. (From the collection of Gerald Granston, currently on loan to the Museum of Jewish Heritage, NY)

The First Class Promenade Deck offered all the comforts of a conservatory at home, but on a larger scale. Despite the enclosed construction, providing weather protection for the worst conditions, this deck was still light and airy. (From the collection of Gerald Granston, currently on loan to the Museum of Jewish Heritage, NY)

These diagrams show the deck layout of the "St Louis", showing the Boat Deck (upper left), the Promenade Deck (upper centre), the Sport Deck (top right) and the four passenger decks. (The US Holocaust Memorial Museum)

Few photographs could be found of individual Ship's crew members, but fortunately, a few more have come to light of some of those who played a significant part in making life more bearable for the passengers of this fated voyage. They include Ship Photographer Paul Bendowski and his wife Irene, the Ladies' Hairdresser; Steward Peter Schmidt is seen here whilst being detained by the British Army at the end of World War Two; and Pastry Cook Christian Muhlbacher. This last picture is part of a snapshot taken by Paul Bendowski and which Muhlbacher carried with him throughout the War. (Authors' Collection)

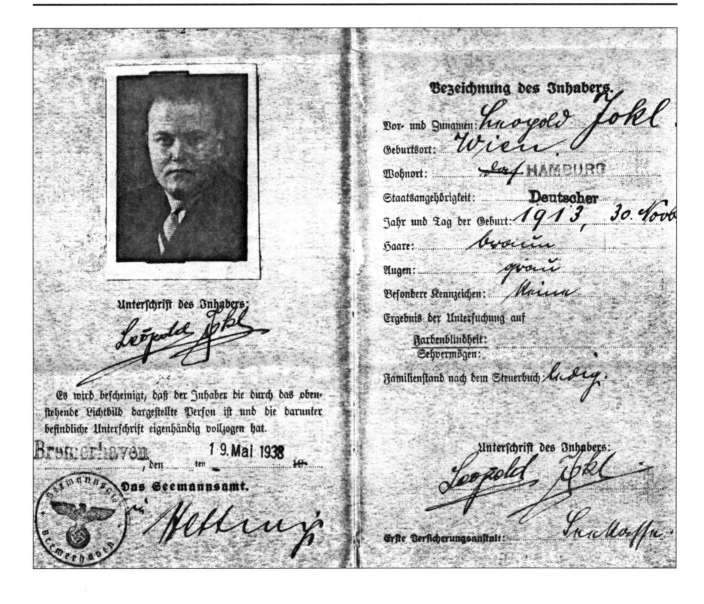

A key member of the Ship's crew was Leo Jockl for, apart from being the Captain's Steward, he was also noted for his kindness and helpfulness with passengers. Here we see two pages of his seaman's passbook, which tell us he was born in Vienna in 1913 and that he "signed on" in Bremerhaven. A death certificate shows that his father Artur Jockl, who died in 1943, was Jewish, but his mother was a Gentile, which may explain the fact that Leo was not recorded as a Jew, but it justifies his fears and anxieties on that voyage. (Mrs Gerda Jockl)

This little group on the right shows Leo Jockl (2nd from right) with three fellow crew members enjoying the sun on one of Jockl's few opportunities to relax (Mrs Gerda Jockl).

The first two pages of any seaman's passbook look like this. It tells us that Seaman Rolf Herrsl signed on to the St Louis on 11th May, just two days before sailing (a quite common occurrence), that he was "signed on" for four months and seventeen days, returning to Hamburg on his final voyage not later than 27th September and that he would be "paid off" on 3rd October. (Authors' collection)

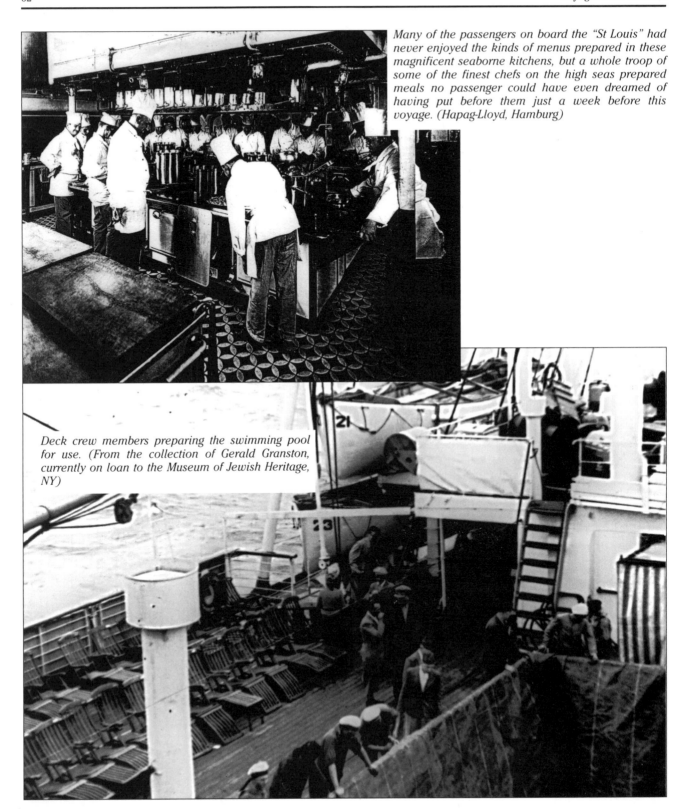

Many of the passengers on board the "St Louis" had never enjoyed the kinds of menus prepared in these magnificent seaborne kitchens, but a whole troop of some of the finest chefs on the high seas prepared meals no passenger could have even dreamed of having put before them just a week before this voyage. (Hapag-Lloyd, Hamburg)

Deck crew members preparing the swimming pool for use. (From the collection of Gerald Granston, currently on loan to the Museum of Jewish Heritage, NY)

SATURDAY, MAY 13, 1939

On Saturday, May 13, the day of departure, from morning to late afternoon, nearly 900 passengers would board the St. Louis. The queues stretched from shed 76 to the gangways and into the ship. Almost half the refugees were women and children. Many men, like Aaron Pozner, released from concentration camps on condition they left Germany immediately, had to travel alone, leaving their families behind to follow later. Many women travelled alone or with their children; their husbands were either still trapped in concentration camps or already in Cuba waiting for them. And two young children were to make the long sea voyage alone.

Seven-year-old Renatta and her five-year-old sister Evelyne entered shed 76 early in the morning, the culmination of months of argument, planning, and scheming by their parents.

Their father, Max Aber, had been a respected and fashionable doctor in the Berlin of the thirties. Despite the Nazis, he and his wife, Lucie, had managed to lead an almost carefree life. But gradually they realised it could not last. Legally, Dr. Aber, like Dr. Spanier, had been allowed to treat only Jews, but because of his reputation, by 1938, S.S. and S.A. officers began to seek his skill as a dermatologist to cure their venereal diseases. They knew he was a Jew, and he knew it was only a matter of time before one of them returned to escort him to Buchenwald or Dachau. In the meantime, they paid well to have their syphilis and gonorrhea treated.

Dr. Aber saved those fees in preparation for an escape. He had handed the money over to a trusted friend, a Berlin lawyer, who passed on the cash to the Brazilian ambassador in Berlin in exchange for American dollars. The lawyer smuggled the dollars to Paris and deposited them in an account in Dr. Aber's name. But after several successful runs, the lawyer was caught by the Gestapo and sent to a concentration camp, where he would die.

When Dr. Aber realised that his house was being watched, he fled. He went to New York, where he spent $500 of the $800 that had been deposited in Paris, on a U.S. Immigration Department bond that guaranteed him a place on the American quota. But until his number came up, the United States ordered, he must leave the country. With his remaining money,

he travelled to Cuba to wait along with all the other refugees.

Dr. Aber had discussed the question of how to get his family out of Germany with two fellow immigrants with the same problem, who had arrived in Havana at about the same time. Dr. Bardeleben was a physician from Berlin, and Hans Fischer had managed a Breslau factory until he was thrown into Buchenwald and later given two weeks to leave Germany. Of similar ages and background, the three men became increasingly anxious about the safety of their wives and children.

But Max Aber had a worry the other two did not have. Like them, he had bombarded his wife with cables and letters about her coming to Cuba, but Lucie Aber's replies had been cool. Finally he had accepted the truth: his marriage was over and his wife loved another man. He did not altogether blame her. A busy doctor in Berlin had many demands on his time; his wife had not always understood the pressures. On occasion he had found solace in other beds. In turn, his wife had also looked elsewhere. Soon after he had left Germany, she had taken up with a German of influence and charm, and with him, she, a gentile, would need no longer face years of humiliation that came from marriage to a non-Aryan.

For Renatta and Evelyne Aber, their father's absence was hard enough to accept, but in late 1938 there had come an even harsher blow. Their mother had packed them away to a children's home outside Berlin, explaining that it was best for the youngsters. From the outset, Renatta hated the home, with its tasteless food, faded linen, and cold corridors, but she put on a brave front for her younger sister.

Her resolve had failed her only on Kristallnacht; now, seven months later, she still remembered the terror she felt on seeing burning synagogues, black-booted men with guns, broken glass, shops smashed, and white paint daubed on buildings.

Dr. Aber had been even more concerned about his daughters when he had learned where they were. He had pondered how to get his wife to agree to their leaving the home, and how to get them to Cuba.

"First you must have permits," a young divorcee had insisted to him one afternoon. "Go and see my former husband. He's got connections."

Dr. Aber had been long enough in Havana to know that on every street corner, besides the pimps offering girls and dirty postcards, there were men claiming to have connections. But he went. The rendezvous was in a shabby sidewalk cafe. The ex-husband was uncouth, uneducated. With paper and pencil provided by the bartender, he wrote out a message to show his "connection." Aber looked at it sceptically. His contact was claiming to know one of the most powerful men in Cuba, Jose Estedes.

To save the ten-cent trolley fare, Dr. Aber walked to Estedes' home. When he presented the slip of paper, to his astonishment he was immediately ushered into the presence of Estedes, who, after hearing of his plight, drove him to the office of Cuba's director of immigration. When he left the office, he had landing permits for Cuba for his wife and children.

Late in February 1939, Max Aber had sent the papers to Lucie, pleading that she book passage on the next available ship. But Lucie had no intention of joining her husband. Finally, his patience exhausted, Dr. Aber had threatened to return to Berlin to collect Renatta and Evelyne, whatever the cost and risk to himself. His wife gave in.

Now, inside shed 76, Renatta and Evelyne looked up at their mother as she repeated to them how exciting it would be travelling alone.

"Then why don't you come, too?" Renatta persisted.

Lucie Aber shook her head. "Maybe later, darling." Then, looking around to see no one was watching, she opened her purse and produced a child's gold watch. "Take this, quickly, put it in your pocket."

"No, Momma," Renatta replied, frightened. "It's not allowed. I know it's not." The child, terrified of the men in uniforms she saw all around, adamantly refused to accept the going-away present.

An elderly couple joined the group. They had agreed to act as guardians to the children. Lucie Aber hugged her daughters and then turned away.

"I'll look after Evelyne," the seven-year-old called to her mother. "I promise."

Taking her sister by the hand, Renatta slowly walked toward the ship. Only once did the two small children look back. Their mother was not to be seen.

By midmorning Saturday, Purser Ferdinand Mueller had achieved the impossible. By bribery, pleading, and manipulation, he had carried out the captain's order to ensure that the ship's larder was properly provisioned. Since dawn he had supervised the loading of pounds of caviar, sides of salmon, smoked and fresh, hundreds of cases of choice German wines and beers, and medical supplies, and he had even managed to scrounge an adequate supply of "fine quality" toilet paper.

Ship's Purser Ferdinand Müller – this photo was taken whilst he was on home leave in 1939, just before this voyage. (Authors' Collection)

Periodically he left the loading bays to watch over the embarking passengers, making sure his stewards settled them comfortably in their cabins. Now, with the last of the supplies safely stowed, he began to knock on those cabin doors, introducing himself, offering to be of service.

When he arrived at the Weilers' cabin and knocked, Recha Weiler opened the door. Behind her, Mueller could see her husband, seated with a leather-bound book on his knees, an embroidered skullcap on his head. Recha explained that they were saying prayers; it was not, she asked anxiously, forbidden?

An embarrassed Mueller said there were no such restrictions on board, and went on to explain that during the voyage the first-class social hall would be converted into a synagogue. The look of utter disbelief on Recha Weiler's face further discomfited the purser; it brought home to him the true meaning, he later told a steward, of what people like the Weilers must have suffered.

Recha asked him for which faith the synagogue would be used: Orthodox, Conservative, or Reform.

Mueller was startled by the question. He had never before considered that Judaism was anything other than a single belief.

Several times during the afternoon, Aaron Pozner tried to ask one of the crew whether the ship would leave on time, but did not dare. Instead, he stood on A deck apart from everyone else, and watched his fellow travellers boarding. One particular group caught his attention: a man in a topcoat, holding a woman's arm. Behind them came two chattering youngsters. Even from that distance, Pozner felt the man's apprehension.

Down on the quay, Max Loewe's anxiety gave way once again to fear. The swastika flag was flying at the stern. He suddenly realised the St. Louis was a German ship; once aboard, he would still be on German territory. Perhaps he had not given the Gestapo the slip after all; perhaps there were Gestapo on the ship who would yet turn him in.

Elise Loewe had had to choose between staying with the aged mother she loved who refused to leave Germany, and going with her husband. She knew that if she had stayed, her husband would have remained as well; eventually he would have been caught, and that might well have meant his death. She had chosen her husband. She felt sure she would never see her mother again.

In shed 76, Elise had shielded her husband as best she could from the officials; fortunately they had seemed much more intent on her pretty, seventeen-year-old, dark-haired daughter Ruth. They successfully passed the emigration formalities, only to receive a cruel blow: the precious container holding everything in the world the family owned had been mistakenly shipped to Shanghai.

The formerly prosperous Loewes were leaving Germany with little more than the clothes they wore. Max Loewe knew there was now nothing left for the Nazis to take but himself and his family. He was barely able to control his anguish as he walked up the gangway.

High above the quay, forward on the promenade deck, First Officer Klaus Ostermeyer and Purser Mueller watched the scenes below. Mueller had tried to explain his problem of a choice of Orthodox, Conservative, or Reform services to Ostermeyer, but the first officer replied merely: "If that's the only problem we'll have, then we will escape lightly." Both men were conscious of the stiff, motionless figure of Captain Schröder standing once again on the nearby bridge wing. Mueller wondered what he was thinking.

The captain was wondering what the people boarding the ship thought. Most moved a trifle too fast or too slow, staring around, turning their heads, looking for a friendly face in the crowd. Though he could not see their faces too clearly, he imagined that not a few were suppressing tears. Gustav Schröder was a romantic man; he wanted to believe that if they had a common thought, it was probably one of sadness that they, Germans, were being thrown out of their country; he hoped any bitterness would be assuaged to a considerable degree by the behaviour of his crew.

Then, by the first-class boarding gate, Schröder saw a photographer taking pictures of the passengers, as many tried to shield their faces from the camera. Sensing trouble, he hurried to the gate to find the man reloading his camera.

"Who are you?" Schröder barked.

The man said he was from the Ministry of Propaganda, and began to explain that his films were to be rushed to Berlin at the "express request of Minister Goebbels."

"Get off my ship!"

The man paused, uncertain, and then, possibly believing that nobody had the authority to countermand an order from Goebbels, prepared to resume photographing. A furious Schröder shoved him toward the gangway. "Get off—or I'll personally throw you overboard. And you can report that to the minister!"

The man slunk off the ship.

As the captain walked briskly toward the bridge, a sixth sense drew him back toward the night-club on B deck, the Tanzplatz. From inside came the sound of a piano and singing. Recognising the words, he hurried the last few steps to throw open the club's door. Inside, grouped around the baby grand, Otto

Schiendick and the Gestapo "firemen" were chorusing their way through a medley of Nazi songs. Their voices died away as the captain entered.

Gustav Schröder walked over and slammed shut the piano lid. Schiendick, a note of defiance in his voice, asked what exactly was the captain objecting to?

Apart from breaking a company rule forbidding crew to make use of passenger areas, they had deliberately flouted his order to cause no embarrassment to the passengers.

"Embarrassment, Captain?" said Schiendick. "Where is the embarrassment? There is no law that forbids us to sing party songs."

The steward produced a piece of paper. It was authority from Hapag for the crew to use the Tanzplatz "when, and if it is reasonable."

Schröder handed it back to the steward.

"Get out! All of you! If I find you in here again you will need more than a piece of paper to save your skins!"

The sullen group filed out.

Down on the quay, in the late afternoon, the man from the Propaganda Ministry continued to photograph passengers as they trudged towards the St. Louis. He chose his subjects carefully, selecting only those who would later, with the help of a Nazi caption writer, be presented as "documentary" pictorial proof that the refugees were "subhuman savages," "furtive looking fugitives," not "worthy" of German citizenship.

The men, women, and children were in fact frightened people whose faces bore the mark of years of stress. The quayside scene was all the more painful for many of them as the Hapag band, present to give the ship its traditional musical farewell, played tunes from a bygone era.

Yet for Babette Spanier, that music suited perfectly her arrival in shed 76. All afternoon she had prepared her husband and children for this moment. She had told Fritz they would leave Germany in a fitting manner so that nobody could say a scion of the Seidemann family did not depart Germany in style.

First she had dressed the twins in their best party frocks. Then she had made Dr. Spanier wear a dinner suit beneath his topcoat. Finally she herself had-put on a close-fitting evening gown and fur wrap.

A taxi had carried them to the Hapag pier.

Inside shed 76, the officials and the other refugees were amazed by the appearance of the four people dressed as if they were going to a ball; the contrast with the shabby dress of many of the other passengers was total. Babette Spanier had inserted a monocle in her eye.

The family were waved through by the cheap-suited party men. Outside, at the foot of the black-and-white cliff of the St. Louis, stewards were ready. Willing hands grasped the Spaniers' luggage; cheerful voices gave their first assurance of friendly service.

In a grand cavalcade the party swept toward the first-class gangway, toward the ministry photographer.

"Excuse me," said Babette Spanier to her husband, "but it looks as if someone is going to take our picture."

She turned to the photographer and asked him how they should pose. He looked away: the Spanier family did not fit the image he required.

At that moment the band, perhaps catching the mood, launched into "Vienna, City of my Dreams."

"Fritz," Babette said with a smile. "Remember the music? The night you proposed."

She began to hum the tune. Her voice shook. And both then realised how frightened she was, that her insistence on a splendid entrance was really no more than a brave try at hiding her fears. Fritz was proud to see that she was still humming as she stepped on board, bestowing a gracious smile on the steward who stepped forward to guide them to their cabins.

During the afternoon, Purser Ferdinand Mueller dealt with passenger inquiries swiftly and sympathetically, though not always entirely to their satisfaction. He had to turn down a request from a couple who wanted to change cabins, making clear that the ship was fully booked and there were no spare cabins available. Recha Weiler came to ask whether kosher food might be served. Mueller regretted that it would not, at least not immediately, but asked if it would suffice to offer a plentiful supply of egg and fish dishes. A group of young passengers came, wanting to know where the swimming pool was. Politely postponing the discussion on kosher cooking, the purser told the group that the pool would be erected in the opening above the cargo hold, aft on A deck, after leaving port; it would be filled with water once the ship neared the warmer Gulf Stream.

By six o'clock Saturday evening, the purser was pleased that many of the passengers were already behaving like the travellers he was used to serving.

Babette Spanier thought the crew acted as if they had been told to put on a show. Since boarding she had watched them, wondering what they really thought. She asked her husband, who said it did not matter.

"All that matters is that we sail on time and get away from Germany," Dr. Spanier said.

Even if the ship was a thousand miles away it could still be recalled by radio. Babette wondered whether her husband had considered that, but decided not to ask him.

Gustav Schröder dined alone in his day cabin. As the steward, Leo Jockl, served him, the captain noticed he was obviously fumbling. What was the matter?

No more than "the general tension of the voyage," he told the captain.

The trip must be regarded as the same as any other. "These people are passengers, no different from others we have carried."

The steward nodded and hurried from the cabin before the captain could pry out the truth that he had been asked to inform on him.

Schröder watched him go with some misgivings. The fact that Jockl was a half Jew made the voyage nerve-racking for him. The captain decided he must watch his steward more carefully. He then made another entry in the diary he was keeping of the trip.

"There is a somewhat nervous disposition among the passengers. Despite this, everyone seems convinced they will never see Germany again. Touching departure scenes have taken place. Many seem light of heart, having left their homes. Others take it heavily. But beautiful weather, pure sea air, good food, and attentive service will soon provide the usual worry-free atmosphere of long sea voyages. Painful impressions on land disappear quickly at sea and soon seem merely like dreams."

He walked to the bridge to prepare for the moment he always enjoyed, the moment of departure.

By half past seven on Saturday evening, the crowd at the railing had grown quiet. From high above came a piercing blast. Below, on the quay, the band struggled to compete. Bellowed commands echoed between ship and shore. Then the gangways were hauled clear and ropes slipped. Still the crowd remained quiet, waiting.

Even the band was now silent, its leader standing stiffly to attention, baton poised. Aaron Pozner felt the deck tremble under his feet, and a sigh stirred among the people wedged around him.

"The ship's moving!" somebody cried. "The space between us and the land is growing."

It widened steadily and surely before their eyes—too wide for anybody to jump from the ship, or onto it.

Babette Spanier looked at her watch. "Right on time. Eight o'clock.

"The Germans are never late, especially when it comes to Jews," her husband replied.

Shortly after 8:30 P.M., the radio room aboard the St. Louis received a priority message from Claus-Gottfried Holthusen. It made Gustave Schröder angry: he had been deliberately deceived by Holthusen at his earlier meeting, for now the Hapag director had cabled in the message the captain decoded:

IMPERATIVE YOU MAKE ALL SPEED HAVANA IN VIEW TWO OTHER SHIPS THE ENGLISH ORDUNA AND FRENCH FLANDRE BOUND THERE WITH SIMILAR PASSENGERS BUT HAVE CONFIRMATION THAT WHATEVER HAPPENS YOUR PASSENGERS WILL LAND. NO CAUSE FOR ALARM .

The cable had come too late to discuss the matter directly with Holthusen, since the St. Louis was not fitted with a ship-to-shore telephone. Schröder believed that Holthusen had timed his message to arrive at the moment when the St. Louis was steadily gaining speed.

The cable had given no positions for the Orduna or the Flandre, but a check in a reference book revealed that both ships were smaller than the St. Louis, and faster. Once the St. Louis was clear of its next port of call, at Cherbourg, she must maintain her maximum speed of sixteen knots all the way to Cuba. Ostermeyer said he would explain to the passengers that they were hurrying because the ship had a tight summer cruise schedule to follow.

It was a relief to have a reassuring and quick-

This picture shows First Officer Ostermeyer at his home near Magdeburg in 1949, some time after he was freed from a Russian PoW camp, where he had been held since 1945. He rejected Communism whilst detained, just as he had rejected Nazism. (Authors' Collection)

thinking senior officer, the captain thought. Ostermeyer had ordered the radio room to locate the Orduna and Flandre as soon as he read the cable; the St. Louis must get to Cuba with its cargo before they did. But no matter how they interpreted the cable's message, its contents seemed to warn of trouble, with its "imperative," "all speed" and "whatever happens." If the fate of his passengers would not be endangered, the captain thought, he would abandon the voyage here and now. He was more than ever determined to resign at the journey's end.

"I'm being used," insisted Gustav Schröder, "and, by God, I don't like it!"

By nine o'clock that Saturday night, news of the ship's departure was being telephoned and telegraphed to various parts of the world.

Claus-Gottfried Holthusen spoke to Morris Troper, European director of the Joint Distribution Committee in Paris.

"All will be well," the Hapag director told him. "They are at sea, which is the main thing."

Troper sensed that they both knew it was not the case, but he kept his reservations to himself. Afterward, he sent a telegram to the American Jewish Joint Distribution Committee in New York stating that the St. Louis would arrive in Havana "around May 27" with almost 1000 on board.

In Berlin, the departure was a signal for action

in the Ministry of Propaganda. Goebbels was telephoned at home. He authorised the Nazi national news agency to carry a long, virulent diatribe on the voyage. Within the hour, newspapers and radio stations through Germany were preparing stories accusing the St. Louis passengers of fleeing with stolen hoards of money, and much else. Aryan Germans were reminded to protect themselves against the "machinations of those still among us."

A ministry official cabled Robert Hoffman at the Hapag office in Havana. Hoffman was instructed to ensure that the fourteen agents provocateurs in Havana created the maximum hostility among the people toward the ship's passengers, and also those on the British and French ships. Further orders were cabled to the German embassies in Washington, London, Paris, and Rome, briefing the ambassadors to exploit the propaganda value of the St. Louis voyage. Those on board were to be branded as criminals; the question was to be planted everywhere: Who would want to take such people? It was crude, but such methods had been effective before.

Commander von Bonin, who had briefed Otto Schiendick about his rendezvous with Hoffman in Havana, learned of the departure over dinner in a call from a duty officer at Abwehr headquarters. There was no need to disturb Admiral Canaris with the news.

Around that time, an Associated Press correspondent in Berlin filed a story to New York on the sailing. He did not give it much play, guessing it might end up as a back page item for the Sunday editions.

In London, Sir Herbert Emerson, like Gustav Schröder, was furious with Claus-Gottfried Holthusen. The director of the International Committee on Political Refugees felt that Holthusen had purposely snubbed him by ignoring his earlier, carefully considered cable warning that the St. Louis should not sail. Emerson believed the refugees on board could jeopardise his negotiations for the wholesale resettlement of Jews outside Germany. Hitler had threatened to withdraw his offer of allowing the orderly emigration of 50,000 a year because of a "lack of response" from other nations.

There had been no lack of response, but how were the schemes to be financed? Official Jewish opinion was divided, and also questioned the suitability of the areas offered.

The refugee director had begun to lose patience, confiding to an aide that there "is always some other scheme in the background for which [the Jews] are prepared to sacrifice schemes which are already in being." Emerson knew the crucially important British white paper on Palestine, due to be published in just four days' time on May 17, was almost certain to exacerbate the situation. The St. Louis was at the very least an irritating distraction. The voyage had come at the worst possible time.

Seated by her husband's bed in cabin B-108 that Saturday night, Recha Weiler kept telling him that the nightmare was finally over, they were out of the darkness into the light.

Professor Weiler nodded, but he was too tired to speak. "Recha," he murmured. "It is enough sometimes just to travel."

Babette and Fritz Spanier settled the twins to sleep and went out to inspect the ship. They walked from one public room to another, most plush-carpeted with crystal chandeliers, gilt framed mirrors, and polished woodwork.

The ship's purser also strolled from deck to deck, pausing to speak with a steward, barman, or cabin boy. Babette wondered if he was briefing them on some anticipated action; the voyage could still be stopped.

But her spirits revived as they inspected the elegant ship. It seemed to represent "the good life ahead," as her husband had promised. "It was glossy and smart, just like America," she later recalled. They would become closer on the voyage. "Fritz was more attentive than he had been for years. He had not even looked at another girl on board, and there were plenty of pretty ones around."

As he walked through the ship, Ferdinand Mueller had been disturbed by the signs of distress or fear on many faces. Even if he had not received clear orders from the captain that everything possible must be done to please the passengers, he was sure he would still have done so. So, when the Spaniers walked into the Schanke Bar on C deck, the purser invited them to join him for a cocktail, "to show we are all Germans."

It seemed a great pity, Dr. Spanier replied, that not until he and his wife were fleeing the country had a German said such a thing.

Two decks above, Max Loewe peered out and

down. The lights onshore blinked, but around the ship, the sea was black.

He wished, he whispered to his wife, that the protecting darkness would never lift. She touched his arm. His children, Ruth and Fritz, although intent on looking toward shore, could not help but overhear what their father had said.

"Do you know what it's like to be a Jew?"

Otto Schiendick's question stunned Leo Jockl. The group of stewards grew silent around one of the tables in the dining salon. Jockl desperately wished he had gone to his quarters instead of remaining to gossip after the last diners had gone. Schiendick repeated the question. One of the stewards looked at him speculatively.

"How do you know what it is like to be a Jew, Schiendick, unless you are one?" he asked.

There was a wave of laughter. Schiendick pushed back his chair and left the group.

EMBARKATION:

Passengers carried passports with a red "J" imprinted upon them and the sign of their impending departure was the exit visa stamp shown here. (Edgar Glucksman)

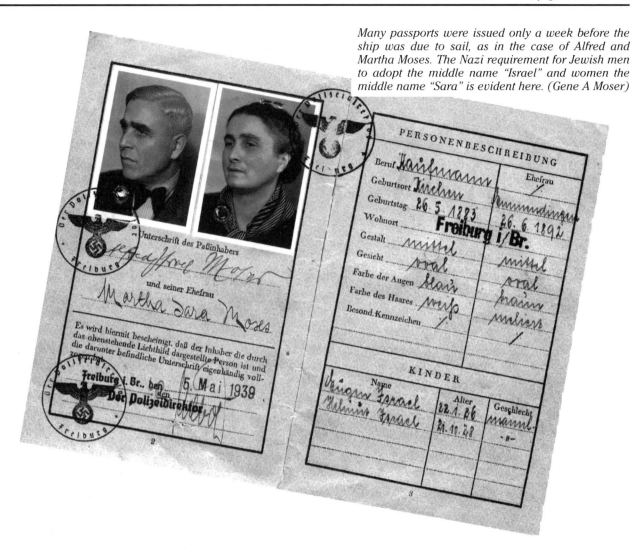

Many passports were issued only a week before the ship was due to sail, as in the case of Alfred and Martha Moses. The Nazi requirement for Jewish men to adopt the middle name "Israel" and women the middle name "Sara" is evident here. (Gene A Moser)

Currency controls were very strict for this voyage and passengers were allowed to take only a 10 reichsmarks each in cash, in additio to spend on board the ship. The Nazis' to render them penniless as they r destination. (Edgar Glucksman)

Before leaving Germany, the documentation had to be complete. Just two weeks before the voyage, Josef Guttmann was issued with this departure certificate, with which he and his family could gain their exit visa. (Harry Goodman)

And then, the passengers began to board on Saturday 13th May... (Authors' Collection)

REPUBLICA DE CUBA

SECRETARIA DE HACIENDA

DPTO. DE INMIGRACION

La Habana, Febrero 28 de 1939.

Sr.Agente General de la
Cia.de Vapores
A quien pueda interesar.
Ciudad.

Señor:-

De conformidad con lo que disponen el Apartado
(A) del Artículo Cuarto del Decreto #55, del 13 de
enero del año en curso y el Párrafo Tercero del Decreto #2507, del 17 de Noviembre de 1938, esta Dirección
General ha tenido a bien, permitir la entrada y estan-
cia en Cuba, por el tiempo que autorizan las leyes de
la República, en calidad de turista y al objeto de ges-
tionar su visado y entrada en los EE. UU., u otro país
cualquiera,de la señora GERTRUD SCHEUER,que por su na-
cionalidad de origen no usa otro apellido,natural y
ciudadana de Alemania,de veinte y cuatro años de edad,
soltera,del comercio y residiendo en la actualidad,en
la Ciudad de Kowln-Muehlein,Alemania,calle de Ruchheimer
número seis;siempre que no sufra enfermedad ni defecto
físico alguno, que porte su pasaporte y que no venga a
dedicarse a trabajos de ninguna clase durante el tiempo
que se encuentre en el Territorio Nacional.-

Lo que digo a usted, por si estima oportuno cur-
sar el cable a su Agencia en el puerto de embarque,a fin
de que le sea expedido el boleto de pasaje al menciona-
do pasajero.

Atentamente de usted,

Manuel Benitez González.
DIRECTOR GENERAL DE INMIGRACION.

This is the transit visa issued to most passengers by the corrupt Director General of Immigration in Cuba, Manuel Benitez Gonzàlez. Some passengers had legal entry permits, but most had this type, as issued to Gertrud Scheuer. (Mrs Gertrud Mendels)

The receipt given for payment for the entry visas for the Guttman family. It is interesting to note that all these documents passed through the hands of Luis Clasing, the HAPAG agent-general in Havana – whose assistant, Robert Hoffman was Otto Schiendick's espionage contact. (Harry Goodman)

SUNDAY, MAY 14, 1939

By Sunday, May 14, a bright and sunny morning, the ship had begun to settle down. Captain Schröder was gratified to see that some of the passengers even smiled at the small party of deck officers he led on the inspection tour he regularly carried out on the first full day of a new trip. The inspection was primarily an exercise in public relations.

Within an hour the entourage had put in a brisk appearance in the social hall, peered into the deserted gymnasium on A deck, and strolled around the sports deck, where a few younger passengers tried their hand at shuffleboard. Then he led the officers inside, down to B deck, to the Tanzplatz;,it was being prepared for an afternoon tea dance. They moved farther down, to C deck and the dining areas, where stewards flitted, laying tables for lunch. The arrangement of white linen, crystal glass, and silverware never failed to please Gustav Schröder; it reminded him of his own humble upbringing, when he had eaten from enamelled plates.

The captain led the way past the ship's laundry and into the crew quarters, with its pungent air of men who worked, relaxed, and slept in close proximity. His mellow mood gave way to rising anger as he saw a bulletin board festooned with the current issue of Der Stuermer and party notices bearing the signature of Otto Schiendick.

He ordered the steward to be summoned, and tersely told him to clear the board of all propaganda. Schiendick protested. As the ship's Leiter, he argued, it was his duty to keep the crew informed of party doctrines.

"Take that stuff down."

"But, Captain, I must respectfully—"

"Take it down—now! Like this!"

Gustav Schröder ripped down the pages of Der Stuermer, and dropped them in a trash can.

Crimson-faced, the steward began to remove the offending material.

The Spaniers were among the first to enter the first-class restaurant. A steward showed them to a table and handed around menus.

Babette Spanier was content to watch other passengers arriving. An attractive, well-dressed woman caught her attention; she had a cosmopolitan air. Babette Spanier listened, with shocked disapproval, as the woman spoke to the table steward; for all her elegance, she used the broad, brutal Berlin dialect of the streets.

"Excuse me, but I think we'll have to be careful with whom we mix," Babette said to her husband. Nearby on a podium, the musicians talked quietly among themselves. Soon the diners came in a concerted rush. Stewards advanced, bowing and smiling, escorting them to tables. The orchestra struck up briskly; its clarinettist sang a love song. Babette Spanier thought the performance "far too leery," and gave her attention to the menu.

In the tourist-class restaurant, Renatta Aber solemnly read aloud the contents of the entire menu to her five-year-old sister.

"Can I have it all?" asked Evelyne.

Aaron Pozner watched the two girls. Their innocent enthusiasm reminded him of his own two children. He pushed aside his plate, his appetite gone, and left the restaurant.

Otto Schiendick watched him go and told another steward: "There goes a typical Jew. Ordering all that food and then leaving it."

"I shouldn't let the captain hear you say that," came the reply. "Otherwise you'll be in more trouble."

Schiendick turned away, apparently furious that his latest clash with Captain Schröder had made him the butt of crew gossip. For most of his colleagues, he was only tolerated because of his official party role on board. That knowledge smarted most of all, making him more determined than ever to seek his revenge.

In the kitchen area, which served both first and tourist classes, he cornered Leo Jockl and demanded to know what information he had gleaned.

Jockl replied blandly with a detailed recital of the captain's movements since he had awakened that morning, bathed, shaved, and breakfasted.

"That's not what I want to know."

"But there's nothing else to report," Jockl replied. "Unless you want me to make it up."

Schiendick glared, and for the first time the captain's steward did not avoid the stare.

Alice Feilcherrfeld lunched quickly, having no interest in joining the excited chatter all around her. Afterward she went on deck, but the sight of children playing reminded her of the uncertainty over her own children's future. But, returning to her cabin, she was depressed even more by the empty berths and the folded-up baby's cot in the corner.

Three months earlier, Alice Feilchenfeld had sent her four children to Belgium for safekeeping. They were to join the ship at Cherbourg; in Havana her husband waited to complete the family reunion. But just before boarding in Hamburg, she had received word from Belgium that the Cuban visas for her children had not yet been received. Without them they would not be allowed to board. She wondered whether she should cable her husband to let him know the permits had not arrived, but decided that if he had not already sent them it was now too late.

Rather than sit alone in the empty cabin, Alice Feilchenfeld went for a walk on the promenade deck, where she noticed a man standing alone by the rail. She decided to speak to him and was pleasantly surprised to find that Max Loewe came from her home town, Breslau. She tried to begin a conversation, eager to have a man's advice, but he seemed hardly to comprehend, and fidgeted

nervously. When she began to explain her dilemma about the children, he became even more agitated, as if she had "touched a raw nerve in his mind." Embarrassed, she excused herself.

One-year-old Raphael was the one Frau Feilchenfeld especially worried about; the three older children were tougher, particularly ten-year-old Wolfgang. In Germany, the boy had looked at the world around him and hardened himself to the suffering and taunts. By mid afternoon, she was exhausted and fell asleep in her cabin, as she would recall, "actually trembling with anxiety."

After an excellent dinner, Dr. Spanier and his wife joined the throng heading for the ship's cinema; the main feature was to be a romantic story.

Few noticed Otto Schiendick slip into the back of the dimmed theatre. He wanted to see the passengers' reaction to the newsreel. A murmur of consternation stirred through the audience as the face of Adolf Hitler filled the screen and his voice shrieked familiar invective about "world-wide Jewish influences clamouring for an interventionist war

By Sunday, many passengers had relaxed enough to decide that nothing evil would befall them if they played shuffleboard on the Sports Deck, so they did. (From the collection of Gerald Granston, currently on loan to the Museum of Jewish Heritage, NY)

against Germany." The Fuehrer was followed by shots of German mobilisation, and the strident commentary warned those in the darkened room that the day of reckoning for Jews was at hand.

Dr. Spanier had seen enough. He escorted his wife to their cabin and then stormed to the purser's office.

Mueller was mortified when he heard Fritz Spanier's complaint. In all the careful checks the purser had made to ensure nothing would give offence, he had inadvertently overlooked the newsreel. Dr. Spanier was not placated; nothing less than a personal explanation from the captain would satisfy him. Mueller began to plead there was no need to go to such lengths since the mistake would not occur again. But the doctor coldly insisted that either the purser would take him to the captain or he would seek him out himself.

The captain had years of experience in handling difficult problems involving passengers. Now, he dismissed Mueller; he would deal with the purser later. Alone with Dr. Spanier, the captain listened sympathetically and silently.

But the doctor's anger stemmed from no ordinary complaint. The captain decided to do the only thing he felt proper in the situation: he admitted frankly that there had been a lapse of good taste. It would not occur again.

"A lapse of good taste!" said Dr. Spanier. "Is that what you call insulting people? Do you know what it is really like to be persecuted and then have to endure this?"

The captain conceded that he had no such personal experience. "What further do you wish me to do? You have my assurance it will not happen again. I have apologised. What else can I do?"

There was no more to be done. With a stiff ''Gute Nacht, '' Dr. Spanier left the cabin. Nothing, after all, would be so very different on this ship from life in Nazi Germany. He felt that the captain had behaved correctly, but coldly, in his apology.

Gustav Schröder felt dejected after the encounter. He had tried to avoid just such an incident, and yet it had happened—and early in the voyage. Dr. Spanier did not, however, seem the sort to make further trouble. The captain respected the force of the doctor's words. His eloquence and sense of moral decency made him a formidable figure. He

marked Fritz Spanier as a man of substance.

Fritz and Babette Spanier's exit from the cinema had been witnessed by Otto Schiendick. Others had also left the theatre in disgust, and the steward was pleased that the newsreel had achieved the effect he had hoped for. He had followed Dr. Spanier to the purser's office and watched the two men head for the bridge. When Mueller returned alone, Schiendick had tried to question him, but the usually placid purser erupted in fury.

Otto Schiendick retired to his quarters, determined to add Mueller's name to the captain's as men to be revenged upon.

MONDAY, MAY 15, 1939

The sun sparkled on the wheel house windows. They had not, Gustav Schröder observed to the helmsman, been properly cleaned. It was one of several caustic observations he made early that Monday morning.

The captain had slept badly. He had questioned Jockl about the passengers' mood, and when the steward had not replied quickly enough, he had sharply demanded to know what was the matter.

Jockl then told him of Schiendick's demand that he become an informer. Gustav Schröder listened in stunned silence. His hopes of a peaceful, ordinary voyage faded.

His first thought had been to send for Schiendick, confront him, and then dump the steward ashore at Cherbourg. But he realised that was not possible. Six months ago an order had been issued by Hapag to all its masters that party Leiters on company ships could not be removed without the written authority of the marine superintendent.

If the captain faced Schiendick now, the steward would probably gain the upper hand. He decided for the moment to take no action. His mood was not eased by another cable from Holthusen ordering Schröder to curtail his Cherbourg stop. The 15,507 Orduna, with 154 emigrants on board, was only fourteen hours astern of the St. Louis—and gaining steadily. The Flandre, smaller and faster than either the St. Louis or the Orduna, had 104 refugees, but her exact position was unknown. Suppose they arrived first, and unloaded their human cargo. Would there still be room for the St. Louis's passengers? The message had ended:

REPEAT YOU MAKE ALL POSSIBLE SPEED VIEW FLUID SITUATION HAVANA.

Gustav Schröder dispatched a reply to Holthusen demanding to know what he meant by "fluid situation Havana."

Shortly afterward the Cherbourg pilot came on board and eased the St. Louis toward the harbour. Passengers on deck could clearly see traffic on the waterfront streets, and more than one expressed relief that there were no Nazi symbols in sight.

At 9:30 A.M. the ship was positioned and anchored; minutes afterward the electrically powered starboard accommodation ladder was lowered, and from the shore a number of launches headed toward the liner.

Gustav Schröder summoned First Officer Ostermeyer and showed him the latest cable from Holthusen.

"I want to be out of here in half the usual time," he added. "I don't care how it's done, but I want it done."

Otto and Rosemarie Bergmann watched as the first of the launches rose and fell against the accommodation ladder.

The young couple were happy to have a break from their charges, the two most elderly women on the ship—Rosemarie's mother, aged sixty-nine, and Otto's aunt, Shalote Hecht, eighty. Aunt Shalote had already proven herself particularly trying, and Rosemarie's ailing mother had complained incessantly about having to leave Germany despite the fact that the Nazis had confiscated her home, requiring her to pay rent for living in the house that had been hers for over half a century.

Rosemarie Bergmann, too, gave her husband cause for concern. Superstitious, she had been disturbed by the departure date—the thirteenth—the more so since the journey had begun on the Jewish Sabbath.

They watched the crates of fresh fruits and vegetables being loaded, and she noticed something else that bothered her. No water was being taken on. Otto Bergmann wondered whether the story his wife had heard, at breakfast, could possibly be true—that the ship would not take on water because of a fear that the French could have poisoned it. He discounted it; if someone wanted to kill them all, it

would have been possible for them to poison the stores being loaded.

Yet Rosemarie Bergmann thought it strange that no water was taken on. She decided to note it in her diary of the voyage.

All through the long morning, Alice Feilchenfeld watched the supply boats coming and going. The only break for her had been when the mail was brought on board, the last the St. Louis would receive before Havana. But there had been no letter from her husband in Cuba, and none from her children.

The lunch gong sounded. She refused to leave the rail. Still no one boarded the ship.

Early in the afternoon, a tender filled with people approached. It carried thirty-eight passengers, mostly children and Spanish refugees from the Civil War.

Alice Feilchenfeld saw no sign of her family. In that moment, she made her decision: she would leave the ship and go to Belgium to be with her children, even though it meant she might never see her husband again. With tears streaming down her cheeks, she looked for an officer to whom she could convey her decision.

"Momma! "

She turned, and Judith and Heinz, followed by Wolfgang carrying baby Raphael in his arms, ran down the deck toward her. They had been the last off the launch; their arrival made a total of 937 passengers on board.

Shortly afterward, the St. Louis glided forward into the English Channel toward the Bay of Biscay.

In Havana, some 4000 sea miles away, the news that the St. Louis was on her way did not please the Cuban president; Frederico Bru was determined to stop the ship's passengers from landing.

Throughout the whole of this humid Monday, Manuel Benitez, director of immigration, reassured the refugees and the local Hapag agent, Luis Clasing, that the passengers would land; that President Bru's recently published decree 937, which forbade them entry, was no more than a piece of paper, "just like Hitler gave Chamberlain at Munich."

Clasing had not been amused by the comparison, nor was he able to hide his anxiety that Bru's decree would bar the St. Louis passengers and end the profitable partnership between Manuel

Benitez and Hapag. Benitez had barely concealed the fact that he had amassed a fortune by capitalising on the plight of refugees. He could not accept that he was callously profiteering from their desperation, as had been suggested by at least one of his cabinet colleagues, the commanding Secretary of State, Dr. Juan Remos. Only that day Benitez had heatedly told Remos that in granting refugees sanctuary, however temporary and restrictive it was, he saved their lives. Remos retorted he could not share Benitez's view of himself as an idealistic humanist—or that the money Benitez made was of secondary consideration.

Nevertheless, Remos had promised his support for allowing in the St. Louis passengers. Benitez had been surprised; he knew that Remos usually backed Bru's line at cabinet meetings. The Secretary of State had dryly remarked: "Sometimes conscience is more important than anything. You should try and remember that."

Other cabinet members had proved evasive when Manuel Benitez had tried to enlist their support to have decree 937 repealed. They recognised that the law was more than a device to keep out refugees; it was the instrument Bru wanted to force a head-on clash with Manuel Benitez and, more important, his benefactor, Fulgencio Batista, chief of staff of the Cuban army, and effectively the most powerful single voice on the island.

By late afternoon, having forgone his siesta, Manuel Benitez was tiring of all the unaccustomed activity. Nowadays, the most onerous side of his partnership with Hapag was writer's cramp. In the past months he had signed his name to some 4000 landing permits at $150 a signature, bringing him about $600,000 for an outlay of some seventy-five cents for a new fountain pen.

There had also been periodic and handsome kickbacks from Hapag, and this Monday he received another one when Clasing arrived with $5000 in small bills. The agent explained that Hapag didn't want the "problem" of taking the St. Louis passengers back to Europe, and the company was happy to make Benitez this "gift of friendship" to ensure that the "problem" would not arise.

Benitez had graciously accepted the money, seated Clasing in a corner of his large office, and begun a rereading of decree 937, to see if there was a loophole, to see if a way could be found which would

avoid a confrontation with the president, and yet allow the immigration director to realise his daydream of becoming one of the wealthiest men in the Caribbean.

In the fall of 1938, Benitez had opened a strictly unofficial, private, and illegal "Bureau of Immigration" in the Hotel Plaza, next door to Hapag's offices. He waited for the promulgation of the long-expected decree 55, published in early 1939, drawing a clear distinction between tourists and immigrants.

Decree 55 made it mandatory for an immigrant to have a visa, jointly approved by Benitez, Remos, and the secretary of labour. Further, each immigrant had to post a bond of $500 as a "guarantee of sustenance." Few such legal visas were issued because Benitez, Remos, and the labour secretary disliked and mistrusted each other.

Tourists, on the other hand, were still welcome in Cuba, and could enter unhindered by any such visa restrictions.

Manuel Benitez, with the foresight that made him peculiarly suited to Cuban politics, had prepared his "Immigration Bureau" for just this eventuality. He discreetly let it be known that his "Bureau" would issue not visas, but landing permits, to anyone who paid $150.

The permits were individually typed in Spanish on Department of Immigration note paper which Benitez had purloined. They all carried his flourishing signature. Benitez carefully made sure the permits had the right legal jargon to give them further authenticity; there was a firmly couched warning that the permit holder could not work in Cuba, and that he was only authorised to stay "for such time as may be necessary to obtain a visa for the U.S.A. or any other country."

There had been an immediate rush for the permits. Some of the refugees already settled in Havana, caught up in the spirit of happy corruption, bought them in job lots at $150 apiece, and resold them in Europe at up to $500 each. The profits were reinvested in more permits, and a number of refugees grew prosperous exploiting their kinfolk still in Germany.

Hapag had been quick to see advantages in the scheme, and offered immigrants a bumper package deal—a permit and guaranteed passage on a Hapag ship. The passengers on the St. Louis were just such a package, each of them described on his landing permit—had they known it, it would doubtless have surprised them—as "a tourist, travelling for pleasure."

Manuel Benitez now knew that the "tourist" loophole had been closed. He believed the decree 937 was an act of revenge on Bru's part because Benitez had refused him a share of the profits.

The immigration director lay aside his paper, rose from his couch, and looked quizzically at Clasing. How much would Hapag pay to get decree 937 rescinded? Clasing asked, equally carefully, how much Benitez had in mind.

"Say $250,000," replied Benitez blandly. "You understand it is not for me, but for Bru."

"Impossible! Hapag would never agree to such a figure."

Benitez sighed; with $250,000 from Hapag, he could have made the magnanimous gesture to Bru of "splitting" the profits with the president, while at the same time not actually having to touch any of the money he had already made from selling illegal permits.

Clasing spoke again, and his criticism of Manuel Benitez was barely concealed. "I have given promises to my company on your word and there seems to have been a gross miscalculation about Bru's opposition."

Benitez bridled. The remark hurt his Latin pride. But even if Hapag would not make such a "gesture," it did not matter. Clasing was panicking unnecessarily; he did not understand the Cuban mentality. Benitez argued that Bru could still be outmanoeuvred.

To prove his intention, he telephoned the presidential palace for an "urgent and immediate" appointment with Bru. It was granted. Clasing left, promising to return later that evening to hear the outcome of the meeting.

Shortly afterward the immigration director set out to walk to the palace, content for the moment to be carried along in the undertow of Havana life. On the way he was offered prostitutes, dirty movies, and postcards from pimps who solicited him automatically but with no real hope.

Manuel Benitez enjoyed such experiences. He had grown up with some of the touts, and the sight of them, he often said, was a constant reminder that all men were born equal, and that success, wealth, and position were only a matter of planning and seizing opportunities. Such an attitude had earned him the kind of respect and homage that in America a Mafia clan bestows on its "godfather." And, like all good "dons," he cultivated his popularity.

Along his route this evening Benitez stopped at a news vendor to inquire after the man's family, paused for a chat with a shoeshine boy, slipped a few coins to an old crone minding a coffee stall, and patted a number of children on the head.

Those he touched or talked to were flattered by his attention, and the image of Manuel Benitez as a sharp but likeable wheeler-dealer, an image that he enjoyed, was enhanced by such contacts.

At exactly 6 P.M. he arrived at the palace. From a distance the building gave the impression of solidity and elegance; the walls were thick to resist the summer heat. Closer up, one could see they had suffered the ravages of tropical hurricanes and time. It appeared a quietly crumbling monument to Spanish colonialism.

Frederico Laredo Bru had returned from his siesta to his office late in the afternoon. Now, in the evening sunlight, he stood by one of the tall windows overlooking the landscaped palace gardens, lean and impeccably dressed in a white tropical suit and black bow tie.

He reviewed the reasons that led to decree 937. In part he had published it because the secretary of labour had questioned the wisdom of letting in more refugees—in relation to its size and population, Cuba had more than almost any other country—arguing that though they were legally barred from working, many did in fact get jobs Cubans would otherwise have had. The labour secretary believed public opinion was against further immigration.

Then, the secretary of the treasury had urged a curb on immigrants because of the island's economic stagnation. Finally, Dr. Juan J. Remos, the secretary of state, had eloquently urged the ban on refugees to end Benitez's "disgraceful" flouting of Cuba's immigration laws. That, Bru knew, had been the key factor in his decision, more so because Benitez had refused to share the profits from his private "bureau" with him.

But the mounting public clamour against the refugees had also influenced Bru. What the president did not know was that the outcry had been deliberately whipped up by the fourteen propaganda

Cuban president Federico Bru and his army Chief of Staff, Fulgencio Batista. (UPI)

agents Goebbels had sent to Cuba a full month before, and who had then been carefully briefed by the Abwehr spymaster on the island, Robert Hoffman.

From a Nazi standpoint, the results had been spectacular. An alliance was forged between the newly legalised Cuban Nazi party and the older and stronger National Fascist party to engage in a virulent propaganda war against the refugees. Every move was guided by the Nazi propaganda experts, who, in turn, through Hoffman's office in the Hapag building, received their instructions from Berlin.

The Nazis had persuaded a local press baron to launch a campaign in his three newspapers to drive all Jews out of Cuba. On May 4, one of those papers, El Diario de la Marino, had announced in bold banner headlines that, far from the government driving them out, more would soon be on their way aboard the St. Louis. The Cuban secretary of labour planned to "interfere with the ship." Imprecise though those words were, there was no doubting what was intended when Bru had been asked in Congress to "prohibit repeated immigration of Hebrews who are inundating the republic and making a joke of its laws.

Decree 937 had been passed ten days ago, on May 5. Now, all signs suggested it was a popular move. Yet Bru remained worried because Batista had not yet expressed a view, and the president knew the army chief's attitude was a crucial one.

Ever since Batista had assumed command of the army in the revolt of 1933—the same year Hitler and Roosevelt assumed office—Batista had manipulated political power from behind the scenes. Since 1933, there had been no fewer than nine presidents of Cuba. One had probably the shortest stay in office ever. The first thing he did when installed in the presidential palace was to take a bath in the presidential tub. While he was drying himself he received notice that his term was over.

In 1936, Batista eased the then president from office, and put in his own nominee: Frederico Bru. But by May 1939 Bru had deliberately set himself on a collision course with Batista. He had ousted many of Batista's nominees from office. By stopping Benitez's "bureau," the president would widen the rift, for Batista had also put the immigration director in his post. But Bru was more than a puppet on Batista's string; he was now politically strong enough to show who really ruled Cuba—himself, and not the ex-army sergeant.

Bru seated himself behind his desk to await Benitez, an austere and worried man. He knew that the issue of the St. Louis had brought matters to a head.

He cut short the minister's cordial greeting by saying bluntly that he was already late for a dinner engagement.

"What exactly do you wish to see me about?"

Benitez tried to remain unruffled as he explained that he had come to discuss the "wider implications" of decree 937.

Bru rose, and in his cold, flat voice declared there was nothing to discuss. "The law stays as it stands."

"But Senor Presidente—!"

Bru walked swiftly from behind his desk toward his office door. He held it open.

"I am not going to discuss the matter further with you, or with anybody."

He wished Manuel Benitez a curt good evening.

At around the time Benitez left Bru, American naval attache Ross E. Rowell and his opposite number, Henry Barber, the military attache, kept the cocktail-hour date they had arranged in Havana's American Club to discuss how the arrival of the ship would affect them.

The two intelligence agents liked each other. Rowell was impressed by Barber's long experience of Cuban affairs, and Barber thought Rowell's

enthusiasm for his new job "very commendable." The military attache's field of acquaintances was far wider than Rowell's: he knew many members of Havana's large diplomatic community by their first names, he had carefully nourished friendships among the more influential classes of Cuban society, he knew he could walk into police headquarters and be greeted more like a colleague than an intelligence agent for a foreign power. Barber was also a cautious man. He carefully considered all aspects of a situation before pronouncing, let alone acting. For that reason, the less experienced naval attache was keen to have his views on the St. Louis.

Major Barber believed the passengers would "somehow" be allowed to land. Given that, Rowell inquired, how best to screen them? Clearly he alone could not scrutinise each one as they came ashore. Barber thought little purpose would be served by Rowell's being on hand when the ship arrived.

"If there are infiltraters among them," he told the naval attache, "there will be plenty of time to watch them once they are on land."

Rowell disagreed. He felt the moment of arrival would be crucial: "That is when they will be at their most vulnerable." The two men then debated whether there would in fact be German agents on board. Barber thought it unlikely—"surely there are enough here already"—and then went on to describe a wider view, held by many of his informants, that the voyage was inspired by pure politics.

"Some believe Germany is sending these immigrants here with the express intention of creating the impression abroad that Cuba does not want to accept the very people the world criticises Germany for wanting to get rid of," he told the naval attache. "And remember to Germany, Cuba is part of the United States."

Rowell persisted in his view that the St. Louis was a perfect vehicle for transporting agents under the guise of refugees. "When all these people arrive," he said, "there will be pandemonium. Surely among a thousand people, the chances are there will be at least one agent."

Barber had to admit that on a balance of probabilities, Rowell was right. In the end, the military attache agreed to be on hand with Rowell when the ship arrived: they would split the surveillance duties, then pool the result.

It was a novel arrangement. The main branches of American intelligence were notorious for the way they jealously guarded their secrets, competed with each other, went their own ways, and seldom came together. Even at this meeting, Rowell had not told Barber of his suspicions about Robert Hoffman, or of his continuing surveillance of that most unlikely of all Abwehr agents on the island, the dwarf Otto Ott. Nor had the two men discussed the possibility of checking on St. Louis crew members, as opposed to the refugees, when they came ashore.

Now, as they parted, Barber told Rowell: "The whole matter stinks. I intend to tell Washington in my next report what is really happening here. These forlorn and desperate fugitives are being unscrupulously fleeced by Cuban officials."

As Barber went to send his report to the War Department in Washington, Rowell paid one of his regular calls on the one main Jewish organisation the "fugitives" already in Havana had to turn to: the Jewish Relief Committee. This small organisation, run by two dedicated workers, Milton Goldsmith and Laura Margolis, had become by May 1939 almost alone responsible for the well-being of nearly 5000 refugees. Both officials feared that the St. Louis passengers would strain their meagre resources to breaking point.

Goldsmith was middle-aged, and during his long career in relief work, he had become used to disappointment. Younger than Goldsmith, Laura Margolis had, like him, retained many of the old-fashioned Jewish virtues. She had been taught to feel an obligation to help those worse off than herself, and she continued to do so in the years she had worked with refugees.

Laura Margolis had made repeated requests to New York that someone should be sent to Havana to see the conditions they were labouring under. Goldsmith had asked for more money from the Joint in New York, the agency that financed the committee. Neither request had brought results. As a consequence, the committee was not able to enlarge its overworked and now demoralised staff.

Each day an increasing number of refugees had called at the committee headquarters at Aguiar 556. Some had even followed Goldsmith to his room at the Hotel President. They wanted more money to live on, or information on how to get out of Cuba to the United States more quickly, or how to get relations and

friends into Cuba. Goldsmith found himself painfully inadequate on all three counts.

The harassed committee was besieged by other worries. The Joint in New York had also refused to give Goldsmith the authority he felt he needed to act independently. There were the anti-Semitic newspaper reports: Goldsmith felt he must raise funds in order to "persuade" editors to modify their attitudes. There were the continuous queries from refugees in Havana awaiting relatives on the St. Louis: would they be allowed to land? Goldsmith replied reassuringly that they would, but privately he was far from confident. And finally there was the Advisory Board, composed of eminent Jews living permanently in Cuba, always ready to offer Goldsmith the benefit of their knowledge.

Havana had a nucleus of such wealthy Jews who had established themselves in the nineteen-twenties. They had integrated well into the community, building a synagogue, opening kosher shops, and starting religious schools. But the existence and experience of those earlier immigrants was far removed from that of the refugees who later crowded into Cuba. The established Jews knew the language and had made the island their home, but the new Jews did not speak Spanish, and did not intend to stay. It was the prosperous Jews who advised Goldsmith and Laura Margolis on how to run their Relief Committee, and often those settlers found it difficult to identify with the poverty-stricken refugees.

Now, as Ross Rowell passed through an outer office crowded with people and knocked on his glass door, Goldsmith wondered whether the naval attache had come to add to his troubles; his usual reason for calling was to question him about Nazi agents among the refugees.

To Rowell's "Anything to report?" Goldsmith replied that he had discovered that a person who had recently applied for relief had previously lived for nine years in Mexico. He had been expelled from there for selling secrets to the Germans, and therefore Goldsmith had refused his request for money. Goldsmith told Rowell he believed the man was still a Nazi informer.

Well satisfied with his visit, Rowell thanked Goldsmith and departed to write another report to Washington. As Goldsmith watched him go, and saw at the same time the long queue of refugees outside his office, he must have feared that if the St. Louis was allowed to disembark its passengers, his Relief Committee might collapse altogether.

On this Monday night Luis Clasing and his assistant, Robert Hoffman, came to Benitez's office to learn the result of his meeting with the president.

The immigration director told his visitors that Bru was "just playing politics." In the manner of a born opportunist, Manuel Benitez reduced the whole complicated issue of the St. Louis to a single question. Would Bru allow the ship to enter Cuban territorial waters, let alone Havana Harbour, if he intended to bar the passengers from landing?

It was a tenuous argument and, unhappily for Benitez, Clasing virtually demolished it when he replied that the ship was not yet in the harbour, and even if it were, there was a great difference between the St. Louis's "being there, and actually disembarking refugees."

Benitez brushed aside the comment, believing the German "incapable of appreciating the finer points of argument. He behaved like a permanent tourist," he was to say later. But now the immigration director kept such thoughts to himself, anxious still to appear friendly toward the Hapag men, sensing that at the right moment another generous "gift" would be forthcoming.

It would not be on this night. Before coming to the meeting Clasing had told Hoffman that "tactically" it would be wrong, as the Abwehr agent had recommended, to offer further bribes "at this stage"; Clasing had added that Benitez "must now show results for his money."

Hoffman wanted the St. Louis to have a smooth passage in and out of Havana just as badly as did the Hapag agent; if there were difficulties over the passengers, Hoffman feared that Otto Schiendick might not get ashore to collect the secrets he was holding for him. But how to ensure that the ship landed? Hoffman thought it only a matter of bribing Benitez; Clasing was convinced that to pay more would inevitably lead to further demands later, and would guarantee nothing.

Disagreements between them had become common since Hoffman had been foisted on Clasing a year earlier when the Abwehr spy ring in Cuba was being developed. Clasing, a professional shipping man, had resented such intrusion, the more so as it

had impinged on company affairs on numerous occasions. When he had angrily protested, Hoffman had merely shrugged.

The question of when and whether to offer Manuel Benitez yet another handout had touched a raw nerve in Clasing, further exacerbated when Hoffman had insisted that he come to the meeting. Clasing had objected, and been told curtly by his assistant that Hoffman would not be there in behalf of Hapag.

"Why don't you keep your spying outside my business?" Clasing demanded sourly.

"Why don't you complain to Hamburg and see what happens?" Hoffman retorted.

In Benitez's presence now, both men maintained a seemingly united front, arguing volubly that the St. Louis passengers must land "no matter what happens." Manuel Benitez played his trump card. He reached into a desk drawer and produced a handful of notices.

"These are being posted publicly throughout Havana today," he told them.

The notices stated that though his "bureau" would no longer be issuing landing permits, those Benitez had issued prior to May 6, when decree 937 became law, would be honoured.

"The permits for those on the St. Louis were signed in this office before May 6, my friends. The legislation is not retroactive. Therefore those permits are entirely legal. The passengers will be allowed to disembark."

"And if they are not?" asked Hoffman. "If they are not, I give you my personal assurance I will carry them off the ship, one at a time, myself, if need be."

Dr. Max Aber dressed for dinner with extra care on Monday night. Though the fun-loving doctor looked forward with considerable anticipation to an evening with Benitez's secretary, the vivacious Gloria Spira, it would present only a pleasant interlude in his hours of worry about the safety of his two small daughters, Renatta and Evelyne, now travelling toward him on the St. Louis.

After he had gotten the landing permits at Benitez's "bureau"—seizing the same opportunity to make the acquaintance of Gloria—and sent them off to his wife, he had heard rumours on his frequent visits to the city's gay and gaudy centre that had made him uneasy: there was talk that the permits were "not quite kosher."

Aber had called again on his original Cuban contact, Jose Estedes, to express his concern, and had been taken by Estedes to see the powerful ally of President Bru, Secretary of State Juan Remos. The two Cubans had conversed rapidly in Spanish. Aber, not understanding what was being said, watched Remos carefully; he seemed to display enormous sympathy and friendliness. His kindness and concern was already well known to other refugees.

Do you have enough money to maintain your family? Estedes asked Dr. Aber in English.

Dr. Aber, who was trying to live on the money provided by Milton Goldsmith's Relief Committee, replied that he had virtually none.

Estedes turned back to Remos and said in Spanish: "Yes. He has plenty."

Remos scribbled a message in red ink and ordered a secretary to telegraph it to the Cuban consulate in Hamburg. It was authorisation for bona fide visas to be issued for the Aber children.

Later, Max Aber cabled the prefix number of the telegram to his wife with the request that she collect the visas. Lucie Aber had replied that the original permits issued by Benitez's "bureau" seemed "perfectly adequate." He had not heard from her since.

Earlier that day, he had received a telephone call from a relative in New York. She had just learned from Aber's sister in Germany that Renatta and Evelyne were on the St. Louis. It was enough reason for their father to celebrate tonight, but he still did not know whether his wife had collected the visas from the Cuban consul in Hamburg.

Now, as he dined with one of the most beautiful women in Havana, he asked what could be done for his children if they brought with them only landing permits, and if President Bru enforced decree 937. Gloria Spira laughed—and revealed how Manuel Benitez intended to interpret the decree.

Much later, Max Aber walked back home convinced all would now be well.

TUESDAY, MAY 16, 1939

At first the wind had barely rippled the sea. But within an hour it brought waves rolling against the starboard freeboard of the St. Louis.

In the early hours of Tuesday, May 16, as the motion became more pronounced, First Officer Ostermeyer ordered thirty degrees' wheel to star-

board, bringing the ship head-on into the wind and seaway. Five minutes later he reversed the order, completing a zigzag to port, satisfying himself that the manoeuvre reduced the roll and yet allowed the St. Louis to maintain the maximum speed possible through the Bay of Biscay.

The change of course jolted Aaron Pozner awake. For some minutes he lay still in his bunk in cabin D-375, soaked in a cold sweat, so real was his dream that the screams of his family still rang in his ears.

But the rhythmic motion of the ship slowly relaxed him, reminding him that every rise and fall of the St. Louis brought him closer to Cuba and the chance to earn enough for his family to join him.

Recha Weiler hardly noticed the ship's motion, for by this early Tuesday morning her world had shrunk to her husband's bed.

At some point during the night, Moritz Weiler had begun to sweat profusely, and Recha had given him two of the tablets the ship's doctor, Walter Glauner, had prescribed. She remembered, and had been grateful, that the doctor had been solicitous, insisting that no matter what the hour he would come to the cabin if she felt it necessary. Recha thanked him, but deep down inside her she knew her husband needed more than the ship's doctor and his pills; his frail body required the will to live.

Throughout the night she had sat by his bed, caressing his hand and murmuring gentle encouragement. Now, as dawn lightened the cabin, the tablets took effect; Moritz Weiler fell asleep.

Purser Mueller viewed the heavy swell with unhappiness. Seasickness was the surest way to dampen the growing gaiety among passengers. Since departing Cherbourg, he had been pleased to see smiles on more and more faces. One had even cracked a joke about Hitler. It had brought laughs from the passengers, and also from Mueller, but not from Otto Schiendick. Schiendick had told the passenger the comment was "not funny. All of you owe your lives to the generosity of the Fuehrer for allowing you to travel on this ship."

The passengers had been surprised to be addressed by a steward in this way, but one or two laughed.

Schiendick stalked off, making a further note about the purser in his "book of offences," which he so often flourished in front of fellow stewards.

Down in the crew mess hall, he once again harangued those present on the dangers of mixing with passengers, and especially "polluting our purity by having sexual relationships with non Aryans." He warned that any crew man suspected of such an offence would face severe penalties under the Law for the Protection of German Blood and Honour.

The threat was greeted with barely suppressed grins from some stewards, for by this Tuesday morning the crew quarters were rife with stories that some of the women passengers "were the hottest ever to come on the ship."

Similar stories reached the ears of Babette Spanier, who "could not understand why our nice-looking girls should want to fool around with crew members."

The passengers relaxed after the "St Louis" left Cherbourg and, unaware of the pressure on the ship's captain or the political wranglings going on in Cuba, they moved freely about the decks, meeting other passengers they did not know, making new acquaintances and, ultimately, friendships. (From the collection of Gerald Granston, currently on loan to the Museum of Jewish Heritage, NY)

Fritz Spanier ventured that "even Hitler cannot control the mating instincts of the human race," and went on to point out that he had heard that some of the young refugee men on board had "not been doing badly with the German crew stewardesses."

"That's different," said Babette Spanier.

The conversation was overheard by the Spanier's breakfast steward. When he relayed it to his colleagues, they thought it confirmed their impression that Frau Spanier was one of the most likeable, but "unusual," passengers on the ship. She had an enormous appetite which she maintained despite the ship's rolling, so severe that the wooden sides had been raised around the dining tabletops. Her husband sat patiently while she rapidly ate her way through most courses at every meal. No one could understand how Babette Spanier remained thin.

The eating habits of Otto Bergmann's Aunt Shalote also came in for their fair share of comment by the crew. The night before, at dinner, she had caused raised eyebrows by hectering her steward, demanding that he serve her first, and then sampling all the food as it arrived before deciding what she would eat. When Otto had tried to remonstrate with the eighty-year old, Aunt Shalote had turned on him: "Young man, you don't know how to handle servants."

When the old lady appeared for breakfast this Tuesday, Otto, wanting to be spared further embarrassment, excused himself, saying he was leaving to go to the gift shop to buy a birthday present for his mother-in-law. Aunt Shalote sniffed: "Why all the fuss? Rosemarie's mother is only seventy."

Renatta and Evelyne Aber felt the trip was getting even more exciting than their mother had promised. They had a cabin to themselves, and now, with the storm, the entire ship seemed theirs as passengers slumped on deck chairs or in their bunks.

Sisters Renatta (7) and Evelyne Aber (5). (Dr Max Aber)

After breakfast, Evelyne traipsed behind Renatta on a new adventure: soaping every door handle they passed. They peeped back down a corridor and watched a steward stop at a cabin door, carefully balancing a tray against the ship's motion; he grew angrier the more he tried to turn the handle. Finally his hand completely slid off the doorknob, and he lost his balance, and the tray skidded out of his grasp.

Laughing gleefully, the sisters sought a new diversion. On the promenade deck, they found some string; they dangled it over the rail and let it trail across the passengers dozing in chairs below on A deck.

The high spot of the morning came when they made friends with the Bardeleben and Fischer children. Though they could not know it, their fathers, waiting for them in Havana, had also become friends.

Ten-year-old Marianne Bardeleben and Ruth and Hans Fischer were standing conspiratorially outside the ladies' restroom on B deck when Renatta and Evelyne joined them. Marianne explained that Hans would stand guard while the four girls slipped into the rest room. Inside, each child went into a cubicle, locked its door from the inside, and then crawled out under the door, left the room, and waited expectantly outside.

A woman, clutching at a dressing gown, hurried into the washroom. The children giggled delightedly as they could hear her rushing from one locked door to another. Eventually she was ill in a washbasin.

The gang decided to repeat the prank in another washroom, but a suspicious stewardess followed and caught them red-handed. She threatened to lock them up if they continued. Not very frightened, the children returned to their cabins, whispering to each other that they would meet again.

WEDNESDAY, MAY 17, 1939

After breakfast on Wednesday, May 17, Gustav Schröder remained alone in his cabin. As he peered through the scuttles at the squally weather outside, he speculated on other and more unpleasant possibilities that could soon face his passengers and himself.

He had received no reply to a second and even

terser message to Claus-Gottfried Holthusen, demanding to know the situation in Havana and exactly why the St. Louis was engaged in a race with the two other ships carrying refugees. All Gustav Schröder knew for certain was that the Orduna and Flandre were steadily cutting down his lead, and he had been forced to chart a new course, taking the St. Louis north of the Azores, thus gaining five hours. But even that lead would be cancelled out if the other ships followed a similar route.

The new course had sent the St. Louis plunging through the bellicose Atlantic rollers, setting the breakfast crockery tumbling and bringing from the purser a plea for a reduction in speed during the morning meal.

The captain had brusquely refused, and was irritated with himself for venting his temper and frustration on the person who least deserved it.

By midmorning, the wind and swell held the ship in their sport, sending the few people who had braved it to the sports deck hurrying to their cabins and bringing on a further wave of seasickness throughout the St. Louis.

At noon First Officer Ostermeyer arrived with the daily summary of radio news broadcast to all German ships by the Deutsches Nachrichtenburo, Goebbels' official news agency.

Schröder was horrified to read that the St. Louis was the main item, that its journey was being exploited as part of the gathering Wagnerian murk of Hitler's New Order, and that, in the summary, his passengers were dismissed as Untermenschen, subhuman. He ripped up the news sheet. Turning to Ostermeyer, he snapped: "I'll get these people ashore in Havana even if the whole Propaganda Ministry tries to stop me!"

Unknown to the captain, that Wednesday, in Berlin, the ministry had another, bigger, event on which to comment; it would adversely effect not only the reception his passengers would receive in Cuba, but also the plight of thousands of other refugees.

On May 17, the British government published its long-awaited white paper on Palestine. As Sir Herbert Emerson, director of the International Committee on Political Refugees in London had feared, it further complicated his problems, for the paper set new and stringent limits on the number of Jews to be admitted to Palestine. Worse for Emerson,

Britain and Germany found themselves in unusual agreement with each other, for Hitler welcomed its proposals, and Goebbels exploited the apparent British attitude to the full.

Embarrassed by the German attitude, and by world opinion —apart from Germany almost uniformly critical of the white paper—Britain would quickly offer for Emerson's consideration 40,000 square miles of land in British Guyana for the use of refugees. Most of it was within five degrees of the equator and 250 miles from the sea, but planning soon began for an initial settlement of 5000 people. Not to be outdone, America matched the British offer with the Philippine province of Mindanao. The Dominican Republic, just Southeast of Cuba, then announced it would make room for 50,000 to 100,000 refugees, while suggesting a trial settlement of just over 200 families.

In Cuba itself on this Wednesday, the newspapers concerned themselves with the white paper and mass refugee-settlement areas, and more with the anti-Semitic attacks, which they had begun to narrow down to the St. Louis specifically. Robert Hoffman arranged for the editor of the Havana Avance to write about the ship's arrival:

> Against this invasion we must react with the same energy as have other peoples of the globe. Otherwise we will be absorbed, and the day will come when the blood of our martyrs and heroes shall have served solely to enable the Jews to enjoy a country conquered by our ancestors.

But on the St. Louis, no one yet knew of the white paper, nor of the increasing attacks on the passengers in the Cuban press.

Recha Weiler was so completely absorbed in the matter of administering her husband's medicaments that she did not notice the weather had brightened that Wednesday afternoon.

The ship's doctor, Walter Glauner, had made two visits to her husband's bedside that day, and on the second he had prescribed new tablets, and medicine to be taken hourly.

Now, at 5 P.M., Dr. Glauner returned, this time to give Moritz Weiler an injection. Recha winced as the needle was jabbed into the skin, and later told other passengers she wondered what was the point of it all, for she now believed that no tablet, no sip of medicine, no injection, could alleviate the true cause of her husband's suffering: the pain of having to leave his birthplace.

After the doctor left, she sat by her husband's bed, mopping away his perspiration and struggling to control her own fears. She wanted to say that being together was all she wanted, and that being together was possible only as long as he stayed alive. But when she looked at him, she could find no words. Moritz Weiler had grown more haggard, his eyes more sunken, his bone structure more pronounced, his face more white. It made his words all the harder for her to bear when he whispered: "Liebe, do not be distressed."

The distress Aaron Pozner first felt at the question he had been asked had given way to relief this Wednesday evening. There was, he finally decided, no ulterior motive behind the query; it was no more than curiosity that had prompted Leo Jockl to ask him quietly what it was like to be a Jew in Germany.

Aaron had encountered the steward that afternoon near the first-class restaurant. Seeing the room empty, Aaron had slipped inside to inspect the elegant tableware. The steward had emerged from a pantry and had eagerly conducted Pozner around the gracious salon, stopping with special pride at the captain's table.

Then Leo had invited Aaron for a coffee in the pantry. At first Pozner had refused, suspicious and reluctant to accept that a German could be so friendly. His memory was still fresh of a day in Dachau when a guard had offered a prisoner a cigarette; when he accepted it, it was smashed into his face by a savage blow from the guard's riot stick.

Nevertheless, Leo Jockl's obvious friendliness persuaded Aaron to join the steward for coffee, and he soon found himself unaccountably relaxing. The steward was, Pozner later wrote, "very sincere with his questions." Jockl had listened carefully to Pozner's bald description of Dachau, and how afterward he had fled Germany without his family. Though he had not wished to sound bitter, Pozner had added: "That is what it is like to be a Jew in Germany."

"But have you never lost your faith?"

It was the first time anybody had asked Aaron Pozner such a question, and it left him momentarily

Whilst some on board ship were forming new friendships, other, knowing nothing of the pressure building up in official circles, passed away their time taking photographs. There was always someone happy to be photographed. (From the collection of Gerald Granston, currently on loan to the Museum of Jewish Heritage, NY)

There were always people to photograph, for this was expected to be a voyage of happy memories. (From the collection of Gerald Granston, currently on loan to the Museum of Jewish Heritage, NY)

speechless. He later realised it would have been easy to have said he was a Jew through an accident of birth, but he knew it would have been less than the truth; that for him being a Jew was far more than merely observing the ritual of his faith, that it reached deep into every aspect of his life.

He had decided to say none of these things. Instead he rose to his feet and simply replied: "No, I have not lost my faith, but only a Jew would understand why." Then Aaron Pozner hurried to his cabin, ashamed of himself for the obvious hurt he had seen in Leo Jockl's face. He promised himself that should the opportunity arise, he would redress his rudeness, even thought it seemed baffling to Aaron Pozner why any German should be interested in a religion proscribed by the Nazis.

THURSDAY, MAY 18, 1939

That moment in the afternoon of Thursday, May 18, when Otto Bergmann followed the engine-room officer past the steel fire door leading into the crew quarters, he wanted to turn and run, to leave

behind the raucous singing that swept toward him. He wished he had never asked to visit the engine room.

Bergmann, an engineer, had thought it would be an interesting way to pass the time, and had been pleased when the first officer, Klaus Ostermeyer, agreed to arrange the visit. He was also happy with the prospect of a few hours' respite from the constant all-female company of his wife, his aunt Shalote, and his mother-in-law. After lunch, he had gone to D deck to keep the appointment Ostermeyer had made for him with the engine-room officer. The man had greeted him coolly, and instead of grasping Otto's proffered handshake, he had motioned Otto to follow him down the metal steps, past the sign saying "No entry—crew only," past the fire door, and now into the crew quarters.

Though Bergmann could not see the men who were singing and banging their fists on the table, the sound sickened him much more than the smells of sweat, cigarette smoke, grease, stale cooking, and the sheer stench of close living. Loud and clear, Otto heard with horror the words of the "Horst Wessel," the Nazi rallying song.

He looked back at the fire door, but someone had closed it behind him. Ahead the officer was leading the way toward the engine-room entrance. Bergmann followed him.

"Stop! Passengers are not allowed here!"

He turned to the group of men seated in an opening to his right. Their singing died down as one of them got up, and, staggering slightly, walked up to him. It was obvious the man had been drinking, and although Bergmann did not know it, it was Schiendick. From the end of the room the officer called: "He has been given official permission to visit the engine room."

Schiendick stared balefully at Bergmann, and then returned to his comrades. As Bergmann hurried to catch up to the officer, he heard the men whispering: ''Juden raus, Juden raus!"

With a terrible sense of shock, he realised that "down here, where no passengers had been, it was a totally different world. Up above, the officers, stewards, musicians, bartenders, and bellboys had made us feel welcome. But below, it was different. Perhaps it was more real.

He saw more evidence of Nazism on the crew notice board. In spite of Schröder's specific order, Schiendick had once again plastered it with Nazi slogans and propaganda.

Bergmann finally reached the engine room. He did not enjoy his tour of the boilers, generators, pumps, switch gear, dials, and alarms that made up the mechanical heart of the St. Louis, however shining and spotlessly clean it all looked. Here once more crew members gave him "dirty looks."

As he retraced his steps through the crew quarters, the words of a Nazi song followed him again: "Wenn das Judenblut vom Messer spritzt, dann geht's nochmal so gut. '' ("When Jewish blood flows from the knife, things will go much better.")

FRIDAY, MAY 19, 1939

After breakfast on Friday, May 19, Fritz Spanier was invited to visit the captain l)n the bridge, and his astonishment was equalled only by his curiosity at the purpose of the invitation.

Following that earlier, and brittle, encounter over the screening of the Nazi newsreel, Dr. Spanier had not seen the captain, apart from one glimpse of him standing on the bridge wing.

As he reached the bridge, he found Schröder once more on the wing, this time with two other first-class passengers, Josef Joseph and his pretty daughter, Liesl, aged ten.

Like many on the ship, Dr. Spanier had yet to form meaningful relationships with any of the other passengers, but he immediately liked Josef Joseph, and saw in Liesl a possible playmate for his own twin daughters. Yet he was still puzzled at why he had been asked, and frankly said so to the captain. Gustav Schröder disarmed Dr. Spanier by openly admitting that he hoped the gesture of a tour of the bridge would, in part, go some way toward repairing the damage caused by the newsreel incident.

Josef Joseph followed this exchange literally, and he, too, asked if there was any special reason for his presence. Gustav Schröder laughingly remarked that his only purpose in inviting the Joseph's was simply because on every voyage he had a number of passengers along to see over the bridge.

But there was another reason why Josef Joseph and Fritz Spanier had been invited. It gave the captain a chance to assess them, to confirm for himself the opinion of the first officer, Ostermeyer, that the men were two of the strongest personalities on the ship.

For, by this Friday, almost halfway to Cuba, still with no news from Hapag, still being pursued by the two other refugee ships, with the daily Nazi news summaries still attacking his passengers, Gustav Schröder had begun to plan. Uppermost in his mind was the need to have, should events dictate it, allies among the passengers, men who could firmly quell any trouble. Fritz Spanier was an automatic selection; Josef Joseph had been recommended by Ostermeyer.

Schröder had been fascinated to learn that Joseph was once a friend of Goebbels, initially attracted, as many were, by the man's intellectual brilliance; their friendship had ceased when Goebbels joined the Nazis, and still later, Joseph found his livelihood as a lawyer proscribed by numerous Nazi edicts, trumpeted abroad by Goebbels' machinations.

In spite of his experience, Joseph, like Spanier, simply refused to be cowed by past events, and that, too, had impressed Schröder.

Now, as he led his visitors around the bridge workings, the captain further believed that Joseph would be an ideal man in a crisis; he displayed a lawyer's shrewdness in his questions, yet remained warmly human.

By the end of the visit the captain was satisfied.

Around eight o'clock on Friday evening, the port side of the St. Louis was crowded with passengers peering through a steady drizzle at the Azores. They were close enough to the coast to make out the windmills through the mist.

"We're nearly halfway to Cuba," Elise Loewe told her husband.

SATURDAY, MAY 20, 1939

On Saturday morning, passengers made their way to the first-class social hall, now converted into an Orthodox synagogue. Reform worshipers were in the Tanzplatz, those of the Conservative faith prayed in the gymnastic hall.

The Spaniers had decided to worship with the Orthodox, and were surprised to see the number required before a service could be held—ten men— had been exceeded ten times over. Perhaps they had been drawn by the novelty of worship aboard a ship.

The prophetical reading from Hosea seemed to Babette Spanier particularly appropriate, dealing as it did with infidelity and fornication. She looked at her husband, seated apart with the other men in the congregation, and thought he intentionally avoided her glance. Once more her worries about their marriage returned.

A few of the crew stood above, in the gallery of the social hall, looking down on the scene. Behind them, Otto Schiendick pushed his way to the front. He looked below contemptuously, and told the crew members that their education would be better served reading Mein Kampf.

TUESDAY, MAY 23, 1939

In the three days that followed, Recha Weiler had quietly intoned, in the privacy of their cabin, every prayer she knew for intercession for her husband. She had interrupted her keening only to feed him some broth or the medicine and tablets Dr.

Glauner increasingly prescribed. She had hardly slept, apart from fitfully dozing in her bedside armchair, nor had she eaten properly.

By Tuesday morning, May 23, she was close to nervous and physical exhaustion. When her husband started to moan, a low and choking sound, she leaned forward and gently wiped his face, and then resumed her chanting, her voice rising and falling, corresponding with the laboured breathing.

Once he looked at her and said something. But even when she bent closer his words were too slurred to understand. Recha kissed him gently on the cheek and sat back, looking searchingly into his face. As she watched, his breathing seemed to ease and the pain to go from his eyes.

For a long time she stared at his face, and then, suddenly, Recha began to sob, oblivious to the urgent knocking on the door, or Dr. Glauner standing by the bed, checking and confirming that her husband was dead.

When Gustav Schröder learned of the death, his first thought was to offer what comfort he could to Recha Weiler. Together with purser Mueller, he hurried to cabin B-108, where he found Dr. Glauner trying, and failing, to calm the widow, slumped across the bed on which her husband lay.

The captain motioned Dr. Glauner to join himself and the purser in the corridor outside, and there he quietly explained to them that he believed Recha Weiler's weeping was linked with the "ritual of death" of her faith, and therefore no attempt should be made to curtail her grief. They must give her time "to rend her garments and that sort of thing" before re-entering the cabin.

In the meantime, he told Mueller, the purser should bring a supply of candles. Mueller, surprised, asked what sort.

"It doesn't matter. Just candles," replied the captain.

He was aware that both men were looking at him oddly, and, guessing their thoughts, Gustav Schröder told them that years before he had read a book on the funeral arrangements of various religions.

Then, followed by the ship's doctor, he went back into the cabin. Recha Weiler's face was tear-stained, her neatly coiled hair was now dishevelled, and she had rent her blouse and under-slip to expose the skin.

Gustav Schröder gently explained they had come to offer any help they could, but would leave if she felt they were intruding; or if she preferred to have present any friends on the ship, he would have them called.

"I know nobody," she whispered. "But I will need a rabbi if there is one among the passengers."

"I will see to it," replied Gustav Schröder. "Can we be of any other help?"

She looked at the captain, weighing in her mind a decision. Then she nodded, and said she needed help to lay out her husband.

Together, the three of them moved to the bed. There, sighing deeply, gently removed a feather she had placed on her husband's lips. Looking at her watch, she saw it had remained there well past the ritual eight minutes following his death, a period when, for religious reasons, nobody could touch the body.

Now, she closed her husband's eyes and mouth, and extended his arms beside his body, as Mueller returned with the candles which he had removed from the first-class restaurant.

Recha looked at the captain, thankful and surprised that he had anticipated another of her needs. She took one of the candles from the purser and Gustav Schröder lit it; again Recha glanced gratefully at him.

She placed the lighted candle on a bedside cupboard, murmuring to the three men, standing awkwardly, not knowing what next to do or expect, that for her the candle symbolised the flickering of the human soul.

She then asked them to place the body on the floor, explaining that, that too, was an essential part of the ritual. Under her guidance, Gustav Schröder and Dr. Glauner positioned the body with its feet facing the cabin door, as directed in the Torah.

Recha placed the lighted candle close to her husband's head and draped his body with a sheet. She knelt for a moment in prayer, and then arose. In silence, she took the remaining candles and placed them at various points around the cabin, lighting them as she went along, intoning prayers for the dead.

Gustav Schröder whispered for the doctor and purser to leave and to try to find a rabbi from the passenger list. Then he waited, anxious not to disrupt

the prayers, hating the fact that even with death, bureaucracy still had to pursue Recha Weiler, knowing that no matter how sympathetic he felt, there was no way of avoiding pain for the elderly woman.

"Frau Weiler," he began. "When do you wish the funeral to be?"

She appeared not to have heard the captain's words, as, standing with her back to him, she continued to pray aloud.

Embarrassed, believing he should not have asked the question at that time, Gustav Schröder started to edge toward the door. "Wait. I wish my husband to be buried in Havana."

Recha Weiler turned and faced the captain, and he saw abject misery and pleading on her face. In that moment, he would "willingly have given up my command to have helped her."

Instead, he explained that the ship was still four days from Cuba, that there were no adequate facilities on board for keeping the body, that even when they reached Havana he would still need permission to take the corpse ashore.

What he did not say, but which was also in his mind, was the very real problem of handling the other passengers and crew if it became known they were carrying a dead man. Gustav Schröder believed that the knowledge would create "a low mood," heightened by a traditional belief shared by many seamen that a corpse on a ship was the harbinger of bad luck.

"Please, my husband would have wished it."

The agony behind the words moved Gustav Schröder to promise to try to meet her wish. He hurried to the radio room and sent a priority radio message to the Hapag office in Havana requesting permission to bring the body ashore. The reply came within the morning:

PERMISSION DENIED FOR HEALTH REASONS

The captain returned to Recha Weiler. With her was a tall, well-built, bearded man who introduced himself as Rabbi Gustav Weil, a tourist-class passenger. The rabbi was able to calm the widow. She accepted the decision that her husband must be buried at sea.

Purser Mueller invited Rabbi Weil to his office to discuss the funeral.

Mueller asked whether he should arrange for the ship's carpenter to make up a coffin, "complete with brass handles." The suggestion was gratefully received but delicately refused, by the elderly rabbi, as was the purser's offer to turn the ship's small hospital into a chapel of rest. Rabbi Weil told him, "It is death, not rest, which we are concerned with."

The purser then offered the ship's orchestra to play "somberly" at the service, and was told there should be no music. Next he raised the question of flowers; Rabbi Weil explained that under Judaic law, they would not be required.

Mueller protested that "the body can't just be thrown over the side. It wouldn't be Christian."

Rabbi Weil patiently explained to the purser that a Jewish funeral was an unostentatious rite, a "democracy in death," where no one need be ashamed of the simplicity of the coffin or shroud. Weiler's body, he suggested, should be sewn into a weighted sailcloth, and slid over the side from a plank as soon as possible.

Mueller discussed the timing. "If it is held during the day, it will create a bad effect on everyone. The majority of the passengers are now in good humour. The sight of a body going over the side would be bound to depress them."

The rabbi agreed. Many of the passengers, he observed, had themselves "been recently near to death, the funeral could bring back unpleasant memories. We should try to avoid that."

They agreed to hold the burial service at eleven o'clock that night.

Soon after Gustav Schröder returned to the bridge from his meeting with the widow, a coded cable brought very bad news indeed from Hamburg.

A day of intense telephoning between Hamburg, London, and Paris had preceded that cable. It had begun with Claus-Gottfried Holthusen calling Morris Troper in the French capital to say that Hapag's Orinoco would leave Hamburg for Havana on May 27 with over 200 refugees. Holthusen had added: "So, Herr Troper, you can see there is nothing to worry about over the St. Louis."

Troper was glad to receive some reassuring news; he had been worried ever since reading that morning's Paris newspapers with their reports that Cuban President Bru's opposition to all refugees had hardened.

Holthusen had been placatory, reaffirming that Hapag was in close contact with developments in

Cuba and that the company had "highly placed" connections on the island. He had urged Troper to dismiss the press reports. What the shipping director did not say was that as soon as he was off the line he planned to send Gustav Schröder a cable based on information Hapag had received from Luis Clasing in Havana which clearly confirmed the French newspaper stories.

After Holthusen's call, Morris Troper contacted Sir Herbert Emerson in London to tell him the Orinoco was sailing. The director of the International Committee on Political Refugees replied that the Orinoco's voyage was "just another bit of money-making by Hapag," and in his view it would only worsen the "devilish" situation already created by the St. Louis. Emerson did not reveal that Britain's ambassador in Havana, H. A. Grant Watson, had earlier that week filed a "most confidential" report indicating that he believed President Bru would stand firm on not admitting the refugees. The news had caused a flurry in both the Foreign Office and the Home Office, and Emerson faced a question being asked by more than one Whitehall mandarin: If Cuba would not accept any more refugees, where on earth could they go?

It was against this background that Claus-Gottfried Holthusen sent Schröder the cable. It read:

MAJORITY YOUR PASSENGERS IN CONTRAVENTION NEW CUBAN LAW 937 AND MAY NOT BE GIVEN PERMISSION DISEMBARK. ORINOCO SAILING DOUBTFUL. YOU WILL MAINTAIN SPEED AND COURSE AS SITUATION NOT COMPLETELY CLEAR BUT CERTAINLY CRITICAL IF NOT RESOLVED BEFORE YOUR ARRIVAL.

The captain immediately sent for Dr. Fritz Spanier.

Dr. Spanier faced Gustav Schröder across the captain's desk, uncomfortably aware of the strength of Schröder's argument, yet unable to lend practical support for reasons he knew must sound painfully inadequate.

"No, Captain, I cannot do it," Dr. Spanier said. "I am simply not the right person for such a committee, let alone chair it."

Gustav Schröder hoped his silence would express his disappointment more than words.

"Captain, please understand me. I am not good at such things. My experience of committees is that they spend all their time talking with little result. If I can help, I will gladly do so, but I will better serve you, and the passengers, outside it."

"But you will help?"

"You have my word." "Very well. But I must ask you to treat this talk in the strictest confidence."

Dr. Spanier nodded, still stunned by the cable the captain had shown him. Schröder had also told him of his own fears of "serious trouble" when they reached Havana "unless things improve." He had then explained that he proposed to set up a small passenger committee, made up of lawyers and others, to confer with him in dealing with the passengers should it become necessary.

Fritz Spanier proposed his own choice for the chairmanship of that committee, Josef Joseph.

The captain sent for the lawyer, who immediately accepted the post and went off to select people to serve with him.

At four o'clock that Tuesday afternoon Gustav Schröder welcomed the members of the passenger committee assembled in his day cabin. As Josef Joseph introduced them, each man stepped forward and shook the captain's hand.

As he gripped each hand, Schröder looked into the man's face and was reassured by what he saw. On Dr. Max Weiss's face he saw quiet resolution. Max Zellner and Arthur Hausdorff had the cool, appraising faces of experienced lawyers. The fifth member of the group, Herbert Manasse, though younger than the others, still seemed a man versed in the vicissitudes of life.

Behind them Leo Jockl attended a table set with coffee and cakes. As the steward served, the captain began to explain the reason why they had been assembled. Herbert Manasse interrupted. "Are we here to prepare for returning to Germany?"

The directness of the question and the manner in which it was asked decided Schröder to confide completely in the group.

"At this stage, the answer is no. We will sail to Havana. But I cannot say what will happen when we reach there."

The committee members then listened without interruption as the captain read Holthusen's message. He said it presaged trouble, explained the significance of the reference to the Orinoco—"it means resistance to refugees must have hardened"—and revealed the race for life between the St. Louis and the other two refugee ships. Using a chart,

The Passenger Committee, formed at the suggestion of Captain Schröder and chaired by Dr Josef Joseph (centre). (Mrs Liesl Joseph-Loeb)

Gustav Schröder showed the group that the latest position of the Orduna placed her only seven hours astern with the Flandre twelve hours behind.

The silence in the room, Josef Joseph was to remember was "deadly. The voyage had assumed a menace nobody had suspected." He asked a number of questions: Was decree 937 permanent? What pressures could Hapag bring directly on the Cuban government? What attempts were being made to enlist support from recognised welfare agencies in Cuba and elsewhere? How could landing permits clearly issued by the Cuban authorities be revoked?

Gustav Schröder quietly replied that he had no answer to any of the questions.

Dr. Weiss took up the probing. What would the captain do, if on reaching Havana, they could not disembark?

"We will wait."

"For what?"

"For instructions from Hamburg."

Each man pondered those words. Then Arthur Hausdorff spoke the fear they all felt: "Captain, what if Hamburg insists that you cannot wait and that you must return to Germany?"

Once more, silence. Schröder was uncomfortably aware they wanted a reassuring answer from him. He knew he could not lie to them; to do so now, at the start of their relationship, might destroy any confidence they had in his credibility. Instead, he said, "I give you my word that I will do everything possible to avoid going back to Germany. I am only too well aware of what they would do to you."

"Captain, we thank you for your honesty," said Josef Joseph.

The lawyer had one request: Could they cable the Jewish Relief Committee in Havana for further information on the situation? Gustav Schröder agreed, adding that Hapag would pay for the cost of the radiogram. After some discussion the committee took its first collective action. Their cable read:

WE HAVE JUST HEARD PASSENGERS WITH LANDING PERMITS ON ORINOCO MAY NOT BE ALLOWED TO SAIL. PLEASE TELL US IF WE CAN EXPECT SIMILAR DIFFICULTIES. ST. LOUIS PASSENGER COMMITTEE.

As soon as Otto Schiendick heard of Moritz Weiler's death, he called on the purser. In his capacity as the party watchdog on board, he demanded details of the funeral arrangements. Mueller gave them.

Schiendick said he was satisfied on all but one point. Party regulations stipulated that for burial at sea, the bier must be draped with a swastika flag; he could see "no reason for an exception to be made in this case."

Recha Weiler—indeed, all on board—would regard it as sacrilege if such a thing occurred. Mueller flatly refused.

That afternoon Schiendick called another crew meeting in their mess hall. About fifty attended. He reminded them of the Nazi edict banning Aryans "from attending in any way" Jewish funerals, except in a "professional capacity."

Aaron Pozner heard the news of Weiler's death rom Leo Jockl early in the evening when the steward called to apologise for not keeping their afternoon appointment. "The ship's routine has been disrupted by this unhappy event," he said.

"It is I, not you, who should apologise," replied Pozner, referring to their previous meeting.

Rosemarie Bergmann was told of the professor's death by her husband. Later, while bathing her mother, now bedridden and unable to look after herself, she and her mother agreed it was probably something to do "with our leaving Hamburg on the thirteenth."

Elise Loewe learned the news on a visit to Dr. Glauner after dinner. That morning her husband had complained that he had been unable, again, to sleep the night before. She knew his depression was made worse by lack of sleep, and Elise Loewe was determined to get something to remedy the situation. She had seen Dr. Glauner earlier in the day, and told him she needed "something strong" to help her sleep. Elise Loewe had decided it was better to conceal the fact that it was really for her husband, since his behaviour was already being commented upon by some of the passengers. Dr. Glauner had asked her to return in the evening for the potion.

Now, as he told Frau Loewe of Weiler's death—"he simply lost the will to live"—the doctor handed her a glass partly filled with a milky liquid, and asked her to drink it. Still feeling unable to explain that the sleeping draught was for her husband, Elise Loewe drank it. By the time she got back to her cabin, it had already begun to take effect.

Recha Weiler had spent the day fasting and praying. From time to time Rabbi Gustav Weil had joined her, and they sat beside the body, reading from the Bible or murmuring a prayer. Frau Weiler had covered the mirror over the washstand with a hand towel, drawn the curtains over the porthole, and replenished the candles. Several times during the day she had lifted the sheet to peer at her husband's face; in death it had a peace which had not been there for many years.

At ten o'clock—she later was to remember the time exactly, as she also recalled all the events of that day—Rabbi Weil returned to the cabin. The moment had come for Recha to complete the final preparations for burial. She produced her husband's tallith, the long prayer shawl she had given him on their wedding day, which had served as a canopy during the marriage ceremony.

The shawl was fringed at the corners. Recha pulled the tassels from the cloth, a ritual rending of the garment, and placed it over her husband's body. Then she rose, uttering fresh prayers, and nodded to the rabbi.

He opened the cabin door and motioned inside Purser Mueller and two sailors carrying a folded stretcher and sailcloth. The seamen laid the stretcher on a bed, and rolled out the sailcloth. It looked like a long envelope, open at the top, with iron bars sewn into the sides.

Recha Weiler picked up the candle at the head of the corpse and placed it on a table. At a nod from the rabbi, the sailors carefully lifted the body up from the floor, and slid it inside the sailcloth lying on the stretcher. Screened by Mueller and his companions, the other sailor sewed up the shroud. The purser produced a large Hapag flag, loaned by Captain Schröder, and draped it over the body. Preceded by the stretcher party, Recha Weiler and Rabbi Weil walked slowly from the cabin.

An elevator carried them to aft on A deck, where, waiting by the swimming pool, were Captain Schröder, Ostermeyer, and a handful of passengers, some of whom had also symbolically torn their upper garments.

As the cortege emerged on deck, the ship came to a stop. Captain Schröder had ordered the speed to be reduced gradually, hoping to minimise curiosity

among the passengers, and consequently the St. Louis had steadily lost way for nearly an hour, a fact mentioned to Schröder by Ostermeyer, who also thought the time could be ill afforded with the two other refugee ships now in close pursuit. Schröder had overruled the objections of his first officer. Now he led the way to the ship's railing.

A gate in the deck rail had been opened and a plank placed in position, protruding over the side. The shroud was put on the board, the sailors standing on either side of it, their hands resting lightly on the flag. Mueller stood behind the body, his hands on the end of the plank.

The mourners grouped closer; the ship's officers, bareheaded, stood to one side. The committal service was brief, conducted in Hebrew, and ended with the mourners intoning, "May he come to his place in peace." Rabbi Weil looked to the seamen: they tautened the flag over the shroud, Mueller tilted the plank, and the body slid over the side.

From far below came a dull splash, signal for the mourners on deck to utter, "Remember God, that we are of dust." They stepped to the rail, sprinkling into the sea handfuls of sand which they had taken from the children's sandbox a few feet away. In a series of crisp movements, the sailors folded up the flag and stood to attention beside the plank. During the service Captain Schröder and his first officer had remained rigid; now they turned toward the sea, donned their caps, and saluted.

Schiendick, watching from a position in the shadows of a lifeboat, noticed that the salutes were not Nazi-style, and was seen to enter the fact later in his party notebook.

The formal proceedings on deck ended when Schröder handed to Recha Weiler what was to become for her a treasured memento of the occasion: a map marked with the place where her husband had been buried.

Below in his cabin, Max Loewe had heard the splash of the body as it entered the waters.

His children, Ruth and Fritz, looked down from their upper bunks at their parents. Their father, unable to waken Elise Loewe from her drugged sleep, seemed to cringe, to retreat again within himself. Even twelve-year-old Fritz had come to recognise this as abnormal, and his father's behaviour distressed the boy deeply. It was not until he was older that he could put his feelings into words. "Father was becoming increasingly mentally disturbed. He was paranoiac."

Max Loewe's mind filled with confused thoughts: perhaps the ship had stopped so they could come and get him; perhaps he should hide on the ship as he had had to hide in Germany? His children felt helpless in the face of their father's confused suffering. In the first-class cabin she shared with her mother, the silence before the St. Louis's engines started made ten-year-old Marianne Bardeleben think of the father she had not seen for months.

The girl had much in common with her friends, the Aber children. Like them, her father was a doctor who had fled to Havana. Like them, Marianne had a non-Jewish mother, and had spent time in a home before boarding the ship. During those days, she had become accustomed to "noise, sirens, marching feet, and shouting crowds." For her, the silence of this night on the St. Louis was "ominous and threatening." She waited, almost too frightened to breathe. Only when the engines started up again was Marianne able to shut her eyes to the darkness.

Rosemarie Bergmann had realised that the ship had stopped to bury Moritz Weiler; she carefully noted it in her diary. Her husband wrote in the diary he was also keeping: "At least the old professor has not died or been buried in the hell of the Third Reich."

On B deck, shortly after 11 P.M., Fritz and Babette Spanier took their customary pre-bed stroll, relieved that the ship was back at full speed. It was a cool night, and the deck was now deserted, lit only by a few lights.

Babette Spanier felt like talking. She reflected that their fellow passengers had turned in early possibly because of the funeral, but more likely in order to rest up for the gala costume ball to be held two nights later. She had not yet decided what to wear; she had heard that a number of passengers were going as sheiks or harem girls, but she felt that would be in poor taste in view of the Arab opposition to Jews settling in Palestine.

Dr. Spanier paid little attention to his wife's chatter until suddenly she whispered: "Fritz, did you hear that?"

A giggle, quickly suppressed, came from farther down the deck, straining their eyes in the darkness, the Spaniers could see a close, unheeding couple. They found similar pairs in niches and tucked away under the companionways.

"The whole deck was full of these goings-on," Babette Spanier was to recall. "They were like rabbits in a cornfield."

Suddenly, from the deck above, toward the stern of the ship, came muffled shouting and the pounding of feet. As the runners came closer, Dr. Spanier could make out the words. He turned to his wife and said: "My God!"

The excitement barely ruffled the quiet on the bridge when one of the Gestapo "firemen" reported by telephone: "Man overboard!"

"Did you see him?" asked the voice of the watch officer.

"Yes, he jumped, port side, A deck."

"Thank you," acknowledged the voice with a detached calmness.

The watch officer ordered helmsman Heinz Kritsch to stand by to go hard about, and then contacted Captain Schröder, who bolted to the bridge to take charge of the rescue operation.

Schröder was pleased to see Kritsch at the helm. Apart from the steersman's professional abilities, so necessary in an emergency, the captain had a genuine liking for the young Rhinelander. They shared a common off-duty pleasure, ornithology.

Where the watch officer had been relaxed and easygoing, Schröder moved briskly. The engine room was warned that there was about to be a major course change, extra lookouts were posted, a motorboat was prepared for launching, and, as the ship came around, the bridge searchlight began to sweep the water.

First Officer Ostermeyer established in a series of telephone calls that the jumper was not a passenger but a crew member, Leonid Berg, a kitchen hand.

"Do you know him, Kritsch?" "Yes, Captain. He's a Russian emigre."

A telephone call to purser Mueller provided further details: Berg was thirty years old, on his second voyage, and had jumped from the same spot where Moritz Weiler's body had been dropped into the sea. Mueller believed it "significant" that Berg had experienced frequent attacks of depression during the voyage, a fact which Kritsch confirmed.

Though the night was clear, Schröder thought the chances of finding Berg were slender: there was every likelihood the kitchen hand had been sucked under by the ship's wake. If he was alive, he could be anywhere in several square miles of sea; meantime, the search would cut still further the St. Louis's lead over the Orduna and the Flandre. At 11:55 P.M., the ship hove to. Two illuminated buoys were dropped and the motor launch lowered; it began systematically to quarter the area.

WEDNESDAY, MAY 24, 1939

At 1 A.M. Wednesday, Captain Schröder officially ended the search by ordering three short blasts on the siren to recall the launch. Shortly afterward, the St. Louis resumed course.

By breakfast time, rumours about Berg's death were circulating freely. A favourite story cast the kitchen hand as a victim of a Nazi fight. "With a name like his, what chance did he have?" Shalote Hecht asked. Otto Bergmann wondered whether Berg had been dumped over the side for being "too friendly" with the passengers. Babette Spanier heard a more titillating tale: "Berg was a handsome man who had fallen in love with a passenger, and committed suicide when the other crew told him to give her up." Josef Joseph thought a love tragedy was unlikely. He favoured the theory of a "simple suicide, clean and quick."

"Two deaths are unusual," Aaron Pozner wrote in the diary he kept of the voyage. "It has created new tensions. People are suspicious again. Today there was consternation when two stewards were seen carrying a large portrait of Hitler into the purser's office. People said some Nazi ceremony was being planned, but the portrait was being removed from the social hall for Shabuoth."

Gustav Schröder had ordered the photo to be taken down after Rabbi Weil told him he felt it would be inappropriate for a sacred moment to be celebrated in the "presence of Hitler."

The rabbi had spent much of the morning preparing the hall for the service. It was now decorated with bowls of fruit and vases of flowers; two ornamental palm trees had been borrowed from the Tanzplatz. The service was well attended, and again members of the crew secreted themselves in the gallery, listening to the singing.

Otto Schiendick had not been drawn to the service, but later, learning that the Fuehrer's portrait had been removed, he strongly protested to the purser about "this most serious offence." Once more the usually placid Mueller castigated the steward, telling him it was no concern of his, and that his "days on this ship are numbered."

Schiendick hunted down Jockl and found the

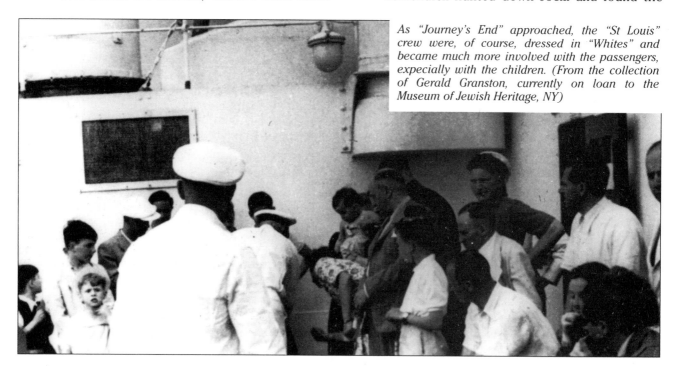

As "Journey's End" approached, the "St Louis" crew were, of course, dressed in "Whites" and became much more involved with the passengers, expecially with the children. (From the collection of Gerald Granston, currently on loan to the Museum of Jewish Heritage, NY)

There were regular children's parties on board, thus reducing the prospect of boredom which, it was recognised by the shipping line, could lead to parental frustration and so passenger unrest. The parties were always quite lavish affairs and so thoroughly enjoyed. (From the collection of Gerald Granston, currently on loan to the Museum of Jewish Heritage, NY)

HAMBURG-AMERIKA LINIE

AN BORD DES M.-S. „ST. LOUIS"
Mittwoch, den 24. Mai 1939

Frühstück

Apfelsinen
Zitronen- und Tomatensaft
Gedämpfte Pflaumen

Haferflocken
Buchweizengrütze
Puffed Wheat   Rice Flakes
Corn Flakes

Gekochte Eier
Spiegeleier
Rühreier mit Wurst
Omelette mit feinem Ragout

Apfelpfannkuchen
Weizenpfannkuchen, Ahornsirup

Gebratene Kalbsleber mit Zwiebeln

Bratkartoffeln

Geräucherte Mettwurst   Leberwurst
Holländer Käse

Gebäck   Röstbrot
Grau- und Schwarzbrot

Butter
Erdbeer-Marmelade
Honig

Kaffee   Kaffee Hag   Tee

Für Kinder:
Milchspeisen zu allen Mahlzeiten

HAMBURG-AMERIKA LINIE

Left: Early mornings would often see several passengers out on deck before breakfast, whilst others would enjoy the comforts of breakfast served at table. The menu above is a typical example of "St Louis" fare – and in fact is the Breakfast Menu from Wednesday 24th May. Note that it offered an additional children's choice. (Edgar Glucksman)

More and more passengers took to the Sports Deck as they approached Cuba, to pass the last few days of their voyage playing shuffleboard and enjoying the sun. Here, a group is watched by crew members as they carry out safety checks on the lifeboats. (From the collection of Gerald Granston, currently on loan to the Museum of Jewish Heritage, NY)

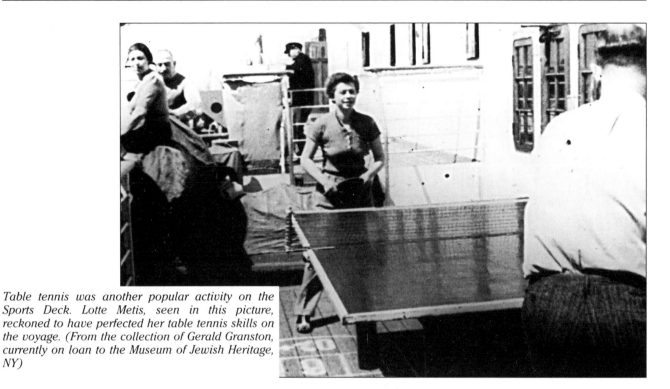

Table tennis was another popular activity on the
Sports Deck. Lotte Metis, seen in this picture,
reckoned to have perfected her table tennis skills on
the voyage. (From the collection of Gerald Granston,
currently on loan to the Museum of Jewish Heritage,
NY)

Sensing that they would soon split up as they went
their separate ways upon disembarkation, groups of
friends began to gather together and take, or have
taken, photographs to remind them of happy days.
(From the collection of Gerald Granston, currently on
loan to the Museum of Jewish Heritage, NY)

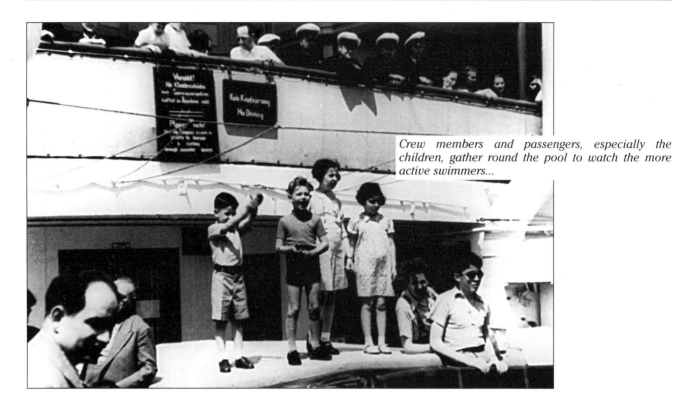

Crew members and passengers, especially the children, gather round the pool to watch the more active swimmers...

...whilst others sit at the poolside and enjoy the sun. (Both from the collection of Gerald Granston, currently on loan to the Museum of Jewish Heritage, NY)

Ship's Photographer Paul Bendowski was also active taking pictures during the voyage. The one on the left is of passenger Kathe Brauer, taken in the ship's studio, whilst the one below shows two young men taking the sun and trying out the cowboy rôle, with hats and neckerchieves. (Paul Bendowski)

The atmosphere became ever more relaxed as Cuba drew nearer, with the sun and the pool during the day and parties in the evenings. (From the collection of Gerald Granston, currently on loan to the Museum of Jewish Heritage, NY)

THE CHILDREN OF THE VOYAGE:

The "St Louis" children's nurse, Monika Schmidt, in the chequered blouse and apron, had a busy time during this voyage; but they were kept occupied with games and tea parties, as well as the adventure of being at sea. (From the collection of Gerald Granston, currently on loan to the Museum of Jewish Heritage, NY)

Children enjoyed the voyage in all kinds of ways, from sitting with a little brother, sipping a cup of tea on the Promenade Deck...

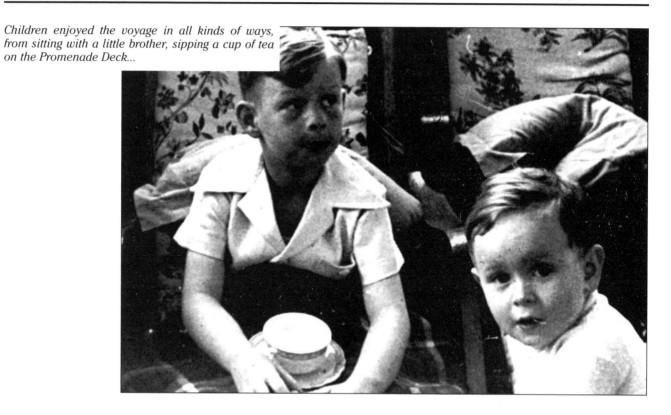

...to exploring the decks and playing pirates, like these two young fellows. (Both pictures from the collection of Gerald Granston, currently on loan to the Museum of Jewish Heritage, NY)

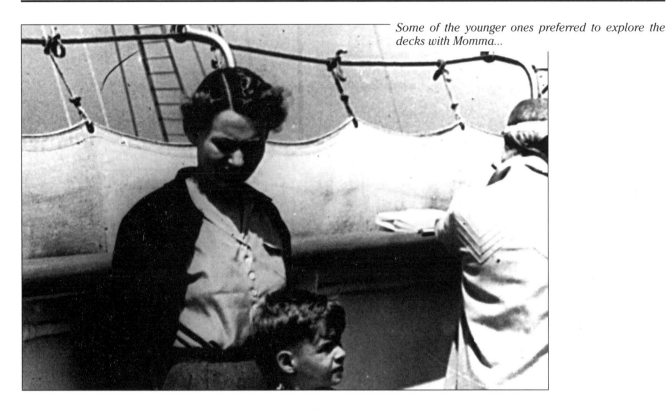

Some of the younger ones preferred to explore the decks with Momma...

...whilst others enjoyed the security and company of Grandma's presence. (Both pictures from the collection of Gerald Granston, currently on loan to the Museum of Jewish Heritage, NY)

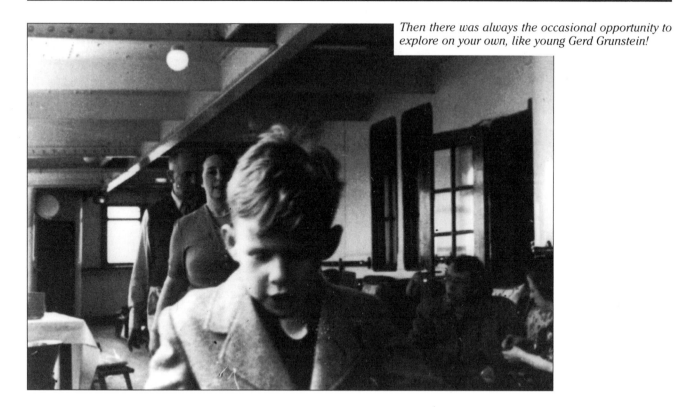

Then there was always the occasional opportunity to explore on your own, like young Gerd Grunstein!

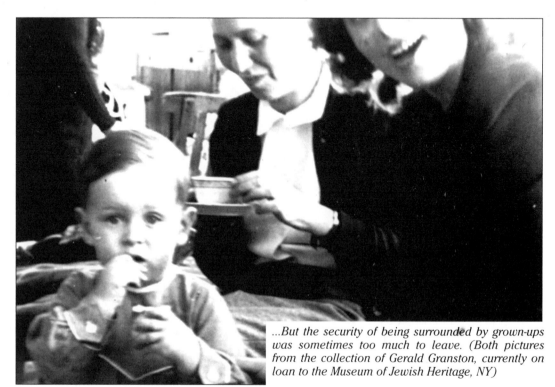

...But the security of being surrounded by grown-ups was sometimes too much to leave. (Both pictures from the collection of Gerald Granston, currently on loan to the Museum of Jewish Heritage, NY)

As the end of the voyage drew nearer, the smaller children had teamed up in pairs (like this duo of cheeky young Gerd Grunstein and friend). The older ones found their own way round the ship and enjoyed the freedom, as with Walter Karliner (right) (two pictures from the collection of Gerald Granston, currently on loan to the Museum of Jewish Heritage, NY) and Vera Hess (below). (Mrs Vera Mahler)

Liesl Joseph at eleven years of age. (Mrs Liesl Joseph-Loeb)

Ruth Isner is the little girl on the right of this picture, on board the "St Louis". (Mrs Ruth Isner-Kissinger)

Towards the end of the voyage groups were being photographed as mementoes. In this picture the boy standing on the right front row is Fred Rief. Two spaces away from him to the centre is his little sister Liane and the boy on the left wearing glasses is Jacques Ring. (Dr Liane Reif-Lehrer)

Another group, this one a group of boys the friends of young Herbie Karliner. Herbie is on the front left. (Herbert Karliner)

captain's steward in a first-class pantry. Here was something he could revenge himself upon. Closing the door, Schiendick angrily demanded to know why Jockl had failed to make any reports on the captain. He was told there was nothing to report.

His voice quite devoid of its usual hectoring tone, Otto Schiendick revealed that he knew about the visit of Josef Joseph and the other passengers to the captain's cabin. Then he raised his voice.

"Why, Jockl, why were they there?" he demanded. "You were there. You haven't mentioned it. Why?"

As he recalled later, at that moment, Leo Jockl felt again the urge to hit the dumpy little man who seemed so bent on destroying the captain. Once more he controlled himself, and calmly repeated what Gustav Schröder had told him to say: the passengers had formed a committee "in case of any trouble in Havana."

At the mention of trouble, Otto Schiendick became uneasy, lowered his voice, and asked what the captain meant.

Sensing that the balance had tilted in his favour, Leo Jockl partly drew upon his own imagination to tell Schiendick that while the trouble was some vague threat against the ship, it had been enough for the captain to contemplate banning all shore leave for the crew.

"Are you sure?" blurted out Schiendick.

"That's what the captain said, but it won't bother me. I hear Havana is not much of a place," replied Leo.

If Otto Schiendick was unable to go ashore, he knew his Abwehr mission would fail, assuring him of unpleasant complications back in Hamburg. In that case not even producing cast-iron proof against the captain or the purser was likely to return him to favour, or get him promoted by the Abwehr.

For the first time since joining the St. Louis, Schiendick felt that it was he who was threatened.

The St. Louis ploughed through a gentle sea toward the Bahamas. After lunch that Wednesday, passengers could choose a tea dance, language classes, or lazing around the swimming pool.

Aaron Pozner spent the early part of the afternoon in his cabin learning Spanish from a phrase book given him by his wife. He found it difficult to concentrate. His mind constantly returned to Leo Jockl. The steward now spent a good deal of his free

time with Pozner, during which a conviction had grown in Pozner's mind. That afternoon, when Jockl arrived, he decided to test his theory. He asked the steward if he was a Jew.

Pozner realised "as soon as I put the question that it was a mistake. Leo was not ready for it. The thought that I was suspicious frightened him. He only shook his head and left the cabin."

Afterward, Leo Jockl felt ashamed he had been unable to admit the truth

Elise Loewe finally awoke late on Wednesday afternoon, dazed from the aftereffects of the sleeping drug Dr. Glauner had given her. She had slept for nearly twenty-four hours.

Her husband's condition had deteriorated. His speech showed he had difficulty in distinguishing between fantasy and reality; his emotional problems were now not just in relation to life. He appeared to have a "death complex," dwelling morbidly on the Weiler funeral and the Berg suicide. Elise Loewe was very frightened.

At exactly six o'clock Havana time on this Wednesday evening, Milton Goldsmith, the director of the Relief Committee in Cuba, ended his telephone conversation with New York.

He had already told the American Jewish Joint Distribution Committee, who financed his work, that without further funds it would be difficult to maintain the 5000 refugees he supported, let alone any newcomers on the St. Louis and other refugee ships. The Joint official had said no extra money was available.

Desperately seeking some concession, Goldsmith had raised again the matter of the shiploads of refugees approaching Havana, but to no avail. Afterward he was left with the impression that the gravity of his situation had completely failed to register with the New York-based committee.

He and his assistant, Laura Margolis, received some financial help from the local Jewish community, but a businessman reflected part of the local feeling when he told Goldsmith, "Over the years we have all sent our donations to the Joint. Let them use that money."

Another had said, "Of course we feel sorry for the refugees, but the whole world should be helping, not just us."

Laura Margolis had wept at those words. Then, on hearing the Joint's reply, she told Goldsmith there was only one solution. The weekly handout to each refugee must be cut from $7 to $4.50. That would eke out a further few weeks' allowance, and in that time they could prepare another appeal to the Joint.

Laura believed that "they won't be able to refuse again. Not with the St. Louis."

Later that same evening, in Havana, Robert Hoffman completed another phase of the plan to carry off one of his biggest espionage coups. He photographically reduced some of the American defence secrets smuggled into Cuba. Then he carefully rolled the films inside the barrels of fountain pens or stitched them onto the spines of magazines. Large documents he had secured in a hollowed-out, carved walking stick.

These were classic Abwehr methods and Hoffman was a skilled hand at such work. Nevertheless he was worried by a number of things, among them the virulent anti-Semitism on the island. He clearly saw the inherent danger in the situation he had helped to create: a climate of hatred now existed which might not only threaten the safety of the St. Louis passengers, but pose problems he had not foreseen in effecting a smooth pickup by Otto Schiendick.

Further, one of his agents, the humpbacked dwarf Otto Ott, reported that the Cuban secret police had started to watch all known Nazi agents on the island. Ott said this surveillance had been started on the direct order of Batista, and Hoffman had no reason to doubt this information, for he had had to pay substantial sums of money in the past for the secret police to turn a blind eye to the Abwehr's activities in Cuba.

What was especially troubling Robert Hoffman was his suspicion that strong American pressure must have been exerted on Batista to make such a move.

There was also evidence of American intervention on other fronts, such as the arrival of a new agent of the U. S. Immigration Service; Abwehr files revealed that the man had a formidable record. Also, the American naval attache, Rowell, was becoming increasingly inquisitive. Overall, the German spy master felt a determined American effort was being mounted to try to recover the secret documents he had now reduced to a few spools of film, secreted in his fancy walking stick.

THURSDAY, MAY 25, 1939

Thursday, May 25, the second day of Shabuoth was also the day of the fancy costume ball, the traditional end-of-voyage party held two nights before landing.

In the morning, on the St. Louis, once again the tables and chairs in the social hall had been rearranged and the room made into a synagogue; once again, despite Schiendick's protestations, Hitler's portrait had been removed.

After the service, an announcement requested all passengers to report to the purser's office to collect their landing cards for disembarkation Saturday morning. By mid afternoon Thursday, the majority of the cards had been given out, and some passengers had even packed most of their clothes, putting aside the costumes they intended to wear at the gala that evening.

Now, seated at a table in the restaurant, Aaron Pozner wondered whether to reconsider his decision that it would be "improper" for him to join the festivities. Everyone else seemed set for a final fling; many were already in fancy dress. Though the dinner menu was not that different from what passengers had come to expect on the voyage, tonight it was particularly tempting after the mainly cheese diet many had maintained during the two days of Shabuoth.

But for Pozner, the contrast with his painful memories of Nazi Germany, of having had to hide among foul-smelling animal skins, of having to grovel in garbage for scraps of food, made it all seem so unreal.

Inside the gaily coloured cover of the tourist-class menu, the refugee from the concentration camp was offered salmon mayonnaise, followed by clear soup with dumplings, veal marengo with buttered noodles and roast potatoes, or fried chicken with grilled tomatoes, cauliflower hollandaise, and chips. For dessert there was orange ice cream, Swiss or harzer cheese, fresh fruit, and coffee or tea.

The Music Programme during dinner featured a wide selection of pieces from Germany, including soft, gentle music and waltzes. It was a few hours filled with nostalgia and hope.

For the man whose memories of Dachau were still fresh in his mind, who had had to leave his family behind, the contrast was finally too much. Unable to finish his meal or to stand the growing boisterousness of his fellow passengers, Pozner returned to his cabin.

After dinner, Leo Jockl joined other stewards in the social hall, putting the finishing touches on the room which had changed its character four times in two days. The palm trees and fruit remained from the morning synagogue service, but now they were hardly noticed among the streamers and balloons suspended from the ceiling and hanging over the gallery rails. The wickerwork chairs, and tables with freshly laundered linen and a spray of flowers on each, had been pushed to the side to make space for the dancers.

Overlooking the entire scene, back in its proper place, was the portrait of the Fuehrer.

The Spaniers and the Josephs delayed going to the ball until it was well under way. Though both couples preferred formal evening attire to fancy costumes, Babette Spanier caused something of a stir by her entrance. She swept down the wide, curved double staircase leading from the gallery to the dance floor with a flourish, raising her long dress as she descended to reveal a pair of high black riding boots. She had exchanged her monocle for a pair of large frame spectacles.

Lilli Joseph thought the overall impression "a little strange." Babette explained that the boots under her evening dress were "because it might turn cool."

Some of the costumes demonstrated considerable invention; Arab djellabahs fashioned out of bed sheets and hand towels; many of the young men came appropriately as pirates and were rewarded by a liberal scattering of briefly clad harem girls waiting to be plundered; two geisha girls were particularly popular.

The band leader raised a cheer with a selection of Glenn Miller melodies. Later, even greater applause came from the younger set as the band swung into rhumbas and tangos.

As the night wore on, the passengers, knowing that what remained of their "shipboard money" would be worthless once they disembarked, spent it on drink. Babette Spanier was disquieted to see the dancing becoming more abandoned. One young couple who had fashioned palm leaves into a Hawaiian type hula skirt were "swinging their hips in a way that was quite revealing." What disturbed her most, however, was the pretty girl dressed in the uniform of a ship's sailor. "Excuse me, " she said to her husband, "but how did she get hold of that" Dr. Spanier thought the answer obvious.

The party finished for all but a few hangers on at three in the morning. Those with energy left began what they thought would be their last full day on the St. Louis by going on deck, from where they could now see the beam from the Bahamas lighthouse.

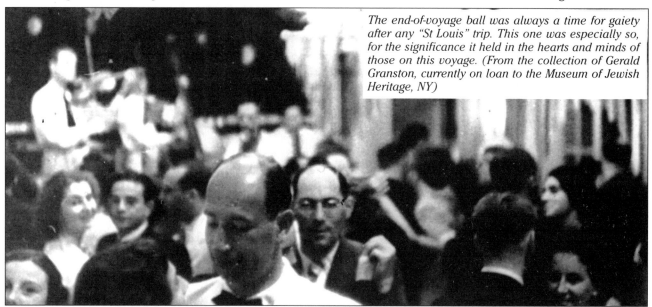

The end-of-voyage ball was always a time for gaiety after any "St Louis" trip. This one was especially so, for the significance it held in the hearts and minds of those on this voyage. (From the collection of Gerald Granston, currently on loan to the Museum of Jewish Heritage, NY)

The mood was positively carefree in the last party of the voyage and revellers kept it going until three in the morning on Friday 27th May. (From the collection of Gerald Granston, currently on loan to the Museum of Jewish Heritage, NY)

An Bord des Motorschiffes „St. Louis"
Donnerstag, den 25. Mai 1939

HAUPTMAHLZEIT

Lachsmayonnaise

Kraftbrühe mit Pfannkuchen

Kalbsragout Marengo, Butternudeln
Röstkartoffeln

Gebratene Poularde, Glasierte Tomaten
Blumenkohl holländisch
Stäbchenkartoffeln

Orangen-Eis

Schweizer und Harzer Käse

Frucht

Kaffee   Tee

This is the menu for the "End of Voyage Ball" used on every voyage's end by Hamburg-Amerika Line on the twin ships "St Louis" and "St Paul". The front face of it takes on a rather symbolic air with this particular voyage, in view of the theatre-like drama about to unfold. (Edgar Glucksman)

II

A Chance

To Die

From the "Daily Mirror" of 6th June 1939. (Mirror Group Newspapers)

The breakfast menu for Friday 26th May. This should have been the breakfast for the last full day on board the "St Louis", had disembarkation taken place as planned, but it turned out not to be so. (Edgar Glucksman)

FRIDAY, MAY 26, 1939

After breakfasting alone in his cabin on Friday, Captain Schroeder went to the chart room. There, as he made his calculations, he was joined by Ostermeyer. The captain said they would arrive in Havana before the two other refugee ships. What really concerned him, he went on to say, was not knowing what would happen when the ship reached harbour. He had sent two further cables to Holthusen, demanding amplification of the director's last radiogram, and the silence, the captain told his first officer, "was deafening."

The conversation then turned to the passengers. Apart from his meetings with Fritz Spanier and the passenger committee, the captain had maintained his stance of remaining aloof from them all, leaving the routine running of the ship to Ostermeyer.

The first officer replied that after some depression caused by the two deaths, all now appeared to be well with the passengers, and that the crew continued to respond to their orders to behave in an exemplary manner. Nevertheless, Captain Schroeder said, Schiendick and the Gestapo "firemen" would be "beached" once they reached Hamburg.

His determination to do so had been furthered by Jockl's recounting that morning his latest encounter with Schiendick.

Gustav Schroeder and Ostermeyer wondered why the party Leiter had seemed concerned over the remark that shore leave might be cancelled. The captain said he had a good mind, in Schiendick's case, to carry out the threat "if there is any more trouble from that man."

Friday the passengers lining the rails tried to identify landmarks as the ship sailed down the Florida coast, passing Miami early in the afternoon.

The sight of the city was a signal scores of them had been waiting for. They hurried to the purser's office and used up the last of their "shipboard money" on telegrams to friends and relatives waiting in Cuba and the United States for their arrival. More than one message contained only the words "Arrived safely."

Late in the afternoon, suitcases were brought up on deck and the deck chairs folded away.

There seemed to Aaron Pozner "a feeling of anticipation, of release from the Nazi horror. People laughed and prayed, and the crew smiled, pretending to understand."

That evening Josef Joseph invited members of the passenger committee to join him for cocktails in the first-class bar.

He raised his glass and thanked them, even though, as he pointed out, there had been nothing in the end for them to do, for since that first meeting with the captain, they had not seen him again, nor had he sent any word of fresh developments.

Only Dr. Max Weiss uttered a cautionary note: "That does not mean there will be no problems." But even he had to agree with Joseph's opinion that it was the "best possible omen" that the Relief Committee in Havana had not answered their telegram. The lawyer believed that in this case the cliché that no news is good news was true.

While the men replenished their glasses, and talked about life after the St. Louis, Gustav Schroeder received a wireless message from Luis Clasing in Havana. It was not in code, and the portent of the words was immediately clear. Clasing had telegraphed:

ANCHOR IN ROADSTEAD. DO NOT REPEAT NOT MAKE ANY ATTEMPT TO COME ALONGSIDE.

The cable Luis Clasing had sent to Captain Schroeder had brought him into direct conflict with his assistant, Robert Hoffman. Hoffman had turned to Clasing angrily, saying the situation would not have arisen if Clasing had offered Manuel Benitez the further bribe he had suggested.

Equally furious, Clasing had retorted that the immigration director wanted $250,000, an impossible sum for Hapag to provide. He had sarcastically suggested that Hoffman should approach his Abwehr paymasters for the money. Hoffman had snapped back that it was a "matter of negotiation," and that he proposed to do just that with Benitez. He stormed out of the Hapag building to see the immigration director.

Luis Clasing spent the next hour preparing a long cable to Claus-Gottfried Holthusen in Hamburg. Now, well into Friday night, he was still unable to find the right words to convey the series of swift-moving developments which had begun earlier in the day.

The first indication of trouble had been a telephone call from President Bru's office to Clasing informing him the St. Louis would not be allowed to tie up at the pier Hapag shared with the American Ward Line.

Clasing made repeated attempts to contact Manuel Benitez, but the immigration director was suddenly unavailable. Next had come a further blunt warning, this time in the evening editions of the local press, that there would be a "dangerous situation" if the refugees landed. That had been followed by a visit from Milton Goldsmith, demanding to know the exact situation.

The relationship between the two men was at best barely polite, kept alive by a common interest in landing as many refugees as possible. It became icy when Clasing refused to give any assurances the St. Louis would berth as scheduled.

"You mean you don't know if they will land or not?" pressed Goldsmith.

"I mean you should put that question to the president," retorted Clasing.

After Goldsmith had gone, the shipping agent had telephoned Bru's secretary and pleaded that it was "now impossible" to turn back the ship, the St. Louis "should at minimum be allowed to anchor in the roadstead, to allow it to revictual, pending a continued search for a solution."

The secretary had telephoned back granting the request on Bru's orders.

Clasing had then cabled Schroeder. Now, he incorporated the substance of that message in his radiogram to Holthusen, adding:

STILL HOPEFUL COMMON SENSE WILL PREVAIL AND ALLOW DISEMBARKATION. ASSURE YOU I AM DOING ALL POSSIBLE AND WILL EXPLORE EVERY MEANS TO ACHIEVE DISEMBARKATION.

A few doors away, Robert Hoffman sipped coffee and shared the optimism engendered by Manuel Benitez.

The immigration director had received him warmly, and asked Hoffman to apologise to Clasing for his earlier unavailability, explaining that he had been "fully occupied with the St. Louis in other quarters."

Benitez did not specify what those areas were, but when Hoffman revealed Bru's order that the ship must anchor out in the harbour, the immigration director had felt it was further confirmation that "Bru was weakening."

Then, in a dazzling display of verbal juggling

An Bord des Motorschiffes „St. Louis"

Freitag, den 26. Mai 1939

HAUPTMAHLZEIT

Salat Monte Christo

Kraftbrühe mit Gemüsen und Eierstich

Mastkalbsrücken, Kartoffelkrusteln
Stangenspargel, Schaumtunke

Gebratene junge Ente

Mirabellenkompott

Maraschino-Eis, Vanillekeks

Schweizer und Kräuter-Käse

Frucht

Kaffee   Tee

MUSIKPROGRAMM

Strand-Idyllen, Walzer . . . .

Der Calif von Bagdad, Ouverture . . Boieldieu

Leuchtkäferchens Stelldichein, Intermezzo Siede

San Lorenzo, Marsch . . . .

. . . . Fetras

. . . . Silva

This is the dinner menu for Friday 26th May, together with the music programme (usually printed on the back of the menu, though the end of voyage ball menu from the previous evening was not). Tomorrow was to be the passengers' last Sabbath on board the "St Louis", but sadly, it was not as they had hoped. (Edgar Glucksman) which had convinced many others and now convinced Robert Hoffman, Benitez went on:

"My friend, Bru has to keep up a pretence. Tonight he lets the ship into Cuban waters. Tomorrow he allows it into the harbour. The next day it will be at the pier. Then, off they will come, and our worries are over."

"You are that sure?"

"Of course. I am a Cuban. I understand the Cuban mind," soothed Manuel Benitez.

Now, as they drank coffee, Hoffman felt especially satisfied that the situation would be resolved after all, that he could keep his meeting with Schiendick. Later, when he wrote his monthly report to the Abwehr, Berlin, he noted he had not even had to offer a small bribe, a nice footnote to his account of Operation Sunshine.

He left Benitez, totally unsuspecting that he had been hoodwinked.

Friday night passed uneventfully aboard the ship. After dinner, served early so that the passengers could get to bed, most of them had laid out their going-ashore clothes and turned in.

Some slept fitfully. Max Loewe had another restless night. Aaron Pozner was a "little anxious" of entering a country where he knew no one, and the Aber children kept each other awake chattering about the sights their father would soon show them.

In his day cabin, Captain Schröder fell asleep in his favourite leather armchair still holding in his hand the cable ordering him to anchor in the roadstead. He had read and reread it, deciding in the end that nothing would be accomplished by contacting Havana at this late stage. After his experience of Holthusen, the captain had little confidence in any Hapag official, especially a "minor one in an outpost like Cuba."

SATURDAY, MAY 27, 1939

At 2:30 A.M., the captain was awakened by the watch officer, who told him the St. Louis had made up for the time lost burying Weiler and searching for Berg, and had actually gained on the other two refugee ships. The Orduna was now six hours behind, and the Flandre nearly twenty-four. There had been no incoming cables except a few of welcome for passengers.

At 3 A.M., Schröder ordered the ship's speed

be reduced to take on the pilot. He looked forward to questioning the Cuban, and as soon as he boarded Schröder asked him why they were to remain at anchor in the harbour, The pilot was noncommittal. His English was poor and his German non-existent. The captain spoke little Spanish, but enough to recognise the man claimed he was "only carrying out orders." The reply rekindled Schröder's fears, but he realised there was no point in pressing the matter.

Precisely at 4 A.M., Captain Schröder ordered the ship's klaxon sounded to awaken the passengers.

Rosemarie Bergmann delayed dressing long enough to capture the moment in her diary: "I have never jumped out of bed so quickly. The sky is dark blue but I can make out a few white buildings stark against it. There are still stars in the sky. It's like a dream."

All over the ship that dream was coming true for its passengers, almost half of whom were women and children being met by husbands and fathers already in Havana.

Soon the decks were overflowing with people trying to recognise landmarks they had seen in postcards. A few car headlights pierced the darkness on the shoreline. Passengers on the port side could see the murky outline of the towering walls of El Morro, the ancient fort guarding the harbour's entrance. The movement of the ship was barely perceptible as it glided through the water, now beginning to sparkle in the dawn.

At 4:30 A.M., the breakfast gong sounded. Despite the hour, there was soon a hubbub of excited conversation in the dining rooms. Some passengers, Babette Spanier noticed, sported the watches and rings they had purchased at the last moment from crew members; the "shipboard money" the passengers had paid for them could be exchanged by the seamen for Reichsmarks on their return to Germany.

With the sound of the anchor being dropped, the Spanier twins rushed to a window in the first-class dining room. Their parents joined them, and on the starboard side, in the half daylight, they could see that the shore was a long way off; away in the distance was Havana Cathedral.

Returning to their table, Babette Spanier asked Leo Jockl why they had not tied up alongside. The steward did not know, he had never been to Havana before, but he suggested that perhaps the harbour was not deep enough to take a ship as large as the St. Louis.

Within minutes, half a dozen theories swept the room. Dr. Spanier, who had see the ship's yellow quarantine flag being hoisted, said that until they had been passed by the port's medical authorities, they would have to remain at anchor.

Rosemarie Bergmann, recalling her doubts about the drinking water at Cherbourg, believed: "We are being kept out now so that no illness is brought on board." Shalote Hecht said she had heard "some story" about the ship's papers not being in order.

By the time that rumour reached A deck, it had changed: now it was the passengers' papers which were in doubt. When he heard this, Josef Joseph kept from his wife his feeling that it "had an uncomfortable ring of truth about it," remembering what the captain had told the passenger committee about decree 937.

The ship's doctor, Walter Glauner, stood at the top of the accommodation ladder, waiting to greet a Cuban in a white tropical suit from the first boat to come alongside. Glauner escorted the Havana Port Authority doctor toward the bridge.

Aft on A deck, the ship's orchestra broke the early morning quiet of the harbour as it struck up "Freut euch des Lebens." Remembering the words of the tune, "Be Happy You're Alive,"

Aaron Pozner "felt good" almost for the first time since leaving Hamburg.

In his day cabin, Captain Schröder gave to the Cuban doctor the thirty-two manifest sheets listing every passenger and containing his sworn statement that none of them was "an idiot, or insane, or suffering from loathsome or contagious disease, or convicted of a felony or some other infamous crime involving moral turpitude."

Despite the captain's signed statement, the doctor insisted that he personally view the passengers. Barely able to conceal his anger over his words being challenged, Schröder curtly ordered the first officer, Ostermeyer, to assemble the passengers in the social hall for inspection. He then abruptly left the two doctors, and returned to the bridge.

Assisted by purser Mueller and his staff, the ship's nurse formed a long snake of people that wound its way around the hall. As the doctors entered, she took up position with them on the bandstand, and the queue began rapidly to file past.

Renatta and Evelyne Aber wriggled themselves near the front of the line, eager to be first. As Renatta looked up to the officials seated behind a table, she "became frightened, as I was in Hamburg, of men in uniform."

Elise Loewe had intentionally chosen a position near the end of the queue for her family. She hoped that by the time they passed the inspection committee it would not be so vigilant, would not see that "Max was not acting normally." The Loewes were passed by the Cuban doctor without comment, as were all the passengers. Satisfied, he authorised Dr. Glauner to arrange for the quarantine flag to be lowered, and left the ship. When Schröder learned that the man had gone, he told Ostermeyer he thought "the entire business was a charade."

Shortly after 6 A.M., Otto Schiendick joined a group of stewards standing by the accommodation ladder watching the approach of a launch flying the Hapag flag. When Luis Clasing reached the deck, Schiendick asked him if he was Robert Hoffman.

"No. And who are you?"

"I'm the Ortsgruppenleiter on this ship."

Suspecting that the steward was involved in Hoffman's Abwehr work, Clasing sourly told him that his assistant had no business on the ship, and if Schiendick wanted to see him he should go ashore; in the meantime he could make himself useful by bringing on board the ship's mail, stacked in the launch.

Then, without waiting for an answer, Luis Clasing went to the bridge.

The captain awaited him in the day cabin, seated behind his desk, on which lay all the telegrams received since leaving Hamburg. He remained seated as Clasing entered. Nor did he offer his visitor any traditional hospitality. He was tired from a night of little sleep, and his mood was not improved by Clasing's breezy reassurance that things "would be well."

Then why, demanded the captain, had Clasing sent a cable ordering the ship to anchor in the roadstead?

Clasing began to explain. The captain interrupted.

"So. This man Benitez tells you it will be all right, and you believe him?"

Clasing, borrowing a sentiment from the

immigration director's fund of reassuring phrases, replied that he understood the Cuban mentality.

"Then, by God, you had better explain these!" roared Gustav Schröder, thrusting the cables at the shipping agent.

Luis Clasing began to wish he had never boarded the ship to face this fierce little man.

"Well? What do they mean," snapped Schröder.

"Captain, the situation is fluid, and there are many problems I have had to overcome—"

"I'm not concerned with your problems. I just want these passengers ashore. Do you understand?"

The telegrams, said Clasing, referred "to events in the past." Then, borrowing another sentiment of Manuel Benitez, he added: "The truth is, you are here, in Havana Harbour. You may regard the voyage as over. The passengers are not your problem any more."

Gustav Schröder rose to his feet, pressing his palms down on the desktop, and looked coldly at the shipping agent. Then, in a measured voice, he said, "These people are my responsibility until they are off this ship. If you ever forget that, I will personally see to it that soon you will be working for somebody else. Now, get off my ship and go back to Havana and get my passengers ashore. And do it quickly!"

At about the time Clasing was receiving his ear-bashing from Schröder, Hoffman, in charge of the Hapag office in Clasing's absence, received his first unsettling news of the day. Otto Ott, the midget spy, telephoned to inform Hoffman in his distinctive high-pitched, panting tone that during the night the Cuban secret police had raided his Swiss Home Restaurant. Nothing had been found, but clearly the restaurant, long a meeting place of the Abwehr, could not be used for the planned Treff between Schiendick and Hoffman.

While Hoffman considered a safe alternative, his phone had rung again. This time a contact in the Havana post office told him that hundreds of. telegrams were being delivered to President Bru urging him to keep out the refugees, and to order the St. Louis to leave.

The information came like a bombshell to Hoffman. The telegrams had probably resulted from the work of the propaganda agents he himself had briefed. Now, despite Benitez's previous assurances, if Bru acted quickly on the advice of those telegrams,

the St. Louis would depart Havana before Schiendick had collected the espionage secrets from Hoffman.

The Abwehr agent cursed himself for not going to the ship with Clasing. He realised he must go immediately, taking the secrets and running the gauntlet of the American agents he guessed would soon be at the harbour.

The U.S. military attache, Major Henry Barber, was already there. He had stopped counting the number of suspected Abwehr agents and contacts on and around the pier. "The place was a bees' nest of them, with the Cuban police and the rest of us playing the keepers."

Naval attaché Ross E. Rowell viewed the Abwehr strength with alarm: "Most of them were there as a smoke screen behind which anything could happen." His confidence ebbed as he realised the enormity of the problem. The plans he had laid—persuading the Cubans to tighten their immigration and custom checks for the St. Louis, having police boats patrol the area around the ship—seemed woefully inadequate to cope with the situation developing this Saturday morning. There was simply no way of properly shadowing all the Abwehr men. Rowell decided that, until Hoffman appeared, he would concentrate on Ott.

The dwarf was difficult to tail. Ott darted around the pier, playing the part of a successful local restaurateur awaiting the arrival of new customers. He greeted a number of people effusively, and waved each one farewell with his fat cigar before busily talking to someone else.

Rowell was disappointed to see that neither Ott nor any of the other agents gave a sign of doing anything unusual. By 7 A.M., Rowell's spirits began to wane.

They would have revived had he seen Hoffman striding purposefully toward the pier head, carrying some magazines and official-looking papers, and forcing his way through the crowds with a carved walking stick.

Hoffman was allowed through the customs point, and waited at the landing stage for the Hapag launch, now returning with Clasing. As the launch pulled alongside, Hoffman told Clasing it was urgent that he go to the ship. Clasing, still smarting from Schröder's tongue-lashing, told Hoffman he was "welcome, but I suggest you avoid the captain. He's not in a very receptive mood."

Just as the launch was leaving, Rowell, talking to Milton Goldsmith and Laura Margolis, caught sight of Hoffman departing. Rowell borrowed the binoculars the refugee workers had been using to watch the passengers now thronging the upper decks of the St. Louis. Angry that he had not spotted Hoffman earlier, he now hoped he could see what the Abwehr agent did, even if he could not overhear what was being said.

"I am Robert Hoffman, assistant manager of the Hapag office," Hoffman told the Cuban police officer confronting him at the bottom of the St. Louis accommodation ladder.

"That does not matter. We have just received strict instructions from the highest authority to allow no one but Cuban officials aboard."

"Then I should like to have a certain crew member brought to me here."

"I am sorry. That is not allowed. There is to be no contact between anyone on the ship and anyone who comes out to it. Please leave."

"But I only want to give a friend these magazines," Hoffman pleaded.

For a moment, the policeman hesitated. Hoffman sensed he might be able to bribe his way up the ladder if the steward was present to receive the documents instantly. He shouted up Schiendick's name. At this, the policeman put his hand on his pistol, and ordered Hoffman back into the launch. Hoffman looked up: there was no reply to his call. He stepped into the boat, and it headed for the shore.

Rowell handed the binoculars back to Milton Goldsmith, relieved that Hoffman had not boarded the ship and had apparently only spoken to the policeman.

Like Rowell, Hoffman did not see nor hear Otto Schiendick approach the top of the ladder and ask Leo Jockl whether it was Clasing who was now returning to the shore in the Hapag launch.

"I don't think so," said Jockl to Schiendick. "He called out for you. I think his name was Hoffman."

On shore, watching the Hapag launch approaching shortly after seven o'clock, Rowell's attention was drawn by an excited murmur sweeping the crowd as people fell back to allow Manuel Benitez to walk to the pier head. Rowell presumed Benitez had come to "make good on his promises." Later, in a

secret report to Washington, he would write that the swashbuckling minister had "arrived on the scene armed with two pistols."

At the pier head, a police captain and a detachment of patrolmen awaited Benitez. The captain saluted the minister and then shrugged apologetically, saying he had orders not to let him through.

"Do you know who I am?"

The captain did, and it was for that reason he was being barred, on specific instructions.

"Who issued them?"

They had come directly from President Bru's office.

"They cannot apply to me!"

The captain was even more apologetic, but stood firm; the president's instructions were that the minister must not be allowed to pass this point.

For a moment it seemed to Rowell that Benitez was about to shoot his way through the police cordon. The minister's hands hovered over the pistol butts. Then, finally, he turned away, and headed toward his office, hands still on his pistols.

Milton Goldsmith had viewed the scene with disbelief, concluding that it was dismal proof that Bru was in total command. He, too, turned and pushed his way through the stunned crowd, pausing only to tell Laura Margolis he intended to telephone the Joint in New York.

By nine o'clock that morning of arrival, the Cuban police already aboard the St. Louis had been joined by immigration and customs officials.

Passengers and crew had watched the small uniformed group make their way up the ladder and then go directly into the first-class restaurant. There they ordered a breakfast of rolls, sausages, and beer. Otto Bergmann noticed that the officials seemed especially to like the German lager. "That will put them in a good mood," he told his wife.

On deck, passengers waited, watching the rowboats which now surrounded the ship offering a variety of fresh tropical fruits. A few tossed money down, and received a bunch of bananas or coconuts, which were passed up the ladder by the now more obliging policeman.

As the Aber children moved close to the companionway, Evelyne caught a glimpse of a black man; she had never seen one before. Clutching her sister's hand, she ran to the safety of their cabin.

Gradually a sprinkling of relatives and friends began to arrive in the rowboats. When they got too close to the St. Louis, the police ordered them back. Their shouted words could barely be understood on the upper decks, some seventy-five feet above the water line. In one of the boats were Dr. Aber, Dr. Bardeleben, and Hans Fischer. They circled the ship, shouting up their names.

Mrs. Bardeleben was the first to see them; she and her daughter Marianne had been standing at the rail ever since they passed the medical examination.

Ten-year-old Marianne was particularly excited. The night before, for the first time in her life, she had been taken to the hairdresser. This morning her mother had given her a further surprise: two Cuban hair clips sent by her father to Germany had been kept secret from her and brought out only as a special treat for this moment. Marianne excitedly peered down at the rowboats, hoping to find her father so he could see her new hair style. Her mother kept saying, "There he is. There!" but the distance was too great for the child to pick out her father; there were so many upturned faces, and so many boats. "There, Marianne, there!" urged her mother. Marianne was broken-hearted, for she still failed to see her father.

Dr. Aber called up to Mrs. Bardeleben, asking for his daughters. "After what seemed like hours," she returned with them, lifting first Evelyne, then Renatta, above the ship's rail so they could catch a glimpse of the father they had not seen for a year. They hardly recognised him.

Almost crying with delight, Dr. Aber then asked whether his children had visas. It took some time before he made himself understood, his companions thought the question irrelevant. Finally Mrs. Bardeleben returned again, waving two green passports. "Yes, they have Cuban visas inside," she shouted. Dr. Aber wept with relief.

Rosemarie Bergmann "hugged with her eyes" those in the boats. "At last we are among friends," she told her husband.

Mrs. Spanier heard someone call, "Don't worry, everything will be all right."

"Of course it will," she said to her husband. "What do they mean?"

Fritz Spanier did not reply.

About ten o'clock, the immigration officials finished their beers and began processing passports, Benitez's landing permits, and the landing cards that had been given out on board. The passports, each stamped in Germany with a red "J," were given a cursory glance, as were the permits. The Cuban officials stamped the landing cards with an "R." Passengers were then given a form telling them where their luggage would be found on the Ward pier.

By ten-thirty, about fifty passengers had been cleared, collected their hand luggage, and were standing at the top of the accommodation ladder awaiting transport from the ship.

Anticipation rose as they saw the launch return which had brought the customs and immigration personnel aboard. An official ran up the ladder, ignored the passengers, and walked into the ship.

Minutes later, he, and all the officials, left the St. Louis. Only the Cuban police remained.

Soon after ten o'clock, Milton Goldsmith telephoned Joseph C. Hyman, the executive director of the Joint Distribution Committee, in New York. Goldsmith explained to Hyman, some 1500 miles away, that "our worst fears have come true. The passengers have not been allowed to disembark."

Hyman liked and respected Goldsmith as an energetic worker for whom years of setbacks had not eroded the enthusiasm essential for the often thankless task of manning a welfare outpost.

Now, as he listened to his voice, he recognised that Milton Goldsmith badly needed help.

Hyman promised that two experienced relief workers, Lawrence Berenson and Cecilia Razovsky, would fly down. Berenson, a lawyer, would "negotiate a settlement." Razovsky was to "help take care of the passengers when they land." The pair would arrive on Tuesday.

Goldsmith quietly pointed out that that was still three days hence: "The position here has been allowed to drift too long already. President Bru is afraid to let the passengers off because of anti-Semitic campaigns. Hapag have told me that if the passengers don't land, they are sure Germany won't have them back."

Hyman agreed there must be "no question" of the refugees returning to Germany. He requested that Goldsmith co-operate fully with Berenson in his "difficult task," and promised the fullest support of the Joint.

Laura Margolis was pleased to learn that at long last they were to receive the help they had repeatedly requested, though the role Cecilia Razovsky was to play did not seem altogether clear. Laura told Goldsmith the woman had "a reputation for forthrightness which might not suit the situation." Nevertheless, Berenson would come with one great advantage. He was a personal friend of Fulgencio Batista, and Batista had recently been warmly welcomed in America by President Roosevelt. With connections like those, if Berenson could not "do a deal," no one could.

A deal, in any form, was furthest from President Bru's mind as he stood at his office window and looked out across the bay at the anchored St. Louis. Behind him, on his desk, were the bundles of telegrams which had been delivered earlier that morning, each one almost identically worded in its warning of "serious consequences" if the refugees were granted permission to land.

The telegrams had not influenced Bru; he dismissed them for what they were, an organised attempt to manipulate the situation. What did concern him were the indications of a possible

alliance aimed at circumventing decree 937.

The first had come, predictably, when Manuel Benitez, after his failure to bulldoze his way on to the ship, demanded another meeting with the president. Bru had refused even to speak to the minister on the telephone.

The next move had caught the president unawares. It came when Dr. Juan Remos, the secretary of state, had telephoned to express his opinion that while legally the refugees should not be allowed to enter Cuba, there "may well be a moral case to let them in." Bru had listened respectfully to the arguments Remos advanced in the quiet, controlled voice which in the past had lent steadfast support to Bru both within and without the cabinet, and had advocated closing Benitez's illegal immigration "bureau."

Remos reminded Bru that Batista had yet to pronounce on decree 937, and there was "also the question of the American attitude to consider."

Bru had replied that he believed Cuban public opinion was largely in favour of banning the refugees, whatever Batista might say, and that he did not share the secretary of state's fear of pressure from the United States. America, he told Remos, was

On the right of this picture is Lawrence Berenson, the Jewish Joint Distribution Committee representative, dining with Under Secretary of State Welles in New York in 1939. No doubt, the topic of conversation revolved around the "St Louis" refugees. (The US Holocaust Memorial Museum)

increasingly sensitive to the immigration issue. Opposition had quickened in the past months across the United States in spite of a lobby demanding extra admissions for European refugees.

The telephone call left the president uneasy. Without the total support of Remos, his cabinet might be split, and that could be a critical factor with elections pending. Bru sensed that any alliance which came about because of Remos and Benitez's common aim would likely have the support of Batista, and together, if that happened, the three would make a coalition powerful enough to end Bru's hope of a further term in office.

And yet, with a politician's instinct, Bru still believed he was right to maintain his stand, and that in the end he would be proved right at the ballot box. Nevertheless, he decided that the ship anchored out in the bay must not become an election issue, must not split his cabinet, must not even be allowed to remain as an offending presence for a moment longer than necessary.

By the end of this Saturday morning, Manuel Benitez was concerned, to varying degrees, on three counts.

First, President Bru had effectively barred him from both ship and palace. Benitez was upset by such banishment, but he had been long enough in the rough-and-tumble of Cuban politics to know it would not be an impossibility, given the right moment, to reinstate himself in the presidential favour.

Second, Dr. Juan Remos had told him that the interests of the Cuban nation must come above any support he might tender for the refugees.

Benitez had pleaded that his only concern "was helping the refugees as a matter of conscience."

Remos said he was astonished that Benitez had the gall to offer "such a high-flying excuse for larceny on a grand scale."

Benitez had learned in his political life to ride with such insults, but the immigration director had made a third, and more unpalatable, discovery. His benefactor, Batista, had gone to ground. It had dawned on Manuel Benitez that it was a deliberate move on the part of the army chief, one designed to avoid Batista's becoming involved with the St. Louis, or with the way Benitez had handled matters. That did worry the immigration director.

Ironically, Batista's move was a parallel one to that which Benitez had himself adopted toward Luis Clasing earlier on Saturday. Benitez had become "unavailable" to the shipping agent, and he planned to remain so until he had found a way out of the crisis. By lunch time Saturday, like Bru, Benitez began to feel that the only solution was for the St. Louis to weigh anchor and take her troublesome passengers elsewhere. Then, when tempers had cooled, he would resume his old relationship with Hapag. But Benitez, an expert on the Cuban mentality, had greatly misunderstood the European mind, in particular that of Gustav Schröder.

At lunch time this Saturday, Captain Schröder spoke frankly to the ship's officers assembled in his day cabin.

"Gentlemen," he said, "I fear trouble."

The first serious sign of trouble, he said, had come when the Cuban officials had abruptly departed, leaving only the police behind. The captain had sent for the senior policeman, and the man had been unable, or unwilling, to explain why the customs and immigration officials had left. Under Schröder's pressing questions, the policeman had pleaded the language barrier; the only sense the captain had gleaned from him was a repeated, "In Cuba, things go lower than in Europe."

Next had been the arrival of the Orduna; she had also been ordered to anchor out in the harbour, and now a police detail guarded her gangway.

The captain revealed that Luis Clasing had made no further contact since returning to Havana. Gustav Schröder wondered whether his earlier blistering attack on the shipping agent, far from galvanising Clasing, had merely had the opposite effect, sending him bolting for cover. Now, to the assembled officers, he returned to that thought, producing and reading Clasing's telegram, which ordered the ship to anchor in the roadstead.

"I don't think we can expect much from him," Schröder said, "or it seems, from Hamburg," referring to Holthusen's cables.

He went on to reveal the existence of the passenger committee, which brought surprised murmurs and questions. One officer asked what authority the committee had; the captain replied that its sole function was liaison. Another wondered if it gave pass-engers "a status on the ship they did not have in Germany." Gustav Schröder answered sharply, "We

HAVANA AT LAST:

Above: this is what the passengers saw as the "St Louis" slipped into the roadway to await its turn to pull alongside to disembarkation. (From the collection of Gerald Granston, currently on loan to the Museum of Jewish Heritage, NY)

Right: coming down the channel into the roadway, passengers saw this lighthouse and buttresses to mark the approach to Havana harbour... then, as they rounded into the bay, this is one of the views that confronted them. (Mrs Gertrud Mendels)

The "St Louis" surrounded by small boats. (Wiener Library, London)

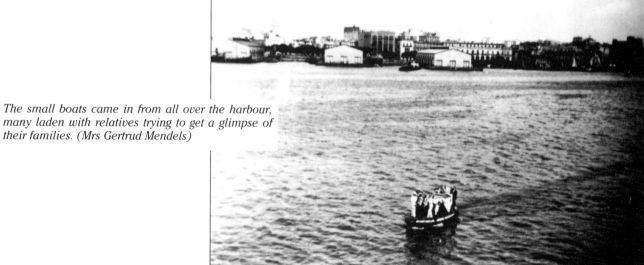

The small boats came in from all over the harbour, many laden with relatives trying to get a glimpse of their families. (Mrs Gertrud Mendels)

Above: by Saturday evening, the Jewish Sabbath, there were more and more boats closing in on the "St Louis", whilst (below) traffic built up on the waterfront. (Herbert Karliner)

These are two more views the passengers were able to enjoy from the rail of the "St Louis" while waiting to disembark. (Mrs Gertrud Mendels)

are not in Germany now." Nor, he reminded them, would he tolerate any sign of "the sort of thing some of these people have experienced back home."

Nevertheless, he went on, if the daily Nazi radio summaries were to be believed, a similar climate existed in Havana. He now personally discounted much of the broadcasts as typical propa-ganda, yet he admitted that if they contained even some truth, the situation could become unpleasant.

Therefore, he continued, he had decided to cancel all shore leave until further notice.

Another murmur rippled through the room, and purser Mueller, remembering the repeated inquiries he had had from Otto Schiendick about going ashore, expressed the view that the captain's decision would not only be unpopular but might lead to tension between crew and passengers.

"It's your job, all of you, to make sure that does not happen," retorted Gustav Schröder.

In the meantime, he concluded, in spite of his fears, he was confident about one thing: "These pass-engers are eventually destined for America. If the situation here deteriorates, I am sure the United States will resolve matters by accepting them a little sooner."

The office of the American consul general in Havana, Coert du Bois, was on the first floor of the consulate at the foot of Obispo Street, near the docks, and from it he could clearly see the St. Louis.

Like Goldsmith's Relief Committee, du Bois's consulate was constantly besieged by refugees; on his decision depended which, and in what order, refugees left Cuba and were allowed into the United States. The consul general carried a further burden: the ailing American ambassador relied on him heavily for advice and daily information, information that was pass-ed to the government in Washington and that would critically affect the future of the St. Louis passengers.

Early on the day of arrival of the St. Louis—which, unhappily, coincided with the removal of the American embassy to another building, and with the beginning of the Whitsun weekend—Coert du Bois cabled to Cordell Hull at the State Department in Washington an assessment of the St. Louis situation. It was to become typical of the attitude of the American government to the entire affair.

THERE APPEARS TO BE NO ACTION THAT THE EMBASSY OR CONSULATE GENERAL COULD PROPERLY TAKE AT PRESENT.

In the British legation, Ambassador H. A. Grant Watson discussed with his consul general the difficulties of the St. Louis in relation to the Orduna.

The important thing, stressed Watson, was to make absolutely clear the difference between the two ships: "The St. Louis is German, the Orduna is British." In addition, the refugees on the Orduna should be allowed to land, said the ambassador, because they, unlike those on the St. Louis, "started their journey before decree 937 came into force. Although the Orduna did not leave Liverpool until May 11, after publication of Bru's decree, many of the refugees were from Gdynia, and they left there before the 5th May. The St. Louis did not leave until May 13."

The consul general conveyed the legal niceties of the British argument to the Cuban government. An under-secretary of state promised it would be "duly considered, but in the meantime, 937 applies to the Orduna."

French diplomats received a similar answer when they raised the question of the Flandre passengers. Like the British, the French saw no way of pressing the matter further, and repaired to enjoy the Whitsun weekend.

The Sabbath service on the St. Louis had been poorly attended that Saturday morning; most passengers were too excited watching the activity surrounding the ship.

Although Alice Feilchenfeld and her four young children had not yet seen her husband, she had decided they should attend. The family were deeply religious, and had managed to eat kosher throughout the trip. Now was not the time to break with their beliefs. Alice Feilchenfeld had been pleased to see Recha Weiler present; she hoped the service would console her.

Elise Loewe had also persuaded her family to attend. She hoped the service would somehow give her husband strength: the prophetical reading dealt with the birth of Samson.

On deck, at one o'clock, the Spaniers and Josephs watched the Orduna weigh anchor and move slowly toward the quay.

"Excuse me," said Babette, "but weren't we here first?"

As always, Dr. Spanier had a comforting

answer: "The Orduna is a much smaller ship, carrying many fewer passengers. I'm sure we'll be off after lunch."

Lunch came and went, and no one boarded or left the St. Louis. The Cuban police were by now freely mixing with the passengers, and to those who asked them when they would get off, their reply was always the same: "Despues de Pentecostes." It was reassuring, and seemed a genuine reason for the delay.

At three-thirty, a launch came alongside and a uniformed official boarded. Shortly afterward, Purser Mueller broadcast an announcement requesting Mrs. Meta Bonne, her children Beatrice and Jakob, and four Cuban passengers, to come to his office. About fifteen minutes later, the group were swiftly escorted to the launch, and their suitcases handed down by policemen.

They were the first passengers from the St. Louis to disembark.

Their departure caused immediate hope. Clearly it was possible to get off, but how? The reason the Cubans had been allowed to go was taken for granted, but the departure of the Bonnes was a mystery. Mrs. Bonne had kept to herself during the voyage; some knew five-year-old Beatrice had had her birthday the day before, as a party had been arranged in the ship's kindergarten for the child by a St. Louis stewardess. But there was no apparent reason why this one family had been singled out for special treatment.

Captain Schröder sent for Mueller and demanded an explanation. The purser described how the immigration official had asked to see the Bonnes' passports, and looked at the visas inside. Mrs. Bonne had also produced her landing permits, each signed by Benitez, but, the purser reported, they were of no interest to the Cuban, who then said they could leave the ship.

Captain Schröder shook his head, surprising the purser by saying the disembarkation of the passengers was a "bad sign," and asking Mueller to find out which other passengers had visas.

Dr. Max Aber had not seen the passengers come ashore. Along with many others, he was at Benitez's "bureau."

Much as Gloria Spira liked the refugee doctor, she could only tell him: "The situation is serious. President Bru won't let the people off. Minister Benitez has given me orders not to be disturbed. There is nothing I can do."

Max Aber walked back to the cafe where his friends, Dr. Bardeleben and Hans Fischer, were waiting to tell him of the disembarkation of the seven passengers.

From their sidewalk table, the men could see the St. Louis, its swastika hanging limply in the Cuban heat. All around them were relatives and friends of the passengers, bartering with the owners of rowboats for a trip out to the ship; twenty-five cents was the going rate; a few who had boats with outboard motors charged more.

From time to time, an agitated immigration officer passed the cafe. One stopped at Max Aber's table and told the doctor Gloria Spira had asked him to help get Renatta and Evelyne Aber off the ship. The official told Aber to meet him at noon the next day, Sunday.

During Saturday afternoon, refugees came off the Orduna and were greeted by people on the shore who had helped swell the crowd on the waterfront to some two thousand onlookers. But no more left the St. Louis.

As Max Aber returned to his room in the Havana suburb of Vedado around nine o'clock, he saw the Orduna slowly sailing past the St. Louis and out of the harbour; the German ship remained.

SUNDAY, MAY 28, 1939

The worry that the St. Louis might also sail while he was asleep kept Aber awake much of the night, but Sunday morning it was still anchored in the bay. Walking back to the harbour, a reverberating bang repeated again and again, made him quicken his step. He broke into a run. Guns were being fired. Dr. Aber relaxed only when he reached the waterfront: an arriving American warship had received a military salute.

Another ship also arrived that Sunday, May 28. The Flandre was now tied up where the Orduna had previously been berthed.

Max Aber went straight to the cafe where the immigration man had agreed to meet him. Just after one o'clock, Aber saw him, but the official brushed him off, saying he was "too busy with the French ship," and entered the customs area, where Aber could follow him no farther.

With growing concern, the doctor called on

Luis Clasing, but the Hapag agent offered no help. Aber protested that "as a German and a holder of the Iron Cross I received while fighting for Germany in 1915, I deserve treatment for my daughters at least as good as those who've already gotten off."

Clasing told him that those who had disembarked from the St. Louis "were Cubans," and only forty-eight passengers had been allowed off the British Orduna; the others had been ordered to remain on board and the ship had gone in search of another port.

The doctor returned to the waterfront, depressed, and, after again visiting the St. Louis with his friends, saw the Flandre leave the harbour.

"Each day a ship comes in, disembarks passengers, and goes," said Dr. Bardeleben. "Why can't the same happen with ours?"

"Because they were English and French ships. Ours is German," replied Hans Fischer.

MONDAY, MAY 29, 1939

By nine o'clock in the morning of Monday, May 29, Max Aber had left his pension and was knocking on the door of the residence of Jose Estedes, the well-connected Cuban who had originally purchased the Benitez landing permits for his family, and then later introduced him to Secretary of State Remos, who had arranged the visas.

A maid answered the door. "Senor Estedes in Havana," she told the doctor.

"Where?" he asked.

The maid did not know.

Max Aber hurried to the town centre, searching for the only man he now believed could help him. He walked the full length of the main business street, Obispo, without success. He tried the adjoining streets. By lunch time, he had still not found Jose Estedes. Aber decided to try the better restaurants and hotels, and just after noon, he found Estedes at the Hotel Sevilla-Biltmore.

"Dr. Aber was in tears," Estedes later recalled. "He told me how his wife had left him for a German, and about his daughters on the St. Louis with no one to look after them. He seemed to me a fine, cultured man of capacity. He was in bad shape." Jose Estedes took Max Aber to see Cuba's secretary of defence, the elderly, aristocratic friend of Batista, General Rafael Montalvo. Aber waited in an outer office while

Estedes spoke to the general.

Montalvo listened as Estedes explained Aber's plight, then summoned two aides, an army captain, Gomez Gomez, and Captain Eiturey of the Cuban police. The general told them to go with Estedes and Aber and "get the girls off the ship."

The party travelled in the general's official car to Benitez's "bureau." Startled, Gloria Spira asked them to wait, but Aber was staggered to see his three companions sweep past the secretary and into Benitez's private office.

Benitez was not impressed that they had come at the "suggestion" of General Montalvo.

"I will not permit anyone off the ship," he told the group. "If they put their money on the table—I want two million dollars, yes, that's what I said—they can come in. Otherwise there is no way they can come in."

At that point, Estedes was to recall, "Captain Gomez pulled out his revolver and said, 'You are under arrest.' It was unbelievable. Benitez went red in the face. He was speechless."

If the minister thought of using one of his own pistols, he gave no sign. Gomez kept his revolver trained squarely on the minister and, without taking his eyes off him, told Captain Eiturey to take Dr. Aber to the St. Louis and return with his daughters.

Max Aber followed the police captain to the crowded pier head. There the police motioned them through. They boarded a launch. "A little motor boat with a flag on," Dr. Aber noted, "steered by a huge Negro with only two teeth."

Standing at the top of the accommodation ladder of the St. Louis, waiting for them, was Captain Schröder, surrounded by police, passengers, and crew.

At first, Max Aber thought the ship's captain "a Hitler man. He was in uniform. He clicked his heels together and said 'Good afternoon.' I was astonished. Then he talked to Captain Eiturey in broken Spanish. I couldn't understand. I just told him, 'I have come to pick up my daughters. They have visas.' Captain Schröder said, 'Yes, you can take them.' He was very nice and friendly."

When Evelyne and Renatta were brought to their father, they were in bathing suits, and seemed to Aber "to be more interested in the fun they were having on the ship."

As they went away to change, passengers collected around the doctor, besieging him with questions: "When will we leave? Can you help us? What is going on in Havana?"

Max Aber hid his doubts:

"I tried to give them some consolation. I told them other refugees from Germany had been allowed in. They were crying. I didn't want to discourage them."

Renatta and Evelyne returned, dressed in lace dresses and light coats. When they got in the launch, Evelyne clung to her father, frightened of the big, black, toothless helmsman.

On the way to the shore, Dr. Aber remembered something "strange" his wife had written from Germany, telling him to "look carefully in Renatta's new coat." The doctor felt the lining. Sewn in the seams was jewellery. Though the little girl had refused to take the gold watch her mother had offered in Hamburg, she had been an unwitting accomplice in hoodwinking the Nazi customs officials.

Now, Cuban customs checks were waived as Captain Eiturey led the group through, and then escorted them across the street to Benitez's office.

Gomez had kept his pistol pointed at Benitez the whole time Aber was away, Jose Estedes recalled, "and Benitez did not move or say a single word."

The party then drove back to Montalvo's office. Dr. Aber introduced his daughters to the general, and thanked him for "making me the happiest man alive."

The general telephoned Benitez:

"Thank you, Minister, for your co-operation and generous help.'

There was a short pause before Montalvo put down the receiver.

"What did Benitez say?" asked Estedes.

"He said," replied General Montalvo, that "it was a pleasure to be of service."

President Bru had not allowed the weekend at his country estate to be disturbed by the refugee ship, but when he returned to the palace Monday afternoon, he learned that the saga of the St. Louis had been reported by The New York Times, and reporters were arriving in Havana from other newspapers to cover the story.

Bru did not welcome their presence. He still smarted from press jibes that he had often in the past demonstrated the courage of Batista's convictions. That sentiment, he mused, would soon be given the lie.

Even so, Bru was relieved to be told of Batista's "indisposition." Like Benitez, the president diagnosed it as one of convenience, and the danger of a head-on clash with Batista over the St. Louis seemed to Bru, at minimum, postponed. He was further heartened by the news that Benitez had been seen hightailing it out of Havana that afternoon. The only decision remaining was whether Bru should order the ship to leave harbour before "Batista had a chance to surface." As he considered the question, Bru overheard his secretary taking a call from the Hapag office.

It was Robert Hoffman. The Abwehr agent had had a worrying weekend. Ever since his rebuff by the Cuban police on the St. Louis, Hoffman had considered how he could transfer the secret documents to Schiendick, what reason he could invent that would allow him onto the ship. A few moments before his call to Bru's secretary, Luis Clasing had provided the answer: he mentioned in passing to Hoffman that he had heard from Milton Goldsmith that a passenger committee had been formed on the St. Louis; Goldsmith had been given permission to board the ship to meet them.

Preoccupied with the problem of what to do with the 250 passengers in Havana who had booked passage on the St. Louis for its return voyage to Hamburg via Lisbon, and wishing not to face Captain Schröder again, Clasing had agreed that Hoffman might try to visit the ship to meet the committee as his representative.

Hoffman's inquiry to Bru's secretary brought a favourable reply. With Batista and Benitez out of the way, Bru decided to be "generous." If Hoffman went to the ship at once, and did not stay aboard longer than the time the president had granted to Milton Goldsmith, he could visit the ship.

The German agent was jubilant. Taking his cane, magazines, and pens containing the secrets, he went immediately to the pier head. There he was stopped. Though the Cuban police officer, on checking Hoffman's credentials, agreed that permission had been granted for him to go to the St. Louis, he "regretted nothing could be taken to the ship."

Hoffman realised that if he objected too

strongly, the police might become suspicious. He handed over the walking stick; the officer requested the magazines as well. Watched by press men, Hoffman did as he was asked, pleased at least that there seemed no American agents present. With two pens which contained microfilm in the barrels protruding from his handkerchief pocket, the Abwehr agent walked to the Hapag launch.

From the bridge wing the captain watched Robert Hoffman climbing the accommodation ladder, and ordered that he should immediately report to his cabin.

There, after a perfunctory introduction, the captain demanded to know what news Hoffman brought from Luis Clasing about disembarking the passengers.

"None," replied Hoffman. "And I will be perfectly frank. Your passengers do not interest me."

"What!" stormed Schröder. "My God, they had better —otherwise I'll have you thrown off this ship."

"I don't think so, Captain," replied Hoffman. "I don't think you have the authority to do that."

Hoffman then identified himself as the senior Abwehr agent in Cuba, and made it clear that, should the situation arise, he could rely "on the backing of Admiral Canaris himself."

Unable to assimilate what he had heard, the captain remained silent, feeling the atmosphere in his cabin had been "poisoned." Then Gustav Schröder asked how the Abwehr was involved with his ship.

"There is no need for you to know that, Captain," said Hoffman. "All you need to know is what you will do now—"

"By God, you're not giving me orders!"

"They are not my orders. They come from Berlin. If you choose to disobey them, that is a matter for you. And so will be the consequences."

The oppressive silence returned to the cabin as Gustav Schröder weighed what he had been told, bitterly regretting that he had let this self-assured, arrogant man on his ship, hating his power to summon help from Canaris, a figure the captain knew only by reputation as a member of the Nazi clique now ruling Germany.

Hoffman spoke again, asking if the crew had been granted shore leave.

Schröder shook his head.

"Then you will do so."

The captain made no reply, merely nodding agreement, not trusting himself to speak.

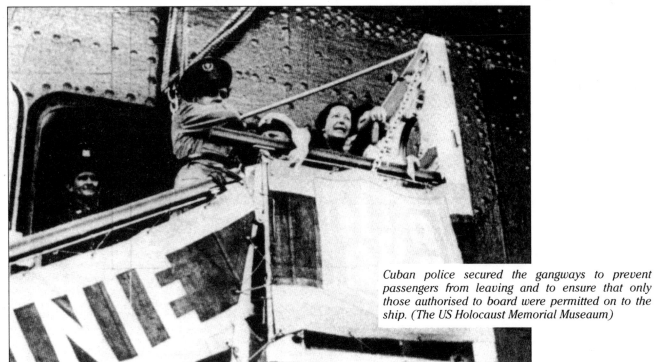

Cuban police secured the gangways to prevent passengers from leaving and to ensure that only those authorised to board were permitted on to the ship. (The US Holocaust Memorial Museaum)

"Thank you. The first group will go ashore this evening. I will settle arrangements with your purser."

"And then?"

Hoffman looked puzzled.

"What happens to my passengers?"

"Captain. I have already made it clear they are no concern of mine. But, if it will help you, the Americans are sending two people down here from New York tomorrow. No doubt they will find a solution."

With that, Hoffman walked out of the cabin.

For the first time since leaving Hamburg, Gustav Schröder felt beaten.

Being deceived by Holthusen was one thing; being exploited by Goebbels was another; they were events outside his immediate influence.

But Hoffman was different: he was immediate; he had stood in the captain's cabin, and threatened him. Hoffman had introduced the presence of the Abwehr on board. And, Schröder thought bitterly, "I had been unable to overcome those threats, or excise the Abwehr." He had a deep sense of failure, an attitude of mind which already had begun to affect his decision making and would later make him appear even more isolated to the passengers he wanted to help.

His first decision after Hoffman left was to abandon any thought of going ashore to investigate matters for himself, and to remain on board pending the outcome of any discussions the American negotiators would have with Cuban officials.

It was his second error of judgement since the start of the voyage, and it was a far more serious one than his first mistake, his decision to stay aloof from the passengers. For what the captain did not appreciate was that on this Monday afternoon, his "view from the bridge" of the worsening crisis was increasingly confined.

Robert Hoffman found Purser Mueller in his office, explained that the captain had granted shore leave, and suggested that a launch filled with crew should go ashore that evening.

"Would you also like to pick those to go?" inquired Mueller sarcastically.

"I'll leave that to you. But make sure the ship's Orstgruppenleiter is among them. I want to talk to him about crew morale."

"You can do that now," retorted the purser.

In uncomfortable silence, the two men waited for Otto Schiendick. When the steward arrived, Hoffman pointedly asked the purser to leave.

Mueller was about to protest, saw the look on Hoffman's face, and slammed shut his office door.

Hoffman looked carefully at the man who had come over 4000 miles to keep this Treff—and was, as an Abwehr report later showed, singularly unimpressed.

Years would pass before the substance of their meeting, as with much else involving the two men, became available, pieced together from information provided by their former colleagues and from the files of German, American, and British intelligence. From these, it is clear that Hoffman summed up Schiendick as a servile, self-aggrandizing man. Schiendick had produced his notebook, filled with the trivia he had written down about Schröder and Mueller, adding: "They are not party men and should be removed."

Hoffman indicated he was not interested in such tittle-tattle, and handed over the two fountain pens and their precious microfilm, no doubt saying that his only concern was the completion of Operation Sunshine. He briefed the steward on the pickup and on the situation ashore, telling him about the American and Cuban secret service men prowling the Havana waterfront.

However little Hoffman thought of Schiendick, like Gustav Schröder, the spy master found himself in a situation over which he had no control. There could be no question of aborting the mission, nor was there any way of replacing the steward as a cour-ier. He, like Schröder, was saddled with Schiendick.

At the same time another meeting was taking place on board between Milton Goldsmith and the passenger committee. The refugee director had been blunt from the outset, underlining that even with the imminent arrival of the Joint representatives from New York, the outlook was grim.

The committee members, their belief that the delay in disembarking was only caused by the holiday weekend now shattered, waited uneasily for the tired, middle-aged man to continue.

Goldsmith wished he had not been so outspoken. The men grouped around him explained that they had received no indication from the captain, or anyone else, that for the last three days their fate was in the balance. Milton Goldsmith guessed, accurately,

Friends and relatives of passengers, having hired boats to take them alongside the "St Louis", shout messages up to the pasengers (Stern Archiv)

that the captain himself was probably unaware of the true situation.

Into this already tense and depressed atmosphere walked Hoffman. Goldsmith introduced him as the assistant manager of Hapag in Havana, and expressed surprise when Hoffman "regretted" he had no positive news.

"When will these people get off?" pressed Goldsmith.

Hoffman shrugged. It was "all a matter of the proper authorities."

"Who, exactly, are they?" demanded Josef Joseph.

"Ultimately, the president of Cuba," replied Hoffman.

"Has he been approached by your office?" asked Goldsmith.

"Yes—and by others."

"And?"

"Herr Goldsmith, this is Cuba. You know as well as I that you cannot push. Cuba didn't ask these people to come."

"But Cuba, like Hapag, was quite happy to take their money.

Hoffman shrugged again.

"What will happen?" asked Josef Joseph.

Robert Hoffman said he did not know, nor, it seemed to the dejected passenger committee, did he much care.

With growing alarm they turned to Goldsmith, who outlined a plan to bring public pressure to bear.

Into a notebook, Dr. Max Weiss wrote the minutes of the proposal: "Goldsmith asks us to obtain three hundred names of friends or relatives of passengers in U.S. to give to the Joint, who will then cable influential Americans for help. Goldsmith says if we can't land in Havana he will work night and day to land us somewhere else. He says there is no question of us returning to Germany, and we must impress that upon the passengers."

The meeting ended as purser Mueller and a Cuban policeman arrived to say that Hoffman and Goldsmith's visiting time was over. While the committee members walked with Goldsmith to the accommodation ladder, Robert Hoffman again told Mueller to see to it that Otto Schiendick was among those crew members granted shore leave that night. By way of explanation, Hoffman added: "We did not complete our talk about crew morale."

After Schiendick's meeting with Hoffman, and while Hoffman was with the passenger committee, the steward arranged to see the ship's first officer, Klaus Ostermeyer, about the subject of crew morale. He was to find Ostermeyer surprisingly receptive to his scheme.

During his regular tours of the St. Louis, Ostermeyer had become aware of the increasing tenseness aboard ship. Since Captain Schröder had delegated to him the responsibility for gauging the passenger's mood, Ostermeyer had mixed frequently with them, taking tea and coffee and buying drinks, and come to the conclusion that the monotony of three days' inactivity was causing tension.

There had been complaints from the tourist passengers that those in the first class were receiving "better treatment," when, under the circumstances, they argued, all should be treated equally. Ostermeyer ordered that the usual demarcation between the classes should be abolished, with passengers of both classes allowed to make equal use of all the ship's amenities.

But it was Schiendick who suggested to Ostermeyer that the ship itself and, more particularly, its crew were in danger. Reminding the first officer of his responsibility for the crew's morale, Schiendick told Ostermeyer he believed that a search of the ship should be made for "explosives or other dangerous devices." Such a search, he went on, was necessary "because of the situation we find ourselves in as a result of carrying these people." It would go some way toward alleviating the foreboding of crew members who "fear for their lives because of the way some passengers are acting."

Ostermeyer thought Schiendick was exaggerating; still, the seeds of uncertainty had been sown, and he authorised a spot check of passenger cabins and public areas, unaware that Schiendick's reasons for suggesting the search were virtually the opposite to those he had given the first officer.

At four-thirty in the afternoon, Robert Hoffman left the St. Louis, having delayed his departure in the Hapag launch until Milton Goldsmith had made his way ashore in the boat that had brought him. The Abwehr agent was anxious to ensure that as few per-sons as possible saw him collect the cane and maga-zines containing the secrets for Schiendick which he had left with the Cuban police at the pier head.

As he walked with them to the Hapag office, he was again relieved to see that his arrival back on shore had not been witnessed by either Rowell or Barber, the American attaches.

At the office, Hoffman found Luis Clasing too busy. He did not ask how Hoffman's visit to the ship had gone.

During the afternoon, Clasing learned that Manuel Benitez had disappeared, and received two cables from Claus-Gottfried Holthusen, each impatiently insisting that he extricate the company from any blame in the situation. Holthusen had granted Clasing's request that the St. Louis's departure be delayed a further two days. Trusting that the American negotiators would have succeeded by then, Clasing now cabled Hamburg:

HOPEFUL SITUATION RESOLVED BY WEDNESDAY. AM IN CONTACT HIGHEST CUBAN AUTHORITIES. SITUATION ON SHIP CALM. CAPTAIN AND CREW DOING ALL POSSIBLE TO ASSIST PASSENGERS.

Clasing then set out to make good his boast of top-level talks. A telephone call to Bru's office brought the response that the president did not discuss "such matters with commercial companies." Another call to the secretary of labour's office, drew the reply that if Clasing cared to read the newspapers, he would find that the secretary's views had already been stated: he was firmly opposed to further immigration.

Soon after five o'clock, he reached the secretary of state, Juan Remos. Clasing had held no great hope of getting past the outer secretariat and was astonished to be put through to the minister.

Remos listened sympathetically to Clasing's suggestion that 250 passengers be taken off the ship and put in a quarantine camp, so making room for the 250 passengers in Havana waiting for passage back to Europe on the St. Louis.

The minister said the idea would be considered, but it would be agonising to have to select who would be allowed to leave the ship, and who would have to return to Germany. Clasing suggested that the passengers draw lots; Remos told him that that attitude hardly suggested that he cared in any way for his charges.

By late Monday afternoon, Max Loewe's paranoid schizophrenia, with its symptoms of being watched, followed, talked about, and plotted against, was acute. He told his wife there were "S.S. and Gestapo on board," specifically there to search him out and take him back to the concentration camp he had managed to avoid when he had been in hiding in Germany. Every moment longer he was detained on the St. Louis, Loewe believed, brought him closer to detection.

Desperately trying to conceal her own distress over his suffering, Elise Loewe tried hard to divert her husband's thoughts. That Monday morning she had organised a small family party in their cabin to mark the thirteenth birthday of their son, Fritz. It had not eased her husband's burden, and only reminded him they had lost everything of value when the trunk containing their belongings had been sent by the German authorities to Shanghai; the group had barely a change of clothes among their hand luggage, let alone a present to give Fritz for his birthday.

Max Loewe's fantasies were not far from the truth. The six Gestapo "firemen," who hated all the passengers on the ship, had managed to hide those feelings on the journey from Hamburg from all but a few, who simply thought them "different somehow from the rest of the crew." Since docking in Havana, the "firemen" had made their presence increasingly felt. They had patrolled the ship in pairs, unsmiling, chivvying passengers at every opportunity. They were, according to Babette Spanier, especially threatening toward children. She had warned her twin daughters to keep well clear of the patrols.

Now, with Ostermeyer's authority to search the ship for bombs, the way was open for the "firemen" to do as Schiendick had planned, while posing as the official protectors of the passengers and crew. Two of them called on Recha Weiler and abruptly blew out the candles she was burning to mourn the death of her husband. The candles were, they sharply reminded the old lady, a "dangerous fire hazard." When she tried to explain the reason for them, one of the men interrupted: "Candles won't help him where he's gone."

But it was Aaron Pozner the men singled out for the toughest treatment.

He was standing at the stern of the St. Louis, not far from where the ship's swastika hung. During the three days they had been in port, Pozner had eaten little, spending as much time on deck as possible, moving from one shaded spot to another. Down below where the restaurants were, the ship was hot and airless, and many passengers had complained that the heavy food was totally unsuitable in the humid Havana heat. The sun had sent the temperature to nearly 100 degrees on the decks.

"You are to come with us."

The hand on his shoulder combined with the tone of the voice made Pozner swing around in fright.

"We must search your cabin. You have the key?"

The "firemen" placed themselves on either side of Pozner, and motioned him forward. To his repeated "Why my cabin?" they gave no answer, speaking only once when he walked toward a lift. He was told they "preferred to go down by the stairs, where we can look out for other suspicious persons." Pozner unlocked the door to D-375, an inside cabin on the lowest passenger deck on the ship, and let the men in. They shut the door behind them, locked it, and ransacked the room, throwing everything on the floor, smashing against the washbasin a framed picture of his wife and children. As he bent down to pick it up one of them knocked Pozner to the floor. The other opened his suitcase, neatly packed ready for disembarkation, and scattered its few contents around the cabin, pausing only to rip to pieces a letter he had received from his wife at Cherbourg, and the Spanish phrase book. They missed the diary in his pocket.

Satisfied, the Gestapo men left. It was time Pozner had his head shaved again, the last man said as he went out. The former inmate of Dachau then knew why he had been beaten.

Even the crew were too frightened to object about the "firemen's" maltreatment of passengers; they too, they later admitted, feared revenge if they protested.

Not everyone on the St. Louis knew of the "search." With more than 1100 on board including crew, scattered throughout a large ship, many events took place of which the majority were totally unaware. What was not known was later invented and passed on, making it difficult to disentangle the truth from fiction. Passengers began to mingle less among themselves, preferring to keep to their established friends whom they knew they could trust.

On deck Rosemarie Bergmann looked excitedly down at a small boat bobbing amidships. Standing in the boat was a man holding a white dog.

"It's Oshey," shouted Rosemarie to her husband.

It was their fox terrier, which had travelled ahead of them on a freighter from Bremen. From now on, it would be brought out each day for them to see, but even Oshey was not allowed onto the ship.

At about five-thirty, Purser Mueller and a bevy of stewards and seamen took up position at the top of the accommodation ladder. Minutes later, fifteen passengers, most of whom had boarded at Cherbourg and were either Cuban or Spanish, stepped down the ladder into a waiting launch, which sped toward the shore. Their departure was so quick that few passengers noticed it. Aaron Pozner was one who did.

Trying to take his mind off what had happened to him, and afraid the Gestapo men might return, he had left his cabin to be among the security of other people. Now he watched the launch return empty after discharging its fifteen passengers. Stewards and seamen began loading cases into the launch. When his time came, Pozner wrote later in his diary, "I will carry my own case ashore."

Around 6 P.M. the launch returned to take a party of crewmen into Havana. Otto Schiendick was among them. As the launch sped across the bay he warned the seamen that they must not comment to any waiting newspaperman about the ship or its passengers because it would "only be used to Germany's detriment." As the launch edged toward the Ward Line pier, his colleagues noticed that Schiendick grew restive.

His anxiety further increased when they were each subjected to a thorough search by Cuban officials, and questioned and photographed by the newspapermen keeping a vigil outside the immigration hall.

Seeking an interview, the reporters were balked by the crew's insisting in German that they did not understand English. Those same reporters would undoubtedly have been intrigued by Otto Schiendick's first action after he left the pier. At a news-stand he bought a number of English-language magazines, explaining to the other crewmen that he wanted to "show his friends back home the sort of lies

foreigners write about Germany."

Next he led them to a gift shop, and there Schiendick surprised his colleagues by buying, and handing them, walking sticks. It was the first time they could recall the steward's ever showing such generosity, but they accepted it at face value, never suspecting they had become pawns in Robert Hoffman's plan to complete the last stage of Operation Sunshine.

As they filtered into the town, the crewmen split up into smaller groups, and somewhere along the way Schiendick detached himself from one of those groups and made his way to the Hapag office.

Inside, in Robert Hoffman's office, Schiendick exchanged his recently purchased cane and magazines for the identical ones Hoffman had carefully prepared to hold the remaining American secrets.

Moments later Schiendick was back in the crowded Havana streets, joined up with other members of the crew, and together they returned to the Ward Line pier, their shore leave at an end.

Again the seamen were subjected to a thorough search, but the Cubans hardly glanced at their walking sticks or the magazines under Schiendick's arm.

Robert Hoffman watched from a safe distance and shortly afterward cabled Berlin that his part in Operation Sunshine was over.

Neither Rowell nor Barber had followed Otto Schiendick. To them, he was just one of the crew who had gone ashore, and there was no reason for them to suspect that he was any different from the others.

As the crew returned, they saw that the number of police boats circling the ship had increased. Many swept the hull and superstructure with searchlights.

To Rosemarie Bergmann, it seemed the passengers were now imprisoned; Aaron Pozner, in his cabin, saw the lights pass his porthole and was reminded of those that scanned the Dachau compound.

Max Loewe's thoughts of being a wanted man remained with him: he often wandered off alone. Ruth and Fritz had gone in search of their father, but the ship had any number of hiding places. When he returned, he could not explain where he had been or why he had gone. Of all the people on the St. Louis, none was so tragic and pitiful a figure as this prematurely aged man.

HAMBURG-AMERIKA LINIE

Die Schiffsleitung hat die nachstehend benannten Herren gebeten, zwecks einer schnellen Abwickelung der Landungsangelegenheiten die Interessen der Passagiere wahrzunehmen :

Herrn Dr. Weis
Herrn Herbert Manasse
Herrn Rechtsanwalt Josef Joseph
Herrn Rechtsanwalt Zellner
Herrn Rechtsanwalt Hausdorff

Diese Herren werden durch die Schiffsleitung von allen Maßnahmen laufend unterrichtet. Die Passagiere können davon überzeugt sein, daß von der Schiffsleitung und der Agentur in Verbindung mit dem jüdischen Hilfskomitee und der Deutschen Gesandschaft nichts unversucht gelassen wird, um die Landung zu beschleunigen.

Die Passagiere werden gebeten, sich nur auf die authentischen Mitteilungen zu verlassen, die von der Schiffsleitung durch das bestehende Komitee bekannt gegeben werden.

Die Schiffsleitung

This document, issued by the "Ship's Management", announced the formation of the Passenger Committee, naming the Committee's members. (Mrs Liesl Joseph-Loeb)

TUESDAY, MAY 30, 1939

On Tuesday morning, the passenger committee filed into the captain's day cabin. Still shocked at Hoffman's revelation that the ship was somehow involved with the Abwehr and espionage, he had, nevertheless spent time preparing himself for this meeting, the first he had convened since forming the committee.

Mueller, the purser, had briefed him on the committee's earlier meeting with Milton Goldsmith. Of necessity the description was sketchy; the purser had gleaned sparse information by adroit questioning of the members after the meeting had ended. But the captain realised that Goldsmith's attitude had brought gloom.

Now, he found them not only anxious but also resentful. They believed he had been less than forthcoming in his earlier promise of regular consultations. Schröder saw the justice of their complaint and conceded that, on reflection, he should have summoned them earlier; he had not done so because he had hoped he would have better news if he waited. "And have you?" asked Josef Joseph somberly.

The captain, with no news from Luis Clasing, and having decided not to go ashore and seek his own answer to that question, could only reply: "Things don't look good, but we must never lose hope."

It was honest enough, but it gave rise to new uncertainties. They had expected more than talk of hope. Some even wondered whether this little man facing them really had the stature to resolve the crisis. They mistook his tiredness for lethargy, and his silence for indecision.

Like Milton Goldsmith, the captain was convinced that the committee would carry out specific tasks well, but would be unable to initiate their own ideas. Therefore, he reasoned, if they could be imbued with a sense of purpose, one he must give them, it would communicate itself to the other passengers.

Taking pains to convey a feeling of being "part of an equal partnership," Gustav Schröder proposed that the committee itself cable influential figures to intercede. Goldsmith had suggested a similar idea, but this time the initiative would be in the committee's hands, and it would "be seen by all on board that you are striving to solve matters."

The committee accepted the idea, and decided the first message should go to the wife of President Bru, the man they knew controlled their immediate fate. To her they cabled:

OVER 900 PASSENGERS, 400 WOMEN AND CHILDREN, ASK YOU TO USE YOUR INFLUENCE AND HELP US OUT OF THIS TERRIBLE SITUATION. TRADITIONAL HUMANITARIANISM OF YOUR COUNTRY AND YOUR WOMAN'S FEELINGS GIVE US HOPE THAT YOU WILL NOT REFUSE OUR REQUEST .

Similar telegrams were sent to public figures in the United States, though the committee decided it would be premature at this stage to call for the help of President Franklin Roosevelt.

While they drafted their messages and dispatched them, taking care, at Schröder's suggestion, to post carbons for other passengers to see on the ship's notice boards, a seaplane landed close to the ship.

It brought Lawrence Berenson and Cecilia Razovsky from New York. Ashore, they went directly to the Relief Committee office, where Milton Goldsmith and Laura Margolis carefully briefed them on all developments.

"It will take money more than anything else to buy them their freedom," Berenson said.

On board the St. Louis Max Loewe had watched the plane land with great excitement. But at three o'clock this Tuesday afternoon, the day after his son's thirteenth birthday, Max Loewe entered a lavatory on A Deck. He locked the door and slashed his wrists with a straight razor. He walked past the ship's doctor's office on his way to the deck, and at exactly the spot where Moritz Weiler's body had been put over the side, and where Leonid Berg had jumped to his death, Max Loewe leaped over the rail.

Captain Schröder and the first officer, Ostermeyer, standing on the port bridge wing, heard Max Loewe's scream as he entered the water. The captain shouted for a long blast on the ship's siren— traditional signal for "man overboard"—and then followed Ostermeyer, who was already racing along the promenade deck.

Purser Mueller was on the boat deck, near lifeboat number 8, when the siren sounded. He peered down at the water and saw nothing. He looked toward the bridge, where the entire watch was crowded on the port wing, gesticulating and shouting toward the sea. He looked down again and saw Loewe thrashing in "a pool of his own blood." Mueller rushed to the nearby officer's quarters, where the night watch were still asleep, and bellowed: "Out! Out! Man overboard!"

In the stern of B deck, stewards and deck hands, including Otto Schiendick, were spending an off-duty period sunbathing. They jumped to their feet and ran to the rail. Below, a police boat went into a sharp turn as other launches also made for the St. Louis.

Some sixty feet below Otto Schiendick, a couple of cable lengths out from the hull, Max Loewe had somehow raised his arms over his head and was clawing at his exposed veins, "pulling at them like rubber bands."

Above, from A deck, came a woman's anguished voice, almost lost in the piercing cries from Max Loewe.

On B deck, the powerful figure of leading seaman Heinrich Meier elbowed Schiendick aside.

"Nein!" Otto Schiendick's shout halted Meier as he clambered on top of the rail. He turned for a moment to look at the steward and then dived into the water, dimly aware of the uproar sweeping the ship's upper decks.

Meier was one of the ship's best swimmers. Even so, the impact of the sea from the height he dived slapped hard against him. Underwater for seconds, he shot to the surface, and found his hands and body stained with Loewe's blood. Shouting filled his ears; Meier looked up, but could not make out the words. Then, from close by, he heard: "Murderers! They will never get me!"

The seaman reached Max Loewe and lunged at him, seeking a hold. Loewe spun away and plunged beneath the water. Meier dived after him, grabbed him by the hair, and pulled the desperate man to the surface. Max Loewe called out again: "Let me die!" as another sound came to Meier, blocking out the shouting. He turned and saw the police boat; hands reached down and pulled Loewe out of the water. Moments later Meier too flopped into the launch.

Loewe lay moaning in the boat's well, blood draining from his wrists. A policeman began to bandage his wounds, but with a sudden burst of strength, Loewe kicked the officer clear, tore at the

tourniquet, and went toward the water, screaming again and again, "Let me die, let me die!"

Meier grabbed him and the pair rolled back into the boat. Two policemen straddled Loewe, re bandaged his wrists, and held him down as the boat turned to the shore.

At that moment the St. Louis's siren stopped.

On the boat deck, purser Mueller and the off-duty watch he had roused swung number 8 lifeboat back on its davits. On the promenade deck, Schröder and Ostermeyer walked past weeping passengers back to the bridge.

Otto Schiendick made the only immediate comment on the tragedy. Turning to the other stewards, he said: "Meier was a fool to risk his life. He won't be thanked for it." Schiendick was wrong.

The ship's siren had caused consternation along the Havana waterfront, where several thousand people kept vigil over the St. Louis. Word spread like a brush fire that the siren signalled the ship's departure.

Robert Hoffman heard the blast and left immediately to investigate; President Bru's siesta was disturbed and he told his secretary to warn Hapag that such "demonstrations" would not help matters; Laura Margolis stopped the discussion she was having with Cecilia Razovsky about where the passengers would be accommodated on landing.

When Hoffman reached the Ward Line pier he found an ambulance backed close to the water. Standing nearby were attaches Powell and Barber. Terrified that something had happened to Otto Schiendick and the secret documents, he pushed his way forward to look inside the ambulance. Max Loewe lay strapped on a stretcher, barely conscious. Seated beside him was Meier and two policemen. One of them warned everyone to stay clear, and pulled the door shut as photographers jostled for position. Its siren wailing, the ambulance drove from the pier to the Calixto Garcia Hospital.

On admission, Max Loewe was sedated and put in a guarded room; Meier was given a pair of pyjamas and coffee while his clothes dried.

The drama provided reporters with the break they needed. They pooled their resources to cover the hospital and comb the waterfront for eyewitness reaction. Two of them talked and bribed their way through the police cordon on the pier and chartered a

CAMEO 1: THE GOLDSCHMIDTS:

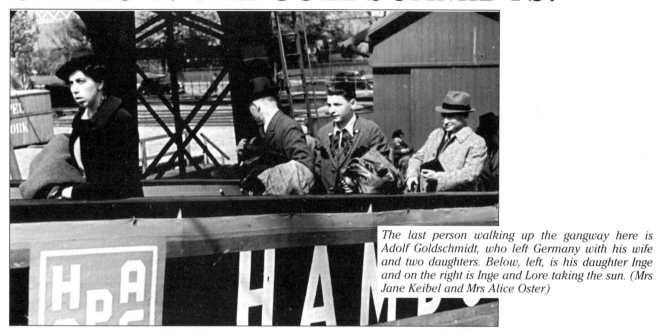

The last person walking up the gangway here is Adolf Goldschmidt, who left Germany with his wife and two daughters. Below, left, is his daughter Inge and on the right is Inge and Lore taking the sun. (Mrs Jane Keibel and Mrs Alice Oster)

Here is Lore with her parents on board the "St Louis", sitting in the shade on the Sports Deck. The Goldschmidts were finally allowed to settle in the United States. (Mrs Alice Oster)

Ruth and Inge Heilbrün travelled alongside the Goldschmidts and were friends. Inge was settled in France, with her parents, from the "St Louis" and they were later deported from the South of France. (Mrs Jane Keibel) boat to take them to the St. Louis. They nosed their way through the flotilla of craft around the ship and tied up at the accommodation ladder. With that confident manner peculiar to police and press, they went aboard, telling the Cubans guarding the ladder top that they had been sent to investigate the incident. They bluffed a gullible ship's officer to direct them to Elise Loewe, and then asked him to muster other eyewitnesses.

Elise Loewe, Fritz and Ruth, had gone to their cabins as soon as they heard the news. When the reporters arrived, they found two well-built passengers, George and Carl Lenneberg, standing in their way. Fearing just such an intrusion, they had stationed themselves outside the cabin. They eyed the reporters coldly. The newsmen tried another bluff, but the brothers would not move. Just as a scuffle was about to break out, the ship's officer arrived to say he had assembled some eyewitnesses on deck.

Realising that they could not see Elise Loewe, the reporters admitted their identity, and silenced the angry murmurs by changing the subject to mention the arrival of Berenson and Razovsky. Many passengers did not know of this development, and directed a barrage of questions at the reporters, who did little to dispel their anxiety.

First Officer Ostermeyer ordered the newsmen off the ship, a gesture misunderstood by a few passengers, who from then on believed that the ship's officers had a policy of keeping the outside world uninformed of their plight.

But the reporters had seen enough to draw a graphic picture of the ship "that shames the world." Within hours of their returning to shore, that description was radioed to a dozen countries. It was almost opposite to the news reports Gustav Schröder had become used to hearing; ever since the St. Louis had arrived on Saturday, Nazi news broadcast summaries to the effect that Cuba, "and soon the whole world," would show its attitude toward the refugees by rejecting his passengers.

Though the captain hoped this confident prediction would be proven wrong by the efforts of Berenson, his private diary spoke of "going back to Hamburg and having to live with my conscience." Like everyone else on the ship, the captain still found himself short on facts in a sea of conjecture. His notes to Clasing had brought only the vaguest of replies; his

latest cable to Hamburg demanding to know what action he should take when the two-day extension expired had elicited no reply whatsoever. Conditions on board added to his worries. Instead of relying solely on Ostermeyer, he had begun to take soundings himself among officers and a few passengers.

Assistant purser Hans Reich, who had established a convivial arrangement with several of the prettiest girls on board, told the captain he had the impression they thought the delay was due solely to Cuban inefficiency; certainly, from Reich's point of view, they seemed happy enough to while away their days by the pool, and their evenings in his company.

Dr. Spanier took the more guarded view that the general feeling was "not uniform throughout the ship. It differs from person to person, and from moment to moment." The relationship between the two men had been maintained, even strengthened, despite Dr. Spanier's refusal to serve on the passenger committee. The captain genuinely liked the soft-spoken doctor, finding him not only a useful sounding board but a valuable independent, and outspoken, voice. Dr. Spanier for his part looked forward to any meeting with the captain because, as he said, "I thought he was in an impossible position and I wanted to be of use to him in any way I could—apart from serving on the committee."

From his soundings, and those of Ostermeyer, the captain judged the mood of his ship as "fragile."

Max Loewe's action had broken that fragility. Within an hour of the incident, Schröder received reports of passenger reaction; many said Loewe jumped through a combination of fear of the future and harassment from the crew.

The last charge produced an explosion from Schröder. He summoned all deck officers and blasted them in his saltiest language, warning of the severest reprimands if such conduct continued. He had the Gestapo "firemen" marched before him. Although word had not reached him of the way they had carried out their "search for explosives," the captain knew their reputation, and threatened to put them ashore if he heard the slightest criticism of their behaviour. Then he sent for Schiendick and subjected him to the most violent tirade of all for not maintaining the "proper standards" as ship's Ortsgruppenleiter.

The steward, doubtless anxious only that the St. Louis returned to Germany quickly, mumbled to the captain that he would "be more observant in future."

Loewe's jump and the arrival of Berenson and Razovsky brought home to the passengers the real gravity of their position: those who had been quiet now became militant; the outspoken and confident became silent.

Leo Jockl, during a later afternoon visit to the bridge with the captain's tea tray, felt a ray of hope about the outcome of the voyage. He found Schröder and Ostermeyer poring over charts of the American coast.

Purser Mueller contacted the senior Cuban policeman on the gangway and pleaded with him to let Elise Loewe go ashore to see her husband. The officer eventually agreed to convey the request to the authorities, but returned with the answer that no passenger would be allowed to leave the ship under any circumstances.

Unaware of Max Loewe's act, or its repercussions, American ambassador Butler Wright waited at home for the Cuban secretary of state, Juan Remos. Wright had carefully prepared himself for the "informal meeting" during an all-morning conference with his consul general, Coert du Bois.

Du Bois had explained that telegrams were beginning to flood into his office on behalf of the St. Louis passengers. Because there were so many he had drafted a standard reply to be used for all of them, which the State Department in Washington had approved. It read:

ACKNOWLEDGING YOUR TELEGRAM RE EUROPEAN REFUGEES ON BOARD STEAMER SAINT LOUIS PLEASE BE ASSURED CONSULATE GENERAL DOING EVERY-THING IT PROPERLY CAN ALONG THE LINE OF UNOFFICIAL GOOD OFFICES. HUMANITARIAN ASPECTS OF SITUATION HAVE BEEN EMPHASISED TO CUBAN GOVERNMENT. DEPARTMENT OF STATE IS BEING KEPT CURRENTLY INFORMED.

Despite approval for his statement implying that pressure was being brought to bear on the Cuban government by America, du Bois was told that Under-secretary of State Sumner Welles was "distinctly against making representations" to the Cuban authorities about the refugees.

Ambassador Wright had wondered whether the view of Welles, notoriously ambitious and jealous of the power of Secretary of State Cordell Hull, coincided with that of President Roosevelt. Du Bois replied that the State Department had told him that various organisations were requesting eminent Americans to speak to the president, urging him to make direct representations to the Cuban government, but "no instructions along those lines had yet come from the White House."

The two men had then discussed whether, in the circumstances, the matter could properly be rais-ed by the ambassador during his meeting with Remos. Much, they decided, depended on Remos himself.

Forty-three, a former university professor, Remos was known as a liberal intellectual. He had a considerable reputation as an author; at the age of fifteen he had written a history of the fall of the Bastille, and soon after he produced a standard work on the life of Donizetti. More important, Wright knew that Remos had the confidence of Bru. A few months earlier, Batista had announced the resignation of Remos; the president had refused to accept it, and Remos stayed on. The ambassador felt, therefore, that Remos was a man of considerable courage, to whom a carefully chosen word or two would not go amiss.

Secretary of State Remos arrived at the ambassador's residence precisely at four o'clock. After a suitable time exchanging pleasantries, Wright "improved the opportunity to inquire about the present status of the refugees on the St. Louis."

Remos expressed "deep concern," and regretted that the situation had arisen through the "pernicious practice of a member of my government, compounded by Hapag's willingness to accept bookings without ensuring that passengers had a visa, in direct violation of my requests to them."

Wright asked for the secretary's own view on what should happen. "My personal opinion is that the aliens on the St. Louis should be admitted," Remos told Wright. "If they are not, the outcry in the press, and the statements which would be made about the way the Cuban government conducted itself, would be most derogatory."

Ambassador Wright hinted agreement. Then, calling on the skill thirty years in diplomacy had taught him, and while delicately affirming that he was acting "without instructions," the ambassador gently reminded the secretary of President Roosevelt's appeal to all nations to take into account "humanitarian considerations" when dealing with the refugees.

Juan Remos thanked the ambassador for his "informal good offices," making it clear that he appreciated that the observations were made "solely in a desire to prove of assistance to my country." As he left, he said the entire matter was to be discussed by the cabinet the next morning, and in the meantime the departure of the St. Louis would be delayed.

Ambassador Wright was pleased with the outcome of his talk. In a confidential report to Secretary of State Cordell Hull, he wrote: "I gained the impression that the awkwardness of the situation is becoming increasingly evident to Cuban government authorities."

Lawrence Berenson and Cecilia Razovsky had checked into adjoining suites in the Hotel Sevilla-Biltmore, one of the best in a city of expensive hotels. On the same floor were three of Hoffman's agents, who spent an anxious time believing the Joint representatives were from the F.B.I.

After checking in, Razovsky had gone back to see Laura Margolis, while Berenson began a marathon telephone session to his contacts. They were many. Berenson spoke fluent Spanish, was a prominent New York lawyer, and had been president of the Cuban Chamber of Commerce in the U. S. For all his flamboyant manner, he was a shrewd judge of when to act the corporation lawyer, and when the public relations man.

Berenson soon had little doubt that his original assessment was right. Money would be the key, probably the only, factor. The question was, To whom should it be offered, when would be the right moment, and above all, how much? He had come to Havana with no fixed sum in mind, simply authority from the Joint in New York "to negotiate." That, he knew, would mean having to go through the tedious procedure of regularly contacting and keeping informed the head office in New York. And the head office, Milton Goldsmith had told him, was "not always understanding."

Berenson's first contacts in Havana warned him that any approach to President Bru would be rebuffed at this stage. Nor was a search for Manuel Benitez to be seriously considered. He had left town, trumpeting that he wanted two million dollars to "guarantee" the passengers' freedom. It was a figure that Berenson believed showed at least a temporary aberration.

Berenson's feelers among other cabinet ministers left little doubt that they would follow Bru's dictates. He did not know Remos. That left Batista.

After several calls, Berenson realised Batista was avoiding him. Though they were friends, intermediaries hinted that the army chief saw no political gain to be made from the St. Louis, at least not for the moment. Batista, it seemed, was content "to sit this one out and watch Bru wriggle." Berenson was not despondent. He knew Cuban politicians well enough to know they would change their position with the first shift in public opinion. Max Loewe's action might provide the impetus for that change.

When reporters knocked at Berenson's door, he was friendly and forthcoming. He had come, he said, from New York to avoid just such tragedies How desperate the position already was could be judged from Loewe's behaviour. The issue now was, How many more would follow Loewe's example rather than be returned to Germany?

At 5;30 P.M., leading seaman Heinrich Meier returned to the St. Louis and a hero's welcome from crew and passengers alike. He brought the news that Max Loewe would "probably live."

The passengers had taken up a collection for Meier, and Captain Schröder presented it to him. It totalled 150 Reichsmarks, a considerable sum considering the financial state of the refugees.

Schröder, outwardly relaxed and smiling, hoped his public appearance would diffuse the tense atmosphere on board. Earlier he had listened in silence as the passenger committee had spoken of an "impending disaster unless good news came soon."

Now, as he returned to his cabin, Schröder was met by Ostermeyer, who informed him that cabin 76 on A deck was locked from the inside and had not answered the purser's repeated knocking. The cabin was only a few feet from the spot where Max Loewe had slashed his wrists.

Captain Schröder ordered the door be forced open and the ship's doctor despatched to the scene. A seaman jimmied open the door and Dr. Glauner and Purser Mueller entered 76. Its sole occupant, Dr. Fritz Herrmann, a middle-aged physician from Munich, lay undressed on the bed, unconscious. On a side table was a syringe and a row of empty ampoules.

151

"Will he live?" asked Mueller.

"Who knows? And how many more will there be?" demanded Dr. Glauner, echoing Lawrence Berenson's earlier question to the reporters.

Captain Schröder asked the committee later what could be done to ensure that no further suicide attempts were made. The reply was unanimous: news of this second suicide bid must be concealed from the passengers; the ship's hull must be lit by powerful floodlights at night; lifeboats must be prepared for instant launching in anticipation of further jumpers.

Schröder agreed to the suggestions.

Fritz Herrmann survived and was kept in quarantine; few on the ship ever knew of his suicide attempt.

That Tuesday evening, lifeboats were lowered to the deck and sailors stationed by them; when darkness fell, lights were dangled over the side, illuminating the water.

By then, Aaron Pozner was not the only person to think the St. Louis now resembled a floating concentration camp.

That same Tuesday night, Lawrence Berenson and Cecilia Razovsky dined in the Sevilla-Biltmore. Over crayfish cocktails and steaks they assessed the situation.

For Cecilia Razovsky the critical factor was the attitude of the local relief committee and its advisory board.

"Worthy, and well-intentional," was her verdict on the board. "But out of touch, and with nothing to contribute—unless, of course, it's money."

It was a typically blunt judgement, the sort that had made Cecilia Razovsky a respected, if not universally liked, refugee worker. Berenson agreed with her assessment. The advisory board was to be shunted aside—a decision that later would lead to friction and the eventual resignation of its most prominent members.

But on this clammy Tuesday night, even if the couple dining in a quiet corner of the dining room had anticipated such an outcome, they would not have changed their minds. Both saw themselves as professionals, facing a professional problem which needed totally professional answers.

By the end of dinner, after less than a day in Havana, they came to a conclusion both crucial and far-reaching: Milton Goldsmith and Laura Margolis

were undoubtedly dedicated, but in Cecilia Razovsky's eyes they "did not have the professional experience necessary to solve the crisis."

Berenson agreed. If they were too closely associated with the committee, "we lose the respect of the Cubans." But possibly his legal training caused him to hedge. "If we ignore the committee completely, we sever our connections with the other refugees on the island. The main thing is for us to be seen by all to be impartial."

Cecilia Razovsky had one further suggestion. Berenson should ignore what everybody had toldhim and make a determined attempt to contact President Bru. They left the dining room and went to Berenson's suite to telephone the palace.

Bru's secretary was courteous but evasive: the president's engagement diary was full "for the foreseeable future."

Berenson ignored the snub, and decided not to force the issue. Instead he thumbed again through his "contacts book." Eventually he produced a name: Garciá Montes, the secretary ofagriculture.

Berenson explained to Cecilia that he had a "close personal relationship" with the secretary, and also with his predecessor, Amadeo Lopez Castro. He had met the two men when they had visited the United States to negotiate a sugar agreement.

As Cuba's acknowledged sugar expert, Lopez Castro was a man of immense influence. Both he and Montes were confidants of Batista and, Berenson believed, might provide an entree to the army chief. Equally important, Montes, as secretary of agriculture in Bru's cabinet, would have direct access to the president.

With skilful handling, Lawrence Berenson believed, Garciá Montes and Lopez Castro would provide him with the hourly attitudes of the two men in Cuba who mattered, Bru and Batista, without "having to take sides or ostracise either of them."

He telephoned Montes. The secretary confirmed he was on "good terms" with Bru, and agreed that he and Lopez Castro could be of assistance. All he asked for was time "to assess the situation." He promised to bring Lopez Castro to his home to meet Berenson the following night.

It was, Lawrence Berenson told Cecilia Razovsky, "the first step on the road to a solution."

CAMEO 2: HEINRICH GLUCKSMANN:

"Heini" Glucksmann was born in Pless in 1909. As he left school in Oppeln, he went to work for a local cigar maker as a cashier and is seen here (left) at his 21st birthday party. His employer is seated at the right-hand end of the table, next to his brother Max, who is holding up Heini's birthday card. Heini is sitting fourth from the left. The right hand picture shows Heinrich outside his employer's premises with his workmates. (Edgar Glucksman)

Heini was a keen sportsman and swam, cycled, skated and skiied. This is just one of the certificates he won for swimming, when he placed third in a regional competition in November 1936. (Edgar Glucksman)

This was Heinrich Glucksmann's employer, whose name is lost in the mists of time, for all Heini wrote on the back of the picture was: "Mein Cheff". (Edgar Glucksman)

This pretty young lady accompanied Heinrich in many local skating competitions and helped to win on several occasions. (Edgar Glucksman)

Heinrich was interned in Buchenwald on "Kristallnacht", like so many other German Jews, but his employer managed to find out where he was and paid for his release, on condition that he left the country. This was a passport picture taken just after Heinrich was released, hence the very short hair. (Edgar Glucksman)

This was the passport issued to Heinrich Glucksmann in January 1939, preparatory to his departure on the "St Louis". On the third page is the bank's endorsement of his cash allocation of 9 Reichsmarks, issued on 9th May. His exit visa is stamped on the fourth page, along with the entry visa and aliens registration in Great Britain in June after the epic journey. (Edgar Glucksman)

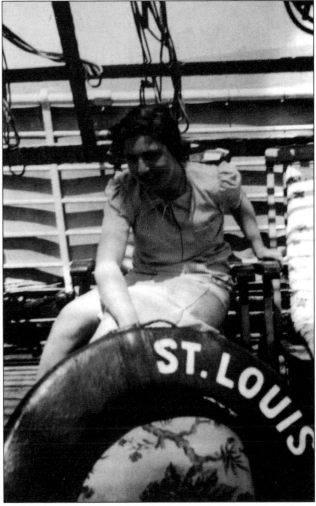

On board the "St Louis", Heinrich seems to have enjoyed himself and seems to have enjoyed female company, too! (Edgar Glucksman)

WEDNESDAY, MAY 31, 1939

By midmorning Wednesday, the bridge of the St. Louis registered a blistering 102 degrees, and the decks shimmered in the heat. Around the ship a flock of boats maintained watch, offering fruits and bringing relatives to wave and shout encouragement.

The response on board was subdued. Babette Spanier felt, "There was no more to talk about, because there was no real news. We had done all the waving, the calling of greetings, the chasing after rumours, the speculation about Berenson and Razovsky, and, after five days, we were still on board. We didn't know why—and that was the worst thing. Suicide attempts we could live with; none of us were strangers to death. That a few had got ashore, we could rationalise. But out there, on the decks, in the heat, near exhaustion, with no appetite, just not knowing, that was the terrible thing."

Yet for Babette Spanier there was one personal consolation. Her marriage seemed to have revived; her husband had never been more considerate or attentive, and that made everything else bearable.

Some passengers, though, were finding the situation on board intolerable, and began to blame everything on the passenger committee, feeling, as Otto Bergmann felt, that "they don't tell us anything and they don't do anything."

In some ways the committee was secretive. After discussions with Schröder, they had decided not to spell out that decree 937 was the stumbling block to disembarkation. The captain felt the information might further depress passengers whose experiences in Germany had made them well aware of the futility of challenging laws. Nor had the committee explained in detail their initiative in telegraphing public figures. It might suggest a desperate situation. Nor were the implications behind the arrival of the Joint negotiators circulated in committee bulletins. The committee did not wish to postulate what Berenson and Cecilia Razovsky might or might not achieve.

Dr. Spanier's clinical experience made him believe much of the mental stress on board was closely associated with the deaths of Weiler and Berg, and Loewe's attempted suicide.

Passengers became obsessed with indefinable fears and fantasies. Those passengers—shy, timid people often without emotional reserves—especially worried Dr. Spanier. He felt that unless they received swift assurances they too might try to end their lives. Dr. Spanier did not mention his fears to the passenger committee, but he did convey them to the captain. Schröder was horrified by the doctor's prognosis because, he explained, it matched his own.

That morning the captain had received a letter from a passenger saying that the man's aged mother, who was travelling with him, was on the verge of suicide, and "others will undoubtedly follow her lead." Schröder sent the overworked Dr. Glauner to sedate the woman, a move Dr. Spanier thought "hardly satisfactory." He told the captain: "You may have to sedate the whole ship if we don't get off soon."

Some thousand miles to the north of Havana, in Atlantic City on America's Eastern seaboard, the saga of the St. Louis finally stirred the general public into action. That day, The New York Times had carried a sober account of Loewe's suicide attempt.

Atlantic City's liberal community became one of the first to show public concern over the St. Louis with ~ protest meeting and march. Other demonstrations followed in New York, Chicago, and Washington. Messages were sent to President Roosevelt, Cardinal Spellman of New York, Cardinal Mundelein of Chicago, Secretary of the Interior Harold L. Ickes, labour leader John L. Lewis, and Supreme Court Justice Ferdinand Pecora. They were urged to telegraph President Bru asking him to repeal decree 937, and many did so.

As the media sensed a bigger story developing, more reporters and radio crews were dispatched to Havana. In London, the press was slower; only the Times had mentioned the St. Louis. Its brief report was read by Sir Herbert Emerson, director of the International Committee on Political Refugees. He saw the item as "the public tip of a private scandal." Emerson had kept up to date on events in Havana through copies of Ambassador Watson's reports to the Foreign Office. Watson believed decree 937 was "of a temporary nature."

Emerson did not share the view. His sources among President Roosevelt's Refugee Advisory Committee told him Bru was unpredictable. The committee was "not optimistic" about the refugees' chance of entering America "before their quota numbers came up." Presumably the committee reflected the American president's personal stand on the matter.

In Paris, the newspapers handled the St. Louis story coolly. Although the anti-Semitism of some stories disturbed Morris Troper, he had other worries. The Orinoco had sailed from Hamburg with 200 refugees on May 27 as scheduled, but the Hapag liner seemed in no hurry to set course for Cuba, and was still hovering off the coast of France. Claus-Gottfried Holthusen had been blandly evasive about the ship's intentions, and Troper wondered whether he might soon have to assume responsibility for the Orinoco's passengers.

In Germany, Der Stuermer urged that the 200 be sent to Dachau or Buchenwald if they set foot again in the Reich. The newspaper predicted the same fate for the St. Louis passengers if they returned. The Nazi-controlled press in Germany followed Goebbels' edict to use the St. Louis as a handle to attack all Jews remaining in the country. The campaign outside Germany had also satisfied the propaganda minister's instructions. In South Africa, South America, the Middle East, as well as Europe, the St. Louis was now a Nazi cause celebre, used as proof that it was not just Germany who did not want the Jews.

Late on Wednesday morning, President Bru went to the cabinet room to join his ministers. The only absentee was his director of immigration, Manuel Benitez.

Bru gave a comprehensive resume of the St. Louis affair. At the end, he blamed Hapag "for bringing these passengers here with documents obtained through bribery." The president reaffirmed his determination not to be influenced by "external forces," and asked for cabinet backing.

Secretary of Agriculture Garciá Montes did not speak, deciding, for the moment, to keep to himself his telephone conversation with Lawrence Berenson.

Secretary of State Juan Remos raised the suggestion Luis Clasing had made to him: that 250 refugees on the St. Louis be allowed to land so that an equivalent number of travellers wishing to return to Europe could embark.

Bru rejected the idea: there were other ships available on which they could travel; if 250 refugees were allowed to land it would negate the very meaning of decree 937. The cabinet agreed with him.

Remos then stated the American government's "unofficial position as conveyed to me informally by their ambassador."

The president listened thoughtfully, then replied, "I appreciate the concern for 'humanitarian considerations.' I feel deeply the pitiable situation of the refugees. However, I believe this is an opportunity to end once and for all the abuses that have led to it. Sending the ship back to Germany is the lesser of two evils."

Juan Remos accepted the president's arguments. With a sense of relief, the president saw there would be no split in his cabinet. It voted unanimously to exclude the refugees.

Ever since arriving in Havana, Gustav Schröder had eaten his meals alone in his day cabin, and lunch this Wednesday was no exception. Leo Jockl served the meal in silence, realising that the captain did not want his thoughts disturbed. In fact, Schröder was brooding on the meeting he was about to have with Juan Estevez Maymir, President Bru's special plenipotentiary. Schröder had been told that Maymir would bring him news of the government's official position.

It would be the captain's first contact with the Cuban regime, and he recognised an important opportunity to make known his own views and perhaps change the situation.

Juan Maymir arrived just after lunch. He was much taller than the captain, and, even at sixty, he held himself as rigidly as the younger man. His face betrayed nothing of his real thinking. He conveyed the current Cuban position in a few sentences: the cabinet had just endorsed a decision to bar the refugees; a law had existed before the ship sailed, precluding such immigration; Hapag had chosen to flout it, therefore the company was now totally responsible for the refugees.

Schröder argued that, blame apart, the refugees were in Havana Harbour.

Then, in the face of Maymir's silence, Schröder showed him the passenger's letter containing the suicide threat. Maymir read and reread it before handing it back. The captain expounded on his fears of a "collective suicide pact." With slow deliberation, Maymir remarked that the Cuban government would not be blackmailed; a wave of suicides would be laid at the door of Hapag.

Schröder sought another opening. World opinion might apportion blame differently; even if the shipping line had disregarded a Cuban law, in doing so it gave "these people an opportunity to begin a new life." If Cuba refused them sanctuary, "the world will say your president has acted inhumanely."

Maymir thought it was an "interesting view," and he promised to convey it to Bru, along with a personal letter the captain had written to the president, saying there was a "state of mutiny aboard" which he feared he could not control if he was forced to leave the harbour without disembarking his passengers.

The shadowboxing with Maymir was over; Schröder felt he had never really gotten to grips with his opponent.

Shortly afterward, the S. S. Iller arrived from Bremen with twelve passengers. They too were barred from landing. The Iller's captain signalled the St. Louis, asking how long he should wait in the harbour. Schröder replied: "That is a matter for God and your conscience.'

The St. Louis, anchored five days in the centre of Havana harbour, was now a tourist attraction. Friends and relatives of the refugees, lining the waterfront, were joined by Cuban sightseers. They produced a carnival atmosphere. Fruit and nut vendors set up shop on the Prado Promenade. Boats of dubious seaworthiness augmented those already offering trips to the ship; the price rose to one dollar. Binoculars and telescopes were rented. Entertainment was provided by street musicians and performing monkeys. The ship had fostered a shore-based industry.

For those who were waiting for loved ones to disembark, the noise and frivolity was cruel. Goldsmith's Relief Committee continued to be besieged, and continued to counsel patience. On Wednesday afternoon, after hearing of the Cuban cabinet's decision, Luis Clasing decided he would give the crowd outside his office clamouring for news "something to think about." He posted a notice saying the St. Louis would sail "tomorrow, Thursday, June 1, for Hamburg."

The notice caused near-panic among those who read it. Clasing had the announcement removed, but the damage was done. Hysterical relatives tried to bribe policemen to get their families off the ship; the U.S. consulate was flooded with requests that America call a halt to all immigration from Germany so St. Louis passengers could enter without delay, taking priority over all others.

The most desperate turned to anyone who might offer hope or consolation. Some even sought the advice of a refugee fortune-teller, a middle-aged woman from Prague who had made quite a name for herself in Havana s refugee community. She was not optimistic. Mysteriously swinging a lead weight on a string above her left hand, she predicted that the passengers would not be allowed off the ship, and soon they would be returned to Europe.

The fortune-teller's predictions drove many of her clients to despair. A few openly vowed they would "commit murder" if they could not board the ship to see their relatives. One of them was actually to do just that. Twenty-seven-year-old Hildie Reading had found a way around the president's ban. Her mother and father, an aunt, an uncle, and a former boy friend were all on the ship. She had personally paid Benitez $750 for their landing permits. Hildie Reading, herself a refugee, had learned Spanish while in Cuba, and earned a comfortable living giving facial and body massages; there was a regular demand for the beautiful Jew's services.

During the siesta hour on Tuesday, she had made her way to the home of the Secretary of State Remos, an elegant mansion guarded by six soldiers. She had to see the secretary urgently, she said, and she meant him no harm. The soldiers had searched her and found no weapon. She invited them to accompany her to the door. Instead they had waved her by.

A maid let her in and told her the secretary's office was at the top of a spiral staircase, directly in front of her. The young woman had knocked on the door, and gone straight in: "Dr. Remos was sitting in a huge, heavy, green leather armchair. Before he could say anything, I apologised for disturbing him, told him not to be angry with his soldiers for letting me in, and said I would only take five minutes of his time, and then burst into tears."

Remos listened sympathetically to Hildie Reading's pleading for permission to visit her relatives on the St. Louis, and finally agreed that she could board the ship for three hours the following day.

On Wednesday afternoon, accompanied by two soldiers, she boarded the ship and located her parents. There was a tearful reunion, while scores of passengers crowded around.

"I climbed onto a box, and told them they had nothing to fear. It was just the Cuban mentality. I knew because I had lived there for months. I spoke to them for a long time, and then I said they must understand I wanted a little time with my parents."

Hildie Reading explained to the two soldiers that she would like to see her mother and father alone. They agreed. Inside her parents' cabin, she gave her father $1700. It was her entire savings, and in the end it would make the difference between whether they lived or died.

The reason for her visit accomplished, the young woman left the ship carrying dozens of unstamped letters from passengers, which she promised to post. As she climbed into the launch, she broke down. One of the soldiers put his arm around her. "He was very upset by what he had seen on the ship, and said it was only a temporary hitch— 'Someone important who has to sign something is asleep in his hacienda'—and I believed him."

That "someone important," President Bru, had in fact allowed his Wednesday afternoon siesta to be disturbed when he agreed to take a telephone call from his secretary of agriculture and Lawrence Berenson's contact, García Montes. Afterward, Bru spent the afternoon alone in his office, placing Montes' call in context with, among other things, the morning cabinet decision, and the stack of newly arrived telegrams on his desk.

The telegrams particularly troubled him. They bore the names of influential people, moved to protest over the St. Louis, and, unlike the previous batch, most were from America. To one side was the cable the passenger committee had sent to Bru's wife the day before. It remained unanswered. Bru and his wife had been too upset by the message's reference to the children on the ship to reply; it reminded them that they had no children of their own.

President Bru, behind his narrow vision and stubbornness, was a sensitive man, capable of acts of generosity. So far he had resisted such feelings over the St. Louis. He had been able to sweep aside the protests from the British and French governments, but there remained a nagging unease about the attitude of the American ambassador. For all his outward independence, Bru was receptive to American thinking. At the cabinet meeting, Remos had made clear Ambassador Wright's feelings: the

diplomat had appealed for compassion. That sentiment remained with Bru, and so far he had issued no instructions for the cabinet decision to bar the refugees to be carried out.

The letter from Schröder added to Bru's concern. In conjunction with Juan Maymir's report on his visit to the ship, the letter had to be taken seriously. For the first time Bru accepted that the refugees were desperate enough to contemplate seriously mass suicide rather than return to Germany. The thought chilled him.

Further, there was the presence of Lawrence Berenson to complicate the issue; he was not the sort of man with whom Frederico Bru would choose to deal, but as the official representative of such a powerful American organisation, he could hardly ignore him.

Yet Bru actively disliked and mistrusted Berenson. He even help him partly responsible for the St. Louis situation, because Berenson had been told months earlier that refugees arriving without visas would not be admitted to Cuba.

Over all other considerations in Bru's mind loomed the figure of Batista. The army chief had remained publicly outside the controversy, but the president knew there was no reason to believe he would continue to do so.

All Wednesday afternoon, Bru had wrestled with the issue. By five o'clock, he came to a decision of crucial importance to those on the St. Louis. He telephoned García Montes and told him he was willing to discuss the matter with him and Lopez Castro the next morning at nine o'clock. The president made one condition: Lawrence Berenson was not to be present.

Around the time Frederico Bru made that telephone call, the passenger committee on the St. Louis assembled in the captain's day cabin. They found the captain standing between First Officer Ostermeyer and Purser Mueller.

All sensed immediately that Schröder was showing open strain for the first time. His fingers clutched nervously at various objects on his desk. His face was drawn. His shoulders drooped. He appeared "an old man." But it was his voice, above all, that shocked those present. It had lost its confidence, its certainty, its very tone; it was tired and faded as he spoke.

First, he read a copy of the letter he had sent to

President Bru, leaving his listeners in no doubt that Schröder genuinely feared mass suicide. A melancholy silence settled over the cabin. Then, in his precise Hanoverian accent, the captain expressed his "great disappointment" that the Joint team from New York had not yet visited the ship. If they had, he added, they would have seen for themselves that the situation was rapidly worsening.

Mueller stared at the captain and struggled for something to say. Finally, he stammered that the "only expedient thing to do is to return home. We are seamen, not politicians."

Schröder sighed. "Yes, perhaps. But we would reach Hamburg half empty." Then he repeated a phrase he had used before: "Worse, we might face mutiny on the high seas. That is a real possibility." Schröder's eyes searched the faces of those around him, seeking reassurance. He found none. After a long pause, he spoke again.

"Very well then," he said. "Certain further steps have to be taken."

He planned to initiate "suicide patrols" at night. Fifteen male passengers should be selected to augment the Cuban police and crew already patrolling the ship after dark. Those selected were to be able-bodied and discreet.

"Why passengers?" asked Ostermeyer.

"Because they are better able to deal with their own people," said Schröder.

A murmur of agreement came from the committee.

"But nothing must be done to destroy hope," Schröder ended. "Hope must always remain."

Some of the committee felt afterward that those words were little more than an attempt by the captain to sustain his own rapidly ebbing confidence.

As he had done every evening since arriving in Havana, Aaron Pozner made his way to the social hall this Wednesday night, seated himself at a corner table, and listened to the gossip. For some days the hall had become a clearinghouse for rumour, speculation, and the few available facts.

A disquieting hush settled over the huge room as the passenger committee appeared. Its members dispersed and moved from one group to another, repeating a familiar litany: Do not worry, stay calm, do nothing rash.

Pozner admired Josef Joseph's extraordinary self-control. The lawyer gently chided a tearful young woman, smiled understandingly at a couple tightly holding hands, gave an old man a reassuring pat on the shoulder. Joseph gave no hint that in moving around the hall he was in reality choosing members for the suicide patrol. He recognised that the margin for error was high because he knew few on board well enough to make a sure judgement.

He chose a bank clerk; the man was small and wiry but gave an impression of toughness. He picked a tall, sparse, middle-aged man who looked energetic enough to restrain potential suicides. Joseph selected another, a stolid shopkeeper who, he judged, lacked the imagination to consider whether a person had a right to end his own life.

He turned down some of the younger men because he thought them immature: they might panic in an emergency. Others were rejected: they looked right for the suicide patrol, but Joseph suspected them of emotional instability.

The lawyer considered Aaron Pozner. Joseph found him a strange man: polite, apparently in control of his feelings, yet distant. He respected Pozner's right to isolation, but wondered if it masked an urge for self-destruction. He ruled him out.

Joseph turned to Werner Feig, a Berliner with strong opinions about most things on board. Feig was born to travel first class, and had boundless self-confidence. He was asked to Join the patrol.

Fritz Gotthelf, another Berliner, was the last approached. The former sales manager was chosen because he was a man "convinced of the importance of life" and had become a cheering influence throughout the ship.

At eight o'clock, the men assembled in the purser's office, where they were briefed on their duties and assigned to their watches. The patrols began an hour later, and were changed every two hours throughout the night.

CAMEO 3: THE GRUNSTEINS:

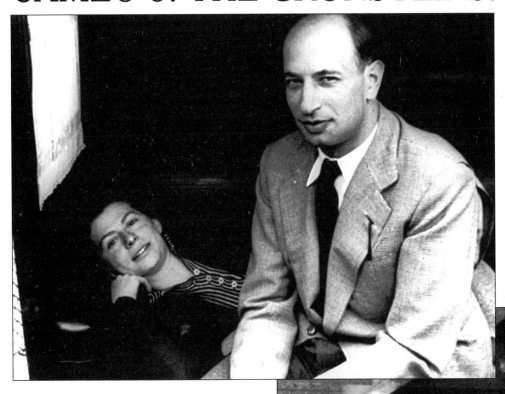

This "Cameo" consists of only two pictures for the simple reason that many of the photographs in this book came from the collection of Gerald Granston, who was born Gerd Grunstein, and are spread elsewhere throughout the book. It is true to say that had his collection not been available to the publisher to reproduce, this book would have been the poorer. Above is his father, with a lady called Lotte Metis. Each was travelling alone with their children and struck up a friendship. The lower picture shows Heinz Grunstein with young Gerd, who appears about ready to go off again on his travels around the decks of the ship. (From the collection of Gerald Granston, currently on loan to the Museum of Jewish Heritage, NY)

THURSDAY, JUNE 1, 1939

The next morning, Leo Jockl approached the captain's quarters. In one hand he balanced a breakfast tray. Its contents never varied: a pot of coffee, black bread, and sliced sausage. In the other, Jockl held a blue book which the watch officer had just given him. It was the night log, recording among other things that there had been no radio traffic during the night, nor had the suicide patrols encountered any difficulties.

Jockl entered the cabin, set down the tray, and drew the thick curtains. He watched as Schröder dwelt over the log, plainly relieved that it had been a quiet night. Yet, Jockl saw, the captain's mood was still sombre. He picked over his breakfast, and then walked listlessly to his bath. It was clear to Jockl that the captain's anxieties were as great as ever; worse, Gustav Schröder showed no signs of overcoming them. The steward left the cabin with the feeling that the ship's master had finally succumbed to the pressure of events that were outside his control.

At nine-thirty, Lawrence Berenson elbowed his way through a throng of excited people stationed outside the Havana Relief Committee offices. Inside, a jubilant Milton Goldsmith showed him the Havana Post. Its front-page headline read:

HOPE IS SEEN FOR HOMELESS ON SAINT LOUIS

The first paragraph stated that the "European refugees will be permitted to land in Cuba."

Consul general Coert du Bois had also read the article. He telephoned Milton Goldsmith for verification of the story, but the call was immediately taken over by Berenson. The lawyer said it was "close to the truth," adding that he had just spoken to Montes by telephone at the presidential palace. There, Garciá Montes and Lopez Castro had come out of their meeting with Bru, where, Berenson reported to du Bois, "They put out feelers on my behalf. Montes told me that 'everything is O.K. above.' I am much encouraged. Negotiations have now formally opened with the president for the passengers' release. The only remaining question is merely one of guarantees, and I will settle that when I see the president at noon today."

The diplomat made no immediate reply, mulling over Berenson's exultant outburst. All Coert du Bois's considerable experience told him that such an explosive situation could not be so easily defused. Yet the confident, experienced man at the other end of the telephone was now emphatically repeating: "It's all over but the shouting."

The consul general murmured, "I hope you are right."

"I'd stake my bottom dollar on it," said Berenson.

Even for a man who had the reputation of being a lucky gambler, it was a rash bet.

"Que hora es?"

Liesl Joseph's question pleased the Cuban policeman on guard at the accommodation ladder.

He told her it was just past "diez hora."

Like many children on the St. Louis, Liesl found the policemen good-humoured and willing to enter into almost any sort of game. Children wore policemen's hats and paraded themselves around the ship. Policemen chased after them shouting in feigned indignation.

Liesl attempted another question.

"A que hora ir Havana?"

The policeman replied in unison with Liesl: "Mãnana."It was the most overworked word on the ship.

Just a few feet away from Liesl, beside the railing, Marianne Bardeleben, Hans Fischer, and Wolfgang Feilchenfeld amused themselves by throwing small coins over the side. Far below, a collection of young Cuban boys dived off their boats into the water, attempting to beat each other to the booty. After a few seconds, one of them surfaced, his face beaming, the coin held high in one hand.

The long stay in harbour had affected the St. Louis children in different ways. The Spanier twins, upset, clung to their parents. Liesl Joseph was unconcerned: "Father and his committee have everything under control." Hans Fischer and Wolfgang Feilchenfeld remained fascinated by the continuous activity in the harbour. Marianne Bardeleben soon found new friends to replace the Aber children, but the memory of Max Loewe's jump still haunted the child: "It was like being surrounded by a ghost you knew was there but couldn't see."

In general, the children accepted their situation

much easier than the grownups. Otto and Rosemarie Bergmann were particularly worried about their "two old ladies." Otto wrote in his diary: "Aunt Shalote is standing up well to the strain, but she is eighty years old. Rosemarie's mother has again taken to her bed. Dr. Glauner fears for her life. She is suffering from pneumonia she contracted before leaving Germany, and keeps repeating she wants to return to her home."

Rosemarie Bergmann could not bring herself to tell her mother that returning to Germany was the last thing anyone else wanted.

That Thursday morning, her husband made another attempt to get his two elderly charges off the ship by pleading his case to assistant purser Hans Reich. Reich was not hopeful, explaining that similar appeals on behalf of the widowed Recha Weiler had been rejected by the Cuban authorities. Elise Loewe had not been allowed ashore even to visit her husband in the hospital.

"They are unbending," said Reich. "They won't make any exceptions, however mitigating the circumstances."

Bergmann, disconsolate, left the office knowing that the two oldest women on the ship were to be treated by the Cubans no differently from anyone else.

Hans Reich was upset by Otto Bergmann's visit. The assistant purser's outward bonhomie belied an inner concern for the passengers. On the way to Cuba he had shown himself willing at every opportunity to go out of his way to be helpful. Tall and handsome, he was also extremely popular with the women.

One of those women, twenty-four-year-old Gertrud Scheuer, thought Hans "exceptionally nice."

She had been told by a steward that he had a Jewish grandmother; his curly hair seemed to confirm the suggestion.

Gertrud Scheuer entered Reich's office as Otto Bergmann was leaving. Hans told her how helpless he felt in the face of problems like the Bergmanns'. To cheer him up, Gertrud showed him a postcard she had received on arrival in Cuba. Its message read: "Welcome to American soil."

Their discussion was interrupted when, at ten-thirty, a seaplane landed in the harbour, once again causing great excitement. It was from New York, and brought mail for the St. Louis. The letters were hardly more welcome than the newspapers. Little groups of passengers crowded together, silently reading over each other's shoulders. Some thought the attention focused on them would lead inevitably to their being saved; others felt the reports simply confirmed the hopelessness of their situation.

Marianne Bardeleben's mother knew at least what credence to put in the Havana newspaper Pueblo. Tucked away on its back page was a reference to the St. Louis. In it, Max Aber—now languishing nearly penniless in Havana with his two daughters—was described as "a millionaire, resident of the United States."

Pueblo's front page was mostly devoted to an explosion in a cinema in Liverpool, England, thousands of miles away. Not for the first time, Mrs. Bardeleben wondered if anyone in Havana really cared about the ship on his doorstep.

Promptly at noon, an immaculately dressed Lawrence Berenson was ushered into Frederico Bru's office in the presidential palace. The lawyer strode across the room to where Bru stood behind his desk, shook the president's hand warmly, thanked him for the interview, and, virtually anticipating Bru's gesture, seated himself in a comfortable chair beside the desk.

His was a brash, hail-fellow-well-met perfor-mance of a man whose manner indicated that it was now only "a matter of tidying up the small print" before catching the first flight out to New York, content in the knowledge that a difficult task had been successfully accomplished.

Bru's opening remarks crushed Berenson's complacency:

"I have asked you here in order to let you know that I have decided not to enter into any negotiations whatsoever about the St. Louis until it has left Cuban waters."

Stunned, failing to immediately comprehend the significance of Bru's words, Berenson automatically launched into his prepared speech:

"Mr. President. The situation on the ship is serious. Already there have been two suicide attempts here in the harbour. My guess is that there may be more. Human feelings make it imperative that . . ." Berenson's voice tailed off as he gradually realised what the man eyeing him from behind the desk had said, that it was far from being all over but the shouting.

In a cold, clipped voice which barely concealed

his dislike for Berenson, Frederico Bru said:

"I do not need to be reminded of the situation by you. However, the prestige of my government is at stake. I have ordered that the ship, and all on board, must leave the port as soon as it gets up steam. After it is outside territorial limits I will be willing to listen to any plan which covers the passengers' maintenance in the Cuban Republic until such time as they can go elsewhere."

"Mr. President, does that mean—"

"It means exactly what I have said," snapped Bru.

"Mr. President, it is a very generous gesture"

"Señor Berenson, do you have any other questions?" Bru asked.

Berenson's instinct to respond intuitively to any situation asserted itself. He asked the president whether the Isle of Pines, off the Cuban mainland, used for centuries as a prison, could be considered as a temporary haven for the passengers.

"Señor Berenson. I have already told you I will not discuss any such possibilities with you, or anybody else, until the ship has left. Nor, I further inform you, will I give you any assurance that its departure will not be permanent!"

"But, Mr. President, you just indicated—"

"Señor Berenson! I know what I have said. Now, if there is nothing else!"

Frederico Bru rose abruptly to his feet. The interview was over.

As he turned to leave, a crestfallen Lawrence Berenson tried for one last concession: Could he be granted permission to visit the ship before it left to allay the fears of its passengers?

"No," snapped Bru, his anger rising. "I absolutely forbid you to go aboard that ship."

Early that afternoon consul general Coert du Bois received a copy of Bru's decree ordering the St. Louis to sail from Cuban waters. It confirmed the diplomat's worst fears: the document was as legally watertight as it was possible to make it. Its lengthy preamble set out the background and justification for the decision to banish the refugees. The nub of the argument was contained in clause 4, a paragraph that effectively sealed the loophole Manuel Benitez had originally used to issue his illegal permits.

The status of tourists claimed by the passengers is in
every sense improper, tourists by definition being persons travelling for pleasure; it is not possible to attribute that characteristic to individuals compelled by superior force to emigrate to regions where the circumstances which caused their exodus do not exist.

The document ordered the ship to sail "this day," Thursday, June 1, and warned that the Cuban navy would "conduct" the St. Louis out of territorial waters if she refused to go.

As far as Coert du Bois was concerned, the decree signalled the end of an unhappy episode. He now believed there was nothing he, or anybody else in Havana who had been involved in the affair, could do. He began to draft a telegram to Washington to that effect.

He was interrupted by a telephone call from Lawrence Berenson. The diplomat was astonished by Berenson's mood. Berenson seemed as confident as ever.

"Forget the decree," insisted Berenson. "It's a piece of paper to save Bru's face. The important thing is what he told me."

Berenson then related his version of the meeting he had with the president, stressing Bru's "promise" to consider letting the refugees return, and stay on the Isle of Pines.

The diplomat pressed. Was it a definite promise? Berenson was confident it was, adding "even if they don't go to the Isle of Pines, I am sure they will be allowed back in."

Then, asked du Bois, what was the point of the St. Louis being drummed out of Cuban waters?

"I've already told you. It's the president saving face! Once they are out, I can work out a deal with him to let them back in and everybody will be happy."

Coert du Bois asked what sort of deal was involved.

"Money. It's just a matter of money. It always has been!"

Berenson concluded the conversation by saying he was leaving at once for the finca of Lopez Castro, where, with Garciá Montes, he would produce "financial guarantees" acceptable to Frederico Bru. Afterward Coert du Bois tore up the draft of his telegram to Washington, persuaded by Berenson's words that the lawyer might well succeed in his mission.

The man who had to act on Bru's decree,

Captain Schröder, was among the last to know of it, and even then, he heard about the order in a roundabout way. A small boat pushed to the ship, and a man shouted up a message for Herbert Manasse, the passenger committee's youngest member. The caller said the St. Louis had been ordered to leave within three hours.

Manasse immediately informed the captain of the news. He reacted with no apparent emotion, simply thanking Manasse for the information. But, in fact, the news came as a bombshell. He could not possibly prepare the ship to sail at such short notice. "There was no one to whom I could turn for help," he wrote in his diary. "Everything was now up to me." At long last, he finally concluded, "the time had come for me to leave the ship."

He took off his tropical whites, changed into civilian clothes, and called in his first officer.

"Ostermeyer, it looks bad. I am going ashore. I will leave alone. In the meantime, please start up the engines."

The first officer did not press for an explanation: "The fact that the captain had changed out of his uniform was enough to convince me the matter was serious." For a moment, he wondered whether Schröder was leaving the ship for good. The captain answered the unspoken question by saying he expected to return "in an hour or so," and then walked out on deck. He was relieved to see the message shouted to Manasse had apparently not yet registered with the passengers. They lined the rails, looking as they had for the last few days—drained of emotion, numbed.

Dressed in a single-breasted grey suit, white shirt, tie, and brown felt fedora, Schröder passed unrecognised among the passengers. His dress made him appear one of them. He hoped his "disguise" would also enable him to remain anonymous ashore, for the last thing Schröder wanted was to be hounded by the press.

Near the accommodation ladder he saw a knot of passengers, mostly women, one of whom he noticed was pregnant. A sailor saluted somewhat hesitantly; the captain looked a tired, insignificant little man as he left his ship precisely at one o'clock to step off his ship for the first time in nearly three weeks.

During Thursday morning, the shifty figure of Otto Schiendick had prowled the ship's decks and public rooms, watching passengers and crew. As the captain left, the steward told one of the Gestapo "firemen," "That man is a fool over the Jews."

In all his time on the St. Louis, the last few days in Havana Harbour were perhaps the most anxious Schiendick had ever spent. He had expected the ship by now would be on its way back to Hamburg, where he would receive a rapturous welcome from the Abwehr. Schiendick had hidden the American secrets in his berth, in a steel box the Abwehr provided. He believed the box contained sufficiently important material for his debriefing officer in Hamburg to forget about the considerable sum of money Schiendick had been given for expenses, and which he had not found it necessary to use.

But the steward knew that his authority as ship's party Leiter was increasingly being challenged. Typically, he looked again for a scapegoat. Early this Thursday afternoon he settled on the person so often the object of his revenge, Leo Jockl.

Schiendick watched the captain's steward using his rest period to amuse children around the swimming pool. A few of the smaller ones called Jockl "Uncle." Schiendick wondered if the word had a deeper meaning than its childish connotation. Jockl, with his non-Aryan nose, could well be, thought Otto Schiendick, a real uncle to some of the boys and girls grouped around him.

No doubt with a sense of satisfaction, Schiendick devised a plan to confirm his theory.

In her first-class cabin, Elise Loewe tried to conceal from her children the anxiety she felt about her husband. Fritz sat on his father's berth, telling his sister and mother he was now the man of the family; he was, after all, thirteen years and two days old.

At about the same time, on shore, in the Calixto Garciá Hospital, Max Loewe was receiving a visit from someone he had never met before. Hildie Reading, the only woman to board the St. Louis, had once more talked her way past administrative restrictions, and into his room.

Only hours before she arrived, Max Loewe had got out of his bed, and with the same resolve which had led him to slash his wrists, he had crossed to a wall mirror, and smashed his head repeatedly against it. The mirror had splintered, and before he was forcibly restrained by nurses, he had nearly succeeded in his second attempt to kill himself. Now, Max Loewe was strapped down in his bed, his arms

CAMEO 4: THE KARLINERS:

Another quite small family cameo, because again, much of the material which came from Herbert Karliner has been used to illustrate other parts of this book, for example his grandmother's shop in the Picture Prologue. This fascinating little tea party consists of Ruth, Else, Herbert and Walter Karliner as very young children. The larger group photo must have been taken in the early 1930s and shows a group of children with their Rabbi. We know who most of them are, but not all. On the back row at the left is Roe Goodman (who finally reached Australia); beside and in front of her are Walter Karliner, Ilse Karliner and Ruth Karliner. Then, seated, is Rabbi Schiftauer and at his side, in front, are Elga Fixler (now Goodman, also in Australia) and Herbie Karliner. (Herbert Karliner)

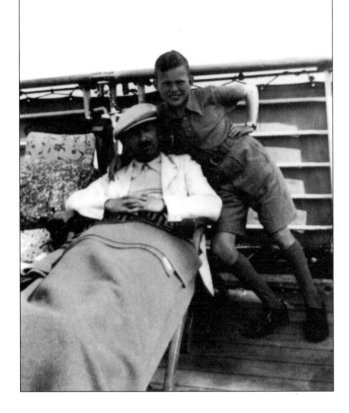

This is young Herbert with his father on board the "St Louis"... (Herbert Karliner)

.......And here is a view of one of their favourite spots, the sundeck. (Herbert Karliner)

bound to his body. Both of his wrists were heavily bandaged, as was his head. On either side of him, a male nurse stood guard.

Hildie Reading gave one of the nurses the flowers she had brought, and then tried to make conversation with Max Loewe, telling him she, too, was from Breslau, but:

"He could barely speak. He said his hopes were shattered. He had a horrible fear of being taken back to Germany and the concentration camps. It was terrible. They had destroyed him."

Babette Spanier awoke with a start. "Fritz, is that you? Did you hear the noise?"

There was no answer. Then she remembered her husband had taken the twins up on deck while she had an afternoon rest. It had been broken by the ship's engines beginning to pulsate six decks below. She scrambled off the bed to the porthole. Outside, nothing had changed. She looked at her watch: it showed 3 P.M.

The vibrations became louder, more insistent. She was puzzled, recalling no warning that the ship's engines were to start up. Suddenly, angry voices drowned the throbbing. She rushed to the porthole again. The shouting came from above, on A deck. Behind her, the cabin door swung open and her husband and the twins rushed in.

"They've gone mad up there," panted Dr. Spanier.

On A deck, Aaron Pozner experienced a similar reaction. The half dozen women passengers who had stood silently near the accommodation ladder since morning had begun to shout and scream as soon as the sound of the engines reached the deck.

The three Cuban policemen guarding the ladder looked uneasily at the women. Then, in a concerted rush, the women stormed the ladder, almost overwhelming the policemen.

In the clawing scramble, Clara Frank, a young married woman who was four months pregnant, was thrust against the rail by the other women, all desperate to escape from the ship they now believed was about to sail.

The policemen bunched together, sealing off the ladder, and drew their pistols.

"Parar!"

The women ignored a policeman's shout to stop.

"Parar!"

The policemen cocked their pistols. Heaving, sobbing, the women fell back. A couple of seamen rushed forward, lifting the unconscious woman, and carried her to the ship's hospital. Though Clara Frank did not yet know it, her baby had been seriously injured in the attempt to escape.

When Captain Schröder reached the Ward Line pier, he was met by Luis Clasing and Hapag's lawyer in Havana, Dr. Jose Tamorga, a sombre man who ushered them into a car and drove swiftly away before the reporters scented a development.

Tamorga briefed Schröder on Bru's decree, and the captain ordered him to drive them to the palace. By the time they arrived, Schröder had gradually worked himself up into a rage that carried them past the palace guards, the secretariat, and into the splendidly cool office of the president's plenipotentiary, Juan Estevez Maymir.

Schröder demanded an immediate audience with Bru. Maymir regretted that was impossible. The captain offered to wait. The president's envoy replied that that was pointless. Controlling his anger, Schröder described again the desperation of the passengers. Maymir made no response. The captain appealed for compassion for at least the women and children. The presidential aide's face remained impassive. Finally Schröder erupted, threatening that Hapag would prosecute the Cuban government.

Maymir rose to his feet. For a long moment he looked at the three men and slowly shook his head in disbelief.

"Prosecute?" he echoed. "Hapag prosecute when it is they who have violated the law?"

He moved from behind his desk and stood in front of Schröder. Speaking slowly, he said: "The decree is irrevocable. You will sail—or you will be forced out. That is the end of the matter."

"Nein!" Schröder flushed. "I need more time!"

"Your time is over," replied Maymir.

"I need time to prepare for sea."

"How long?"

"Water must be taken on. Food, vegetables, fruit . . ."

"How long, Captain, how long?"

"A day, perhaps more."

Maymir abruptly left the room, and returned to say the ship's stay could be extended until 10 A.M. the

Waiting... there was nothing else to do as the negotiations continued and no-one was allowed off the ship. On the right of this picture is Justin Isner, next to him are his daughter Ruth, his wife, then Mrs Bonne (who had a legitimate visa and so was allowed to disembark at Havana and now living in New York). Next to Mrs Bonne is Ruth's sister, Bella. Justin Isner perished in the Holocaust at Auschwitz in November 1942. (Mrs Ruth Isner-Kissinger)

next day, Friday, June 2. He then wished the three men good day.

No one spoke until they were in the car. Then Schröder demanded to see Lawrence Berenson. He found the Sevilla-Biltmore besieged by reporters all awaiting Berenson's reaction to the decree, but the lawyer had left for his meeting with Garciá Montes and Lopez Castro. The reporters failed to recognise the captain of the St. Louis.

Schröder asked to be driven to the German consulate. Clasing protested that it would be a waste of time, that they would be better employed supervising preparations for departure.

"Verdammt! Take me!" Schröder shouted.
Dr. Kaempe, the charge d'affaires, had a copy of the decree before him when Gustav Schröder was shown into his office.

He listened carefully as the captain argued the case for exerting diplomatic pressure to ensure that the passengers disembarked. Kaempe said all such channels had been exhausted.

"These are Jews, Captain," Kaempe added. "Feeling here is against them."

"They are also people, Herr Doktor," retorted Schröder. "And I care about people."

The diplomat bridled. Everybody cared about people, he replied, but there was nothing more he could do: "Take them back, Captain, and let someone else take over their responsibility."

Trembling with anger and nervous exhaustion, Schröder stalked out of the consulate, and told Clasing to drive him to the pier: "I'm going back to my ship. I understand the people there better than I ever will those here."

The clash between the Cuban policemen and the women passengers had created a ground swell of resentment on the St. Louis. Now a large group of police, guns drawn, stood with their backs to the rail on A deck facing a hostile crowd. Between them first officer Ostermeyer and purser Mueller paced, pleading for restraint. From below came the pounding of the ship's engines.

When the captain stepped on deck, Ostermeyer quickly explained developments. Schröder ordered the police to lower their weapons but they did not respond, perhaps not recognising the little man in civilian clothes. Schröder's tension and anger erupted again; this time no one was in doubt he was the captain. He stormed at a police sergeant that if his orders were not obeyed at once, he would have his crew disarm the Cubans and pitch them off the ship. The police obeyed.

Schröder faced the passengers. He expressed deep regret that the incident had happened, but urged them to disperse; their presence would achieve nothing. A man pushed forward and asked whether it was true the ship was about to sail. Schröder ignored him and briefly addressed all the passengers; their committee was the proper medium for information; it would inform them of any sailing date.

Alone in his cabin, sweating profusely, the captain, who now bore more responsibility for the immediate fate of the passengers than President Bru or Lawrence Berenson, sat and agonised with his conscience.

No matter how he reviewed it, the journey ashore had been a disaster. All his plans had collapsed. He had gambled on seeing the president and failed. He had hoped to shame Maymir into granting a worthwhile extension to provide time for Berenson to negotiate, and he had been rejected. His overture to Kaempe had proven fruitless.

Dejected and depressed, he felt "an acute sense of failure," a conviction that he had badly mishandled the voyage. He had failed always to make a clear assertion of his authority. He regretted his decision at the outset not to press Hapag harder for contingency plans for the crisis that now engulfed him. That had been a mistake. There were others: he had not recognised that the German news summaries offered a distinct warning of disaster; it had been a "mistake" allowing Clasing a free hand to conduct affairs ashore.

He paced the cabin, vowing that Clasing would be dismissed if he had anything to do with it. But the heat of the room dulled such thoughts. He was weary. His behaviour had already placed him in conflict with the Nazi party. He had received several warnings. Would he now find himself branded a "Jew-lover"? The thought, with its shadow of the Gestapo and the concentration camps, was a fearful one.

He was painfully aware of his family responsibilities. Added to those were the verities of his upbringing, his belief in Germany and in his officer's code. All these factors he now considered.

His instinct told him to cable Hapag asking whether he should return. But while that would absolve him from responsibility, it would not end the debate with his conscience. He knew he would never forgive himself if he did not keep his promise to the committee that he would make every effort to land the passengers outside Germany.

A knocking on the door cut into his thoughts. Radio officer Fritsch brought a radiogram from Hapag in Hamburg.

By the time he had deciphered it, Gustav Schröder felt a sense of deliverance. He had been temporarily released from his timetable.

It was, he told the passenger committee who later assembled in his cabin, "a free hand to sail to any port that will take us."

They watched Schröder draft a notice for passengers to be posted throughout the ship:

THE CUBAN GOVERNMENT HAS ORDERED US TO LEAVE THE HARBOUR. WE SHALL DEPART AT 10 A.M. FRIDAY MORNING. BUT OUR DEPARTURE DOES NOT MEAN DISCUSSIONS WITH THE CUBAN GOVERNMENT ARE ENDED. ONLY BY LEAVING HAVANA CAN MR. BERENSON AND HIS COLLEAGUES CONTINUE WORKING. THE SHIP WILL CONTINUE TO BE IN CONTACT WITH ALL JEWISH ORGANISATIONS AND OTHER OFFICIAL BODIES. THEY WILL ALL CONTINUE TO TRY TO ARRANGE A LANDING OUTSIDE GERMANY. IN THE MEANTIME THE SHIP WILL REMAIN CLOSE TO THE AMERICAN COAST.

The committee studied the notice with care. Josef Joseph voiced a common thought: Did Schröder have any information the United States would take them?

The captain replied: "Anything is now possible."

When the passengers saw the captain's notice about their departure, not all of them believed it.

Gustav Schröder's early decision to remain aloof had caused most of the refugees to be suspicious of him, and his uniform was a constant reminder of others in uniform in Germany whom they feared and hated. This uncertainty about Captain Schröder as a man, linking him with the unpleasant memories of what they had left behind, was to colour the passengers' view of everything he did or said he would do. As a result, many did not believe him when he said he would "remain close to the American coast"; they were convinced that if they left Havana they would be heading back for Germany.

Some passengers, like Otto Bergmann, questioned the captain's notice even more fundamentally. He thought it "ridiculous.

We cannot leave. It is not true." But as Thursday evening wore on, more and more little boats pulled alongside the ship, and the occupants shouted up good-byes to the refugees. Soon everyone on the St. Louis realised that the unbelievable was about to happen. In the boats, the emotion was equal to that on the ship. Many believed they would never see their loved ones again. Men and women were sobbing openly. Now and then one screamed. Outstretched arms almost beckoned passengers to jump.

Ten-year-old Marianne Bardeleben, still wearing the hair clips her father had sent her, stood by the rail with her mother. Mrs. Bardeleben could hardly hold back her tears; she pointed to her husband. Marianne waved, but she was still unsure which was her father in the sea of faces below.

Dr. Bardeleben was in the same boat as Hans Fischer. Staring up the black, towering sides of the St. Louis, past scores of heads peering down through portholes, Hans eventually spotted his son. The boy was with Wolfgang Feilchenfeld, who was carrying his year-old brother, while Mrs. Feilchenfeld stood nearby with her other two children.

Wolfgang saw his father in a rowboat holding up two pineapples; they were passed to a steward at the foot of the accommodation ladder. Later the pineapples would be cut up by one of the ship's chefs, arranged artistically with cherries, placed on the Feilchenfeld table, and remain in the memories of the four children as one of the most unforgettable moments of the voyage.

Liesl Joseph stood by the rail with her parents. Passengers frequently came up to her father seeking information and advice. Liesl "basked in his importance," unaware of the threat her mother and father were living under.

Lilli and Josef Joseph, using their considerable connections on shore, felt they could have arranged to leave the ship, but had decided against it. "There were dangerous people on board. Especially the ones who had been in concentration camps and who had promised the Gestapo they would never return to Germany. They said we would all leave the ship or no one would. They threatened to kill us if we tried to get off the boat."

Nevertheless, some of the passengers did make secret plans to escape that last night in harbour. Most involved simply dropping or being lowered from a porthole into the water, to be picked up by friendly Cubans. But when the time came, it was seen to be impossible. There were too many police launches and too many searchlights. In addition, at least one woman passenger realised she was too well endowed to squeeze through a porthole.

A steward suggested to Gertrud Scheuer, the shapely twenty-four-year-old friend of Assistant Purser Reich, a more promising proposal. He knew two young Cuban stevedores who had agreed they would smuggle Gertrud off in an empty container. But the steward was unable to introduce Gertrud to them; like all of the eighty stewards on the ship, the night before sailing he was carefully watched. Those not engaged in some necessary activity were confined to their quarters.

On deck, the passengers themselves were watched by the suicide patrols. They escorted anyone acting suspiciously to his or her cabin, and those who were hysterical were taken to the ship's doctor and sedated.

Dr. Glauner's supply of sleeping drugs nearly ran out.

Crowded together in the first-class cabin just after nine o'clock, the passenger committee listened attentively to Milton Goldsmith. The relief worker chose his words carefully, promising the group that after the ship sailed the Joint would work for "an early landing."

Josef Joseph asked why they could not go straight to the United States. Goldsmith said he thought that was out of the question. Dr. Weiss, note-taker of the meeting, pressed him on the point, but Goldsmith refused to elaborate.

Realising it was necessary to end on a more positive note, Goldsmith promised they would be "kept fully informed of developments," and "need not fear a return to Germany." That too, he told them, was "out of the question."

As the meeting broke up, Herbert Manasse commented that it was a pity Lawrence Berenson had not yet seen fit to visit them.

"He has more important work," said Goldsmith. "He holds your future in his hands."

"Fifty thousand dollars is not enough."

Garciá Montes's statement shook Berenson. It

seemed to contradict what the lawyer's other adviser, Lopez Castro, had suggested.

Seated on the tiled veranda of the ranch house, the two Cubans drew with slow deliberateness on their cigars and carefully watched Lawrence Berenson for his reaction. Berenson's face betrayed nothing. With studied indifference he sipped his drink. Then, replacing his glass on the table, he looked at Lopez Castro.

"Are you sure it is necessary to put up any money at all?"

Through a small cloud of cigar smoke, the Cuban repeated arguments now familiar to Berenson after hours of negotiations. A bond, of suitable size, had to be posted on behalf of the refugees before there was any chance of them being allowed on Cuban soil. It could be cashed by the Cuban government if, and only if, the refugees did not leave the country by a certain date—or if they became a charge on the country during their stay.

Though nobody had mentioned it, Berenson believed it represented Bru's solution to the situation; there was every possibility that it might also reflect Batista's wishes.

He had quickly accepted the proposal—with one important proviso. He argued that it would be an act of good faith on the part of the Cuban government to allow the passengers to land before the bond was posted—"before the vultures get in"—or its amount specified. His counterproposal had started hours of protracted, polite, though stubborn, argument. Now, as the evening shadows darkened the veranda, the discussions finally narrowed down to the size of the bond.

Berenson believed that if they could agree to a figure, his other demands would be acceded to; that the bond should also include the passengers on the Orduna and Flandre, and that they should all be allowed to land before the bond was posted.

As the matter was reduced to one of hard cash, Berenson felt his confidence rise; he hugely enjoyed the cut-and-thrust of bargaining over money. He believed he had managed the situation adroitly, allowing himself to be forced to offer $50,000 as a bond, but now, suddenly, as casually as he swatted an insect, Garciá Montes murmured the figure was not enough, that only $150,000 would be acceptable. This was three times what Lopez Castro had suggested.

"That figure is impossibly high," said Berenson. "I think not," replied Montes.

Lopez Castro replenished their drinks, raised his glass, and murmured, "Salud. "

Three hours and several toasts later, the matter was still unresolved.

Finally, at midnight, Lawrence Berenson left the finca, taking with him the draft wording for the bond, with a blank space for its amount to be filled in.

As he drove away, Montes murmured with a shrug: "Fifty thousand, one hundred and fifty thousand. It's up to you."

It seemed inhuman to have to calculate the value of people in dollars, but to Berenson it was a necessity, and he hoped to negotiate the deal as cheaply as possible.

Max Fuld left Germany ahead of his family and found accommodation in New York. His family followed him on the "St Louis" and he travelled to Havana to meet them. Now he was at risk of losing them and so wrote this letter to Captain Schröder in an attempt to make contact with his wife, Julie, who was travelling with their sons Ludwig and Hans, and gain their release. They were not allowed to disembark. (Stern Archiv)

Above: Waiting... this small gorup of friends had a photograph taken as a memento, still expecting to land in Havana despite, but taking heart from, the Captain's notice that the ship would sail up the Florida coast awaiting news. To the right of the picture are Selman Messinger, his wife Paula and their son Salo. On the right is father Sam and son Sol taking the sun as they continue to wait... (Dr Sol Messinger)

III

The Final

Solution

FRIDAY, JUNE 2, 1939

Joseph C. Hyman, executive director of the Joint Distribution Committee, arrived at his office early on Friday morning, knowing it was the day the St. Louis was to leave Havana. He carried a copy of The New) York Times. He was pleased to see that the St. Louis was once again front-page news. Under the heading: "CUBA ORDERS LINER AND REFUGEES TO GO, Ruby Hart Phillips? the newspaper's long-established and respected correspondent in Havana, had sent a comprehensive wireless report describing the situation.

There was little in the story that Hyman was not already aware of, having had frequent telephone conversations with Berenson. But a footnote to the article, datelined Washington and headed "Partial Solution Reported," gave the executive director cause for thought.

It stated that the Cuban government required a bond of $500 per refugee before they would be allowed to land. This was a much higher figure than Hyman had anticipated, and far exceeded the bond he hoped to raise through an insurance company. Nevertheless, Hyman should have realised, it was precisely the sum required of immigrants to Cuba who carried legal visas, and it was also a normal requirement for many other countries, including the United States itself.

The report from Washington also quoted America's most famous and powerful union leader, John L. Lewis. Following the public outcry in the United States, Lewis had cabled Batista asking that "in the name of humanity" the refugees be permitted to land. "I appeal to you because of your well-known feeling for the victims of German Nazism," Lewis went on. "If returned to Germany, these people will undoubtedly be sent to Nazi concentration camps."

Hyman wondered how many readers would understand what "concentration camps" really meant. A telephone call broke his meditation; it was Berenson from Havana. The lawyer spoke quickly and excitedly, outlining the plan he proposed to put to Bru. The bond would run for six years, and would be reduced proportionately as individuals left Cuba. Hyman then referred to The New York Times report, pointing out that in hard cash, it meant raising a total of nearly half a million dollars for the St. Louis

passengers. Berenson told the executive director he planned to negotiate a figure much less than that. Hyman replied that he hoped it would not be more than $125,000, as he had already mentioned that sum to the insurance company. He promised to cable the lawyer as soon as he arranged the bond, and gave his approval for the proposals to go forward to Bru.

In Havana, Berenson went off to deliver the draft to Antonio Bustamente, the Relief Committee lawyer, who would translate it into Spanish.

In New York, Hyman arranged a meeting with the insurance company, when, unknown to Berenson, he planned to ask if the bond could be raised to $200,000 "just in case."

Fifteen hundred miles south, in sweltering Havana harbour, the St. Louis prepared to sail. Its captain, crew, and passengers were convinced that nothing could now alter their situation, that no intercession—financial, political, or spiritual—could halt the departure proceedings.

From his vantage point high in the wheel house, Gustav Schröder felt a great gloom settle over the liner. Forward, on the bridge, the silence was broken by a telegraph ring in the standby to the engine room. At that moment a launch tied up alongside the accommodation ladder and Milton Goldsmith clambered on board, forcing a path through the passengers thronging the decks. He hurried to the captain's day cabin.

In the social hall, the passenger committee struggled to placate a mass of agitated passengers. Some were shouting, a number were crying, a few prayed aloud. In the babble of sounds, a theme gradually emerged—a monotonous, frightening chant: "We must not sail. We must not die. We must not sail . . ."

The refrain carried out to the decks, sending a shiver through many of those lining the rails, too numbed to speak, shuffling their feet on decks vibrating ever louder from the increasing revolutions of the engines. For most of those at the rails, the arrival of Goldsmith and the chanting in the social hall did not matter. Their attention, their very existence,focused on the water immediately around the St. Louis.

It was empty.

A cordon of police launches now kept back all the motorboats, the rowboats, the dinghies, the catamarans, all the myriad little boats which every day had ferried out relatives and friends to wave and to shout encouragement to those on board the ship.

Even to men like Aaron Pozner, who had known nobody in those boats, their very presence had been a comfort. Now, that connection had been suddenly severed. And for Pozner, as for many other men who had endured in silence six days of torment, the absence of the small boats proved to be too much to bear. Tears trickled down his face, the first time he had cried in public since the day he had said good-bye to his wife and children.

Around him other men sobbed with grief.

Suddenly, a police launch left its station and raced toward the ship. As it arrived at the accommodation ladder, six figures, accompanied by Cuban policemen, scurried down the ladder and into the launch. It immediately sped toward the shore, carrying the last passengers to leave the St. Louis.

Their departure had been achieved by the use of personal outside influence and power—something that few others on the ship could have summoned.

The rescue had come through the direct intervention of the Annenberg publishing family in Philadelphia, a mysterious lawyer called Mr. Carson, and the Cuban ambassador in New York, Señor Pedro Fraga.

The exact sequence of events will now never be clear. But somehow Fraga was induced to authorise that Cuban visas be stamped in the passports of the lucky six while the ship was in Havana Harbour. Who they were, what their connection with the Annenbergs was, is also something of a mystery. Carson arrived in a chartered aircraft to expedite the transfer of the group from Cuba to America.

The sight of the police launch spiriting the refugees away sent a shock wave coursing through the St. Louis, halting the keening in the social hall, the sobbing on deck, the very routine of departure. The passenger committee sought an explanation from Purser Mueller, failed to receive one, and burst in upon Captain Schröder and Milton Goldsmith. The refugee director had come on board to urge the captain to remain close to Cuba, "even if it meant sailing around and around in a circle."

The two men turned, somewhat startled, as the committee bunched into the cabin, demanding that if six people had been whisked to safety, then the ship's departure should be postponed to see if new moves could be made to get the other passengers ashore.

"Gentlemen," said Gustav Schröder. "I know nothing about these people who have gone. But one thing I do know. If I stay a moment longer than allowed, then the Cuban navy will force me out."

"Force?" echoed Josef Joseph. "How? By gunfire?"

"I would think that most unlikely," replied Schröder evenly.

"But it would solve your problems, wouldn't it?" pressed Joseph. "If they damaged the ship, we would have to remain here, and even probably be taken ashore."

"An interesting hypothesis, but one I am not prepared to put to the test," retorted Schröder.

Goldsmith shrugged, insisting there was nothing more the captain could do except leave on schedule. Then Gustav Schröder reminded them that America was only a few hours' sailing away.

The captain had intended his remark to be no more than a morale booster, a reminder that the United States was close by. But to the desperate committee members his words raised a burst of questions. Did the captain plan to sail to the United States? Had he reasons to believe they would be admitted? Was some deal in progress of which they were unaware?

To all such questions Gustav Schröder gave a negative answer, stressing that he had no positive information, that he had meant no more than he had said: the United States was a short cruise away. But the listeners were left with the definite belief that, if all else failed, the United States would probably accept them.

The committee men had been too preoccupied to study the American newspapers brought on board the previous day, which would have soured such optimism.

Roosevelt, contemplating running for an unprecedented third term, sensed too clearly the mood of the United States. With war once more brewing in Europe, the majority of Americans favoured a strict isolationist policy, where refugees, however deserving, would at best be an unwelcome reminder of a world the United States wanted no part of. There were also other factors: U.S. business was again in a tailspin, swelling the unemployment figures by four million. The president was ready with appropriate phrases, attacking the "economic royalists" who were choking the Great American Dream. But in spite of progress to help the farmers and provide cheap public housing, Roosevelt's measures simply did not evoke the same confidence as in the early days of the New Deal. To allow a well-publicised shipload of refugees into such a situation would require a great deal more compassion on the part of the administration than had been shown so far.

Goldsmith's offer to address the entire passenger complement before the ship sailed was greeted warmly. The shy and modest relief director found himself invested with power never before accorded him. He planned to use it to full effect when speaking to the passengers.

In the purser's office, Robert Hoffman listened with impatience to Otto Schiendick's diatribe. Hoffman had boarded the ship to express the customary farewell of the local Hapag office, and had been sharing a bottle of Sekt with Mueller when Schiendick arrived. The steward had peremptorily asked Mueller to leave, as he had "confidential party business to discuss," and then had launched into a brutal tirade against Leo Jockl.

Hoffman wondered if Schiendick had gone mad; he tipped back his chair and stared at the steward. In a voice meant to be angry but in reality only resigned, he asked: "You really wish me to contact Hamburg for the Gestapo to check on this man?"

"Yes."

Hoffman's tone became scathing. "All this because you suspect him of Jewish blood?"

"Suspicion can lead to the truth."

Hoffman realised he could not afford to upset the steward. He stood up. He would send the cable. But, he added, "I only hope you will display the same diligence safeguarding the material now in your possession as you have in this matter!"

With that, he walked out of the office.

Word of the meeting in the social hall was announced over the ship's loudspeaker. The room quickly became crowded. Many of the women were crying. A Cuban official stood by the entrance with the senior police officer on the ship.

At ten-thirty, the passenger committee filed in, followed by Goldsmith and Robert Hoffman. They were joined on the platform by the police officer and the Cuban official. There was no officer from the St. Louis present.

The ten men stood where only a week before the Cuban medical officer had "inspected" passengers as they passed in front of him, full of anticipation and excitement. As Josef Joseph surveyed the scene now, the contrast could not have been greater. A week ago, faces had been filled with hope; now it was hopelessness. Then, people had been crying with joy; now they cried from fear. Thirty passengers, including Max Loewe and Moritz Weiler, were no longer on the ship; 907 remained. They included Mrs. Loewe and Mrs. Weiler.

Milton Goldsmith, the American who had for months borne stoically the burden of criticism and helplessness in his Havana relief office, spoke first.

"Sisters and brothers," he began. "Do not give up hope. Be strong. Do not fear a return to Hamburg. The Joint committee here, in New York, and throughout the world, will work so that soon you can land outside Germany. Important people will contact the Cuban president as soon as you leave. Your committee will hear from the United States and us very often, possibly every two hours. The world is watching you. You are 'one family' now."

There was no applause as the speech ended, only a silence broken by sobbing. Then the Cuban police officer spoke.

"I am sorry, but I and my policemen have to do our duty, a hard duty. We wish, from our hearts, that you will soon land."

As the men left the platform, each smiled reassuringly, except for Robert Hoffman. The Abwehr agent led the group out, looking straight ahead, his face cold and unemotional. Hoffman walked directly to the accommodation ladder and down into one of the many official and police launches now alongside.

Milton Goldsmith waited until everyone lined up by the ladder was off, including the fifty policemen who had for so long been guarding the ship. He then shook hands with each member of the committee, and was the last person to leave the St. Louis.

Herbert Manasse looked at his watch. "Eleven o'clock. We're an hour late."

"Late for what?" said Josef Joseph. "We have nowhere to go."

First Officer Ostermeyer reported to the captain that the ship. was ready for sailing.

"Ostermeyer," Schröder replied, "the Cuban president reminds me of a man who invites guests to dinner, but on arrival, he keeps them waiting in the entrance hall, and then throws them out."

"I wonder," said Ostermeyer, "whether we will receive a second invitation."

At two minutes past eleven o'clock, Gustav Schröder gave the order to stand to stations; the ship's engines increased their revolutions, from the bridge came "dead slow ahead," and the St. Louis began to move toward the open sea, observed by an estimated 100,000 onlookers on the shore.

The captain watched helmsman Kritsch responding to the course changes, almost anticipating the ringing telegraph on the port side of the bridge. Schröder wondered how many bearing changes the young steersman would make in the next few days as the ship awaited the outcome of negotiations. It would depend, Schröder believed, on "luck, Bru, and the American president." He had little faith in any of the three.

Below on the passenger decks, the mood was gloomier. The rails were lined with weeping people, or those who stood in silence as Havana steadily receded. The edginess communicated itself to crew detailed to stop any passengers jumping overboard: in their nervousness they plucked at several people leaning over the rails.

Aft, close to where Moritz Weiler and Max Loewe had gone over the side, which had become a symbolic gathering place for some of the more outspoken younger passengers, the rail had been roped off.

Now, as the ship gathered way, a group of youths ducked under the barrier and stood defiantly at the rail. A squad of seamen turned to a deck officer; anxious to avoid trouble, he ordered the ropes removed. A mocking cheer greeted this concession, and somebody shouted: "We'll soon be running the ship—then we can go where we like."

For Dr. Fritz Spanier those words held a chilling element of truth. Ever since the women passengers had stormed the gangway on the previous day, he had detected a growing feeling that some of the wilder elements on board wanted to hijack the liner. Twice this morning he had encountered small groups standing expectantly around, eyeing each other and whispering among themselves about "positive action." Shortly before the ship sailed, Fritz Spanier overheard a trio of youths talking about storming the

engine room in a bid to cripple the ship.

Dr. Spanier firmly believed any such move would be dangerous—and futile. He felt the plotters would be overpowered long before they achieved their aim; worse, their actions would alienate all sympathy among the crew, and, when the outside world learned of the matter, it was likely the passengers would be branded as pirates.

Yet now, as the St. Louis glided out of Havana harbour, he spotted another group of youths, bunched together, looking speculatively toward the bridge. Dr. Spanier walked toward them in a determined way, and warned them that if they caused any trouble he would see to it that "you will wish you had stayed in Germany."

Discomfited, the youths walked away.

Aaron Pozner also watched them disperse with a feeling of relief—but for reasons far different from those felt by Fritz Spanier.

Since the confrontation between passengers and police on deck the previous day, Pozner had concluded that passive resistance was not enough, that violence might now be the only answer, that to seize the ship was the only hope left. He would be quite willing to lead an assault on the crew to force them to sail anywhere but Germany.

Pozner had also concluded it would be better to be branded as pirates, and possibly interned in some foreign jail, than to return to a Nazi concentration camp. Equally, he believed no immediate attempt should be made to capture the ship; that move should come only when all outside efforts had failed, when there was nothing to lose, when it would be better to risk death at sea than at the hands of the Gestapo.

As the youths walked away from Dr. Spanier, Aaron Pozner followed them, anxious to convince them of his arguments.

Below on B deck, in the Tanzplatz, Otto Schiendick and the Gestapo "firemen," the men charged specifically with ensuring the ship's safety, had once more defied Captain Schröder by assembling in the night-club to sing Nazi songs as the ship nosed her way out into the open sea, heading, they believed, for Hamburg.

Schiendick ordered a pause in the sing-song to read out a formidable list of the ship's complement whom he had booked for transgressing one Nazi edict or another. His roll call was headed by the captain and

CAMEO 5: RUTH KEILER

Mrs Ruth Keiler was in the same predicament as many of the women on board the "St Louis" – her husband, Siegfried, had left Germany and gone ahead to establish himself in the United States, awaiting the opportunity of bringing his family to join him there – and, of course, waiting for their visa numbers to "come up". Siegfried was a pharmacist in Breslau, where this photograph was taken, so they had enjoyed a quite comfortable life, though when the Nazi pressures began to be exerted on the medical profession and its associated businesses, there was little alternative than to leave while there was a chance. For his wife, the "St Louis" voyage had seemed to be too good an opportunity to miss and so she had taken it. She, like all the others, could have no idea that the journey would turn sour and had no idea of the mischief created by the Nazis in Cuba before the arrival of the "St Louis". Ruth Keiler returned to Europe, joining the group that went to Holland. Her husband's brother, who lived in England, had a friend who was a postman in Amsterdam. That friend managed to gain her release from the transit camp at Rotterdam West and, at great risk to himself and his family, hid Mrs Keiler for the duration of the war in their third-floor apartment. It was a story very similar to that of Ann Frank who, as the world knows, was found in a house search and later perished. Ruth Keiler was only allowed out of her hiding place at night, but did survive the war and today lives in the United States. The irony of her story is that, as the "St Louis" left Hamburg harbour, she saw another large passenger vessel steaming on an opposite course. That ship, she later learned, was carrying her mother and brother to the relative safety of Shanghai on the Chinese coast. (Mrs Ruth Holman, via John H Wolff)

The lower picture shows Mrs Keiler (later Mrs Holman), aboard the "St Louis" with another family from Breslau, shoe store owners Hans and Selma Rosenfeld, with their daughter, Sheffi. Sadly, the Rosenfelds were not so fortunate. They were also placed in a "transit" camp upon their return to Europe and ultimately were taken back to Germany, where they perished. (Mrs Ruth Holman, via John H Wolff)

This other photograph of Mrs Keiler was also taken on board, resting on the sundeck whilst awaiting news of a future in Cuba. (Mrs Ruth Holman, via John H Wolff)

Mrs Keiler wrote this postcard to her husband whilst waiting for the ship to sail from Cherbourg.. On the front of it was a photograph of the "St Louis". At the time, as can be seen from the address, Siegfried Keiler was still living with a friend. This postcard, from the postmark, is one of those allowed off the ship before it finally departed Cherbourg. That is why this card is clearly postmarked "Deutsche Seepost". (Mrs Ruth Holman, via John H Wolff)

Purser Mueller. It included seven deckhands and five stewards accused of being too friendly with the passengers: Schiendick urged the Gestapo men to report any further infringements to him on the homeward journey so the ship could be purged of such deviants.

Finally, he revealed the inquiries being carried out on his instructions into Leo Jockl's background. The steward promised his companions that if his suspicions were confirmed, they would have "much fun." In the meantime they should continue to harass the passengers; he believed if they were goaded far enough some of them might be bold and foolish enough to retaliate. Then, Otto Schiendick promised, "they will soon remember who they are."

There were many passengers on deck who could never forget who they were. Everywhere they looked the reminder was there: the escorting flotilla of police launches, twenty-six in all, and beyond them the launches filled with press men and newsreel camera teams. From time to time a reporter bellowed out a question, hoping for a reaction or a quotable reply. Receiving no answers, several enterprising journalists invented their own replies, a touch of fiction that suited many of the eyewitness accounts of the St. Louis departure.

In the wake of the press launches came a sizeable armada of small craft, carrying relatives, minor Cuban officials, and a large number of people attracted by the possibility of further drama.

Three miles out, the limit of Cuban territorial waters, the police boats vectored back to shore; the press and public boats rolled gently in the swell, still hoping for a reaction from the St. Louis. None came. Soon, only a handful of boats remained to keep the liner company.

In a Hapag launch were Robert Hoffman, Milton Goldsmith, and Lawrence Berenson; the refugee workers had persuaded Hoffman to take them along. At sea Berenson had maintained a breezy line of small talk, to which Goldsmith did not respond.

During Berenson's time in Havana, the relationship between the two men had grown cool. Berenson felt Goldsmith was out of his depth in the present situation. Goldsmith regarded the lawyer as altogether too brash for a crisis where he believed tact and a real understanding of the Cuban mentality to be essential. Now, as their launch turned away from the St. Louis, the attitudes of the two men were symbolised in their farewell salutes. Milton Goldsmith clasped his hands in prayer, Lawrence Berenson raised his hands in a boxer's victory salute. To those at the rails of the St. Louis, it was the gesture the third man in the boat gave which sickened them. Standing between the two refugee workers, Robert Hoffman raised his right hand in a stiff Nazi salute.

On the way back to Havana, Goldsmith's mood was sombre; there were tears in his eyes. His attitude, Robert Hoffman noticed, contrasted strongly with Berenson's. The lawyer appeared relieved that the ship had left, but as Berenson began to tell Goldsmith of the proposals he would soon put before Bru, Hoffman became uneasy. The lawyer repeatedly told Goldsmith the St. Louis would return within forty-eight hours when he had settled "the money problems."

As Berenson's confidence gradually lifted Goldsmith's depression, it began to alarm Hoffman. He realised that if the ship returned, it could well put at risk the documents Otto Schiendick was taking to Hamburg; the U.S. secret agents could devise a plan to board the ship and retrieve them. Hoffman decided to try to throw Berenson off balance. Pointedly ignoring Goldsmith, the German agent asked the lawyer to join him for lunch, saying he had "information of great importance for your negotiations."

Berenson accepted.

On shore, the huge crowds, mostly Cuban sightseers, were gradually dispersing. For them, the star attraction of the past week had gone, and life could begin to return to normal.

Hoffman took Berenson to the Swiss Home Restaurant, where they were greeted warmly by Otto Ott, the dwarf. Ott motioned with his large cigar toward a secluded corner table. There Hoffman's spy poured Berenson a large rum and Coke. Berenson asked what it was Hoffman had to tell him. Hoffman looked around, as if to make sure he was not being overheard, and then announced that he had a confidential message from the president.

"What most concerns him is money," began Hoffman.

"Money will be no problem," insisted Berenson.

"Señor Berenson, you underestimate what the president wants. He asks me to inform you that unless you are able to deliver a million dollars, then you should save your energy for more worthwhile ventures and return to the United States."

After careful questioning, Berenson decided that Hoffman's claims were a "come-on, that he was just another of those in Havana trying 'to get in on the act.' "

All afternoon and evening, the Joint negotiator was bombarded by other people claiming to represent Bru. Two of them were particularly troublesome, and, near midnight, Berenson finally agreed to meet them in his hotel bedroom.

The men were well-connected; Major Bernardo Garciá, although known as a playboy, was also Cuba's chief of police; Colonel Manuel Benitez was the son and namesake of the former immigration director who had sold the illegal permits to the St. Louis passengers. In the "Sergeant's Revolution" of 1933, the young Benitez had been a renegade officer, siding with Batista, and had ever since been his staunch ally, often acting as Batista's personal aide. Major Garciá told Berenson he had been asked by President Bru to act as intermediary, and that all communications for the President must go through him.

Colonel Benitez apologised for his father's behaviour over the St. Louis, expressing regret that the Cuban government "is unable to make good on the permits." The colonel claimed that the sum required to ensure the refugees' return was "between $400,000 and $500,000.'

Berenson felt that this was yet another attempt to con him and that whatever they or Robert Hoffman or anyone else advised him, it would simply strengthen his resolve to conduct negotiations in his own way. Eventually, at 3 A.M., he told Garciá and Benitez he was not prepared to discuss the matter further, and asked them to leave.

Unwittingly, the lawyer had missed an opportunity to gain two important, if decidedly slippery, allies. Major Garciá had in fact been given authority by the president to handle all further negotiations.

SATURDAY, JUNE 3, 1939

In Hamburg, Claus-Gottfried Holthusen telephoned Morris Troper in Paris. The Hapag director told Troper he had reluctantly decided that the Orinoco, sister ship of the St. Louis, having been kept hovering for days off Cherbourg, must return to Germany with its 2~0 refugees, all of whom had booked passage for Cuba.

"In view of the unresolved situation of the St. Louis, the risk is too great. The Orinoco is now on its way back to Hamburg," Holthusen told the European Joint director.

Troper had anticipated the decision, and inquiries had already been made of the British and French governments as to whether, if the Orinoco was turned back, they would accept its passengers. Both countries had refused. Troper's main concern now was whether the passengers would be sent to the concentration camps, as Der Stuermer had advocated.

That real possibility also upset America's ambassador in London, the founder of the Kennedy dynasty, Joseph Kennedy. He was a man whose anti-British tendencies and defeatist attitude were already causing criticism in British government circles. Kennedy was on record as believing that in a forthcoming war with Germany, Britain "would be badly thrashed," a sentiment he continually impressed on Washington. He was also to state that he proposed to stay in London only thirty days after bombing began, "and not a moment longer." When the time came, he kept his word.

But even Kennedy's greatest critics admitted that he had one redeeming feature: an ability to bypass bureaucracy and, by dealing directly with those in authority, to produce results. This skill he brought to bear on the Orinoco.

In London, negotiations had reached a critical stage over Germany's plan for the wholesale resettlement of Jews. Sir Herbert Emerson, director of the International Committee on Political Refugees, was about to meet Hitler's representative for "final discussions."

Acting in concert with Emerson, Kennedy told the German ambassador in London that it would be "unfortunate if the discussions were marred by maltreatment of the Orinoco passengers" on their return to Germany. Kennedy's message reached Hitler; the Gestapo allowed the 200 refugees on the Orinoco to return to their homes unmolested.

Ambassador Kennedy had achieved his goal for the Orinoco passengers. And that same day, in Washington, his government was taking a decision about the St. Louis passengers.

Although they would not admit it publicly for a week, on this Saturday, June 3, the American government decided that, if the St. Louis passengers were not allowed into Cuba, they would be refused entry into America.

The decision to bar the refugees reflected widespread feeling in the United States toward immigrants. By June 1939, with some thirty million unemployed, opposition came from labour leaders, who claimed that work markets were being depressed by foreigners willing to accept minimum wages. Among the unemployed, as in the rest of the country, there existed a xenophobia which made the United States not so much a melting pot for racial and religious differences but rather a pit for racial and religious antagonisms. On the edge of this caldron perched the 100 per cent American, determined to return the nation to Anglo-Saxon purity. Despite having descended from immigrant stock, they now regarded themselves as native Americans, and were determined to exclude anyone of doubtful origin.

By 1939, the refugees of Europe had fallen into that category. While the average American decried Nazi policies, he was equally opposed to offering its victims a home. For some organisations, like the notorious Ku Klux Klan, which claimed a membership of 4.5 million "white, male persons, native-born gentile citizens of the United States of America," the European refugee posed a greater threat than the Negro. Imperial Wizard Hiram W. Evans explained: "The Negro is not a menace to Americanism in the sense that the Jew or Roman Catholic is a menace." Increasingly, those two groups were to bear the brunt of the Klan's sectarian violence.

Such demagogues as the radio priest Father Charles Coughlin found willing response among the millions who saw refugees like those on the St. Louis as a further threat to the "purity" of the United States.

It was against that background that the State Department, itself filled with its share of prejudiced men, decided to exclude the St. Louis passengers. And Franklin Roosevelt, the "liberal" president, but always a president mindful of public opinion, did not overrule that decision.

The only hope now for the refugees drifting just outside Cuban waters was Lawrence Berenson.

In Havana, Berenson received a visit from Nestor Pou, consul of the Dominican Republic. He arrived with a cable from his government offering sanctuary for the St. Louis refugees at $500 a head.

Pou explained that this was the "going price."

After some debate, he revealed that his government would not adhere strictly to the per capita figure of $500, but was "willing to listen to any sort of guarantee."

Berenson, understandably, felt he had "been here before," that Pou, for all his carefully couched diplomatic language, was "also on the make"; in short, the lawyer believed this was one further example of a Caribbean grafter trying to cash in. Instinct also told the lawyer it was better to deal with "the devil I knew," Bru, than enter into protracted discussions with Pou's government. But, careful to keep open options, Berenson informed Pou he would consult with the Joint in New York.

After the envoy left, Berenson informed Cecilia Razovsky that the Dominican offer would be a powerful factor in settling matters with Bru. For he now believed that when the Cuban president discovered another country was offering to take the refugees, Bru would be only too happy to settle for the bond Berenson would offer. It was, in the lawyer's view, a matter of "how you play these banana republic politicians."

Berenson asked Cecilia to tell Goldsmith about the Dominican offer, and then called on Antonio Bustamente, the Relief Committee lawyer who had translated the bond terms into Spanish. In the space still left blank for the amount of the bond, Berenson wrote in $50,000, the lowest figure anyone had suggested. He told Bustamente to get the papers to Bru "pronto."

Bustamente produced a hand-written document on palace note paper, signed by the president, authorising all negotiations be conducted through Chief of Police García—one of the men Berenson had shown the door to early on Saturday morning.

"This," said Bustamente firmly, flourishing the note, "is the only way open to us."

Berenson shrugged: as far as he was concerned any channel was only a formality; the deal was as good as settled. So confident was he that, with the help of Bustamente, he concluded arrangements for his visit to the Isle of Pines that afternoon to inspect its amenities for the refugees he expected to land there in a few days.

The visit to the island took on all the panoply of a state visit, with Berenson travelling in a motor cruiser crammed with Cuban dignitaries, army officers, and a detachment of soldiers.

Behind came supporting launches of press and newsreel teams.

Waiting to greet them was a smaller, but equally impressive entourage. At their head was the army chief of staff, the bemedaled, potbellied, jackbooted Fulgencio Batista. Smiling impassively, Batista grasped Berenson's hand, pumped it warmly for the benefit of the photographers, turned, and without so much as a word of explanation, led the lawyer on a swift tour of the island's compounds.

Hedged in by soldiers and officials, Berenson made repeated attempts to discuss the deeper implications of the St. Louis affair, but failed utterly to draw the army chief. Thirty minutes after stepping ashore, still dumbfounded, Lawrence Berenson was on his way back to Havana with Batista's parting words ringing in his ears: "This will do them very nicely, Senor Berenson."

It was the one and only time that the éminence grise of Cuba emerged from the shadows during the crisis. To Lawrence Berenson, this appearance by Batista, however brief, was the most significant omen he had received since arriving in Havana. The lawyer believed it a "positive sign" that Batista favoured letting in the refugees, that it was "nothing less than a public declaration of support for our cause." And, he later told Cecilia Razovsky, it would clinch acceptance for his $50,000 bond. There was now no question of offering up to the $125,000 authorised in the latest cable from the Joint in New York. As he and Cecilia Razovsky went for a celebration drink, Lawrence Berenson reiterated to reporters waiting in the lobby: "It's all over but the shouting."

The journalists preferred to wait and see before filing wrap-up stories.

Around the time Lawrence Berenson ordered cocktails, Gustav Schröder was facing a new and serious worry, one that took precedence over the other anxieties he had experienced since leaving Havana.

Purser Mueller had finally confirmed, after a detailed analysis of the stores taken on board before sailing, that, at the present level of consumption, there would be a food and water shortage in about twelve days. The effect if they did not land their passengers before then, Schröder told Mueller and First Officer Ostermeyer, could be disastrous. Faced with such shortages, the passengers might well stage an open revolt.

The three men already knew the seeds were there after Dr. Spanier had reported that some of the male passengers were talking of hijacking the ship. The news had placed the captain in a dilemma. He could not arrest, or confine on suspicion, numbers of passengers; such action could trigger a mass uprising in which, by sheer weight of numbers, his crew would be overpowered. Equally, he could not ignore the warning. Instead, with the knowledge of the passenger committee, he had compromised by increasing the crew security patrols on board and building up a file of possible troublemakers. Included on his list was Aaron Pozner.

Another worry was the total absence of radio communication. For over twelve hours the St. Louis had sailed in ever-widening circles off the Cuban coast, hoping for a message recalling her. Then, in the early hours of Saturday, Gustav Schröder ordered the ship to steer slowly northward toward Florida. At the back of his mind was still the vague hope of intervention by the United States, and he had reasoned that, should that come, he wanted to be well placed to run for the nearest American port.

After his last discussion with the committee on the possibility of an American solution, when they had read more into his remarks than he ever intended, he had decided to keep such thoughts to himself. To the committee's queries about the course change, he answered that the weather would be cooler the farther north they were, providing some respite for the passengers, who were still suffering from the heat.

Level-headed though the committee was, Schröder also felt he should not mention to them the suggestion Ostermeyer had made about introducing rationing.

Gustav Schröder vetoed the idea as potentially dangerous: "If we cut down their food and water, some might even think we're trying to starve them, and that could lead to a riot."

At 4:50 P.M. a cable from Luis Clasing was brought to the captain's day cabin. It read:

INFORMED BY BERENSON VIA GOLDSMITH DOMINICAN REPUBLIC WILLING TAKE YOUR PASSENGERS.

Five minutes later a second cable arrived, this one from the Hapag office in New York:

THERE IS STILL HOPE OF LANDING IN CUBA.

Gustav Schröder summoned the committee, wondering as he did so how the two new members would react. Both Solly Guttmann and Ernst Vendig were first-class passengers who had become outspoken critics of the committee. When news of their feelings had reached the captain, he promptly suggested that they be co-opted onto the committee—a shrewd move which silenced their public carping.

The newcomers, like the other members, regarded the cables as "hopeful." A suitable notice was drafted for their fellow passengers to read. Though no mention was made in the notice about the Dominican Republic specifically, scores of passengers assumed it was the country involved, and were sure they would land there.

By early evening, the ship was near Miami, still heading north, away from The Dominican Republic and Cuba, on a course that if maintained would bring the St. Louis to that point in the ocean where it must either continue northward, reverse course, or swing east—north-east—toward Europe.

Armed with a pair of dividers and an atlas he had borrowed from the ship's library, Otto Schiendick calculated that at its present speed the ship should reach that point in a few hours.

In Havana, reporters cornered Luis Clasing and were surprised to hear the St. Louis was "following her course back to Hamburg." To those who asked about rumours that the ship was off Florida, Clasing replied they were "absurd and false."

Clasing's statements were a curious fabrication, no doubt invented to rid him of the unwelcome attention he and his office had endured during the days the ship was in the harbour.

The reporters returned to the Sevilla-Biltmore for a follow-up comment from Berenson, but the lawyer had told the hotel reception he was not to be disturbed. Alone in his room, Berenson confidently awaited a reaction from President Bru to the proposal given to Major García that afternoon. Soon after 11 P.M., it came. Antonio Bustamente telephoned to say that the president, while accepting in principle the idea of a bond, rejected $50,000 as too low a figure. He added that Bru wished to discuss the matter with Berenson at his country seat the next day, Sunday, at noon.

Berenson was not unduly perturbed by Bru's reaction, but surprisingly, although it was nearly

midnight, he decided to communicate it to the American ambassador, Butler Wright.

The ambassador was not pleased to be interrupted at the party he was attending, the more so as Berenson insisted on talking "for nearly an hour about the St. Louis situation." Nevertheless, as Wright made clear in a subsequent report to Washington, the lawyer was as optimistic as ever, for the ambassador quoted Berenson as saying:

"The president is going to accept the plan as outlined, with certain unimportant modifications, one being that the bond is raised to $150,000."

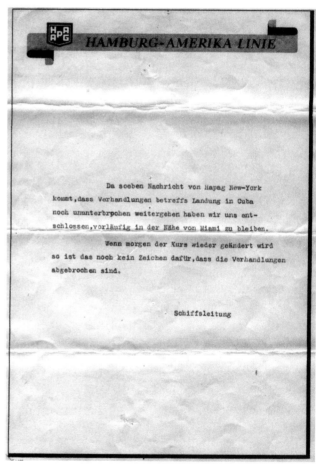

This message from the "Schiffsleitung" (Ship's Management), posted early on Friday 3rd June, explained that news had come from Hapag New York to say that discussions regarding landing in Cuba continued uninterrupted. The ship would now seek temporary cover in the vicinity (presumably offshore) of Miami and so the course would be changed in the morning. (Mrs Gertrud Mendels)

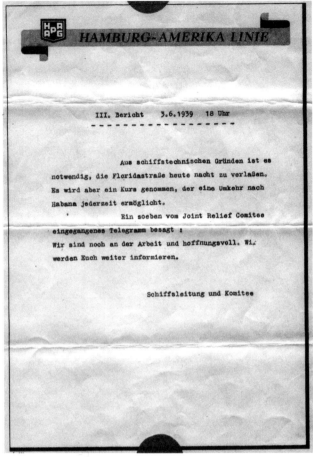

This notice was posted on board ship at 6pm on 3rd June: "For technical reasons, it is necessary to sail up the Florida coast tonight while it is quiet. It is a course, however, from which we can turn back to Havana at any time. News has been received from the Joint Relief Committee to tell us that: "We are still in discussions and are hopeful". (Mrs Gertrud Mendels)

At 9.45pm, this further bulletin was issued jointly by the Company and the Passenger Committee, advising that news had been received from Hapag in New York that there was still hope of a landing in Cuba. But passengers were now becoming restless with news they weren't sure they could believe. (Mrs Gertrud Mendels)

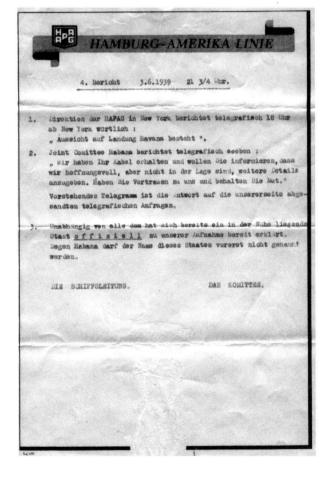

SUNDAY, JUNE 4, 1939

On Sunday morning, the passengers on the St. Louis were relieved to see that they were still near the American coast, and even closer to Miami than the night before. Now the city could be seen without binoculars.

The sight was comforting; the refugees knew where they were, for the miniature Hapag flag pinpointing their position on the map outside Purser Mueller's office was not believed. Most passengers thought Mueller placed the flag wherever he considered it would please them most.

But more important for the passengers than the ship's position was the direction in which it was travelling. Only one passenger on the ship was able to describe their course with any certainty: ten-year-old Wolfgang Feilchenfeld. Wolfgang had won a compass at the children's party held just before arrival in Havana, and after leaving the harbour, he had become a centre of attraction. Sitting unconcernedly at the stern of the ship on B deck, playing chess with his friend Hans Fischer, as the two boys had been when the St. Louis had departed Havana and had continued to do ever since, Wolfgang confidently told inquirers on Sunday morning that they were now heading "south south-west, toward Cuba."

Looking toward Miami, Rosemarie Bergmann said to her husband: "So near and yet so far." The remark prompted Otto to state again his view that the passenger committee was a "forum for polite talk, not action." He wanted to offer his services but Rosemarie restrained him. Instead she drew his attention to the deep-sea fishing yachts from Florida that from time to time came close to the St. Louis. Many, she pointed out, were taking photographs of the passengers; she wondered if they would be sold to the newspapers.

In midmorning, a much larger ship joined the fishing fleet. It was U.S. Coast Guard cutter 244, from the naval base at Fort Lauderdale. Most passengers believed it was there "to protect us, to pick up anyone who jumped overboard." Only a few thought the cutter's presence was to ensure that the St. Louis did not enter American waters.

The sight of the approaching vessel caused Otto Schiendick to panic. He moved to the radio room, where he ordered the duty operator to tune in to the coast guard boat's frequency. The man was

about to comply when First Officer Ostermeyer arrived and ordered the steward out.

Schiendick darted back on deck and saw that the cutter was now cruising close to the ship, a fact which undoubtedly unnerved him further. He doubtless wondered if it was part of a move by U.S. intelligence to apprehend him. For a moment, Schiendick probably considered whether he should follow Abwehr practice and destroy the material if the ship was boarded. The quickest way to do that would be to dump it overboard.

As if anticipating the steward's thoughts, the cutter circled the St. Louis, and Otto Schiendick clearly saw its officers scanning the decks through binoculars.

Then, one of them waved. Soon everyone on the St. Louis was waving back. Schiendick's fears faded. The Abwehr agent managed a nervous smile, and along with all the others, he hesitantly raised his arm in a gesture of greeting.

At noon on Sunday Lawrence Berenson and Antonio Bustamente entered the large, comfortably furnished office which President Frederico Bru used during weekends at his palatial country estate, Parraga. It was to be a meeting of enormous importance to the St. Louis passengers.

The president motioned the two men to sit, and then immediately asked whether Berenson could meet his demands.

The lawyer said he could. As the president had requested, the bond could run for nine years instead of six. Males over twenty-one years of age would be the first to leave the country. Berenson thought it "likely" the bond could be raised form $50,000 to $150,000

Accounts differ about the critical discussion which followed.

According to Bru, he went on to remind Berenson that the $150,000 bond was to guarantee the passengers' sustenance on the Isle of Pines or elsewhere, and that, in addition, he required that the normal $500 in cash to be deposited in the Cuban treasury for each immigrant; it would be returned as they left the country. Further, Bru maintained that at the meeting he had insisted that his demands must be met in full within forty-eight hours or the matter would be closed. Finally, Bru later stated, Berenson had agreed to all his qualifications.

Berenson's recollection of what was said differed fundamentally. He claimed the president made no mention of a deadline, and insisted he had said only that "the St. Louis can be brought back in forty-eight hours." Regarding the money, Berenson maintained that it was left "open to negotiation after speaking to my principals in New York."

What is known is that Berenson was shaken badly by the president's demands but that even so, Antonio Bustamente advised him to accept them. Equally clear, Berenson was left with no doubt that President Frederico Bru wanted $500 per refugee in cash—nearly half a million dollars—plus the $150,000 bond.

After the meeting, Berenson returned to his hotel to seek the advice of the Joint in New York.

Joseph Hyman, executive director of the Joint Distribution Committee in New York, did not react as strongly to Bru's new demands as Lawrence Berenson had feared. The director stated that he was "prepared to deposit up to $250,000 if there were proper safeguards, plus a bond for the further amount required." He would send the cash to Cuba "only as a last resort," and requested the lawyer, "if possible, to eliminate children from the deposit."

Berenson was satisfied. He was now in a position to offer the president real money, as well as the bond that had been requested earlier. The lawyer then asked Hyman whether, apart from the Dominican Republic, any other countries had offered refuge. Avoiding mention of the United States, the director replied that although many approaches had been made, so far Venezuela, Ecuador, Chile, Colombia, Paraguay, and Argentina had all said no. He thought the Dominican Republic need not be considered: "All our efforts should be directed toward Cuba."

That Sunday evening, Berenson once again contacted American Ambassador Butler Wright. At 9:30 P.M., he and the ambassador met at Consul General Coert du Bois's home. There, Berenson told them of Bru's demand "for an immediate deposit in the Cuban treasury of nearly $500,000"—much more than the maximum Hyman had offered—and indicated that this might be avoided altogether if the American diplomats made a personal appeal to Fulgencio Batista, requesting the army chief to instruct the president to waive the cash deposit demand.

The diplomats were not prepared to be drawn

by Berenson. Instead, du Bois commented unhelpfully to the lawyer that his "house of cards, so carefully built up, appears to have fallen down."

At midnight, as the discussion ended, the ambassador told Berenson that the Dominican Republic was his "ace in the hole, and it seems the time has come for you to play it."

The Joint negotiator thought otherwise. He returned to the Sevilla-Biltmore, and began to work out his new offer to Bru.

It was not an easy matter.

Berenson lacked any adviser whom he could trust, having received conflicting advice from, amongst others, Robert Hoffman, Major García, Colonel Benitez, Lopez Castro, García Montes, Antonio Bustamente, and the American diplomats. Batista had seemed to indicate that a solution was possible, but had given no indication how it was to be achieved.

With only the instructions he had received from New York as his guide, Berenson began drafting his revised proposals.

The lawyer estimated, wrongly, that there were 933 passengers on the St. Louis, 26 more than there in fact were, and after "eliminating 162 children and 25 tourists who will go to the U.S.," he calculated that the sum of $500 each would come to $373,000.

Working on the same premise of discounting the children, he calculated that the refugees on the Flandre and Orduna would cost a further $70,000, making a grand total of $443,000.

Berenson then described how the $443,000 was to be paid. Bearing in mind that Hyman had said he could send up to $250,000, Berenson wrote:

From New York	$200,000
From Havana Committee	50,000
From Passengers	40,000
Total in Cash	$290,000
Difference	153,000
Total	$443,000

As with all computations made by a good accountant, everything neatly balanced. Berenson's usual confidence returned. Remembering Hyman's message that he would send the cash "only as a last resort," the lawyer added a rider: any excess funds

CAMEO 6: Dr WERNER LÖVINSOHN:

Dr Werner Lövinsohn practiced in Frankfurt until prohibited from treating all but Jews by the Nazi legislation of 25th July 1938. The first of these two documents, the notice of that prohibition, was the deciding factor in the family's decision that Edith Lövinsohn and their daughter, Hella, should leave Germany as soon as they were able. The second document is, ironically, a "Certificate of Good Conduct" and permit to emigrate. The "St Louis" voyage was the first opportunity they had to leave, though Dr Lövinsohn stayed behind, hoping to join his family later. (Mrs Hella Roubicek)

provided by relatives of the passengers would be used to reduce the amount of money coming from New York.

Early the next morning, Monday, June 5, after a night of little sleep, Berenson confidently delivered the proposals to Bustamente, who translated them and gave them to Major Bernardo García precisely at 2 P.M., for forwarding to Bru.

In Washington, an hour later, a telephone conversation took place between Henry Morgenthau, Jr., secretary of the treasury, and Cordell Hull, secretary of state, two of the most influential members of President Roosevelt's government.

The sixty-eight-year-old Hull considered himself something of an expert on Cuba, having as a young man raised a regiment of Tennessee Volunteers and accompanied them to fight in the Republic. But the millionaire Morgenthau did not think that experience of much help in the present crisis, and considered Hull's State Department "simply not equipped psychologically, or administratively, to handle the refugee job." Nevertheless, he knew State was the department concerned, and at 3:17 that Monday afternoon he called up Hull.

A flavour of the somewhat ambiguous conversation which followed, and the relationship between the two secretaries, is provided by the transcript of the telephone call.

M: Hello, Cordell.
H: Yes, sir.
M: How are you?
H: Fine!
M: Cordell, some of my good friends have called me about this terrible tragedy with those 900 refugees.
H: Yes.
M: And there have been so many things back and forth.
H: Yeah.
M: Guaranteeing money and so forth.
H: Yeah.
M: You see?
H: Yeah. Well I talked with the president about twenty minutes ago . . .
M: Yes?
H: And this morning I talked to old man James Carson, who is in Havana.
M: Yes?

H: He brought up the question they might go out to the—the islands—our islands down there. What the devil are they . . .
M: Virgin Islands?
H: Yeah. I took that up at once and found we couldn't unless they had a definite home where they were coming from, and in a situation to return to.
M: I see.
H: I think the Jewish organisations . . . will work it out if the financing will be made certain . . . They've got a real chance of doing it, that's what I'm trying to say.
M: I see.
H: We'll do what we can, you understand, but they need a man there who knows how to dicker with them on the financing...
M: I see.
H: This is a matter primarily between the Cuban government and these people.
M: I see.
H: And not this government.
M: I see. Well, would you mind if I called you again tomorrow?
H: Yes, sir. I'm keeping up with it the best I can.
M: And I can call you again? H: Yes, sir. Anytime. M: Thank you. H: Yeah. M: Thank you.

The conversation could hardly have been the most illuminating for Morgenthau. Even so, it provided more information than most inquiries made of the American government.

President Roosevelt did not reply to or even acknowledge the two telegrams sent to him by the passenger committee on the St. Louis. Other telegrams were handed down by Roosevelt's personal secretary to the State Department to answer; they often left them unanswered for over a week, and then simply stated that it was "a matter for the Cuban government."

American newspapers attempted to arouse public sympathy by editorials such as the one in the Philadelphia Record:

"Granted that the refugee problem is complex and difficult, there must be a better solution for a civilised people than sending out police boats to pick up those who jump in the water."

Although this was typical of many editorials appearing on this Monday, June 5, neither the Record nor any other American newspaper advocated that the St. Louis's passengers should be given immediate,

Form No. 20.

WESTERN UNION

THE WESTERN UNION
TELEGRAPH COMPANY.

CABLEGRAM

Counter
No.

ANGLO - AMERICAN
TELEGRAPH CO. LD.

THIS FORM IS ISSUED BY THE COMPANY AND MAY BE HANDED IN AT ANY POST OFFICE WHICH ACCEPTS TELEGRAMS.

Date Stamp.	Prefix 4.6.39	Code.	Words.	Sent.	For Postage Stamps.

Service Instructions.
VIA
WESTERN UNION.

Charge.

At...................M.
To.....................
By.......................

To be securely affixed by the Sender.
Any stamp for which there is not room here
should be affixed at the back of this form.

The Sender's Name and
Address, or either of them, if to be
telegraphed, must be written at the
end of the text of the Telegram.

TO {

TO PREVENT MISTAKES PLEASE WRITE DISTINCTLY.

Passengers Committee St.Louis

Berenson had satisfactory conferences today cuban high officials
seeing President sunday. will cable again.

Uebersetzung : Herr Berenson hatte heute zufriedenstellende
Konferenzen mit hohen cubanischen Behörden.Er wird Sonntag
den Praesidenten sprechen, und wird wieder cabeln .

Having read the conditions printed on the back hereof, I request that the above telegram be forwarded by the Western Union Telegraph Company,
subject to the said conditions, to which I agree.

NOT TO BE
TELEGRAPHED

Signature   Address

This Cablegram was received by the Passenger Committee on the "St Louis" on 4th June. Its message is self-explanatory. (Mrs Liesl Joseph-Loeb)

unrestricted admission to the United States.

And the official view was explicitly stated by immigration inspector Walter Thomas of Miami: "The St. Louis will not be allowed to dock here, or at any U.S. port."

At three-thirty Monday afternoon, President Frederico Bru repeated his terms for a settlement to the press in Havana. The president stated he was willing for the refugees to return, and to be housed on the Isle of Pines, as long as acceptable guarantees were given that "they will not become public charges, and that their food and lodging while in Cuba is paid for." Bru added the offer was valid until noon the next day, Tuesday, June 6, and concluded: "I feel deeply the plight of the refugees, but the post that I occupy has painful duties, which oblige me to

disregard the impulses of my heart and follow the stern dictates of duty."

Questioned by reporters, Lawrence Berenson described Bru's statement as an "inspired declaration of a humanitarian and a great statesman."

Thirty minutes after the president's announcement, Major Bernardo García delivered to him Berenson's revised proposals.

That same Monday afternoon, Gustav Schröder closeted himself in the radio room with Ostermeyer, his first officer. Weeks of tension had brought the two men closer together, and now, both were firmly convinced that Hapag was impeding and confusing matters. Their anger was aroused by company cables from Hamburg, Havana, and New York which were contradictory, and, in the captain's opinion, verged on irresponsible meddling.

A message from Claus-Gottfried Holthusen said the company was scouring the" western hemisphere for a suitable port, and warned Schröder to prepare to sail "anywhere at short notice." Luis Clasing cabled that plans to land the refugees in the Dominican Republic "will only go ahead if they all disembark." From New York had come a message that the Hapag office there was ready to process the passengers "if they land."

Gustav Schröder thrust the cables aside, growling that this spate of company interest was even less helpful than Hapag's periodic silences. He turned to a sheaf of cables from newspapers and radio and newsreel companies. The one from the Associated Press read:

KINDLY INFORM US YOUR INTENTIONS IN VIEW WORLD INTEREST YOUR SITUATION.

Those last words stayed Schröder's impulse to ignore the media's request for information. If public opinion could be aroused it could materially improve their chances of landing the refugees in Cuba; publicity might mitigate the unremitting wave of abuse beamed daily in Nazi broadcasts whose tone had become more vehement since the ship departed Havana.

Gustav Schröder replied to the Associated Press, giving the ship's latest position, speed, and course. His cable concluded:

MY INTENTION IS TO DO ALL POSSIBLE TO ALLEVIATE MOUNTING CONCERN OF MY PASSENGERS WHOSE ONLY WISH IS TO FIND A HOME.

Similar replies were sent to other wire and newsreel services and radio stations, though the captain declined requests from American networks to allow their reporters on board. Tropical Radio in Miami then announced that some newspapers had chartered aircraft, and shortly afterward several planes swooped and circled over the St. Louis.

On board, this unprecedented interest buoyed hopes. Babette Spanier probably spoke for all the passengers when she told her husband: "With this going on we must land somewhere."

The possible choice of landing places widened further with a cable from New York philanthropist Bernard Sandler:

URGE YOU SAIL INTO INTERNATIONAL ZONE NEAR BEDLOES ISLAND IN NEW YORK HARBOUR AND STAY THERE WHILE I AND GROUP OF OTHER AMERICAN BUSINESSMEN MEET ALL YOUR COSTS WHILE AT THE SAME TIME MAKING APPEAL TO CONGRESS FOR ASYLUM ALL YOUR PASSENGERS.

Gustav Schröder was nonplussed by the offer. It sounded attractive, but, as he told Ostermeyer: "I can't just sail into New York Harbour on the authority of a cable from a man I've never heard of."

He cabled Sandler:

PLEASE CONFIRM AND FINALISE ALL DETAILS WITH HAPAG NY.

On board ship this Monday, Sandler's offer, when it was posted by the committee, increased still further the mood of optimism.

Schröder and Ostermeyer left the radio room and went to the captain's cabin. Leo Jockl, who served them coffee, noted that "they were definitely in better spirits than before."

Later that afternoon, Otto Schiendick entered the radio room. He ordered the radio operator to show him the morning's traffic log. When the man hesitated, Schiendick said refusal to co-operate with the party Leiter would have serious consequences. The operator handed him the log.

Its recital of press dispatches, Sandler's offer, and Hapag cables, must have confirmed Schiendick's worst fears: the St. Louis was not en route back to Hamburg; the ship could well land in New York or another port with potentially disastrous results for his Abwehr mission.

That is the most likely explanation for the steward's next action: he drafted a message addressed to a secret Abwehr "letter box" in Hamburg, told the operator to send it at once, and walked out of the room.

The message read:

USE ALL INFLUENCE TO BRING SHIP BACK TO GERMANY IMMEDIATELY.

Astounded, believing the steward had gone mad, the radio man took the message to the bridge.

When the captain read it, he too thought Schiendick had taken leave of his senses, or else the steward was indulging in some sinister practical joke. He then reasoned that unless the steward had gone completely berserk, he would never have dared try to send such a message if he was not totally confident of being supported in his action by someone very well placed in Germany.

Later that afternoon, the captain faced Schiendick in his day cabin, but with more caution than he would have preferred. Schiendick stated that as ship's Leiter he had the right to send the message. Schröder pointed out that the steward's influence did not extend beyond the crew. Schiendick hesitated, and then revealed his Abwehr connection and enough of his mission to make the captain realise he was telling the truth.

Schröder was shocked and angry at what he heard. He saw now that not only were his passengers pawns of Nazi propaganda, but his ship had been used by the German secret service. He was powerless to prevent that, but there was one thing he could do. As he dismissed Schiendick, he told him:

"Your cable will not be sent. As far as I am concerned, you are still only a steward with certain political responsibilities. They do not include telling me when or where my ship goes."

At four-fifty that afternoon the ship's radio picked up a news flash from a Miami radio station; it quoted President Bru as saying the passengers could disembark on the Isle of Pines. The news flash confirmed a cable from Havana received a short time before.

Schröder promptly turned the St. Louis south again, heading the ship back to Cuba. At 5 P.M. he informed the passenger committee of the reason for his decision, and earned himself a spontaneous burst of applause. Excited questions followed, but the captain could not answer whether the Isle of Pines would be a temporary or a permanent home, nor could he describe what facilities the island offered.

The committee posted the news at ten prominent points throughout the ship, and by 5:30 P.M. a ground swell of relief and excitement spread throughout the St. Louis. Most people felt, as Babette Spanier did: "we are no longer wandering Jews."

She suggested to her husband that they bring their suitcases on deck so that they could disembark as soon as the ship arrived at the island. Others had the same thought, and by 7 P.M. the decks were cluttered with luggage.

Aaron Pozner felt only tired relief. He would "do anything" on the island to earn enough money to send for his family. He could abandon the desperate plan to

hijack the ship. He, and his fellow plotters, some dozen able-bodied young men, had proposed to storm the bridge in the early hours of the following day, hold the duty watch as hostages, and force the captain to run the ship onto the American coast. Though they had all recognised it as a foolhardy scheme with little chance of success, Pozner had argued that even if they failed, it would make "the world realise how desperate we are." But he feared nevertheless that failure could compel the captain to make full speed for Germany. Once there, the plotters would be doomed.

When Rabbi Weil brought the widow Weiler the news, her first thought was that there might be a synagogue on the island where she could commemorate her husband. The rabbi promised that somehow one would be provided.

Now their future seemed settled, a number of the younger passengers went to the after deck, where couples danced, and some of the men indulged in playful roughhousing. This joyful mood carried on into the evening meal. Leo Jockl had not seen such high spirits in the first-class restaurant since the gala dinner just before arrival in Havana. The air of conviviality brought smiles from Purser Mueller and his assistant, Hans Reich, when they toured the social hall after dinner. How long, they were repeatedly asked, would it take to reach the Isle of Pines?

"Not long," was Reich's unfailing response. "But won't you be sorry to leave us?" More than one pretty young passenger said they would be.

By 10 P.M. First Officer Ostermeyer had revised his estimated time of arrival at the island; he now calculated that with her present speed of twelve knots, the St. Louis would arrive soon after 9 A.M. the following day.

"An early breakfast and then they can go on their way," Ostermeyer told Schröder. "And we can go home."

"I hope so," replied the captain. "I really do hope so."

With that he retired to bed.

Josef Joseph and his fellow committee members had spent part of the evening combing the ship's library for information about the Isle of Pines. Later they pooled their knowledge: all they had gleaned was that the island was thirty-five miles wide, with tropical vegetation, and had been a penal colony, information which brought a wry smile.

Dr. Max Weiss, who had uttered a restraining note when the ship had first approached Havana Harbour, again urged caution: "Let's get our feet on the ground before we celebrate." Once more he was a lone voice. His colleagues pointed out that in the "most unlikely event" of a new failure, there were still offers from Sandler and the Dominican Republic. "Cuba, Dominican Republic, New York. It doesn't matter in the end so long as it isn't Germany," insisted Josef Joseph.

By midnight the last of the passengers were in bed and the ship was left to the security patrols.

TUESDAY, JUNE 6, 1939

At 5 A.M. Tuesday, the cleaners swept, dusted, and polished their way through the public rooms, followed by stewards laying up for breakfast. At 6 A.M. the radio room received its first message of the day. It came from Havana.

ISLE OF PINES NOT CONFIRMED.

Schröder studied the cable. If disembarkation was "not confirmed," it did not mean it was cancelled. Still, "not confirmed," could be the precursor to cancellation. For fifteen minutes he debated what action to take. At 6:30 A.M. he ordered the ship to reduce speed.

To an Associated Press cable which arrived soon afterward requesting the latest information, Gustav Schröder replied:

SHIP REMAINING BETWEEN CUBA AND FLORIDA PENDING CLARIFICATION.

At 7 A.M. the captain assembled the passenger committee in his quarters and showed them the cable. The shocked silence was broken by Josef Joseph's question: "What about the Dominican Republic and New York?" There was no new information. Herbert Manasse asked what they should tell the passengers.

"Nothing for the moment," Schröder said. "Let us wait and see what develops. In the meantime, he suggested, the committee should continue to cable influential figures to intervene. No one could think of

a suitable name. Then Ernst Vendig, a new member of the committee, suggested the mayor of St. Louis; the town, after all, had the same name as the ship and might be moved to take an interest.

That Tuesday morning, Lawrence Berenson arrived at the Havana office of Antonio Bustamente just before ten o'clock, the hour when Major Bernardo García had promised to telephone with President Bru's reaction to the revised proposals submitted to him the previous afternoon. At ten-thirty, having heard nothing, Bustamente telephoned the palace and was told the president was still in conference with García and his secretary of the treasury.

There is no record of what was said during that meeting. No doubt Bru was aware his public announcement stating that the refugees could return to the Isle of Pines had not been favourably received by the general public; Havana newspaper morning editions were distinctly critical of the offer.

Waiting with Bustamente, as time passed, Berenson's optimism began to wane. Just after noon, as Bustamente was reminding Berenson that was the hour Bru had said the offer would expire, the telephone rang. It was García. Bustamente watched Berenson's face gradually go pale as he listened. After a long pause, Berenson spoke: "Major García, I don't believe it. The president promised. I must see him immediately." Then the line went dead.

"A statement has just been put out from the palace," Berenson told Bustamente. "It says the government has terminated the matter. The president refuses to see me."

The telephone rang again; the press wanted Berenson's reaction. The lawyer told them: "The declaration has come entirely unexpectedly and I have no explanation for it." He then tried to contact Coert du Bois, eventually locating him at the American Club at 1:30 P.M. Soon after, the two men met in the consul general's office.

Berenson was disconsolate, and du Bois gave him little reason to feel otherwise.

"In my opinion," du Bois said, "you and your co-religionists in New York had better prepare for the worst. You have removed this matter off the plane of humanitarianism and onto the plane of horse trading."

In Washington, unaware of the latest development in Havana, Henry Morgenthau again telephoned Secretary of State Cordell Hull:

M: Cordell?

H: Yes, sir.

M: How are you?

H: Good!

M: I'm calling you about this St. Louis, the German boat.

H: Yeah.

M: My friends in New York say they are having some trouble, the Cubans demanding cash.

H: The situation, you see, is that the—the folks in New York don't want any money to get in the hands of the Cubans, and the Cubans do.

M: Uh-huh.

H: My men . . . are working down there . . . with the—the man who represented the New York people.

M: That's right.

H: I forget his name.

M: Well—there's nothing that I could do, or that they should do?

H: Nothing I see right now. If I find out anything I'll let you know.

M: Thank you so much.

H: Yeah.

M: Thank you.

H: Yeah.

M: Good-bye.

Soon after, an assistant handed to Cordell Hull a cable from Coert du Bois setting out President Bru's midday announcement.

A further announcement was made at 6 P.M. The Cuban government stated:

"Agreement was reached two days ago with Sênor Berenson to land the exiles on the Isle of Pines after he had deposited $500 in cash per person, with a subsidiary guarantee with regard to their food and lodging. He was given forty-eight hours to meet these requirements. Yesterday Sênor Berenson made an alternative proposal, offering $443,000 for the St. Louis passengers, plus 150 additional refugees on the Orduna and Flandre, the sum to include expenses for food and lodging. The Cuban government could not accept the proposal, and having passed excessively the time allowed, the government terminates the matter."

The next day, the Joint in New York would cable President Bru directly, offering to fulfil his each and every condition. By then it would be too late.

But, on this Tuesday evening, after telling Cecilia Razovsky and Lawrence Berenson that he proposed to inform the St. Louis of Bru's decision, Milton Goldsmith looked to Berenson for approval. Lawrence Berenson, now tired, humiliated, and beaten, could merely nod.

Captain Schröder received Goldsmith's cable at 8 P.M. He kept its contents to himself. At 11:30 P.M., he received a second cable, this time from Claus-Gottfried Holthusen in Hamburg. Again the captain kept the contents to himself.

But as a result of that second cable, at 11:40 P.M., Gustav Schröder walked from his cabin to the bridge, and ordered helmsman Heinz Kritsch to bring the ship onto a heading of east north-east, a change of course which would take the St. Louis back to Germany.

WEDNESDAY, JUNE 7, 1939

The message Holthusen had sent Captain Schröder ordered:

RETURN HAMBURG IMMEDIATELY.

Even before he had heard from Clasing of Bru's decision, the Hapag director had been under considerable pressure to recall the ship. He had estimated that the St. Louis would need to leave for Germany on this Wednesday night at the latest in order to disembark its passengers there and sail to New York in time to meet its scheduled summer cruises. Further, Captain Schröder had informed him that the constant changes of course and manoeuvring had reduced his fuel to such an extent that he could "hold out for little longer than a week before being forced into port to refuel."

Holthusen had heard from the Hapag office in New York that reservations for the St. Louis's Caribbean cruises were in danger of falling off, due to adverse publicity; some American newspapers placed Hapag's advertisements for the pleasure cruises on the same page that reported the plight of the refugees on the "pleasure liner."

Hapag was never a company to court publicity, and now Holthusen hoped that with the return of the ship the matter would fade from the headlines. Instead, newspaper coverage increased. In Germany, President Bru's rejection of the passengers, coupled, by inference, with that of President Roosevelt's, gave Goebbels' propaganda machine a field day. How could the world criticise Germany for its treatment of Jews, Goebbels asked, when the world could see how other countries rejected them? It was not a question easily answered.

For internal consumption, Goebbels took a different tack, stoking hatred against the returning refugees. German radio stations announced:

"Since no one will accept the shabby Jews on the St. Louis, we will have to take them back and support them."

It was not difficult to guess where they were to be "supported": in the concentration camps. The relatives of the St. Louis passengers, most of them elderly parents who had stayed behind in Germany, knowing this, suffered with the refugees on the ship as it travelled homeward.

Elise Loewe's mother in Breslau, knowing nothing of her son in-law's attempted suicide, feared for his life on his return. She knew he was on the Gestapo's wanted list before he left, and believed there was no doubt the Gestapo would take him away when the St. Louis reached Hamburg. The same fear gripped Rachel Pozner in Nuremberg, Lilli Joseph's sister and mother in Berlin, and Josef Joseph's sister in Duesseldorf.

In London, the press, while mentioning Bru's decision, devoted more space to the crucial talks about to take place with Hitler's representative on the plan for the resettlement of all remaining Jews in Germany.

Paul Baerwald, the highly respected chairman of the Joint Distribution Committee, had arrived from New York for the discussions, and was staying at the Savoy Hotel. On this Wednesday, he read with resignation the newspaper reports of what had happened in Cuba. A cable arriving from Joseph Hyman, Baerwald's executive director in New York, suggested that Baerwald "test" the attitude of the British and French governments toward giving the St. Louis passengers asylum.

During the afternoon, the chairman spoke to various of his contacts in London on the possible British position. Sir Herbert Emerson, director of the International Committee on Political Refugees, about to embark on the most delicate of all negotiations affecting "not just a few hundred, but hundreds of thousands of refugees," thought it "a most inappropriate moment to raise the matter."

In the late afternoon, Baerwald cabled his colleagues in New York telling them the response to his first tentative inquiries "did not seem promising."

At about the same time, on the St. Louis, Captain Schröder called the passenger committee to his cabin, and told them the ship was returning to Europe. "I have left it as late as possible," he said, "in the hope the position would change, but I can no longer keep it from you."

Some of the committee had already guessed the worst, noting the ship's direction, but after so many hopeful signs in the past, they could not at first bring themselves to believe what the captain had said. Josef Joseph asked Schröder how he could ignore the offer of the island off New York, and the Dominican Republic.

"That is why I delayed telling you until now," the Captain replied. "I have just had a cable from Hapag in New York saying that both these possibilities are now extremely remote." Answering the unspoken question, he went on: "I do not believe you will disembark in Germany. I believe you should now pin your hopes on Great Britain."

A terrible, personal realisation touched each member of the passenger committee. They dared not say it openly, even to each other. Some could not bear even to mention it to their wives and children. It was inhuman, degrading, and endured in private, but it cut deeply into one of the most basic of all human needs: the need to be wanted. Instead, they had been rejected. Even the New World did not want them; now they must rely again on the Old. The committee suffered in silence, knowing it was not just an anonymous group of people who had been turned down, but that they, individually, each one, had had the open door shut in their faces; through them, their entire race had been judged, and found wanting. If some other country accepted them, they now believed it would be on sufferance.

Joseph advised they should not yet inform the passengers. Dr. Weiss agreed: "We need time for our own strength to return."

The captain watched them leave. He knew, as they did, that the only certain gate that remained open to welcome the passengers on the St. Louis was the gate to a concentration camp.

DEBEG
BERLIN

Durchgangstelegramm

Seefunkstelle

Lfd. Nr.:

Befördert

Aufgenommen

am
um
an
durch

am
um
von
durch

Nr.   /   mit   W.

Art   von

den   um   via

6. Juni 1939 Vormittags 11 Uhr

Wir kabelten soeben erneut an folgende Adressen :

Joint Relief Committee   H a b a n a   National Coordinating Committee
Razkowsky
Praesident Roosevelt   Washington
Oberbuergermeister   St.Louis Minnesota
Associated Press   New York   das Committee

Bemerkungen:

Debeg Nr. 6. 3000 Bl. A 50. 10. 37. J. S

This radio-telegram was sent out by the Passenger Committee to the Jewish Joint Relief Committee in New York on June 6th, to tell "the Joint" to whom the Passenger Committee had sent appeals for help. (Mrs Liesl Joseph-Loeb)

HAMBURG-AMERIKA LINIE

8. Juni 1939 12.00 Uhr mittags

Die HAPAG New York telegraphierte soeben :

> Joint Distribution Committee has placed on deposit
> 500 U.S.A. Dollars for each refugee and money is in
> the bank subject to call from Cuban Government. They
> have telegraphed Cuban president and are taking every
> possible action which they think is helpful stop.
> Constantly we are in touch with committee and convinced
> that they are doing utmost, therefore we can only ask
> passengers to have confidence and patience.
>
> Johs. Schroeder

Die Übersetzung lautet :

> Das Joint Distribution Committee hat 500 U.S.A.-Dollars
> für jeden Auswanderer deponiert und das Geld liegt bei der
> Bank bereit zum Abruf der cubanischen Regierung. Das Komi-
> tee hat dieses dem Präsidenten mitgeteilt und unternimmt
> alles, was Erfolg verspricht.
> Die Hapag New York ist ständig in Verbindung mit dem Komi-
> tee und ist davon überzeugt, dass dieses das Alleräusserste
> tut; deshalb kann den Passagieren nur gesagt werden, Ver-
> trauen und Geduld zu haben.
>
> Johs. Schroeder
> Direktor der Hapag New York.
>
> gez. S C H R O E D E R
> Kapitän.

Captain Schröder put out this bulletin at mid-day on June 8th, hoping to calm the fears of many passengers, who were beginning to believe they would soon be on their way back to Hitler's Germany. It had come from the captain's namesake, Johannes Schröder, Hapag's Director in New York and was transmitted in both German and English. (Mrs Liesl Joseph-Loeb)

CAMEO 7: THE REIF FAMILY:

Dr Gerschon Reif qualified in Histology in 1920 at the University of Vienna, as the diploma below shows, after his military service in the Great War. The picture above shows Dr Reif with his son, Fred, in June 1932, before Hitler's rise to power brought so many problems to the Jewish communities in Germany and Austria. (Dr Liane Reif-Lehrer)

Above is Dr Gerschon Reif with his daughter, Liane, in 1936. Sadly, he died in September 1938, just a week after receiving an exit permit for the USA. Below is his widow, Chaje, in a portrait taken in Vienna, of her and her children, shortly after Dr Reif's death. (Dr Liane Reif-Lehrer)

Der Polizeipräsident in Wien.

K.B.19758 F.3. (R). Wien, den

Zeugnis.

Dem Herrn   Dr. Gerschon R e i f

Der Frau

Dem Fräulein

am 9.VIII.1894   in   Serafince   geboren,

zuständig nach   Wien

in   Wien, II., Reichsbrückenstr.Nr.28   wohnhaft,

wird auf sein Ansuchen zum Zwecke der   Erlangung des amerikanischen

Einreisevisums

hiemit bestätigt, daß gegen ihn

Nachteiliges nicht vorgemerkt ist.

Above, right, is a photo of young Fred Reif with his baby sister Liane, taken in June 1935. Below is a snapshot of Liane at three years of age. Immediately above is the emigration certificate the Reifs were unable to use and left is Mrs Reif's passport, which finally brought them out of Austria. (Dr Liane Reif-Lehrer)

THURSDAY, JUNE 8, 1939

The next day, Thursday, in New York, the executive committee of the Joint met to review matters. On Wednesday, they had received an offer from the quarantine station at Balboa, in the Panama Canal Zone, to house the refugees at a cost of $1.50 per day for those over twelve years of age, half price for children. The offer had been declined by the Joint because "negotiations in Cuba are continuing."

Now, there were two new offers to consider: the president of Honduras said his country was willing to take the passengers, but did not specify terms; Bernard Sandler, evidently unsuccessful in his bid to persuade Congress to accept the refugees, stated that he could provide a ship for them to transfer to if $50,000 was forthcoming. It was reported that singer Eddie Cantor had offered the money. Both suggestions were refused by the Joint. Then they examined the earlier offer of the Dominican Republic. After careful consideration, it too was rejected: the country did not have the facilities to accommodate them, the $500 deposit for each passenger was not thought to be returnable, the deposit applied only to Jews and might therefore set a precedent to be followed by other countries.

Having disposed of that matter, the Joint executive committee turned its attention to more "positive" action. A cable was sent to their chairman in London, Paul Baerwald, criticising the British government's failure to co-operate. In light of their own country's decision to keep out the refugees, and subsequent events, it seemed singularly inappropriate.

As the Joint executive committee was meeting in New York, on the St. Louis the ship's loudspeakers summoned all passengers to the social hall for an announcement of extraordinary important. Dr. Fritz Spanier, like many others, suspected what it would be. Their fears were swiftly confirmed by Josef Joseph's stark announcement that they were heading back to Europe.

An audible gasp swept the room. A voice cried out: "You mean we are going back to Germany!"

"Not necessarily. But we must stay calm."

Joseph's appeal was lost in voluble protests from a group of young men. One of them, Aaron Pozner, was thrust forward as their spokesman. In an impassioned voice, he argued that many men on board had been in concentration camps, and only released on the strict condition that they left Germany forever. His words rang through the social hall: "For us to return means one thing—returning to those camps. That could also be the future of every man woman and child on this ship!"

His statement brought an anguished chorus. Babette Spanier tearfully begged her husband to promise her their twin daughters would not face that fate. Embracing his wife and children, Fritz Spanier found no words of reassurance.

Shalote Hecht turned to her nephew, Otto Bergmann, and vowed fiercely: "If the worst happens we'll stay together. After all, they can only kill us once."

Recha Weiler, leaning on the arm of Rabbi Weil, murmured quietly she was only glad her husband's death had spared him from the fate now facing them.

Little Judith Feilchenfeld asked: "Momma, if they put us in a camp will they let Papa come and see us?" Alice Feilchenfeld held back her tears and gently told her daughter she was not to think such things. Judith's eldest brother, Wolfgang, looked at his compass and said it was pointing east north-east. For the first time in several days, nobody paid any attention to the boy's news.

Elise Loewe felt her children's arms slip protectively around her, and Ruth whispered: "Somebody will think of something."

For their sake, she did not say what she had thought for many days: that the future held no personal interest for her from that moment her husband, Max, had plunged overboard in Havana Harbour.

Around the Loewes, the low-keyed chant first heard when the ship had sailed from Havana took on a new life as scores repeated: "We must not die . . . we will not return . . . we must not die."

Herbert Manasse, the youngest member of the committee, demanded silence. The sound of his strong, confident voice stilled the crowd.

"Ladies and gentlemen," Manasse said, "the news is bad. That we all realise. But Europe is still many days away. That gives the Joint, and all our other friends, time to make new moves to help us. In the meantime this sort of behaviour will do nothing to alter or help our situation. The committee will welcome practical suggestions—but we cannot tolerate rash behaviour."

One of the men elbowed his way to the rostrum where Manasse stood. He had, he said, a suggestion: a number of the best swimmers should volunteer to jump overboard at selected intervals; the ship would be forced to stop and pick them up; in that way they could delay almost indefinitely their return to Europe.

Manasse quashed the idea: "That is an example of the sort of suggestion we will not act upon. It is foolhardy and futile!"

The man stormed out of the social hall, followed closely by Pozner and the rest of his group.

That morning, like the passengers, steward Leo Jockl also faced a threat to his future.

It had arrived in a coded cable addressed to Gustav Schröder, from Hapag, Hamburg:

POLICE REQUEST FULL DETAILS OF YOUR PERSONAL KNOWLEDGE STEWARD JOCKL'S FAMILY BACKGROUND AS THEY HAVE REPORTS HE IS OF JEWISH ANTECEDENTS. MATTER REGARDED MOST SERIOUSLY AS POLICE SAY COMPLAINT BASED ON SOUND SOURCES. IF NECESSARY CONSULT ORTSGRUPPENLEITER SCHIENDICK TO CLARIFY JOCKL BACKGROUND AND RADIO ALL INFORMATION IMMEDIATELY.

The request sickened the captain; for him it was further proof that the company he had served so proudly was now "acting as a messenger service for the Nazis." His determination to resign at the end of the voyage grew even stronger.

Schröder guessed, correctly, that somewhere behind the cable was the hand of Otto Schiendick. But a confrontation would probably simply bring the response that the steward had a right to be involved in such a matter; undoubtedly Schiendick would relish the prospect of interrogating Jockl.

Yet the cable could not be ignored; that would certainly raise the curiosity of the Gestapo. The captain sent for Jockl, showed him the message, and watched with compassion as the steward read it. Then, with a sigh, Schröder drafted a reply and handed it to his steward:

FULLEST QUESTIONING REVEALS STEWARD JOCKL LOYAL TO PARTY AND COUNTRY NO EVIDENCE OF SEMITIC BACKGROUND.

The two men looked silently at each other. Then the captain began to encode the message. He paused only once to say to the steward: "God help us both if they discover the truth."

That same morning Otto Schiendick told Purser Mueller that, in his capacity as Ortsgruppenleiter, he was banning all further "social intercourse" between crew and passengers. Mueller retorted that Schiendick needed the captain's permission for such an action. "In such party matters I do not have to consult the captain," the steward replied.
Shortly afterward the ship's loudspeakers announced the ban.

At lunch time, passengers learned of another development. The menus, formerly individually printed for each meal and offering a choice of food, were now on single mimeographed sheets. All three meals were typed on the page, and there was no longer a choice. Stewards explained: "We face a food shortage due to our hurried departure from Havana."

That evening the ship's orchestra played to a virtually deserted dance floor; the cinema was almost empty. A mood of lethargy steadily tightened its grip on the St. Louis as hour by hour, knot by knot, Germany came closer.

FRIDAY, JUNE 9, 1939

The next day, Friday, the first formal meeting took place at the Home Office in London to discuss the St. Louis. After pressure from Paul Baerwald, chairman of the Joint, allied to that of American ambassador Joseph Kennedy, the British government had agreed the matter could be raised at a "low level" by a representative of the German-Jewish Aid Committee with a junior member of the Home Office staff, Mr. Cooper. Baerwald's earlier impression as he had reported it to New York was confirmed: the Home Office's initial attitude was "not promising."

Cooper thought it "significant" that the Joint itself had not "been prepared to secure the refugees' admission to Cuba on the terms offered." Why, therefore, should Britain, a country with no real knowledge of the passengers, put itself out when, in Havana, the responsible American relief organisation had been unable "to lend a helping hand."

It was an embarrassing question for the British relief worker to answer. He also found it impossible to tell Cooper whether the passengers "were of a desirable, or undesirable, class." The Home Office official believed they "might well be, in fact, something in the nature of a general jail delivery at the insistence of the Gestapo who had forced the voyage on the Hamburg-American Line."

What Cooper did not state, but later included in his report of the meeting, was his "feeling" that if the British government were to "accede to the request at the instance of the Aid Committee, the ruse once practised and proved successful would be repeated ad infinitum."

The two men agreed it was of paramount importance that Sir Herbert Emerson's discussions on the plan for orderly emigration from Germany were not upset. As they parted, they also agreed it would be "altogether wrong to come to any decision with regard to these people while the vessel is on the high seas; if steps were taken to ensure their admission to the United Kingdom, it should only be done after their return to Germany, when individual cases could be investigated."

The words would have chilled the passengers on the St. Louis, but, fortunately, they had no knowledge of the meeting. Nor, again fortunately, did they know what was said when the executive committee of the Joint met in New York the same day to bring themselves up to date on developments.

Morris Troper in Paris had cabled again that if the passengers were returned to Germany, the entire shipload would be sent to the concentration camps. However, it was his impression that if the British government were prepared to offer help, the French might also. Troper reported that Baron Robert de Rothschild was attempting to persuade the authorities to make available a French colonial island off South America, or, failing that, perhaps Tangiers in North Africa.

There was little the executive committee could usefully do. They sent a cable to Troper requesting that they "be assured no single possibility of escape should fail to be given utmost consideration." The Joint decided to hold another meeting, three days later, on Monday, at 4 P.M., "inconvenient and troublesome as it is," because, the acting chairman wrote, "I want the record to show our unremitting efforts."

By midday of that Friday, June 9, unable to afford the luxury of any postponement of action, the St. Louis passenger committee had made the radio room their virtual headquarters, as the latest salvo of appeals was sent to Prime Minister Neville Chamberlain in London, the governments of France, Belgium, and Holland, and religious and civic leaders throughout Europe. Extra care had been taken to make the messages brief as well as poignant, for Hapag had refused to grant the committee further free cabling facilities.

Money to pay for the radiograms had been raised by passengers, who pawned their jewellery, cameras, and even their clothes with crew members. Now, with no more cash available, all on board knew those cables contained their last hopes of intercession.

The cable to Prime Minister Chamberlain was typical:

907 PASSENGERS ON S.S. ST. LOUIS HALF WOMEN AND CHILDREN REFUSED LANDING IN CUBA IN SPITE OF PERMITS AND NOW ON RETURN VOYAGE TO HAMBURG BEG TO BE SAVED BY BEING GRANTED ASYLUM IN ENGLAND OR AT LEAST DISEMBARKATION AT SOUTHAMPTON AS RETURN TO HAMBURG IMPOSSIBLE AND ACTS OF DESPERATION WOULD BE UNAVOIDABLE.

But around the time it was transmitted, the final stages of one act of desperation were already under way. Singly, at intervals, one young man followed another down a corridor on D deck to cabin 373, where Aaron Pozner greeted them. When they were assembled, twelve in all, they stood with heads bowed as Pozner prayed for divine help for the violent action they planned.

Close by in the crew's quarters, violence, verbal but no less wounding, was also in the air as Otto Schiendick briefed the Gestapo "firemen" before they fanned out in pairs through the passenger decks to carry out the steward's orders. By mid afternoon a number of passengers had been told by the "firemen": "These are your last free days. Enjoy them. After you return to Hamburg you won't be heard of again." The refugees, apart from Rabbi Weil, were too terrified to make any protest. And, when he remonstrated, he was warned: "In Dachau they'll shave off your beard if you open your mouth."

The majority of the crew continued to behave

This is the Cablegram sent to British Prime Minister Chamberlain by the Passenger Committee, written in Dr Josef Joseph's own handwriting. (Mrs Liesl Joseph-Loeb)

in an exemplary manner, and there were many acts of generosity. Stewards and cabin boys smuggled in the last of the fresh fruit from the kitchens and placed them in children's cots; the Spanier twins were each slipped five Reichsmarks by their table steward; Carl Lenneberg, who had run out of money for pipe tobacco, found a one-pound tin left for him by his table steward; Assistant Purser Hans Reich took a bottle of Sekt to a couple of pretty girls in their cabin.

Leo Jockl had obtained a special gift for Aaron Pozner, a couple of slices of smoked salmon on black bread. There had been no opportunity or time since Havana for the steward to visit Pozner. But, unexpectedly, on this Friday afternoon Jockl found himself free. He hurried to Pozner's cabin, anxious to know how the teacher was bearing up. There was no reply to Jockl's knocking; impulsively he opened the door, and found the cabin empty, but showing signs of recent occupation by several persons. Jockl knew Pozner was a non-smoker and usually a tidy man; his visitors had shown no such fastidiousness in grinding out their cigarette butts on the carpet. The steward clearly recalled that Pozner had no friends on board. The more he thought about it, the stronger his feeling grew that Aaron Pozner was involved in something out of character. He put the sandwiches on the bed and left.

Later, when Jockl brought tea to the captain, he mentioned his suspicions. Schröder consulted a list on his desk, stabbing a finger against a name halfway down the paper. Aaron Pozner, he said, was one of the passengers he had been warned might try to sabotage the ship.

"Find him, Jockl, and bring him to me before he does anything foolish," ordered the captain.

At that moment, Aaron Pozner and the other

plotters were waiting in the nearest public room to the bridge, the gymnasium. At 4:30 P.M., they slipped out of the gymnasium and entered the bridge area. First Officer Ostermeyer looked up from a map as the man appeared in the chart room. Before he could move, two of them bundled him through the bridge. Helmsman Kritsch gasped at the sight. As he moved to ring the ship's emergency system—designed to warn of fire at sea—he was sent flying into a corner. In minutes the rest of the watch was overpowered. Pozner ordered Ostermeyer to send for the captain. When Captain Schröder appeared he was surrounded by Pozner and two other men. The captain demanded to know what they hoped to achieve.

"To save our lives," said Pozner, "by taking over the ship and sailing it to any country other than Germany."

Schröder looked carefully at the slightly built, tense young teacher, and in a flat and resigned voice, began:

"The other passengers will not support you. You have not seized the engine room. My crew will overpower you. All you are doing is laying yourself open to a charge of piracy."

The group looked uneasily at each other. One said defiantly that they would hold the captain and those on the bridge as hostages.

"I will give no order, no matter what you do, that will take my ship off its set course," insisted Schröder, "and without that order you can do nothing."

The captain walked over to Kritsch and guided him back to the wheel, painfully aware of how frightened the helmsman was. He then said to Pozner:

"You have done enough damage already for me to prefer serious charges. If I do, I can assure you that you certainly will be taken back to Germany. And you know what that means. I understand and sympathise with your desperation. But you have behaved in a criminal manner. However, I am willing to overlook that in all the circumstances if you leave this bridge, having given me an understanding that you will take no further such action. You have exactly one minute to accept this offer."

He deliberately turned his back on the group, who began to whisper among themselves.

"Captain, we cannot return to Germany," pleaded Pozner.

Schröder turned and saw the fear in the young man's face. At that moment First Officer Ostermeyer began to struggle with his captors. The captain sharply ordered him to desist, then, in a softer voice, he told the group he would do everything possible to land the passengers in England. That promise ended any further resistance. The men gave solemn pledges about their future good conduct, and filed off the bridge.

The captain saw that the crisis had deeply affected all the watch, particularly helmsman Kritsch; even the usually cool Ostermeyer was making a visible effort to control himself.

"The incident is over," said Schröder firmly. "There is no cause for further worry."

Nodding for Ostermeyer to follow, the captain left the bridge, aware that he, too, was now showing signs of reaction. He knew that the attempted hijacking might be the prelude to similar acts unless he acted swiftly and surely. Pausing only to pour himself and Ostermeyer large brandies in his day cabin, he made rapid plans. There was no time to convene the committee; in any case, they would be powerless to quell further trouble. Nor could he muster the crew to guard the bridge and engine room; that might well lead to a violent reaction from other headstrong passengers. Schröder decided it was time to follow up a suggestion made to him a number of times in the past.

"I must talk to the passengers myself," he told Ostermeyer. It would be the first time the captain had done so on the voyage; he believed that would be a factor in his favour. "When I speak they will believe me," he said to his first officer.

At 5 P.M., some 600 passengers—the absentees were mostly children—assembled in the social hall to hear the captain. As he stood beneath the huge portrait of Hitler, Schröder experienced a great "sense of hopelessness. It was as if the whole St. Louis had been cast out of this world and must now leave this inhospitable planet. It was this feeling which gave me complete understanding for the desperate position of my passengers and led me to the correct words to say."

His speech was brief; whatever happened they would not be returned to Germany.

The sheer confidence in his voice brought the reaction he desired—"an almost physical wave of relief was felt when I finished speaking." His words carried far more conviction than he really felt, but no one knew that.

Schröder left the social hall to plan his most crucial move. Later, he would not be able to recall how long the idea had been in his mind, or what placed it there. But his promise to Pozner's group to land the refugees in England had given impetus to his schemes.

That evening he summoned the first officer, the purser, and the chief engineer to his cabin, and swore each of them to secrecy over his intentions. Schröder decided not to inform the passenger committee until the last possible moment about the course of action he proposed: he felt they might leak his intentions to some of the other passengers.

Instead, he sent for Dr. Fritz Spanier. The captain had come increasingly to trust the doctor's medical judgements of how passengers would react to a given situation. The doctor listened without interruption as Schröder unfolded his scheme. The

This radio-telegram was sent to Dr Herbert Manasse by Milton Goldsmith, from the Jewish Joint Relief Office in Havana on 10th June. (Mrs Liesl Joseph-Loeb)

advice Spanier then proffered was short and simple.

"Don't tell the committee. Don't give anybody any warning.

That includes the crew. When it happens, treat it as a real emergency. The risk of panic will be higher, but in the circumstances that will be beneficial."

The "circumstances" Dr. Spanier and the three ship's officers had approved was the captain's plan to run the St. Louis close to Beachy Head on the Sussex coast of England, set the ship on fire, and evacuate the passengers ashore.

SATURDAY, JUNE 10, 1939

On June 10, four weeks to the day after the St. Louis had set sail from Hamburg, Morris Troper in Paris spoke by telephone to Max Gottschalk in Brussels. Gottschalk was president of the Refugee Committee, and already knew of the St. Louis's plight. He promised Troper he would "do what I can." What he did set the seal on the future of everyone on board the ship.

At ten-thirty, Gottschalk spoke to Belgian Minister of Justice Paul Emile Janson. Janson in turn

Max Gottschalk, President of the Jewish Refugee Committee in Brussels. (Mrs Liesl Joseph-Loeb)

promised to bring the matter to the attention of Prime Minister Hubert Pierlot. In less than an hour after it was raised, Belgium made the decision which Cuba and America had debated for days, even weeks, and finally refused to make: King Leopold III and Prime Minister Pierlot agreed that 200 of the passengers could land in Belgium.

Morris Troper heard the news from Max Gottschalk just after noon. The Joint director decided not to tell the St. Louis until it was officially confirmed. By then, it would be too late to stop yet another tragedy aboard the ship.

On Saturday morning, helmsman Heinz Kritsch failed to report for duty. He had last been seen by Leo Jockl near the halyard on the after deck. A search party found him in a locker room—hanging from a beam.

Captain Schröder was too overcome to speak when he heard of the helmsman's suicide. He had been genuinely fond of the young sailor, sharing with him a passion for ornithology and a pride in seamanship. The captain committed his thoughts about Kritsch's death to his private diary, an entry that shows the deep feelings it aroused in him:

"God knows why he did it. His death is an irreplaceable loss for both the line and myself, for there was no more reliable man than he. Thoughts about the terrible finality of death depress me for the third time on this journey. First Weiler, then Berg, now Kritsch."

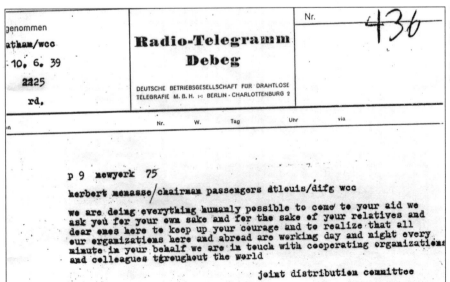

This second message was received from the Joint Distribution Committee in New York at 10.25 in the evening of 10th June. Now, everyone was aware that things were becoming very difficult. (Mrs Liesl Joseph-Loeb)

Shortly before midnight this Saturday, the captain read the burial service and saluted as Kritsch's shroud was dropped over the side to sink beneath the surging bow wave of the St. Louis.

SUNDAY, JUNE 11, 1939

On Sunday, in Paris, Morris Troper continued to press representations to other governments. Belgium had provided the necessary initial breakthrough, and now France, Holland, and Great Britain were actively considering the question.

Troper knew the matter was still urgent, for he had been told by an emissary from Berlin, a Jewish relief worker with suspiciously close and reliable ties with the Gestapo, that the German secret police intended to intern the St. Louis passengers if more than half of them were returned to Hamburg.

The Gestapo also claimed that the ship had been ordered by them to proceed slowly until noon on Monday; after that, unless $50,000 was provided to purchase oil, it would be instructed to head immediately for its home port. Troper told the intermediary to "inform the Gestapo no such money would be forthcoming."

In London, American ambassador Joseph Kennedy met with the chairman of the Joint, Paul Baerwald, and received a letter from him guaranteeing that any of the St. Louis passengers who were permitted to disembark in Britain would be maintained and cared for by the Jewish relief agency. Kennedy promised to arrange that the letter was put before the proper authorities in the hope that "the British government will receive some or all these people here."

After The Joint Distribution Committee's message was received on the evening of 10th June, the Passenger Committee put out this bulletin at lunch time on the 11th, seeking to reassure the passengers. Roughly translated, it read: "Hapag in Hamburg are helping by passing cables received from the Captain, aimed at opening negotiations with the British government, giving details of families – the numbers of men, women and children under 16. An appointed count-master is gathering passport details immediately for these statistics.

"A number of private telegrams have been received from New York, and we confirm to you that Hapag and ourselves have been in contact with the governments of the USA and England. Even a cable, for example, from State Secretary Strauss of the American Interior Ministry, has made enquiries of friends on board. All are doing everything possible to seek a temporary stay in an international safe place until a final solution is found.

"A general message from a reliable source in New York tells us: 'Keep calm, an immediate solution is at hand'" (Herbert Karliner)

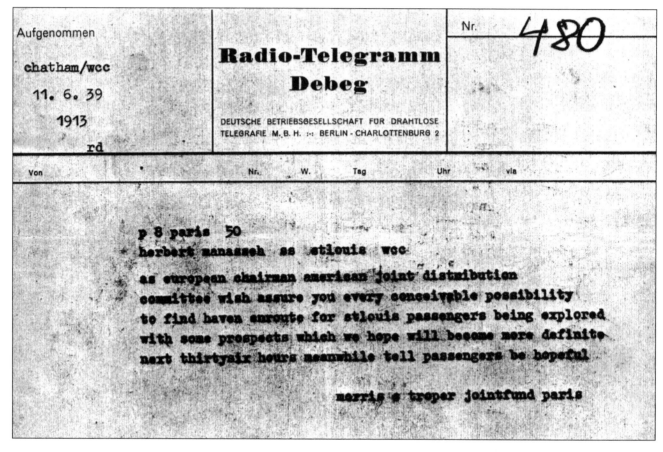

MONDAY, JUNE 12, 1939

The next morning, Monday, June 12, Morris Troper heard from Holland that Queen Wilhelmina and the Dutch government had agreed to give temporary asylum to 194 of the refugees. With this knowledge, Troper cabled the St. Louis.

EVERY CONCEIVABLE POSSIBILITY TO FIND HAVEN BEING EXPLORED WITH SOME PROSPECTS WHICH WE HOPE WILL BECOME DEFINITE NEXT THIRTY-SIX HOURS.

At about the same time in London, the passenger committee's cable was delivered to Prime Minister Neville Chamberlain. After reading it, Chamberlain approved a high-level meeting to be held that afternoon at 3 P.M., to be chaired by the British prime minister's permanent under-secretary at the Home Office, Sir Alexander Maxwell. Among those present were Sir Herbert Emerson, chairman of the International Committee on Political Refugees, Paul Baerwald, chairman of the Joint Distribution Committee, and their various advisors.

Cooper, the junior official who had earlier reported his doubts about letting the refugees in, now repeated his argument that they should be returned to Germany before any promises were made. He told the meeting:

"It is probable that a proportion of the passengers are undesirable. It would be easier to reject such individuals while they were on German soil than to refuse them admission to this country and enforce their return to Germany."

Sir Alexander Maxwell overruled Cooper's objections. Instead, he stated that he would recommend to the British government that they accept up to 350 of the St. Louis passengers. The British government agreed.

That evening, at 6:30 P.M., the French government officially announced that it would take

250 of the refugees.

On the St. Louis that Monday night, none of these decisions was yet known. Even so, Troper's cable with its promise of definite news "in thirty-six hours" had changed everything: Captain Schröder shelved his plan to set fire to the ship; the refugees no longer worried that, with the water shortage and the ship's laundry unable to accept their clothes, even their dress was now beginning to show the effects of the voyage.

That night, many went to the ship's cinema. Ever since Havana, it had been running and rerunning the same films. Even Liesl Joseph, who had often sneaked out of her berth when her parents were asleep to go to the films, had become bored with seeing the same ones over and over again. But tonight, Burser Mueller provided a film which had not been seen before, Ihr Liebhusar, a comedy starring Magda Schneider.

The showing was well attended. One particular

line caused an outburst of laughter: "Travelling by sea makes one nervous."

The tension on the St. Louis had been broken.

TUESDAY, JUNE 13, 1939

On Tuesday, the world learned that the "wandering refugees" would not be returning to Germany. In Berlin, Propaganda Minister Joseph Goebbels ordered that the British and French governments in particular should be heavily criticised in the German press for selling out to the Jews."

In Paris, Morris Troper cabled the ship:

FINAL ARRANGEMENTS FOR DISEMBARKATION ALL PASSENGERS COMPLETE. GOVERNMENTS OF BELGIUM, HOLLAND, FRANCE, AND ENGLAND CO-OPERATED MAGNIFICENTLY WITH AMERICAN JOINT DISTRIBUTION COMMITTEE TO EFFECT THIS POSSIBILITY.

The passenger committee replied that their "gratitude is an immense as the ocean on which we

With the lead set by the Belgian government, others in Europe rallied to the aid of the "St Louis" passengers and now, Morris Troper was able to send the following happy message to Dr Josef Joseph. (Mrs Liesl Joseph-Loeb)

```
018 / Telegramm         Deutsche Reichspost

  LONDON 1618 42 13  8,37
a
        Aufgenommen              RP 26,25 =      REFUGEES              Übermittelt
  Tag  Monat Jahr Zeit                                           Tag:        Zeit:
   13  VI 39    42             LEADER ST LOUIS  VIA HAMBURG       an:         durch:
  von:           durch:
     L dn                      AMERICAN LINE HMB =
  Amt Hamburg

    Ldn

   ANNOUNCED IN LONDON TODAY THAT BRITAIN FRANCE HOLLAND

   BELGIUM HAVE AGREED GIVE REFUGEES ON ST LOUIS

   TEMPORARY ASYLUM IN FOUR COUNTRIES APPRECIATE YOUR

   COMMENT PLEASE GIVE YOUR PRESENT POSITION =

   NEWS EDITOR NEWS CHRONICLE LONDON +

   Raum für dienstliche Rückfragen
                                          CT    RP = 26.25 +    +    +
        8. 38. 3000                                                        x C 187 Dis A3
```

On June 13th, the news broke to the world's press, with the result that the News Editor of London's "News Chronicle" sent this message, seeking comment from the ship's Captain, Gustav Schröder. (Mrs Liesl Joseph-Loeb)

have been travelling since May 13." They decided to inform all the passengers the next morning after breakfast in the social hall.

WEDNESDAY, JUNE 14, 1939

At 10 A.M., in the presence of Captain Schröder, the telegram from Troper was read aloud. From every corner of the large room came cheering and sobs of joy. Josef Joseph asked for silence, and then expressed the gratitude of everyone present to

Schröder and his crew. the captain smiled but did not speak.

That night, a celebration party was held in the jam-packed social hall. There were singers, magicians, classical pianists, and comedians. Most of the jokes had to do with holiday cruises to Cuba. But the biggest laugh was raised by one of the refugees simply reading from a Hapag brochure. The handout stated:

"The St. Louis is a ship on which one travels securely, and lives in comfort. There is everything one can wish for that makes life on board a pleasure."

TELEGRAM RECEIVED

1—1836

FROM

CJ

GRAY
LONDON

DIVISION

THE AME... REPUBLIC
DEPARTMENT OF STATE

Dated June 14, 1939

Rec'd 2:25 p.m.

Secretary of State,

Washington.

Doc. 6

134

830, June 14, 8 p.m.

FROM PELL.

My 822, June 13, 5 p.m.

Arrangements have now been completed for the ST. LOUIS to proceed to Antwerp, where the selection of the various contingents will be made on board. The Belgian and Netherlands contingents will be disembarked and the French and British contingents transferred by tender to a smaller vessel of the Hamburg-Amerika Line which will take them to a French and British port at the expense of the line.

H PD

KENNEDY

With the news out that refuge had been guaranteed by Britain, Belgium, France and Holland, Joseph Kennedy, the US Ambassador to Britain had this message sent to the Secretary of State in Washington. He was no doubt greatly relieved as it eased the embarrassment felt by many in the US, as it would be seen to lead to an opportunity for a controlled inflow of immigrants to the United States. It was Kennedy, of course, who said he would depart London the moment bombs began to fall – and he did, leaving behind not just the bombs falling on Britain, but also several hundred of those "St Louis" passengers who were in Belgium, France and Holland at the time to the very fate they had feared before they left Hamburg on May 13th. (Mrs Liesl Joseph-Loeb)

CAMEO 8: ELLI & RENATE REUTLINGER:

Elli and Renate Reutlinger had also hoped to follow their breadwinner, Gustav, to the United States via Havana. Here they are on board the "St Louis". Below is Elli's identity pass for the Rotterdam Quarantine Station where she awaited her visa to the United States. Top right is the telegram she sent to her husband on arrival in Antwerp and below it is the joyous news from him that her quota number had come up and she was granted a visa – in the nick of time, for the Second World War had now begun. (Renate Reutlinger)

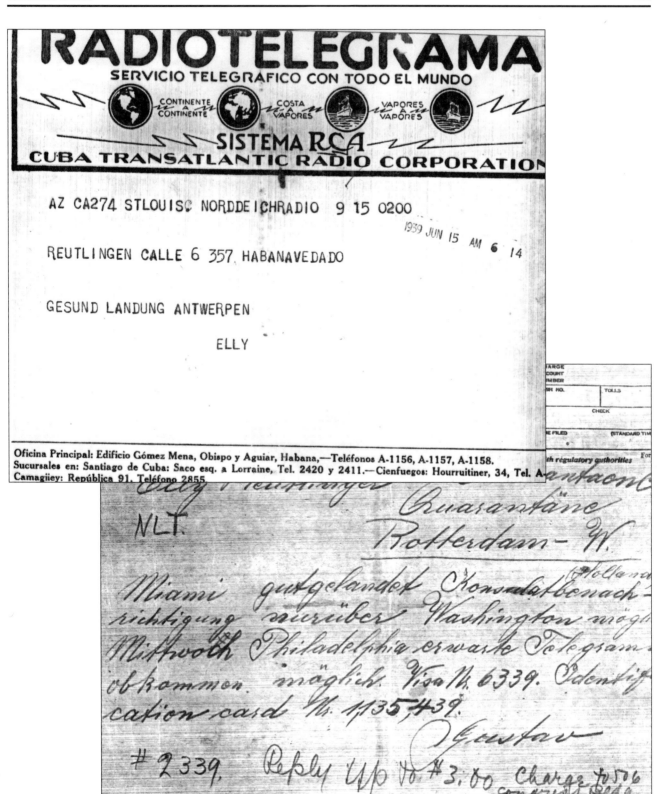

THURSDAY, JUNE 15, 1939

In Paris, the French national chief of police, exercising considerable restraint, told the press that he "regretted our American friends, to whose country the majority of the refugees were eventually going, stopping at Cuba only en route, were not able to direct them to one of their ports instead of sending them back to Europe."

Dr Joseph must hardly have been able to contain his sheer exhilaration as he wrote this message, for now he and his Passenger Committee were almost through their task. Passengers were now to be dispersed in friendly countries and the gratitude they all felt was beyond description. Soon, Morris Troper would be on board the "St Louis" and they would meet, though the bond of friendship was already firmly sealed between them. (Mrs Liesl Joseph-Loeb)

Aufgenommen	**Radio-Telegramm Debeg**	Nr.
	DEUTSCHE BETRIEBSGESELLSCHAFT FÜR DRAHTLOSE TELEGRAFIE M. B. H. :-: BERLIN - CHARLOTTENBURG 2	

Von		Nr.	W.	Tag	Uhr	via

15/6. 20⁵
June 15,

Morris C Troper
                    jointfund   Paris

We all are glad and very calm receiving your and mr. Rosenbergs radiograms from yesterday and today. Desired lists are ready. How are you thinking about passenger distribution. Many many thanks. Cordial greetings.

Committee J.

US President Franklin Delano Roosevelt (above) was the man who finally prevented the "St Louis" from discharging its passengers on to US soil, fearing the political backlash which could result from what would be seen as a violation of the established quota system, quite apart from the effects on his potential third term in office. There must have been serious discussions behind the scenes in the White House, as his First Lady, Eleanor (below), was renowned for her involvement in humanitarian causes and passengers' wives had sent a direct appeal to her by telegram. (Franklin D Roosevelt Library, New York)

This is Lilli Joseph, wife of the Passenger Committee Chairman. The photograph was taken before the Josephs embarked on the "Voyage of the Damned". It was she alone who shared many of his burdens and sleepless nights as he wrestled with the problems of finding a solution to the nightmare prospect of 907 people facing a return to Hamburg and the fate which certainly awaited them there. She also had the task of keeping the reality of the stiuation from her daughter, Liesl who, on her eleventh birthday, presented a small bouquet to Morris Troper upon his arrival on board the "St Louis". (Mrs Liesl Joseph-Loeb)

CAMEO 9: THE RING FAMILY:

Erich and Erna Ring lived near to the Glücksmanns and were good friends. The upper photo shows a picture of proud parents with water-sporting son, Jacques, in the early 1930s. Below it, you see Erich Ring on the right, leaning against the car (a Mercédès-Benz 170). Next to him is Heinrich Glücksmann and the young man on the left, wearing spectacles, is Jacques Ring. Below is another Benitez Cuban visa, but this one is quite interesting, in that it includes someone of a different family name, Flora Karliner. We must presume that Mrs Karliner was related in some way to the Rings for her name to appear on their visa. (Edgar Glucksman)

The upper picture shows the Ring family in a little private party on board the "St Louis" – probably a birthday party. Below is Erich and Erna at the end-of-voyage party, just off Cuba. (Edgar Glucksman)

This is Erich and Erna Ring in much later years, having survived all and settled into retirement. (Edgar Glucksman)

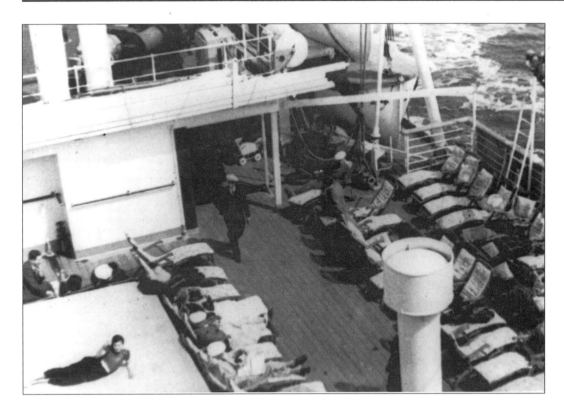

On the return voyage, whilst it was now summer, there weren't many people taking the sun on deck any more and pictures taken now reflected a more pensive mood – a sense of relief, mixed with apprehension. (Four pictures from the collection of Gerald Granston, currently on loan to the Museum of Jewish Heritage, NY)

FRIDAY, JUNE 16, to
SATURDAY, JUNE 17, 1939

Morris Troper left Paris on Friday and spent the night in Antwerp. The next morning, at 4 A.M., he and his party, along with representatives from all the countries concerned, travelled by car to the Dutch port of Flushing at the head of the estuary leading to Antwerp in Belgium. There, at nine o'clock, a tug took them out to the St. Louis.

On the St. Louis, Thursday and Friday had been spent on the ship packing and preparing lists itemising which of the four countries each passenger preferred to go to.

On board the ship, now, the passengers lined the rails to catch their first glimpse of "the man who had saved our lives." A reception line of small children waited to greet Troper. At its head was Liesl Joseph, chosen because she was the daughter of the passenger committee chairman, but also because Liesl was that day celebrating her eleventh birthday.

As Morris Troper stepped onto the ship, Liesl moved forward, and made her prepared speech:

"We thank you with all our hearts. I am sorry that flowers do not grow on ships; otherwise we would have given you the largest and most beautiful bouquet ever."

The sea odyssey was almost over. But for many passengers on the St. Louis, it was, at best, only the end of the beginning.

As the St. Louis steamed slowly toward Antwerp, Morris Troper and the relief workers from France, Belgium, the Netherlands, and the United Kingdom began sorting out which of the passengers were to go where. Though they did not know it, they were, in effect, sitting in judgement on who would live and who would die.

After the welcoming ceremony, Captain Schröder had stepped forward and told Troper, "The entire ship's complement is at your service." He suggested that Troper and the relief workers use the

After the formalities of the welcome to Morris Troper were complete, there was a brief moment for a picture of Dr Joseph (left), Mrs Joseph and Liesl with the man who had done so much to save the lives of 907 people. (Mrs Liesl Joseph-Loeb)

social hall as their office, ordered Purser Mueller and his staff to make the necessary arrangements, and then returned to the bridge to guide the St. Louis up the Schelde estuary to Antwerp.

The social hall, where in Havana the Cuban doctor had inspected the passengers before their expected disembarkation, where afterward so many momentous announcements had been made, now was the setting for the final decisions about the fate of each individual St. Louis passenger.

At the centre table sat Morris Troper and his assistant Emanuel Rosen, both Americans. To their right were the tables of the Belgian and Dutch representatives. To the left, those of the British and French. Hovering in the background was the passenger committee, offering help and advice. In all there were twenty-six officials present; the only member of the ship's company continuously on hand was Assistant Purser Hans Reich. In front of each table was a long line of anxious passengers, all talking at once and hoping to influence the representatives of the country of their choice. Behind the tables, overlooking the entire scene, as usual, was the portrait of Adolf Hitler.

Morris Troper made only one promise to the assembled passengers: he and his co-workers would do their best to keep families together. The first two hours were spent deciding who would be sent to Great Britain. Although the representatives of the four countries gave an outward appearance of friendly compromise and reasonableness, beneath the surface there was tension. From time to time it appeared, especially between the British and the French, Emanuel Rosen noticed, that they barely concealed their competition for those passengers who had the lowest numbers on the U.S. quota list and could therefore be expected to leave after minimum of delay.

The Dutch representative, Alfred Moser, had orders to accept only those with a U.S. registration card, preferably with a low number, because, he explained:

"We already had so many refugees and refugee camps, and now another two hundred! So we tried to get people we could, so to speak, get rid of quickly, in order to comply with the wishes of the Dutch government. But in any case, it was no real solution.

Then, there was the more public happy picture of Morris and Mrs Betty Troper with the children of the voyage. (Mrs Liesl Joseph-Loeb)

Hamburg-Amerika Linie

Drahtwort: Oceanfahrt Hamburg

Ihr Zeichen: Unser Zeichen:

An Bord der St. Louis
16. Juni 39.

Herr Rechtsanwalt Josef Joseph war
... ... der Rückreise des h.S. St Louis von

On Board of the St. Louis
16. June, 1939

Mr. Josef Joseph, Esq. was the Chairman of the Passenger Committee,
and during the time of the return trip of the M.S. St. Louis from Havana,
where permission for the passengers to land was denied, the Committee
under his leadership, was the liasion body between the ship's personnel and
the passengers and established an atmosphere of calm and order.
It was especially during the critical days when all hope of a landing in
America had to be abandoned and an aura of panic prevailed, that Mr.
Joseph displayed the most outstanding service by his exemplary devotion
and transmission of communication between the Captain's Staff and the
travelling guests, so that we are deeply obliged to thank him for this service.

G. Schroeder
Captain. M.S. St. Louis.

... ...
... ausserordentlichen Dienst erwiesen,
sodas wir ihm zu ganz besonderem Dank
verpflichtet sind.

Schröder

Captain Schröder wrote this letter of reference to Dr Josef Joseph on 16th June. The translation came from Dr Joseph's daughter, Liesl. (Mrs Liesl Joseph-Loeb)

Only a delay in the fatal solution."

Not all the passengers on the St. Louis held U.S. quota numbers. Those who did not were barred from Holland.

Soon after two o'clock, Captain Schröder nosed his ship alongside Antwerp Harbour's pier 18. For the first time since leaving Hamburg, the St. Louis had been allowed to tie up at a quayside. Police and customs officials flocked onto the ship, but, as in Havana, friends and relations on the shore, and the press, were not allowed on board.

Just before the ship berthed, there had been ugly scenes near pier 18 when Antwerp's Nazi-inspired National Youth Organisation staged a demonstration protesting the arrival of the refugees. Handbills had been distributed containing the message: "We too want to help the Jews. If they call at our offices each will receive gratis a length of rope and a long nail."

The handbills were confiscated and their distributors dispersed by the Belgian police. Passengers on the St. Louis knew nothing of the demonstration, nor did they see the parade of the black-shirted Fascists which passed through the main streets of Antwerp just at the time the ship arrived. In this case, the police did not intervene.

During the afternoon, the atmosphere in the social hall became more feverish as passengers learned that, in many cases, they were not to be allowed to go to the country of their choosing. Sometimes there were even arguments within families: Rosemarie and Otto Bergmann wanted badly to go to Britain, but the domineering aunt, Shalote Hecht, had her heart set on France, and as the young couple had promised to look after her on the voyage, they felt obliged to do as she wished.

Even so, Rosemarie Bergmann had other worries on her mind, as she made clear to Emanuel Rosen.

"She amazed everyone," he recalled, "because in the midst of the excitement and confusion, she asked what would become of her dog, which Hapag had forwarded to Havana separately, and please could I do something about it?" Rosen could not. Oshey, Rosemarie's fox terrier, would have to fend for herself without the benefit of the relief worker's efforts.

In the calm of his day cabin, Captain Schröder reflected on the trip and his future. He had received

This touching letter of thanks to Morris Troper, for all he did in achieving a place to go for the passengers of the "St Louis", was written by Liesl Joseph, actually on her eleventh birthday. (Mrs Liesl Joseph-Loeb)

instructions from the head office not to return to Germany from Antwerp before proceeding directly to New York, to begin the season of summer cruises to the Caribbean. In the circumstances, he decided not to resign until he could hand in his resignation personally to Holthusen when he returned to Hamburg in the autumn. Having made that decision, the man who had done as much as anyone and more than most to save the lives of his passengers now, typically, began to write individual, private letters to each member of the passenger committee thanking them for what they had done for him.

At five o'clock in the afternoon, Morris Troper announced by loudspeaker the names of the 214 passengers selected to go to Belgium. They were given a last dinner on the St. Louis, and at seven o'clock began filing off the ship, the envy of many

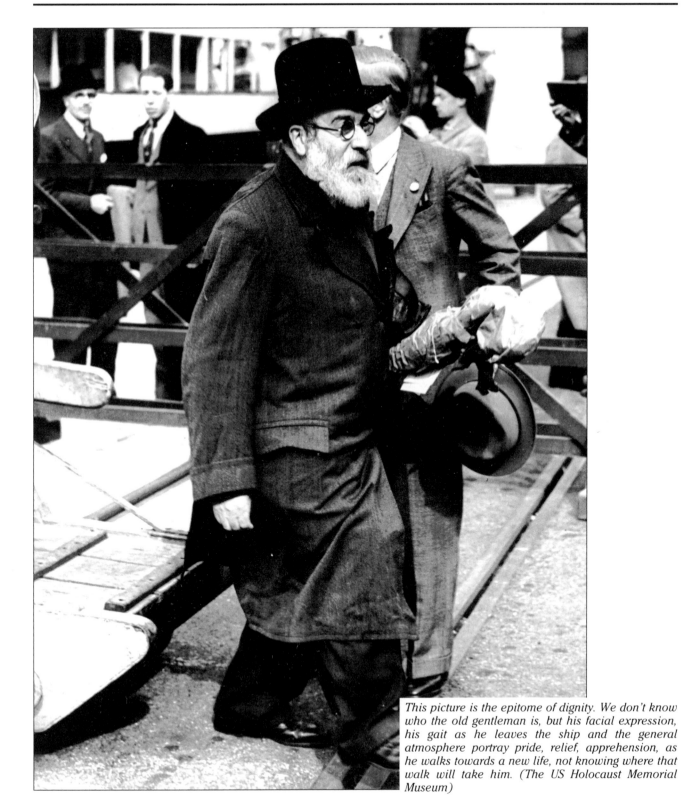

This picture is the epitome of dignity. We don't know who the old gentleman is, but his facial expression, his gait as he leaves the ship and the general atmosphere portray pride, relief, apprehension, as he walks towards a new life, not knowing where that walk will take him. (The US Holocaust Memorial Museum)

fellow passengers for being able to leave so soon.

Among the first down the gangway were George and Carl Lenneberg, the brothers who had prevented reporters from interviewing Elise Loewe after her husband's attempted suicide in Havana Harbour. They wanted to go to Britain but had been chosen for Belgium. The brothers reflected that they had travelled 10,000 miles since leaving Hamburg without setting foot on land, and now as they stepped ashore, they were only 300 miles from where their journey had begun.

One mishap occurred as the passengers disembarked. The woman the children had christened "Big Bertha" fell heavily and broke her leg. She was taken to hospital by the Belgian Red Cross. She was, at least, spared the indignity that awaited the others on their journey to Brussels.

The special train waiting to take them away was on a siding, shielded from the street by iron barriers. The train's appearance reminded the refugees of their status: all the coaches were third class, with wooden seats; the manner in which it had been prepared reminded them of the suspicion with which they were still viewed: all the windows were barred and nailed firmly shut. Once the passengers were on the train, they were locked inside. The police who accompanied them, and watched their every move on the way to Brussels, told the refugees the precautions had been taken for their own safety. Those who had been selected for Belgium would spend Saturday night in various hotels in the capital, before being moved on the next day.

By nine o'clock in the evening, a little before the Belgian passengers arrived in Brussels, the relief workers on the St. Louis had completed the final reckoning. A French consular official boarded and gave those who would be bound for France a card stamped "Refugees from the St. Louis."

Otto Bergmann received his, and observed later in his diary: "In order to get permission to enter France we had to come to Antwerp in Belgium. And to get to Belgium, we had to travel to Cuba."

SUNDAY, JUNE 18, 1939

On Sunday, the 181 passengers who were to travel to Holland were awakened at 5 A.M., and given breakfast an hour later as the little steamer which was to take them to Rotterdam, the Jan van Arckel, came alongside the St. Louis. Although it would have been quicker, and more convenient, for them to travel by land, the Belgian authorities had decreed that only those destined for Belgium could actually land at Antwerp.

Before boarding the Jan van Arckel, Gertrud Scheuer, the popular girl who was friendly with Assistant Purser Reich, had a proposition put to her by one of the crew. He offered to hide her in a cleaning cupboard, to feed and look after her, and then to smuggle her off when the ship docked in New York. Although she did not want to go to the Netherlands, she turned down the offer, believing, "he might throw me overboard or something if I didn't do what he asked."

Accompanied by Alfred Moser, the Dutch contingent left at nine-thirty in the morning and began the journey through the complicated waterway system to Rotterdam. In front of and behind the Jan van Arckel was an escort of river-police boats reminiscent of the departure from Havana; along both sides of the narrow canals, the now famous refugees were waved at and called to by hundreds of well-wishers.

They arrived at Rotterdam at five o'clock in the afternoon, and were immediately interned in the quarantine station of Heijplaat, where many hundreds of other German refugees already languished, all awaiting somewhere to go. Most would remain in the camp for weeks, and few would ultimately survive. Up to fifty people were crowded into some of the long, barrack like rooms.

Outside, the camp was surrounded by barbed wire, and watched by guard dogs.

Back on the St. Louis, the remaining passengers, feeling very strange in the ship that for so long was packed to capacity and now was half empty, had an early lunch in preparation for boarding the Rhakotis—the Hapag passenger/cargo vessel which they had been told had been specially prepared to take them to France and England.

In fact, the Rhakotis was an eleven-year-old freighter, with first-class cabins for 28 and tourist cabins for 24. Soon it would carry 512 people. In three days, Hapag had hastily converted the ship, filling its two large cargo holds with rows of double-decker steel bunks, and long tables for eating on in the centre. The women would be segregated from the men and sleep communally in the forward Hold, the men

CAMEO 10: GERTRUD SCHEUER:

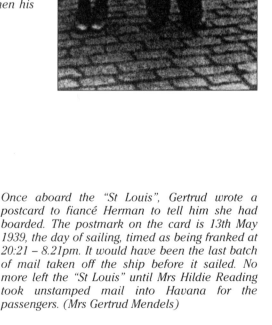

This is the Scheuer family, a portrait taken in Mainz in 1936. Gertrud's brother, Fritz and her father, Edmund Scheuer are standing. Sitting is Mrs Hedwig Scheuer, flanked by her daughters Ruth (left) and Gertrud. The photo was taken just before Fritz left Germany to live in South Africa. Hedwig and Edmund fell victims to the Holocaust in October 1944. Pictured right are Gertrud and her fiancé, Herman Mendels, in Frankfurt in 1938. Herman left Germany shortly afterwards when his visa was issued for migration to the United States. (Mrs Gertrud Mendels)

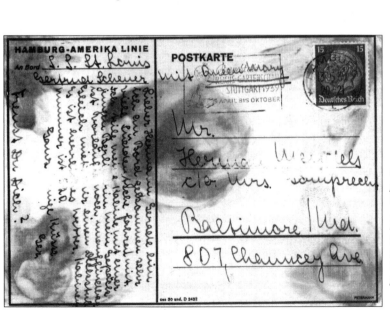

Once aboard the "St Louis", Gertrud wrote a postcard to fiancé Herman to tell him she had boarded. The postmark on the card is 13th May 1939, the day of sailing, timed as being franked at 20:21 – 8.21pm. It would have been the last batch of mail taken off the ship before it sailed. No more left the "St Louis" until Mrs Hildie Reading took unstamped mail into Havana for the passengers. (Mrs Gertrud Mendels)

Halve schon Kaffee am Bord getrunk

This is the front face of another postcard which Gertrud Scheuer bought, with the intention of mailing them on arrival in Havana, to tell friends and family what the ship looked like. She, like others, often wrote down on anything that was available, their impressions of certain things or events. Gertud Scheuer was moved to scribble a little note on this card about the excellent quality of the coffee on board the "St Louis" (Mrs Gertrud Mendels)

On the way out to Havana, whilst Atlantic breezes still blew cool, this picture was taken of Gertrud on deck on 19th May 1939. (Mrs Gertrud Mendels)

And this is the happy ending that many people dream of – just after the wedding of Gertrud to Herman Mendels, who had joined the US Army as the United States entered the Second World War. He was promoted to Master Sergeant during his short service and was sent to Europe, where he found Gertrud again after she emerged from hiding. They were married on October 18th 1945, after hostilities had ceased in both European and Pacific theatres of war, at the synagogue in Utrecht, in Holland. They had both travelled over 10,000 miles to be married less than 400 miles from home. (Mrs Gertrud Mendels)

Here, the children disembarking at Antwerp are greeted by Baroness Rothschild, who provided a great deal of aid and support. (Mrs Alice Oster)

aft. There was nowhere to change. The too-few lavatories had been set up on deck.

Boarding began about two o'clock Sunday afternoon. Purser Mueller and his staff handed out a box containing sandwiches and sweets to each passenger as the last of them finally took their leave of the St. Louis. By mid afternoon, all had boarded the Rhakotis, and the cargo vessel was towed upstream, where it was to spend the night; for security reasons, the Belgians did not allow it to remain alongside the St. Louis after four o'clock. For the rest of the day and into the early evening, the passengers' luggage was taken from the St. Louis and put on the quay, awaiting collection in the morning by the Rhakotis.

The last message Captain Schröder received before sailing for New York was from Hapag director Claus-Gottfried Holthusen in Hamburg. In part, it read:

The Board of the Hamburg-America Line wishes to express its thanks to you for bringing back the St. Louis safely. The purser's report gives a perceptive picture of your journey, and we give you our fullest sympathy. We congratulate you for the way you dealt with your crew and passengers, and hope that on your journey to New York, you will find new strength to fulfil the pleasure cruises.

Just after midnight, on the very day the St. Louis had always been scheduled to leave Europe for New York, the ship began slowly to pull away from pier 18. On the Rhakotis, passengers silently watched her go with, according to Rosemarie Bergmann, "one dry and one wet eye." The St. Louis crew lined the rails, and as they passed the Rhakotis they shouted: "Good luck to the Jews." It was a moving moment, and one even the most bitter of the refugees would never forget.

Most of Captain Schröder's crew had decided to stay with him, partly fearing a return to Germany, where they would almost certainly have been severely criticised for their generally compassionate treatment of the Jewish passengers. One of the few who did sign off at Antwerp carried a Cuban walking stick, a sheaf of magazines, and a pocket full of pens—Abwehr agent and ship's Ortsgruppenleiter Otto Schiendick. Captain Schröder was not sorry to lose him.

The air in the overcrowded converted cargo holds had soon become stale and unbearable. Many of the refugees on the Rhakotis chose to spend the night in the open air on deck, sleeping on mattresses and deck chairs. The few cabins which were not allocated to the extra crew were used by the more fortunate passengers. Each member of the passenger committee and his family had one, as did Rosemarie

Hamburg-Amerika Linie

Drahtwort: Oceanfahrt Hamburg

Ihr Zeichen: Unser Zeichen:

Antwerp, 18th of June 39
M.S. - St. Louis

To Mr Morris Carlton Troper
Chairman European Executive Council
American Joint Distribution Committee
Paris

Before I leave Antwerp I take the opportunity to thank you once more sincerely for the cooperation we have received from you personally and the different Committees in organizing so efficiently the distribution of my passengers and with this helping to arrange their debarkation so speedily. The Rhakotis has taken the contingents for France and England already.

I am sure with this satisfactory ending I join the passengers with my personal thanks and appreciation for all you have done.

Sincerely

G. Schröder -

Captain Schröder, clearly greatly relieved at the outcome of the voyage, and deeply moved by the efforts made by Morris Troper to accommodate the passengers outside Germany, wrote this letter. It needs no further explanation. (Mrs Betty Troper-Yaeger)

Bergmann's mother and Aunt Shalote; two stewardesses gave up their berths so the elderly ladies could have a restful night.

MONDAY, JUNE 19, 1939

On Monday, the passengers were awakened as the Rhakotis moved in to the quay, berthing at pier 18, which the St. Louis had vacated the night before.

Although conditions on board left much to be desired, spirits remained high. Passengers commented on the superior quality of the food: "We had fresh eggs for the first time in three weeks." The meals were served on the long tables in the holds: "We practically had breakfast in bed."

At two o'clock in the afternoon, Morris Troper came to the ship. He shook hands with each member of the passenger committee, and then the American who had succeeded where his own country had failed was applauded and waved good-bye to as he left by car for Paris. An hour later, the Rhakotis departed for Boulogne, travelling close to the Belgian and French coasts. Soon it began to rain heavily, driving the passengers down into the cargo holds. In the confined atmosphere, Otto Bergmann confided to his diary: "I fear it is still possible for a cable to recall us to Germany."

TUESDAY, JUNE 20, 1939

The Rhakotis arrived in Boulogne at four-thirty on Tuesday morning, and was ordered, as the St. Louis had been so many weeks before at Cherbourg, to anchor out in the harbour. At ten o'clock, the purser and stewards on the Rhakotis gave a packed lunch to each of the 224 passengers to disembark in France.

As they boarded a small tender for the trip ashore, Raoul Lambert, the Secretary-General of the Comite d'Assistance aux Refugies, welcomed them with the words: "I greet you on Free French soil." Lambert himself would soon die in a Nazi concentration camp.

On shore, the French porters refused to accept tips for carrying the passengers' luggage.

The refugees would spend Tuesday night in hotels around Boulogne before being moved the next day.

The remaining 288 refugees, the largest contin-gent, departed from Boulogne for Great Britain Tuesday evening just as, in New York, the Joint was releasing an official communiqué stating that the "St. Louis rescue operation is not to be taken as a precedent, and would not be repeated in the future."

WEDNESDAY, JUNE 21, 1939

The passengers were greeted in Southampton at noon on Wednesday—midsummer night, the longest day—by a spectacular display. The harbour was gaily decorated, sirens wailed, the fire fighting boats sent sprays of water dramatically high into the air. It was not until they had landed that the refugees learned it was actually a rehearsal for the arrival of King George VI and Queen Elizabeth, due in Southampton the next day. They too had been on a trip to the "New World."

As the passengers stepped ashore, at least one of them, Fritz Gotthelf, the Berliner who had been a member of the suicide patrol, "knelt down, and kissed the earth." At two o'clock, they left by train and arrived at London's Waterloo station—platform 13—at 3:45 P.M. There some sixty of the single, able-bodied men were immediately dispatched to the famous "Kitchener Camp" at Richborough, which was to become a temporary home for nearly 5000 men awaiting emigration to the U.S.A., Palestine, or South America. The rest of the passengers were housed in small hotels and private houses.

After precisely forty days and forty nights of wandering on the high seas, the last passengers from the St. Louis had found their Promised Land.

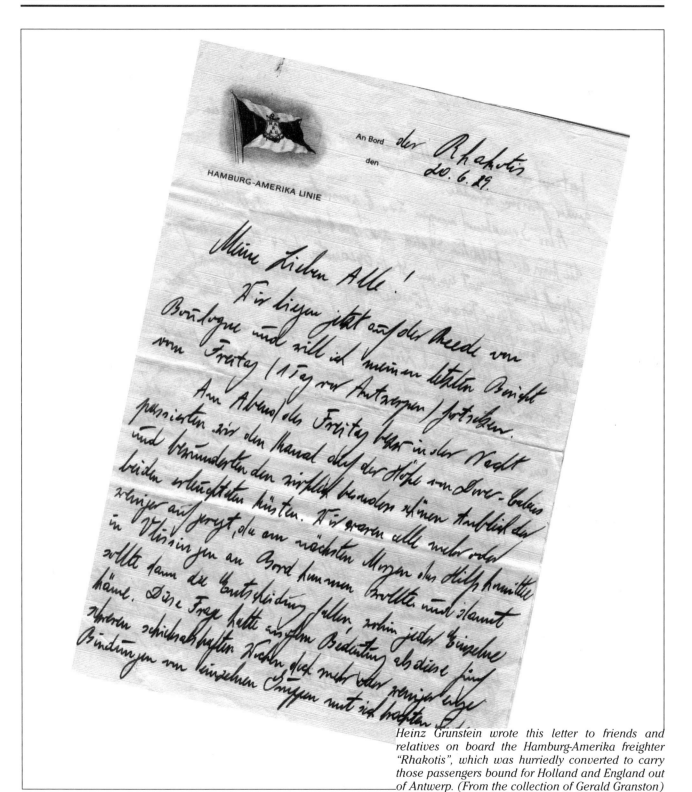

Heinz Grunstein wrote this letter to friends and relatives on board the Hamburg-Amerika freighter "Rhakotis", which was hurriedly converted to carry those passengers bound for Holland and England out of Antwerp. (From the collection of Gerald Granston)

EPILOGUE

For many of the refugees on the St. Louis, their rescue proved to be the beginning of the end.

The 288 who went to England were the luckiest, although at first it must not have appeared so to them. Soon after war was declared, early in September 1939, as German nationals, they were all classified as enemy aliens, and the men interned.

At Kitchener's camp at Richborough, an Aliens Tribunal was set up to examine the internees. Of the 3500 men then there, the loyalty to Britain of only one was found to be doubtful. The first Alien Companies of the Pioneer Corps—initially organised as a non combat military force—were raised and trained. More than half the refugees in the camp volunteered, although they knew that if they were caught by the Germans they might be tried as traitors and shot.

In 1940, the first Alien Pioneer Company went to France, under the leadership of Major F. J. Brister, the man who had represented Britain on the St. Louis in Antwerp Harbour, and who now had in his command men from the ship he had chosen for Britain when the allocation of passengers was made. During the retreat to Dunkirk, they were given arms and, according to all reports, fought bravely. Later they were dispersed among regular British army regiments. Some even went into a special unit of commandos composed exclusively of refugees, mostly German Jews, whose burning hatred of the Nazis made them formidable fighters. Half of them died.

Elise Loewe and her two children were among the St. Louis passengers fortunate enough to be chosen for England, the country Max Loewe had thought too close to Germany when he decided originally to take his family to Cuba. In England, Elise Loewe still did not know the fate of her husband in Havana after his suicide attempt, but in 1940 he was released from the Cuban hospital and somehow made his way to London to be reunited with his family. There, in 1942, aged only fifty-one, he died of a heart ailment probably stemming from his suicide attempts in Havana. In 1947, Elise Loewe took her children to the United States, where they reside today.

The head of the passenger committee, Josef Joseph, and his wife Lilli and daughter Liesl were, after landing in Britain, guests on the estate of the millionaire Rowntree family in York. Though they were

offered a stay there for the duration of the war, Joseph was anxious to emigrate to the United States, and after three months they moved to London. In May 1940, just a year after boarding the St. Louis, Joseph was interned on the Isle of Man as an enemy alien. In September, the family was allowed to book passage for New York, and Lilli and Liesl left London in the middle of an air raid, to travel in a blacked-out train filled with refugees to Glasgow where all the families were to meet their husbands, travelling from internment on a separate train.

When they arrived in Glasgow, it too was having an air raid. After many delays and anxious moments caused by the bombing the families were united, along with 350 British children being evacuated to America. Vastly overcrowded, unarmed, without convoy or escort for two days the ship was shadowed by a U-boat, but it was not torpedoed and arrived safely.

Josef Joseph later died in America. Lilli remarried, and today, in her seventies and still beautiful, she lives in a suburb of New York, where she trustingly loaned us original hand-written passenger committee notes and the drafts of their telegrams to world leaders, as well as much else to do with the St. Louis. She and her daughter Liesl were fortunate to survive. Both of Lilli's sisters, their husbands and children, her mother, and her husband's sisters died in German concentration camps.

In France, after the first night in Boulogne, most of the St. Louis refugees went either to Laval or Le Mans, arriving after midnight.

Herbert Manasse, the youngest member of the passenger committee, continued to carry responsibility for certain St. Louis passengers, leading and looking after the group who went to Laval. When France was occupied, he attempted to escape with his wife and two young children to Italy, but they were caught and sent to Auschwitz, where the entire family was gassed.

Rosemarie and Otto Bergmann, the newly married couple who had promised to chaperon eighty-year-old Shalote Hecht for the two weeks of the voyage, found themselves instead taking care of her for almost two years.

Soon after war was declared, Otto was interned in France as an enemy alien. Rosemarie, with her ailing mother and aunt Shalote, moved into a hotel room in Vichy, paid for by money sent from friends in the United States. There the young woman looked after her "two old ladies" for thirteen months until Otto bribed his way out of internment in October 1940, made his way to Marseilles, and at the U.S. Consulate, managed to get his group on the American quota. At Bordeaux, he got a temporary visa for the Dominican Republic, allowing them to wait there until their U.S. quota number came up.

Aunt Shalote refused to leave France, choosing instead to go to friends in Nice, where she died three months later.

In the meantime, Otto and Rosemarie Bergmann and Rosemarie's mother began the long journey to freedom. First they travelled to the south coast and near Perpignan, hired two French fishermen to row them by night to Spain. They made the journey without being discovered and continued on to Lisbon.

In Lisbon, Emanuel Rosen, the man who had helped Morris Troper on the St. Louis, and who had not been able to offer Rosemarie advice regarding her dog Oshey, had set up an office of the Joint when the Paris office was closed. Between 1940 and 1942, Manny Rosen guided many hundreds of refugees through Spain to North Africa and Portugal, among them passengers he had met on the St. Louis.

The Bergmanns and Rosemarie's mother made their way to Portugal. From there they got a ship to New York, where they stayed only long enough to transfer to another ship for Santo Domingo. In Santo Domingo, they were, at last, reunited with their dog Oshey, who, according to Rosemarie, was "skinny as a chicken. It had pined for us ever since Havana. It, too, had suffered because of the Nazis."

The group was finally allowed into the United States in 1941; six months after arriving, Rosemarie's mother died.

Marianne Bardeleben, the ten-year-old who had been barely able to recognise her father in one of the little boats in Havana Harbour, found herself, the day war was declared, alone and frightened in a cheap lodging house room somewhere in France—she did not know where—with only her nine-year-old friend from the St. Louis, Ruth Fischer, for company. Their mothers had gone to Paris to get bona fide visas for Cuba, where their fathers still were, and were unable to return to the children for a week. Travel had virtually come to a halt. The girls were alone in a strange country whose language they could not speak.

Four months later, on Christmas Eve, both families left Le Havre on the liner De Grasse in a convoy of nearly 100 ships bound for the United States. Most of the ships in the convoy were sunk in the English Channel by U-boats, but the De Grasse got through.

During the trip, the ringworm which Marianne had contracted while living in the louse-ridden room in France grew worse. The ship's doctor promptly shaved her head. It was covered with open sores. When they arrived at New York, because of the ringworm Marianne and her mother were confined to Ellis Island. Marianne described it:

"A sort of prison. I was put in the hospital and remember finding a dead mouse in my slipper one morning. I was still only ten. Every day they shaved my head and put red iodine on it. The pain was excruciating. I could only speak German. No one talked to me. No doctor, no nurse, no one. My mother wasn't allowed to visit me. They put me in a Boy Scout uniform, short pants, and took me out into the snow for exercise. At ten years of age, with my open sore shaved head painted red, in my Boy Scout uniform, the humiliation was terrible."

Marianne and her mother left Ellis Island when their American visitors permits expired and they were forced to leave the United States.

"Then, only then," Marianne recalled, "the doctor spoke to me. In German! He could speak German, but all the time I had been in the hospital he had never said a word to me. I thought he was crueller than the Nazis."

In Havana, Cuban officials once again told them they could not enter the country to join her father, this time because of Marianne's head wound. The child was overcome with guilt; she believed all the family's troubles were her fault. Her mother assured her they would both commit suicide if they were not allowed in. The next day, they were admitted. Marianne's father had bribed officials.

In 1942, when their quota number finally came up, they returned to New York. But even then, Marianne's sense of humiliation was not over. Because her English was still not perfect, she was put in the first grade, a twelve-year-old with children half her age. For her, the humiliation was complete.

In Belgium, the Joint paid for the upkeep of the St. Louis refugees. Among them was passenger committee member Ernst Vendig, his wife and their three children. After Belgium was overrun, he was interned, escaped, collected his family, and made his way to freedom by crossing the Swiss Alps on foot.

Carl and George Lenneberg, who had been in Dachau before joining the St. Louis, made their escape in April 1940, just before the Germans arrived. They got out via Dunkirk, as did so many others.

The father, mother, aunt, and uncle of Hildie Reading, the girl who had boarded the St. Louis in Havana and given her parents $1700, also tried to escape through Dunkirk. They failed. Her uncle was caught and sent to a concentration camp, where he died.

Hildie Reading's mother, father, and aunt returned to Belgium and went underground. They lived in an abandoned store, its front boarded up, its back looking onto a cemetery. There they stayed for five years. Only one Belgian family knew where they were, and with the $1700 Hildie had given them, they paid the family to keep quiet, and bought food. Without the money, they might not have survived.

Alice Feilchenfeld and her four children spent the entire war in Brussels. Although the dollars she received weekly from the Joint were enough to pay for a decent apartment, she chose to live in a rooming house in a poor district because, she recalled, "there the Germans didn't seem to trouble us much, and the poor non-Jewish Belgians did not 'squeal' on anyone. Not like some of the rich people did." For a time, Alice Feilchenfeld and her children lived in their top floor room by day, and by night they hid in a morgue beside a hospital filled with German soldiers.

When the Germans arrived, the Joint left. From then on, the Belgian government made regular welfare payments to the Jews, never divulging their names or addresses to the Germans. In 1946, Alice Feilchenfeld took her children to America, where they rejoined their father, from whom they had been separated since late 1938. Today, she lives in the New Utrecht area of Brooklyn, with memories of looking after her four children for seven years, alone, bravely, most of the time in hiding—an example of courage for her daughter Judith, who lives nearby; now grown up, and with her own family of nine children.

In Holland, Gertrud Scheuer also spent the war in hiding, part of the time in a house near the one in which Anne Frank was writing her famous diary. She

survived and now lives in a Baltimore suburb. She had worked as a maid, moving from family to family, always one step ahead of the Germans.

She was in the minority. Most of the refugees in the Netherlands were to die in the gas chambers, after first passing through Holland's notorious transit camp, Westerbork. Westerbork was planned and built by the Dutch government before the outbreak of war to house German refugees. It opened in October 1939, and among its first inmates were the Dutch contingent from the St. Louis.

The 250-acre camp was completely isolated, set on a windswept plain in an area little better than a peat bog, and from the beginning, conditions were deplorable. The place was a haven for disease-carrying flies and vermin of all kinds; when it rained, it became a swamp. Even so, when the Gestapo took over Westerbork in 1942 from the Dutch, staying in the camp would be safer than leaving, though the refugees did not know it.

But they were not allowed to stay. For two years, every Tuesday, week in, week out, the cattle trucks at Westerbork were loaded with their human freight and trundled off to the gas ovens of Germany and Poland. Westerbork became another word for purgatory.

Alfred Moser, the Dutch relief worker who had shepherded his St. Louis flock to Antwerp, was interned in Westerbork. From there, he was taken to Belsen, but he miraculously survived. On the basis of a fake Paraguayan passport purchased for him by a friend in Switzerland, Moser was taken by train with some 300 other Jews from Belsen, to Berlin, and then to Switzerland. Many of his fellows had typhoid and died on the way before the Swiss Red Cross could save them.

Aaron Pozner was also interned in Westerbork. Before he was taken by cattle train to Auschwitz, he gave his diary to a friend, and it survived. Aaron Pozner, along with the hundred thousand others who passed through Westerbork, did not. The fate of his family is not known.

Fritz Spanier, his wife Babette, and their twin daughters went to Westerbork.

The girls had looked forward to their time in Holland on the St. Louis in Antwerp. Dr. Spanier told them it was a beautiful country of tulips and daffodils. Years later, they found their experiences in

Westerbork too painful to recall, remembering only "the bloodhounds and the rats."

They survived because of the extraordinary power Fritz Spanier wielded in Westerbork. At one point he was even able to have his wife and the children removed from one of the cattle trains bound for Auschwitz; S.S. guards obeyed his order to unbar the door and let his family out.

Dr. Spanier became the chief medical doctor of Westerbork, in charge of a large hospital with 1725 beds, 120 physicians, and a general staff of over 1000. He had a mysterious influence over the camp commandant, and did not even bother to stand in his presence, something no one else dared. He held the power of life and death over his fellow refugees, because those he accepted into his hospital, or whom he told the camp commandant were too ill to travel, generally were not put on the trains to the concentration camps.

In 1944, Dr. Spanier called together five of his doctors and told them they had been ordered to sterilise all the Jewish women in Westerbork who were married to non-Jews. Once sterilised, so the Gestapo said, they would not be subject to deportation. If the doctors refused to carry out the order, it would mean either deportation or death.

One of the doctors, a woman, did refuse to carry out the sterilisation order, and her decision caused it to be re-examined. Surprisingly, the order was withdrawn. The refugees who chose sterilisation instead of deportation had the operation performed by Jewish or Dutch doctors outside Westerbork, and for a time received special privileges. But in the end, they too were sent to the concentration camps.

Dr. Spanier was later accused of abusing his power in Westerbork, of helping those who had the "right connections," of being too friendly with the S.S. If he was, perhaps he remembered that in a way he and his family owed their life to the young S.S. officer who had originally driven them to Hamburg to board the St. Louis. Whatever the truth, Dr. Spanier's hospital in Westerbork was a model of efficiency, though in fact it only kept people alive for the gas chambers.

Fritz Spanier and his family stayed in Westerbork throughout the war. When Holland was liberated, Dr. Spanier returned immediately to Germany, to the terrible extermination camp of Belsen. There he worked with survivors, especially the young, and became almost as well known as he had been in Westerbork. Later, having decided once again to make his home in Germany, he opened an office in Duesseldorf. He died in 1967.

Today, the Spanier twins are both married and live in the United States with their families. Renee and Ines still find it too upsetting to recall what they experienced in the Dutch transit camp.

Their mother lives alone in a modest apartment in Cologne, West Germany, wasted by time and experience, leaving only her eyes to remind one of those news photographs on the St. Louis when her bright stare had looked out of scores of front pages. For several hours, virtually without interruption, she told us of events surrounding the voyage, with that attention to detail that makes a born raconteuse. She conjured up the feeling of 1939, that harsh time when no Jew would have dared enter the Dom Hotel, where she talked to us. Did we realise, she asked, that on the balcony of the very room next door to where we sat, the balcony of suite 108, Hitler had delivered some of his most virulent anti-Semitic propaganda?

It sounded an improbable story until we checked with the Dom's head porter. He could still clearly remember Hitler standing on the balcony and haranguing 50,000 people below in the Grossplatz of the cathedral.

Babette Spanier urged us to call on Dr. Spanier's second wife, Njuta. We found her near the Hofgarten in Dusseldorf, a small, tidy woman whose only bond with Babette Spanier is that they both loved the same man.

Njuta Spanier's memories are kept alive by fading newspaper reports of the St. Louis saga; she also has a collection of letters, documents, and snapshots, all of which have a curious, two-dimensional effect, heightened by the knowledge that although she had not been on the ship, for years afterward she had acted as a sounding board for Dr. Spanier, faithfully storing in her mind all that he had told her about the event.

From a corner of the apartment a caged parrot suddenly screeched, interrupting our discussion. Njuta Spanier explained that her late husband had taught the bird to speak "so that his voice would live on for me after he was gone."

In Cuba it was not easy for a middle-aged man

with no money to learn a new language, study for American medical examinations, and cook for, keep amused, bathe, and clothe two young girls—all on a few dollars a week. Dr. Max Aber looked after his daughters, Renatta and Evelyne, as best he could and by 1941 he was in America, a practising doctor.

In 1973, at the age of seventy-eight looking much younger than his years, still attending to patients in Cape Cod, Dr. Aber described the Cuban newspaper report of 1939 that he was a "millionaire" as a "prognosis not altogether incorrect."

No one can say with certainty how many of the St. Louis passengers eventually perished. One estimate states that of the 907 who were returned to Europe only 240 lived. Those who died became part of the "final solution"—a total of six million Jews who perished as a result of Hitler's policies.

If those from the St. Louis survived the war and the concentration camps in the same proportion as did their fellows, then in France, 180 would have lived out of the 224 who went there; in Belgium, 152 out of 214; in Holland, only 60 out of 181. Most of the 288 who went to Britain lived. What is certain is that if Cuba or the United States had opened their doors, almost no one from the ship need have died.

A disproportionate number of those featured in this book survived, for it was largely from personal interviews with them or their families and from accounts written by them at the time that we were able to piece together Voyage of the Damned.

Today, scattered throughout the world, mostly uncertain of each other's existence, the survivors tend to have one thing in common: a love of life and an enthusiasm for living it every day to the full. Having been near death, escaping through a miracle of chance, they realise how precious and precarious life is. They also have an uncommon respect and affection for the people and countries that gave them the chance to live.

Most members of the crew of the St. Louis served in the German armed forces in the war, among them Leo Jockl. In 1941, plumper, his receding hairline more pronounced, he joined the German navy. By then he had fallen in love with a beautiful Aryan girl, Gerda Kickbush, whose father was a high-ranking Nazi official in Berlin. He soon told her of his background, and she insisted that it made no difference to their love. But her family was not so tolerant.

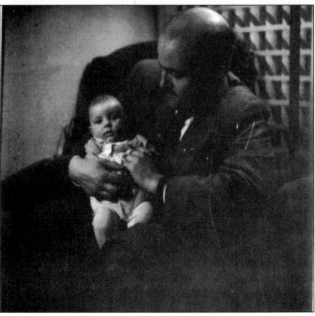

These three pictures show Leo Jockl and his family. Firstly, Leo himself photographed for an identity card, but now with a moustache, and then with his baby son, Frank. The other picture is of Gerda Jockl with the baby. The quality of the pictures is poor, for which the editors apologise, but they felt they should be included. (Mrs Gerda Jockl)

Gerda's mother denounced Jockl to Nazi party headquarters in Berlin. Soon afterward Gerda found she was pregnant. Unable to marry because of the infamous Nuremberg Laws forbidding unions between Jews and gentiles, ostracised by her family, Gerda stood by her man. They lived a cat-and-mouse existence with the Gestapo.

In January 1944, Jockl was drafted into a road gang of "half Jews." Their role was to act as human mine sweepers for German troops trying to stop the Allied invasion of the Fatherland. At three minutes past 2 P.M. on November 17, 1944, near Aachen, an American fighter strafed the road gang, killing Leo.

Today his widow—they were one of the first couples to be "married posthumously" in post-war West Germany—lives in West Berlin with her son Frank and her memories and mementoes. Among them is a letter a St. Louis passenger wrote to Leo: "I think my whole life will never be enough to thank you

for what you did for us." Gerda Jockl believes it is the finest epitaph she would ever want for her husband.

Otto Schiendick has many epitaphs among surviving crewmen who remember and disliked him. Men like former steward Paul Zochert, pastry cook Christian Muhlbacher, stewards Hermann Kempe and Pieter Schmitt. Paul Bendowski, the ship's photographer and his wife, Irene, who was the ladies' hairdresser on the St. Louis, told us that Schiendick was "as nasty as they come—and a bully, too."

Around 1940, Schiendick worked in the overseas Message Centre, the nerve centre of the German secret service, a massive underground concrete cavern below the tree-shaded suburb of Wohldorf in Hamburg. In early 1945, British troops occupied the city as the Germans were demolishing the centre. Among the sabotage squad was Otto Schiendick. As he scrambled clear of the ruins, a British patrol shot him dead.

Purser Mueller and First Officer Ostermeyer survived the war only to fall into Russian hands. The last they were heard of by other crewmen, they were living quietly in East Germany; their material was made available to us by sources that must remain anonymous.

Captain Gustav Schröder survived.

After taking the St. Louis from Antwerp to New York in June 1939, he carried out the planned summer cruises to the Caribbean. He was forbidden by the German embassy to refer in public or in private to the refugee trip. Cruise passengers reported him charming and the ship gracious, although the crew was "jittery" after the Cuban voyage.

On August 26, 1939, the St. Louis was scheduled to depart New York for Bermuda, but its passengers were abruptly told the trip had been cancelled. The next day, the ship sailed empty, departing her pier at Forty-sixth Street at 8 P.M., and was at sea when war was declared on September 3.

Captain Schröder ran the British blockade and reached safety in Murmansk, Russia. There, all but the engineers on the St. Louis travelled by train to Leningrad, and on to Germany. After a stay of four months in Murmansk, still under Schröder's command, the St. Louis made a dash for Hamburg, arriving on New Year's Day, 1940, the last of the Hapag ships on the North American run to reach home port. Schröder took a desk job, never to return to sea again.

The St. Louis was badly damaged by the Royal Air Force in 1944, and at war's end lay as a burned-out hulk in Hamburg Harbour. For a time, after part of it was renovated, the ship was used as a floating hotel. In 1950, it was sold for scrap and broken up.

The Rhakotis, the freighter that had taken the passengers to France and England, was sunk by a British cruiser in 1943.

After the war, Schröder tried to make a living as a writer, sometimes using parts of his diary of the voyage in his books. However, they were not very successful financially, and some of his refugee passengers helped by sending him food and clothing. They also came to his assistance when, under the de-Nazification process, he was put on trial; their testimony helped to acquit him. In 1957, two years before his death, Gustav Schröder received a citation and medal from the West German government for the part he played in saving the lives of his passengers on the voyage to Cuba.

PICTURE EPILOGUE:

The Press had varying levels of interest in the "St Louis" story, but this headline from "Der Stürmer" of May 1939 tells its readers "Jews Emigrate", or more literally: "Jewish Wanderers Out", which seems more appropriate to the mood of the paper, which went on to say in one of the sub-headings below: "When Jews Pioneer the Jewish Opposition in all the World". This attempt to stir world hatred was part of Josef Goebbels' campaign plan attached to the "St Louis" voyage. (Authors' Collection)

ES JUIFS ERRANTS DU "SAINT-LOUIS"

e Passagiere an Deck der St Louis kurz vor der Landung in Antwerpen. Manche
sichter lächeln, denn die schlimmsten Schrecken sind überstanden, aber viele spiegeln
ch noch die Sorgen und Ängste wider, welche hinter ihnen liegen. Die Sorge auch,
was man weiter werden soll.

The photo above, taken from a copy of the "Schweizer Illustrierte Zeitung" ("Swiss Illustrated Times"), shows the passengers at the rail of the "St Louis" prior to disembarkation at Antwerp. (Mrs Hella Roubicek). The small lower picture is from a French newspaper of unknown origin. (Mrs Renate Breslow)

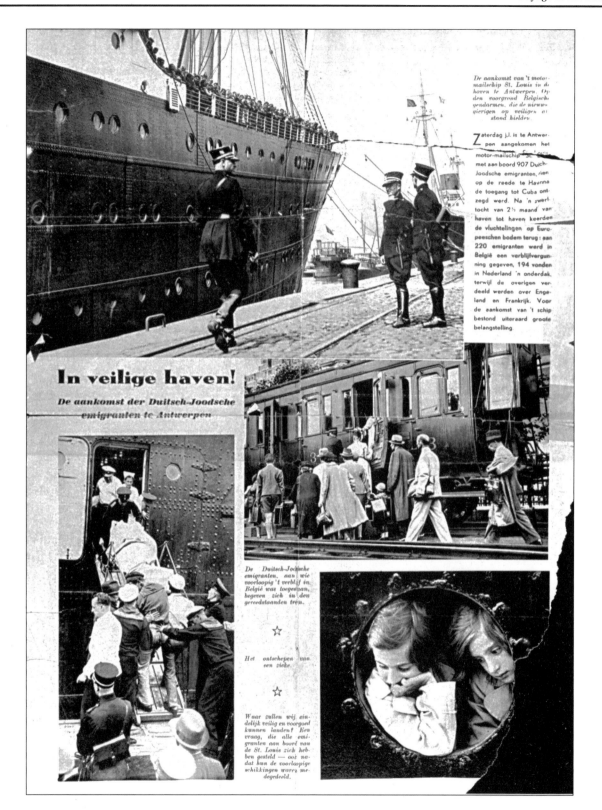

De aankomst van 't motor-mailschip St. Louis in de haven te Antwerpen. Op den voorgrond Belgische gendarmen, die de nieuwsgierigen op veiligen afstand hielden.

Zaterdag j.l. is te Antwerpen aangekomen het motor-mailschip St. Louis met aan boord 907 Duitsch-Joodsche emigranten, wien op de reede te Havanna de toegang tot Cuba ontzegd werd. Na 'n zwerftocht van 2½ maand van haven tot haven keerden de vluchtelingen op Europeeschen bodem terug: aan 220 emigranten werd in België een verblijfvergunning gegeven, 194 vonden in Nederland 'n onderdak, terwijl de overigen verdeeld werden over Engeland en Frankrijk. Voor de aankomst van 't schip bestond uiteraard groote belangstelling

In veilige haven!

De aankomst der Duitsch-Joodsche emigranten te Antwerpen

De Duitsch-Joodsche emigranten, aan wie voorloopig 't verblijf in België was toegestaan, begeven zich in den gereedstaanden trein.

☆

Het ontschepen van een zieke.

☆

Waar zullen wij eindelijk veilig en voorgoed kunnen landen? Een vraag, die alle emigranten aan boord van de St. Louis zich hebben gesteld — ook nadat hun de voorloopige schikkingen waren medegedeeld.

For a day or two, the Dutch press gave quite a lot of space, as shown in these two clippings (opposite and above), to the "St Louis" story, then it faded from the headlines. (Mrs Gertrud Mendels)

THE REFUGEES

ST. LOUIS VICTIMS LAND

Temporary Homes in Four Cou[...]

GENERAL SYMPATHY AROUS[...]

[From our Correspondents]

The tragedy of the 907 Jewish refugees on the Ham[...] liner St. Louis, which has been roaming the high sea[...] Hamburg for Cuba on May 13, has been ended—for th[...] by the kindly gesture of four Governments: the Belgia[...] the initiative in allowing 250 to land in Antwerp, th[...] French, and the Dutch.

The liner arrived at Antwerp at about 2 o'clock last [...] noon with all the passengers on board, but it was not [...] hours later that the first batch began to disembark. In[...] hundreds of persons, most of them Jews, were crowding[...] near the quay, watching the passengers, who were w[...] They were kept away by strong forces of police. [...] occurred, but anti-Jewish leaflets were distributed. No[...] arrived some years ago has such interest been aroused[...]

The chief Alderman of Antwerp was present, and am[...] went on board was the Commissioner of Emigration,[...] thirty years, has been protecting the interests of em[...] through Belgium, and representatives of the Jewish emi[...] Ezra, and of the refugee committees. A represe[...] American Joint, which made the landing of the passe[...] and delegates of various Jewish and non-Jewish bodies[...] including the Quakers, had already boarded the steame[...] launch at Flushing, where the arduous work of selecti[...] suitable for each country had begun.

The passengers had only been informed a few days [...] long period of anguish and anxiety, that they would [...] Germany, and there were moving and touching scenes [...] came on board. The children were placed in rows to g[...] passengers speak well of the treatment they received or[...] the kindness shown by the captain. They are not [...] emigrant class, and as one scanned their faces one realis[...] bestiality but also the stupidity of the Nazi regime. They[...] dressed, but neither this nor the fact that thousands [...] unloaded was any indication of their means, becau[...] remembered that their personal belongings were in ma[...] that they could save.

Whilst the rescue work proceeded, a swastika flag wa[...] the mast of the liner. The irony of it became more app[...] recalled that the St. Louis belongs to the Hamburg [...] which the Jew, Albert Ballin, made into one of the [...] steamship lines.

T[...] 270 refugees to whom Belgium is giving sanctu[...] by special train to Brussels, and they are now at th[...] owned Chateau de Marneffe, in the province of Liège[...]

Arrival in Holland

Some 180 refugees arrived in Rotterdam, Holla[...] evening, and temporary accommodation was found f[...] quarantine station. They were isolated there, and not [...] relatives were allowed in to see them. According to a [...] by the Minister of Justice, it is intended to distribute[...] among the existing camps, and to prepare them for emigration else-where.

Two hundred and twenty-three of the St. Louis passengers landed in France on Tuesday morning from the tender Rhakodis. They were permitted to take up residence anywhere in France, except in Paris.

To demonstrate their sympathy with the refugees, the Boulogne dock-porters declined to accept payment for their work of transferring the baggage. The local authorities are providing free accommodation.

The French officials, co-operating with representatives of the American Joint and the Hicem, expedited the formalities so that all passengers were disembarked within half an hour.

Mr. Morris C. Troper, Chairman of the European Executive Council of the Joint, who supervised the arrival of the St. Louis passengers at Antwerp, paid a high tribute to the co-operation given by the French and Belgian authorities.

Some 250 in England

---

40 DAYS WANDERING ON THE SEAS

German Refugees Find Peace In York At Last

TO the peace of a big house overlooking Knavesmire, York, there came yesterday three people—a man, a woman and a child—for whom in the past few weeks peace has been little more than a word.

They are Herr Josef Joseph, until last November a lawyer with a large practice in Freydt, North Germany; his wife, and their little girl, and when I called on them last night at Chalfonts, The Mount, home of Mr. Arnold Rowntree (writes a "Yorkshire Evening Press" reporter) they told me a little of what it feels like to lose one's wealth, friends and country.

The Josephs were among the party of more than 900 men, women and children which left Hamburg on May 13 in the German liner St. Louis, for Cuba, where many of them had relatives and where they hoped to stay until they could enter the United States.

BLOW TO THEIR HOPES

The liner reached Havana on May 27. Early in the morning Customs and quarantine officials came aboard, and the process of issuing a landing permit for each passenger began. It had already proceeded some way when the blow fell—a telegraphed message from the President ordering that no one should be allowed to land.

For six days, during which the ship remained in full view of the beautiful Cuban capital, urgent efforts were made to obtain a reversal of this decision. An appeal was even made to the President's wife, but to no avail. Then came the next order—the ship must leave Cuban waters within six hours or warships would be sent.

During the days in harbour relatives—often husbands, wives and children—of many of the refugees came as near to the ship as possible in boats. They could not even shake hands.

Eventually, despite the efforts of Cuban and American friends, and of the ship's captain, the liner had to leave, while sympathetic crowds waved a farewell. She cruised slowly back on her course, and appeals for help were sent to the world's capitals.

Herr Joseph told me that he thought the only place left where German refugees could now go freely was China, and many were, in fact, going there, principally to Shanghai.

FILLED WITH DESPAIR

On board the liner, as the prospect of a return to Germany became more and more likely, despair seized many of the refugees who, released from concentration camps, had undertaken never to set foot in the Reich again.

A close watch had to be kept for possible suicide attempts. One unfortunate [...]

had made one at Havana. He had been taken ashore to hospital—but his wife had had to remain on board.

Herr Joseph told me that this was a particularly anxious time for him, as he was chairman and speaker of a committee, consisting of three lawyers, three merchants and a doctor, formed by the passengers themselves. Each day he had to address them, and try to keep up their spirits.

On June 13, however, came news from Paris that negotiations were in progress for four countries, Britain, France, Belgium and Holland, to offer a refuge to the wanderers. Arrangements were eventually completed, and on arrival at Antwerp the party split up, those for Britain and France—about 600—transferring to a smaller ship, and the others going overland.

Herr Joseph and his wife paid a tribute to the kindness of the German captain and crew of the St. Louis, who had done all they could for the refugees.

"The Children of Israel were wandering for 40 years in the Wilderness," said Herr Joseph with a smile, "and we were wandering 40 days over the seas." He also recalled that the refugees had left Hamburg on the 13th, had taken 13 days to reach Havana, and had heard the good news of their admittance in Europe on June 13!"

Herr Joseph told me that he and his family were hoping to go to the United States, where they had friends, but that quota restrictions might mean a delay of a year. His wife stressed the fact that enforced idleness was a factor of their position which they felt most keenly.

Herr Joseph asked me to express the gratitude of himself and his family for the opportunity afforded them of coming to Britain, and to York.

The sum of £25 sent anonymously to the subscription list opened by the Lord Mayor of York in aid of the Baldwin Refugee Fund is already being utilised to aid refugees received locally.

The "Jewish Chronicle" reported in detail on the arrangements made for refugees from the "St Louis". On the same day, this report was carried in the "Yorkshire Evening Post" about the Joseph family being taken in by the Rowntree family, of confectionery fame, long benefactors of humanitarian causes. (Mrs Liesl Joseph-Loeb)

L'ODYSSÉE DU « SAINT-LOUIS »
s'est terminée à Anvers

L'histoire de l'exode des populations juives chassées d'Allemagne, au mépris de tout humanité par le gouvernement du Reich, comporte peu de pages aussi émouvantes e aussi douloureuses que celle de l'odyssée du vapeur « Saint-Louis » parti d'Allemagne pour l'île de Cuba avec mille passagers juifs à bord. Alors que toutes les autorisations semblaient avoir été obtenues, le gouvernement cubain refusa sans explication de laisse débarquer ces malheureux. Alors le navire, durant des jours et des jours, erra littérale ment dans l'Océan, en attendant le résultat de l'intervention pressante du Comité Interna tional des Réfugiés Juifs.

Enfin, la Belgique, la Hollande, l'Angleterre et la France ont accepté d'hospitaliser chacune pour une part, les Israélites chassés de leur patrie et refoulés du Nouveau ... Le « Saint-Louis » est arrivé, samedi, à Anvers ... débarquement émouvant rend ...rès long par suite des mesures à prendre. Environ deux cent cinquante réfugiés, accueil lis par la Belgique, sont aussitôt partis pour Bruxelles, par train spécial.

Le vapeur « Saint-Louis » arrive en vue d'Anvers, ayant à bord environ mille réfugiés juifs chassés d'Allemagne.

Dans le train spécial qui va les amener à Bruxelles, les réfugiés s'installent avec des gendarmes et du personnel du train.

Que de tristesse dans ces deux jeunes visages : elles regardent par un hublot du « Saint-Louis », cette ville inconnue où le destin les amène, après tant de jours incertains, telles des épaves que la vague jette enfin au rivage.

Les autorités belges arrivent à bord du « Saint-Louis » pour prendre les mesures de débarquement et examiner les papiers des réfugiés qui vont débarquer à Anvers.

Au fur et à mesure que le « Saint-Louis » approche, les réfugiés témoignent une joie plus vive et saluent cette terre libre où ils vont être accueillis.

Avec grand soin, on descend les malades qui sont à l'infirmerie.

— 14 —

In France, "Le Soir Illustré" ("The Evening Illustrated") came back to the story on the eve of World War Two, with this full-page spread. (The Gordon Thomas Collection)

Woman Who Escaped 'No Refugee' Decree Hysterical With Joy

By STEPHEN TRUMBULL
Herald Staff Writer
PICTURES ON PAGE 10-A

HAVANA, Cuba, June 7.—A trim, alert-eyed little woman in a neat print dress sat on a wooden cot in a tiny room here Wednesday and gave The Herald the first story to come from a passenger on the refugee ship St. Louis.

A once-wealthy woman, all of her earthly possessions are now in a battered bag at the foot of that narrow cot—yet she is so hysterical with joy she can scarcely speak. There are only moments of doubt when she appears struck with the obsession it might be a dream, from which there will be an awakening.

She is one of the 22 persons who were permitted to land in Havana from the refugee ship when authorities were convinced their papers were in legal order, having been issued and validated well in advance of the "no more refugee" decree of May 5. Despite the legality of her presence here she begs to remain nameless, fearing that to stand out in a city with a refugee problem might bring complications that would break her fleeting grasp at freedom.

Photographs Only Mementos

There is one more dress besides the one she wears. She shares the apartment with a dozen other refugees. The only links with the past are some faded photographs that show a beautiful and spacious German home, an automobile and the faces of relatives she may never again see. She was permitted to sail with the munificent sum of $4, yet she is treading on air in her joy.

She leads you through the maze of cots and the luggage of the others to an open window. Beyond is an azure sea, palm trees and sunshine. She points to the northward, beyond Morro Castle.

"Out there is America, yes? Some day—maybe."

It is with difficulty her attention is brought back to the story of her days on the heartbreak-ship St. Louis, the days of hope and the days of despair while she and 913 other fugitives from the land of the Swastika were under guard in Havana harbor, with all hope dwindling.

CUBA ORDERS JEWS TO GO

Ship Carrying 917 Frantic Refugees Must Leave Havana Harbor

THREATENS FORCE

Police Watch To Prevent Frantic Group From Trying Suicide

BY THE ASSOCIATED PRESS

HAVANA, Cuba, June 1.—A tragic shipload of 917 German Jewish refugees Thursday night faced return to the land from which they fled.

President Federico Laredo Bru coupled an order for their ship to leave with a threat to use gunboats if necessary to tow it from Cuban waters.

The presidential decree came during a day of uncertainty in which the captain of the German liner St. Louis, expressing fear of a "collective suicide pact" among his refugees, sought in vain to [have the] government rescind its [order] landing them.

Held Ready

[The] president directed [the ship] leave "within the [hours]" [as gunboat]es were held ready

Refugee Vessel Rides At Anchor Off Miami Beach

Ship Carrying 907 German Jews Halts For Two Hours While Coast Guard Planes and Ships Patrol Near[by]; Sails South and Then Returns

By STEPHEN TRUMBULL
Herald Staff Writer

[S]ick and bewildered Jewish refugees from Nazi[land] wandering SS. St. Louis saw day break over [l]ast Sunday.

[Th]e ship bearing the cargo of the unwanted was [several m]iles off the Miami Harbor light, while United [States pa]trol boats clustered about. Then the anchor [came] up and it slowly edged its way to the southeast, in the general direction of Havana, the port from which they were banished Friday.

The appearance and departure of the ship here wrote another mysterious chapter in the story of hate, double cross and rumored graft that has been shaping itself since the ship sailed from Hamburg May 15.

Officers Silent

Officers at the Fort Lauderdale coast guard base, who rushed a patrol boat to the ship when it was sighted off that port at 6 a. m., flatly refused to talk.

"We can give no information on this matter," they stated briefly, but firmly.

At nightfall the coast guard boat reported it was dropping the trail of the liner and returning to its Fort Lauderdale base. The St. Louis then was about 10 miles offshore from the Florida keys, continuing its southeasterly course.

American press cuttings which were drifting into Europe at the time of the ship's landing carried stories of Cuba ordering the vessel to go, of it riding at anchor off the Miami coast and of one woman who was allowed to disembark into Havana with a legal visa. The distress still comes across even after so many years. (Herbert Karliner)

On June 5th, the "Miami Herald" carried this front-page spread on the "St Louis", its plight and its passengers. (Herbert Karliner)

These are the visas which finally saved the lives of the Moses family – the United States visas issued to them in Paris in March 1940. Just a little longer wait and their opportunity to leave France would almost certainly have been lost. (Gene A Moser)

As passengers began to find their way into the countries where they were to be settled, the arduous routine of documentation began all over again. In Belgium the identity cards served also as ration cards and looked like this. (Jules Wallerstein)

Heinz Rosenbach was granted his exit permit in this form on 25th April 1939. He finally made it to the United States, as his Alien Registration Card shows, and was able to file his petition for Naturalisation in 1945. (Stephen Rosenbach)

Gültig für Auswanderungszwecke und gültig für drei Monate, vom Tage der Ausstellung an gerechnet.

Polizeiliches Führungszeugnis

Es wird hiermit bescheinigt, daß der kaufm.Angestellte Heinz Jsrael Rosenbach geboren am 16.11.1919 in Hoof , wohnhaft zu Kassel

1. nach dem Strafregister im Geburtsort nicht wegen gewöhnlicher Vergehen, die eine Gefängnisstrafe nach sich ziehen, bestraft oder verurteilt worden ist, noch sich im Anklagezustand befindet,

2. nicht während der der Einschiffung vorhergehenden 5 Jahre unter der Anklage wegen politischer Vergehen gestanden hat,

3. nicht der Bettelei obgelegen hat.

Kassel , den 25. April 1939

Der Polizeipräsident
Jm Auftrage

Verwaltungsgebühr: 0.50 RM.
HAMBURG-AMERIKA LINIE, HAMBURG

R. 852   (Argentinien)   Hö

This was typical of the kind of card index record kept on "St Louis" passengers awaiting entry into the United States. This particular one is for Mrs Lotte Metis. (Herbert Karliner)

S.S. ST. LOUIS
TRISCORNIA

Surname	M.	W.	Maiden Name				
Metis		Lotte					

ADDRESS

England

Relatives on S. S. St. Louis

1st Name	Date of Birth	Nativity	Passport	Occupation	Date	Place	Waiting No.
M Felix	in U.S. on v v.						
W Lotte	7/24/00	Lissa				Berlin	5447
CH.Wolfgang	8/8/25	Grunberg					5448
2 Annette	12/30/30	"					5448

Registration with Consul

	Name	Address	Contact Through	Result of Contact
Affiants	Block Dr.Fritz 134 Elm Av. Mt Vernon			
	Dr.Walter Eckstein Ethical Culture So. N.Y			Deposit 85.
	Dr. Loewenfeld Self Help of German Emigres			Guaranteed 100
Relatives in U.S.	Husband in New York 1st. name not given or address. 2on 74 85th St. nyc			Guaranteed 300
Relatives in Belgium	Herman Hyman 211 Central Park West Holzer 206 Rue de La Poste Brussels			
England	Wittenberg.C. 10 South Rd.Handworth Birmington 15			
Holland				
France				

Having travelled such a huge distance just to come back to Europe – and then go back to the United States – Liane Reif seems to have taken her journey well, as this happy photo shows of her with the parents of Ruth and Bella Isner. Liane, her mother and brother were finally able to return to North America in 1941. Behind the photo is the bank declaration which had to be provided by their sponsor. (Dr Liane Reif-Lehrer)

D/ 41

NEW CHAIRMAN
DUNHAM B. SHERER
PRESIDENT
RALPH PETERS, JR.
FIRST VICE PRESIDENT

FOREIGN DEPARTMENT
EDWARD B. MACKENZIE
VICE PRESIDENT
GEORGE B. McGOWAN
ASST. VICE PRES.
EDWIN S. McMANUS
ASST. VICE PRES.

EXCHANGE BANK TRUST COMPANY

WILLIAM & BEAVER STREETS

CABLE ADDRESS
CORNEXBANK, NEW ...

NEW YORK   June 19, 1941

Information for the American Consul

at   Lyon, France
XX   Dr. Benedict B. Drob

has requested us to give you the following information in connection with the application for entry into this Country of his aunt and her two children, Chaje Leja Reif, Friedrich Reif and Lione Reif, all of Poste Restante Limoges, Hte. Vienne, France.

Checking Account:

In the name of   Benedict B. Drob
Opened   July 5th, 1935
Average balance   six   months
Present balance on   June 18th, 1941 ———— $ 350

Interest Account: Nil $ 739.

In the name of
Opened
Average balance
Present balance on   months
                                         $

Remarks: We are told that Dr. Drob is a D
             at 300 East 56th Street, New York
above account has been conducted in a satis

The above information is supplied by request, and not with the inten merits of any application.

HMA:

Copy sent direct - American Consul, Lyon
Copy sent direct - Sutton Place Branch.

When World War Two began, Heini Glucksmann was interned by the British government, for now he was a German alien. After initial confinement on the Isle of Man, he worked for a time at Warth Mill, in Lancashire as canteen manager, from which he received this reference, Whilst there, he volunteered for military service in the British Army, as the recruiting card here shows. He was accepted and enlisted into the Pioneer Corps for "the period of embodiment" (or put more plainly, for the duration of the war) on 1st October 1940. Many Jewish refugee enlistees were transferred to reserve service as the build up to D-Day began, simply because the senior field commanders were concerned about how they might react to what they were likely to see as the Allies would advance, knowing the concentration camps were there and that troops would find them and relieve them. (Edgar Glucksman)

TO WHOM IT MAY CONCERN.

By kind permission of the Commandant I have much pleasure in placing on record the fact that the undermentioned Internees have rendered valuable service to this Camp by their willing assistance and co-operation in the work of running the Canteen, which has been able to supply necessities and luxuries to their fellow Internees and thus helped to maintain good morale under conditions other than propitious.

HEINRICH GLUCKSMANN,   Manager.
RUDOLPH JACOBSON,   Assistant.
KURT WEIHS,   Assistant.
HEINZ LOESER,   Orderly.

Geo Bancroft
Lieut R.A.
Company Officer & Officer i/c Canteen.

WARTH MILL INTERNMENT CAMP,   CANTEEN
BURY, LANCS.   WARTH A.I. CAMP
1.8.1940.   BURY.
JHS.

CENTRAL OFFICE FOR REFUGE
(National Service Department)

Recruiting No.   Man 64

This is to certify that
Mr. r. Heinrich Glucksmann
of 126 Broughton Lane, Broughton, Manchester.
has this day signed a form offering his services to
HIS MAJESTY'S GOVERNMENT
for Enlistment with the Forces of the Crown.

Signed: for the CENTRAL OFFICE FOR REFUGEES
JGafan   Registrar.

Date: 24/5/40

Duplicate

(I) SOLDIER'S NAME and DESCRIPTION on ATTESTATION.
Army Number 13803304
Surname (in capitals) Glucksmann
Christian Names (in full) Heinrich
Date of Birth 25.11.09.
Place of Birth. { Parish
                { In or near the town of
                { In the county of
Trade on Enlistment. Book Keeper

Nationality of Father at birth
Nationality of Mother at birth
Religious Denomination Jewish
Approved Society
Membership No.
Enlisted at Douglas I.O.M on 1.10.40
For the NS
* Regular Army.   * Supplementary Reserve.
* Territorial Army.   * Army Reserve Section D.
* Strike out those inapplicable.
For years with the Colours and years in the Reserve.
Signature of Soldier
Date 10.10.40.

This is a group photograph of Heinrich Glucksmann's platoon, taken after he had been promoted Corporal and below is a portrait taken of him with his beloved Queenie, the girl he married whilst serving in the army. The amusing tale to that is that when Queenie, who was also a refugee from Central Europe, married her British soldier, she was immediately granted British citizenship. Heini had to complete his qualifying period and was finally granted naturalization in 1946! His certificate of naturalization is opposite. (Edgar Glucksman)

G.18159.

Certificate No. **AZ** 20508

12

BRITISH NATIONALITY AND STATUS OF ALIENS ACT, 1914

CERTIFICATE OF NATURALIZATION

Whereas

Heinrich Glucksmann

has applied to one of His Majesty's Principal Secretaries of State for a Certificate of Naturalization, alleging with respect to **him**self the particulars set out below, and has satisfied him that the conditions laid down in the above-mentioned Act for the grant of a Certificate of Naturalization are fulfilled in **his** case:

Now, therefore, in pursuance of the powers conferred on him by the said Act, the Secretary of State grants to the said

Heinrich Glucksmann

this Certificate of Naturalization, and declares that upon taking the Oath of Allegiance within the time and in the manner required by the regulations made in that behalf **he** shall, subject to the provisions of the said Act, be entitled to all political and other rights, powers and privileges, and be subject to all obligations, duties and liabilities, to which a natural-born British subject is entitled or subject, and have to all intents and purposes the status of a natural-born British subject.

In witness whereof I have hereto subscribed my name this   16th   day of November, 1946.

HOME OFFICE,
LONDON.

Under Secretary of State.

PARTICULARS RELATING TO APPLICANT

Full Name	Heinrich GLUCKSMANN.
Address	314, Littleton Road, Salford 7, Lancashire.
Trade or Occupation	Shirt and pyjama maker.
Place and date of birth	Pless. 25th November, 1909.
Nationality	German.
Single, Married, etc.	Married.
Name of wife or husband	Queenie.
Names and nationality of parents	Eduard and Minna GLUCKSMANN. (German).

(For Oath
see overleaf)

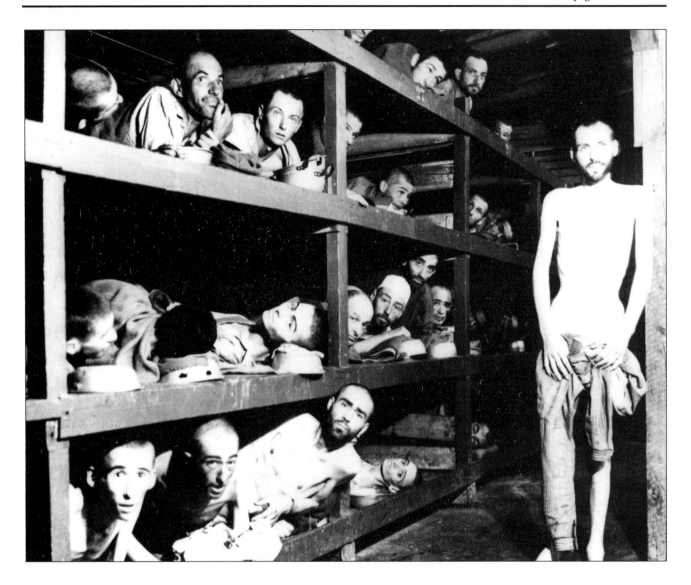

This was the fate of many of the passengers who were rounded up in Belgium, France and Holland as Hitler's armies overran those countries. But these were some of the 'lucky' ones, in that they survived the horrors of Buchenwald, where this picture was taken as the Allies advanced through Germany in the closing stages of World War Two. Miraculously, some did survive the Holocaust and attended a "St Louis" reunion in 1989. (The US Holocaust Memorial Museum)

Captain Schröder's last visit to the "St Louis" must have been a bittersweet memory. Having suffered bomb damage from an RAF raid in 1944, it looks a sorry sight in this picture. (Author's Collection)

The Captain's dress uniform cap was present to a reunion of "St Louis" survivors in 1989, which took place at Miami Beach, a place they were prevented from setting foot on fifty years before. The cap is today in the United States Holocaust Memorial Museum, in Washington DC. (Herbert Karliner)

The last thing to show in this picture epilogue is happiness – in the form of all the faces of people who attended the 1989 "St Louis" Reunion. (Herbert Karliner)

APPENDICES

SPECIAL THANKS

Those that follow were either spoken to by telephone, corresponded with, or interviewed in person.

Crew:
Bendowski, Irene
Bendowski, Paul
Kempe, Hermann
Muhlbacher, Christian
Schimon, Josef
Schmitt, Pieter
Zochert, Paul

Passengers:
Alan, Rolf
Altschul, Hans
Aron, Alfred
Aron, Sofi
Brauer, Kaethe
Buff, Fred
Falk, Eugene
Frieberg, Regina
Freund, Charlotte
Fridberg, Ruth
Friedman, Lillian
Geismar, Sonja
Goldberg, William
Goldman, Renee (nee Spanier)
Brady, Kathryn
Clyma, Frances
Eckstein, Nelly
Egelert, Karl
Estedes, Jose
Felton, Anton
Field, Harold
Friedlander, Albert
Froehlich, Henry
Gantz, Sarita
Gilbert, Martin
Goetz, Harald
Goldstein, Charlotte
Gottschalk, Max
Guttfeld, Martin
Hamel, Otto
Heald, David

Greilsamer, Erich
Herz, Theresa
Hurtig, Herta
Jacobson, Greta
Jacoby, Innes (nee Spanier)
Jacoby-Byk, Regina
Jungerman, Harry
Kadden, Leah
Kahn, Arthur
Karliner, Herbert
Karliner, Walter
Kassel, Fritz
Langnas, Leon
Lavatch, Herma
Leyser, Fred
Lichtenstein, Norbert
Mahler, Vera
Marcus, Ilse
Oster, Alice
Oyres, Herbert
Phillipi, Margarete
Pommer, Martin
Prager, Margarete
Rosenback, Harry
Heilbronner, Marie
Jacob, Johannes
Jacoby, Golda
Jellin, Fred
Jockl, Gerda
Kallman, Charlotte
Karetsky, David
Karetsky, Geraldine
Kramarsky, Lola
Kraner, Joachim
Kruger, Inge
Lenz, Gunther
Leopold, S.
Lewin, Henri
Luftig, Lillian
Man, John
Marx, Sidonie

Safier, Jakob
Schwager, Reni
Schwartz, Hilda
Shilling, Maria
Sichel, Beatrice (nee Bonne)
Sondheimer, Alse
Sternberg, Alice
Strauss, Fred
Strauss, Joseph
Wallerstein, Anton
Weil, Ernst
Zellner, Ruth

Others:
Adler, Inge
Aldoughby, Swy
Altmann, Hilde
Annenberg, Walter
Babish, Reuben
Band, Harold
Barrocas, Jack
Ben-Johoshna, Margot
Bieber, Konrad
Blackburn, Pitch
Miron, Chia
Montagu, Ivor
Moser, Alfred
Neuberg, Gertrude
Pearlman, Moshe
Piton, Mary
Prinz, Arthur
Rosen, Emanuel
Samson, Rita
Sanders, Frank
Schiller, Harriet
Schuster, Max
Seligman, Jenny
Simon, Arthur
Slee, Mac
Spanier, Njuta
Weigall, Michael

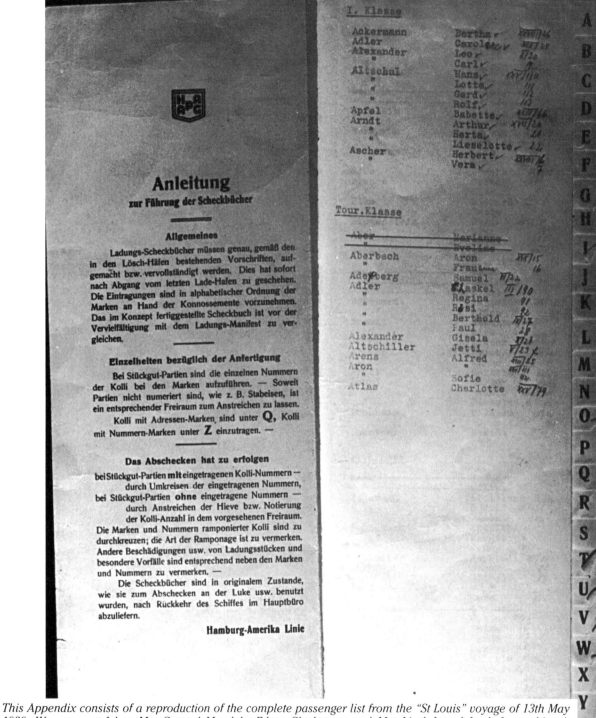

This Appendix consists of a reproduction of the complete passenger list from the "St Louis" voyage of 13th May 1939. We are grateful to Mrs Gertrud Mendels, Edgar Glucksman and Mrs Liesl Joseph-Loeb for making it available to us. The names deleted seem to be for those people who left the ship in Havana. The dual numerals at the sides of the names were thought to be cabin numbers, but careful checking has proved this not to be so. It can only be concluded that they therefore represent shipping line manifest information of another kind.

I. Klasse

Bach	Willy	XIV/30
Back	2 Stella	XXVI/100
Bardeleben	Anna	III/2
"	Marianne	3
~~Baruch~~	~~Ludwig~~	
"	~~Frieda~~	
Bendheim	Ludwig	XIII/16
"	Bertha	7
Berggrün	Ludwig	XVII/24
"	Antonie	25
Bergmann	Otto	VIII/21
"	Rosy	22
Bibo	Günther	XII/35
Biener	Selmar	III/1
"	Elsa	2
Blum	Richard	XIII/1i
"	Betty	2
Blumenstein	Regi	XVII/13
"	Elsa	14
"	Heinz	15
Boas	Benno	XVIII/15
"	Charlotte	16
~~Bonne~~	~~Meta~~	
"	~~Beatrice~~	
"	~~Jakob~~	
Borchardt	Heinrich	VII/31
"	Alice	34
Brandt.	Johannes	XVIII/4
"	Lina	5
"	Dieter	6
Brauer	Erich	XIX/10
"	Käthe	11
Brück	Herbert	IX/37
Brühl	Walter	IX/40
"	Hedwig	41
"	Lieselotte	42
Buchholz	Wilhelm	XI/41
"	Auguste	42
Bukofser	Martha	III/9

Tour. Klasse

~~Back~~	~~James~~	
"	~~Cilly~~	
Bajor	Ladislaus	II/16
Ball	Rudolf	IV/13
"	Aagaraben ~~Paula~~	13 2
IA Bannemann	Phillip	I/2
3 "	Margit	3
4 "	Jenny	4
Begleiter.	Naphtali	VII/81
"	Sara	82
"	Alfred	83
Beifus	"	V/2a
"	Emma	6
~~Benjamin~~	~~Adelheid~~	
Bernstein	Julius	I/25
"	Salmy	26
"	b no	27
"	Margot	28
Bornsborn	Wilhelm	XVIII/3
Blachmann	Arthur	II/35
"	Erna	36
"	Gerda	37
Blatteis	Elias	XII/73

Blatteis	Gerda	XIV/74
"	Claus	75
Blaut	Arthur	X/30
blaut	Arnold	IX/29
Blechner	Oskar	In/86
Blumenstock	Michel	VI/136
"	Lea	137
"	Ruth	138
Bohm	Kurt	I/14
"	Heinz	15
Braun	Alfred	XI/40
Breitbarth	Arthur	II/19
Buff	Fritz	VII/15d
Buxbaum	Levi	XVII/126
Brenner	Blanka	VI/134
Broderova	Elisabeth	IV/17
Bak, Brunk	Bianka	XIX/100

C

. Klasse

Chaim	Georg	xxvii/1
Chraplewski	Siegfried	xii/6
"	Clara	7
"	Jan	8
"	Peter	9
Cohn	Georg	xxiii/13
"	Johanna	xxiii/14
"	Walter	xxviii/8
"	Rita	9
Collin	Auguste	xx/44

✓

our. Klasse

Camnitzer	Siegfried	iii/114
"	Rosalie	115
"	Edith	116
Cohen	Rudolf	xxiv/27
Cohn	~~Israel~~ Eugen	xi/38
"	Helene	39
"	Louis	II/43
"	Lydia	44
"	Sara	xi/74
Cohnstaedt	Fritz	xiii/33
"	Nelly	34
Cunow	Carl	I/47
Czerninski	Max	xiii/10
"	Hilde	11
"	Inge	12

✓

I. Klasse

Danziger	
"	
Davids	
Dörnberg	
Dublon	
"	
"	
Dzialowski	
"	

Karl	xii/33
Rosa	34
Emma	xiiv/72
Gertha	xv/51
Erich	xx/37
Willi	33
Erna	34
Lore	35
Eva	36
Bruno	xx/5
Lici	6

✓

Tour. Klasse

Daniel	
Dingfelder	
"	
"	
Donath	
Dresel	
"	
"	
Dubiecki	
"	

Frau Anna	xiii/13
Leopold	V/26 a
Johanna	b
Rudi	c
Paul	
Richard	xi/20
Ruth	iv/27
Zilla	128
Alfred	129
B.	130
G.	iii/139
B.	140
	141

✓

D
E
G
H
J
K
L
M
N
O
P
Q
R
S
T
U
V
W
X
Y
Z

D

I. Klasse

Danziger	Karl	XII/33
"	Rosa	34
Davids	Emma	1/IV/72
Dörnberg	Gertha	XV/57
Dublon	Erich	XV/32
"	Willi	33
"	Erna	34
"	Lore	35
"	Eva	36
Dzialowski	Bruno	XII/5
"	Lici	6

Tour. Klasse

Daniel	Frau Anna	XIII/13
Dingfelder	Leopold	V/26a
"	Johanna	b
"	Rudi	c
Donath	Paul	IX/20
Dresel	Richard	IV/127
"	Ruth	128
"	Zilla	129
"	Alfred	130
Dubiecki	B.	III/139
"	G.	140
"	B.	141

I. Klasse

Eckmann	Egon	X/13
Edelstein	Ida	XXII/44
Eisner	Ludwig	1/IV/44

Tour. Klasse

Eichwald	Fritz	XII/32
Einhorn	Arnold	IV/12a
"	Gitel	b
Epstein	Moritz	V/40
"	Bettina	61
Erdmann	Simon	VIII/5a
"	Reisel	b
Eskenazy	Albert	
"	Gertrud	
"	Nissun	
~~Engelbert~~	~~Friedl.~~	XIV/8

F

I. Klasse

Falkenstein	Max	*II/2*
"	Hilda	3
Feig	Werner	*XV/12*
Finkelstein	~~Sara~~	*XVII/1*
Fischer	Johanna	*XVII/21*
"	Hans-Hermann	22
"	Ruth	23
Fraenkel	Hans	*XXV/99*
Frank	Manfred	*IX/94*
Freiberg	Regina	*IV/34*
"	Herta	35
"	Gisela	36
Freund	Terese	*XV/19*
"	Philipp	20
"	Lieselotte	21
~~Fried~~	~~Engelbert~~	~~XIV/18~~
Friedheim	Alfred	*XVIII/11*
"	Hertha	12
~~Friedmann~~	~~Amalie~~	
	~~Bruno~~	
	~~Georg~~	
	~~Lillian~~	
Fuchs-Marx	Walther	*XVII/31*
	Anna	32
Fuld	Julie	*XIV/57*
"	Ludwig	58
"	Hans	59
Fried	*Engelbert*	*XXIV/8*

Tour. Klasse

Falk	Eugen	*II/4a*
Fanto	Julius	*III/20b*
Feilchenfeld	Alice	*XIII/14*
"	Kind	18
"	Wolf	15
"	Berta	16
"	Heinz	17
Fink	Manfred	*II/18a*
"	Herta	b
"	Michael	c
Fischbach	Jonas	*IV/65*
"	Amalia	67
"	Moritz	66
"	Amalia	69
Flamberg	Braudla	*V/29a*
	Fella	b
Fränkel	Leon	*VII/9a*
	Alice	b
Frank	Max	*II/11*
"	Moritz	*V/8a*
"	Clara	b
"	Ursula	c
"	Siegfried	*XXVII/3*
Frankfurter	Lilly	*XXII/8*
Friedemann	Walter	*III/10a*
Friedheim	Edith	*II/21*
Friedmann	Rosi	*XIII/2e*
"	Eva-Ruth	g
	Willy	*VII/i*
Fröhlich	Max	*X/24*
		30

I. Klasse

Gabel	Heinrich	*XII/44*
"	Beate	45
"	Gerhard	46
Caubitz	Max	*XII/9*
"	Martha	10
"	Heinz	11
Glade	Bruno	*XXVIII/11*
Glass	Herbert	*IX/11*
Glücksmann	Hans	*XXVIII/27*
	Margarete	28
Goldbaum	Anna	*IV/66*
Goldberg	Wilhelm	*XXI/76*
Goldschmidt	Adolf	*XXIV/49*
"	Gerda	50
"	Inge	51
"	Lore	52
Gottschalk	Jacob	*XII/3*
"	Regina	4
"	Erika	5
"	Charlotte	6
Grünstein	Heinz	*IX/43*
	Gerd	44
Grünthal	Else	*XIII/12*
"	Walter	*XII/7*
"	Margarete	8
"	Ruthild	9
"	Sibyll	10
"	~~Wolf~~ *Adolf*	11
"	Bertha	12
"	Lutz	13
"	Horst	14
Gutmann	Martha	*XXIV/61*
Guttmann	Sally	*IV/45*
Guttmann	Ruth	46
		34

Tour. Klasse

Gelband	Benjamin	*XVI/115*
	Chana	116
Gerber	Rosa	*XXV/90*
"	Ruth	91
~~Gimenez Espinosa~~	~~José~~	*I/10*
Glaser	Arthur	*V/10a*
Glaserfeld	Max	*III/159*
Glücksmann	Heinrich	*IV/119*
Goldreich	Rudolf	120
	Therese	
Goldschmidt	Alex	*V/5d*
"	Helmut	e
"	Else	*XXI/1*
"	Fritz	2
"	Hermann	*XII/91*
Goldstein	~~Rita~~ *Recha*	92
"	Heinz	93
"	Julius	*I/38*
	Rosa	*I/39*
Gottfeld	Fritz	*XIII/5*
	Käte	6
Gotthelf	Sally	*I/11*
"	Erich	*XI/6*
Gottlieb	Walter	*XII/1*
Greilsamer	Johanna	2
Greve	Heinz	3
"	Eveline	4

H

I. Klasse

Haas	Leo	xxV/82
"	Elisabeth	83
Haendler	Fritz	XXII/14
"	Marie	15
Hecht	Charlotte	XIII/45
Heilbrun	Leon	xxIV/69
"	Berna	70
"	Ingeborg	71
"	Norbert	xXIII/7
"	Johanna	8
"	Günther	9
"	Bruno	xXV/84
"	Grete	85
"	Ruth	86
Heinemann	Hilmar	XII/50
Heldenmuth	Alfred	XI/31
"	Selma	32
"	Lilio	33
Hermann	Julius	xXIII/16
"	Sophie	17
"	Gerda	18
Herrmann	Fritz	xXIII/6
Herz	Walter	XXI/29
"	Anna	30
Heymann	Arno	III/10
"	Dorothea	XVIII/1
"	Hedwig	II/9
Hirsch	Max	XII/97
"	Margot	98
"	Joachim	99
Hofmann	Zilly	XV/26
Hopp	Margarethe	XI/43
Huber	Lilly	xXIV/68

Tour. Klasse

Haas	Anton	IV/5
Haber	Nathan	III/135
Händler	Georg	V/4a
"	Rosamunde	b
Heller	Franz	VI/14a
"	Irma	b
Hamburger	Israel	xXII/7
Hammerschlag	Max	I/1
"	Moses	V/76
Hausdorff	Arthur	VIII/1a
"	Gertrud	b
Hauser	Hermann	VII/29
"	Cecilie	30
Heidt	Fritz	xXII/16
"	Else	17
Heim	Emil	XIV/62
"	Gerda	63
Heimann	Erwin	V/62
"	Bella	63
Heller	Moritz	XV/64
"	Frieda	65
Hermanns	Julius	III/37
Herz	Amalie	XIV/59
"	Max	III/107
Hess	Adolf	129
"	Jette	130
"	Vera	132

Hess	Ilse	III/131
"	Martin	II/111
Hesse	Robert	II/145
Hilb	Fritz	VII/15c
Hirsch	Hermann	III/128
Hirschberg	Julius	VI/3a
"	Regina	b
Hirschfeld	Siegfried	VIII/4a
"	Ruth	b
Hoffmann	Selma	VIII/7b
"	Karl	c
"	Emma	xXIV/54
Hofmann	Siegfried	I/18
Hüneberg	Walter	VII/8a

I. Klasse

Issner   Austin   77
"   Babette   10
"   Bella   9
              Ruth   9

Tour. Klasse

Isakowski   Kurt   XIII/9
Israel   Hugo   XI/28

I. Klasse

Jacobowitz   Martin   VII/1
"   Mathilde   2
Jacoby   Otto   VII/12
                       Regina   13
                       Käthe   14
                       Susanne   15
Joel   Leon   VIV/13
"   Johanna   14
Jordan   Günther   15
Joseph   Johanna   VIII/53
"   Josef   VIII/25
                       Lilly   26
Jungermann   Liesel   27
"   Chaim   VIII/22
                       Susi   23
                       Moscheck   24

Tour. Klasse

Jacobowitz   Walter   I/20
Jacobsohn   Erich   XIV/24
"   Thomas   26
                       Margarethe   25
Jonas   Julius   I/29
Josef   Fritz   II/32
"   Frieda   33
"   Kurt   34
Joseph   Benno   X/73
"   Hertha   74
Jungermann   Brigitte   75
                       Alois   IV/121

I
I
C
R
S
T
U
V
W
X
Y
Z

K

I. Klasse

Kahnemann	Paula	XVII/23
Kaim	Hans	XXVIII/14
Kaminker	Berthold	XV/13
Kassel	Fritz	XIV/81
Keiler	Ruth	XXVII/20
Kochmann	Friedrich	XII/6
"	Alice	7
"	Hilde	8
Kohorn	Paul	IX/16
Kugler	Marie	XXII/21

Tour. Klasse

Kahn	Gustav	XIV/60
"	Elsa	61
"	Willi	VII/4
"	Arthur	XI/27
Karliner	Flora	III/88
"	Joseph	XIII/101
"	Martha	102
"	Ilse	103
"	Walter	104
"	Herbert	105
"	Ruth	106
Karmann	Richard	XXVII/15
"	Sidonie	16
"	Annemarie	17
"	Karl	18
"	Käthe	19
Kassel	Arthur	II/45
Katz	Siegfried	I/13
"	Julius	VIII/76
Kaufherr	Joseph	XIII/32
"	Betty	33
"	Hannelore	34
Kaufmann	Nathan	VII/6a
"	Adelheid	b
Kirchhausen	Hermann	
"	Karl	
~~Klein~~	~~Niklas~~	
~~"~~	~~Hermania~~	
~~"~~	~~Maria~~	
"	Hans	IV/20a
"	Leopold	VII/2a
"	Luise	b
"	Hannelore	c
Köppel	Josef	III/103
"	Irmgard	104
"	Judith	105
"	Jacob	106
Kohn	Maximilian	I/1
Kormann	Osias	XV/75
Krebs	Günter	XIII/26
Krohn	Regina	XIV/46
Knepel	Sheja	XI/12
"	Gisela	14
"	Sonja	13
Kutner	Hans	I/19

I. Klasse

Lauchheimer	Ida	XXX/14
Lebrecht	Max	XXX/15
Lenneberg	Hans	XVII/13
"	Julius	11
"	Gisela	12
Levin	Kurt	X/14
Levy	Ernestine	XIV/
Lewith	Julius	VII/25
"	Valerie	26
Leyser	Erich	XVII/6
"	Margot	7
Lichtenstein	Fritz	IV/33
"	Lucie	134
Liepmann	Herbert	XII/3
"	Erna	4
Lissberger	Hedwig	XVIII/25
Loeb	Olga	XXVIII/
"	Hans Otto	16
Löwenstein	Ernst	XIV/92
"	Alice	93
"	Otto	94
"	Kurt	XIV/6
"	Ida	7
Loewinsohn	Edith	XXII/24
"	Hella	23
Löwisohn	Martha	XIV/60
Luft	Gerhard	XX/6
"	Margot	7
Lustig	Egon	XI/21
"	Elsa	22

Tour. Klasse

Langnas	Leon	XI/15
Laskau	Benno	I/31
Lehmann	Salomon	XIV/57
"	Mina	58
Leindörfer	Hugo	XII/5
Leinkram	Aron	III/118
"	Mina	119
Lenneberg	Georg	VII/5a
"	~~Karl~~	keine
Levin	Mirjam	V/6d
"	Rachel	c
"	Hilde	V/6a
"	Ilse	
Leyser	Friedrich	II/40
Lichtenstein	Norbert	I/5
Litmann	Lajlich	I/16
Löb	Bella	XIV/54
"	Armin	55
"	Ruth	56
"	Isidor	XIV/50
"	Karoline	51
"	Marie	52
"	Anneliese	53
~~Loewe~~	~~Max~~	
"	Elise	XIV/12
"	Ruth	13
"	Fritz	14
Loewenstein	Ernst	VII/107
"	Regina	108
Löwy	Carl	V/72

M

I. Klasse

Maier	Ludwig	XVIII/20
"	Freya	21
"	Sonja	22
"	David	23
"	Pauline	24
"	Helene	XI/45
Mainzer	Ernst	12
"	Olga	XIII/2
Manasse	Alfred	
~~Mankiewitz~~	~~Siegfried~~	
"	~~Johanna~~	
Mannheimer	Siegfried	XII/24
Marx	Salomon	XVIII/12
"	Flora	13
"	Emil	VI/4
"	Arthur	XVII/4
Maschkowsky	Toni	5
May	Ludwig	XVIII/10
Mayer	Samuel	12
"	Ludwig	XI/i
"	Fanny	2
Meyer	Stephanie	XVIII/i/3
"+	Berthold	1
"	Elfriede	2
Meyerstein	Ludwig	XXIV/41
"	Alice	42
"	Hans	43
Michaelis	Walter	XI/17
"	Caecilie	18
Moskiewicz	Ismar	XXV/28
Mühlenthal	Charlotte	XXIV/65
Müller	Ernst	XVIII/10
"	Margot	11

Tour. Klasse

Manasse	Herbert	XXI/36
"	Emmi	37
"	Wolfgang	38
"	Ida	39
Marcus	Friedrich	IIV/45
"	Kurt	XXIII/4
"	Ilse	5
Marx	Simon	VI/8
Mayer	Adalbert	IV/110
Mendel	Christine	VII/8
"	Elisabeth	b
"	Karl	c
~~Menendez Barrio~~	~~Mercedes~~	
"	~~Ramiro~~	
"	~~Cesar~~	
Messinger	Seimam	IX/17
"	Fossla	18
"	Salo	19
Metis	Lotte	X/55
"	Wolfgang	56
"	Anette	57
Meyer	Joseph	II/41
"	Anna	42
"	Ernst	XVIII/3
Meyerhoff	Charlotte	I/30
Moser	Edmund	VII/94
"	Rosalie	95
Moses	Alfred	XVIII/2

Moses	Martha	XXIII/3
"	Eugen	4
"	Helmuth	5
"	Georg	II/70
"	Thea	71
Motulsky	Rena	VII/i/a
"	Arno	b
"	Lothar	c
"	Lea	c
Mück	Joachim	IV/133
Münz	Karl	XII/17
"	Sophie	18
"	Paula	19
"	Meta	20

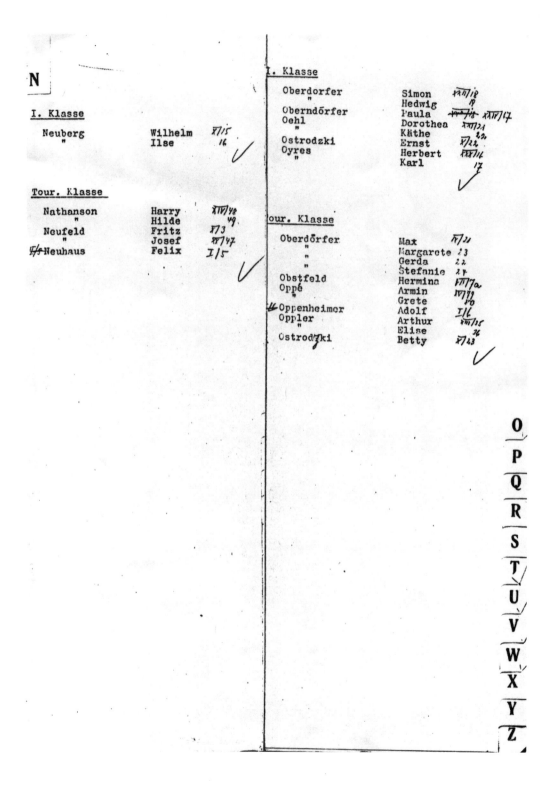

N

I. Klasse

Neuberg
" Wilhelm   XI/15
     Ilse   16

Tour. Klasse

Nathanson
" Harry   XIV/48
     Hilde   49
Neufeld
" Fritz   I/3
     Josef   III/47
Neuhaus   Felix   I/5

I. Klasse

Oberdorfer
"
Oberndörfer
Oehl
"
Ostrodzki
Oyres
"

Simon   XXII/18
Hedwig   19
Paula   XXII/17
Dorothea   XXII/21
Käthe   22
Ernst   XI/22
Herbert   XXII/16
Karl   17

Tour. Klasse

Oberdörfer
"
"
"
Obstfeld
Oppé
"
Oppenheimer
Oppler
"
Ostrodzki

Max   IV/21
Margarete   23
Gerda   22
Stefanie   24
Hermina   XII/7a
Armin   IV/99
Grete   10
Adolf   I/6
Arthur   XII/15
Elise   36
Betty   XI/43

O
P
Q
R
S
T
U
V
W
X
Y
Z

P

I. Klasse

Pommer	Martin	XI/53
Präger	Siegfried	XII/4
"	Margarethe	5
Preiss	Gerhard	III/88
"	Lisbeth	89

Tour. Klasse

Pander	Max	F/27a
"	Berta	b
"	Hilde	c
Philippi	Ernst	XII/4
"	Margarethe	5
"	Hans	6
"	Gert	7
Pick	Elise	XVIII/14
Pintus	Heinz	IV/135.
Preger	Alexander	III/126

Q

Tour. Klasse

| Quintero | Laguno |
| Chacón de Quintero | Ileuna |

I. Klasse

Rebenfeld	Kurt	XIII/10
Reif	Chaje	II/6
"	Friedrich	27
"	Liane	28
Reutlinger	Elly	XVIII/29
"	Renate	30
Rinteln	Walter	XVII/1
"	Elisabeth	2
Rosenbaum	Rosa	XVIII/11
Rosenfeld	Hans	XVII/12
"	Selma	13
"	Steffi	14
Ross	Heinrich	XIV/8
Rotholz	Berthold	XVII/8
"	Margarete	9
"	Günther	10
"	Horst	11
Rothmann	Martin	XVII/3
"	Jenny	4
Rothschild	Eva	
"	Frieda	XXV/80
Ryndsionski	Ferdinand	XXII/23

Tour. Klasse

Rabinowitz	Harry	II/81
Recher	Moritz	VII/3a
"	Irene	b
Reichental	Josef	VIII/5a
"	Betty	b
Reingenheim	Fanny	III/113
"	Jacob	III/114
"	Selma	115
Renner	Blanka	
Richter	Maria	III/127
Riegelhaupt	Cypora	III/184
"	Israel	85
Riesenburger	Hermann	XII/74
Ring	Erich	III/85
"	Erna	86
"	Jaques	87
Ritter	Wilhelm	XVII/107
Roeder	Elisabeth	
Rosenbach	Heinz	IV/17
Rosenberg	Louis	II/58
"	Ricka	59
"	Selig	III/117
Rosenthal	Max	XII/11
"	Kurt	XV/71
"	Johanna	72
"	Margit	73 VII/15a
"	Rolf	
Rosensweig	Siegfried	III/93
Roth	Ernst	V/24a
"	Camilla	b
"	Harry	c
Rothholz	Siegfried	XIII/62
"	Margaret	b
Rothschild	Erwin	XVI/30
Roubitscheck	Richard	IV/124
"	Pauline	125
"	Ernst	126

S

I. Klasse

Salomon	Moritz	XIX/22
"	Sybilla	23
Sandberg	Delta	LV/55
"	Ruth	56
Schafranik	Heinrich	XVII/24
"	Leontine	25
Scheyer	Martha	XVIII/16
Schillinger	Samuel	XXI/80
"	Marie	16
"	Jan	2
"	Jiri	XIV/62
Schoeps	Kurt	63
"	Anni	64
"	Beate	
Schück	Gertrud	III/100
~~Schüfftan~~	~~Walter~~	
"	~~Therese~~	
"	~~Wolfgang~~	
Schwager	Albert	XIV/38
"	Resi	39
Schweitzer	Max	XV/77
"	Jenny	78
Secemski	Aron	VIII/3
"	Louise	4
"	Hanna	5
Seliger	Walter	IX/79
Seligmann	Siegfried	XXV/105
"	Alma	106
"	Ursula	107
"	Max	108
"	Rosie	109
Sietz	Lea	XII/26
Silberstein	Kurt	XXIII/19
"	Thea	20
"	Renate	21
"	Gert	22
Sklow	Betty	II/135
Springer	Julius	XII/20
Stahl	Rosa	XVII/7
Sternberg	Alice	XIV/29
Sternlicht	Gertrud	XVIII/9
"	Lotte	10
Strauss	Alfons	XXVII/9
"	Heinrich	XXIV/28
"	Emma	29
"	Kurt	IV/6
Sydower	Wilhelm	XIV/1

Tour. Klasse

Safier	Jacob	V/28a
"	Zypera	b
"	Eva	c
Salm	Leopold	XIII/27
"	Jana	28
Salmon	Erna	XII/18
"	Egon	19
"	Edith	20
Schapira	Julius	V/23a
"	Henriette	b
Schelansky	Frieda	XII/89
"	Hans	90
Scheuer	Gertrud	XIV/40
Schild	Ison	IV/96
"	Irma	97

18	"	Hermann	I/18
	"	Max	VII/3
Schlesinger		Max	XIV/38
"		Friederike	39
"	1	Richard	VIII/10a
"		Meta	b
Schönberger		Moritz	XIII/47
Schönemann		Siegfried	II/48
"		Gertrud	49
"		Wolfgang	50
~~Schönemann~~		~~Siegfried~~	
Schott		Kurt	XIII/22
"		Siegfried	XIII/11
"		Else	
Schulhof		Julius	II/124
"		Stella	125
Schumanovsky		Emil	VII/1
Schwalbendorf		Josef	XII/41
Schwartz		Oscar	XVII/108
"		Regine	109
Schweiger		Sophie	IV/70
Segal		Moses	XII/27
"		Sabine	28
Seligmann		Sieghert	III/102
Siegel		Arthur	V/25
Silber		Salomon	VII/2a
"		Cheje	b
"		Leo	c
Silzer		Paul	VII/87
"		Leontine	88
Simon		Rolf	XII/77
"		Karl	I/72
"		Selma	78
"		Edith	79
"		Ilse	80
"		Martin	XIII/23
"		Selma	24
Singer		Moses	XII/87
"		Amalia	88
"		Josef	89
Siperstein		Josefine	XII/15
Skotzki		Günther	I/21
"		Charlotte	22
"		Helga	23
"		Inge	24
Spanier		Fritz	XV/105
"		Sara	91
"			92
"			93
Speier		Loyer	I/11
Spira		Hene	II/81
Spitz		Vera	III/82
"		Ursel	84
"		Erich	83
Sreg		Abraham	XIII/7
"		Mathilde	8
Stark		Moses	II/51
"		Pessel	52
"		Paul	53
Stein		Josef	VII/19
"		Fanny	20
"		Grete	V/23c
"		Erich	c
"		Kurt	V/9a
"		Else	b
"		Werner	c
"		Mauritius	XII/11a

T
U
V
W
X
Y
Z

T

I. Klasse

Tichauer	Herbert	×XIV/45
"	Else	46
Tischler	Harry	XXVII/18
"	Lina	19

Tour. Klasse

Tannenbaum	Carl	VII/2d
"	Malchen	2
Troedel	Leopold	IV/120
"	Blanca	121
"	Walter	123
"	Erich	122
Turkowicz	Joer	III/5
"	Helene	6
"	Edith	7

I. Klasse

| Unger | Berta | IV/45 |

Tour. Klasse

U
V
W
X
Y
Z

V

I. Klasse

Vendig	Ernst	XI/1
"	Charlotte	2
"	Paulina	5
"	Fritz	3
"	~~Heber~~ Heinz	4

Tour. Klasse

Velman	Walter	IX/117
"	Hilde	118

I. Klasse

Wachtel	Joseph	XVIII/2
"	Amanda	3
Waldbaum	Victor	XXVIII/17
"	Marga	18
"	Gerda	19
Warschawski	Hans	XXXI/1
"	Johanna	2
"	Ursula	3
"	Franz	4
Wassermann	Paula	XIV/23
Wechselmann	Oskar	XXIV/47
"	Margarete	48
Weil	Eduard	XXII/8
"	Emma	9
"	Julius	XXIV/31
"	Klara	32
"	Susanne	33
"	Felix	XI/10
"	Gustav	XVII/42
"	Arthur	XXIV/34
"	Anneliese	36
"	Ingeborg	35
~~Weiler~~	~~Moritz~~	
"	Recha	XXVII/23
Weinberg	Walter	XXVII/17
Weis	Max	XXI/31
"	Bella	32
Wertheim	Fritz	XX/15
Wilmersdörfer	Siegfried	XX/38
"	Flora	39
Winkler	Istvan	
Wolfermann	Jakob	XVIII/19
"	Flora	20
Wolff	Adolf	XVII/12
"	Else	13
"	Hildegard	14

Tour. Klasse

Wallerstein	Anton	VIII/9a
"	Paula	b
"	Julius	c
"	Edith	d
Wartelski	Leo	XI/48
Wasservogel	Viktor	IV/122
"	Irma	123
Weil	Berthold	XIII/29
"	Thekla	30
"	Ernst	II/47
"	Dina	I/68
Weinstein	Siegfried	69
Weinstock	Arthur	XX/40
"	Charlotte	41
"	Ernst	42
Weisel	Friederike	V/23d
Weiser	Ignaz	24
"	Thawa	25
Weiss	Leopold	XII/11
"	Gerda	IV/136
"	Meyer	XIV/43
"	Ida	44
Weissler	Walter	XII/100
Weisz	Somela	XXI/113
Weltmann	Erich	V/5a

W
X
Y
Z

W

Weltmann	Elly	F/54
"	Renate	c
Wertheimer	Klara	XIII/31
Wiesenfelder	Martin	III/III
~~Windmüller~~	~~Hans~~	
Windmüller	Salomon	XI/23
"	Berta	24
"	Hans	25
"	Rudi	26
Wolf	Moritz	II/66
"	Johanna	67
" *Abraham*	~~Albert~~	XIII/19
"	Lina	20
"	Elisabeth	21
Wolff	Max	II/64

I. Klasse

Zellner	Max	XIV/101
"	Gertrud	102
"	Ruth	103
"	Margot	104

Tour. Klasse

Zweigenthal	Fritz	XX/57

X
—
Y
—
Z

In this Appendix, we reproduce two pieces of music written by Frank Metis long after the event, but which symbolise much of what that awesome voyage was in 1939. (Frank Metis, Carlyle Music and Princess Music)

Frank Metis travelled on the "St Louis" as a young boy. He was among the group which went to Britain after the ship berthed at Antwerp and then travelled to the United States when his visa was issued. He went to live in New York and has lived there ever since. Frank entered the music industry and has a fine reputation as a musical arranger. He wrote these two pieces in 1974 as a commemoration of the voyage, thirty five years after the events took place.

Copyright © 1974 by Frank Metis, 1650 Broadway, New York, N.Y. 10019 (212) 246-3869

The Route taken by the "St Louis". This map shows the outbound route, the local circuits taken by the ship whilst waiting for political decisions about the landing and the return route to Antwerp, then Hamburg. (Author's Collection)

VOYAGE OF THE S. S. ST. LOUIS

KEY TO THE NUMBERS ON THE MAP

1. May 13, 1939, departure Hamburg, 8 P.M.

2. May 15, arrival and departure Cherbourg

3. May 19, pass Azores

4. May 27, arrive Havana 4 A.M., anchored in harbor until:

INSET:

5. June 2, depart Havana, 11 A.M., circle off Cuba

6. June 3, steaming slowly between Havana and Miami

7. June 4, pass Miami going north, and then turn south again

8. June 5, pass Miami heading south

9. June 6, hovering between Miami and Havana ; 11:40 P.M. head back to Europe (Germany)

10. June 17, arrive Antwerp, 2 P.M.

ACKNOWLEDGMENTS

Individuals:

Adler-Rudel, Schalom
Adni, Daniel
Alberti, Frederic
Douglas, Sid
Elon, Amos
Erdman, Fred
Fraenkel, Heinrich

Fredericks, Joan
Harms, Gustav
Japhet, Ernest
Kochan, Lionel
Levin, Marlin
Litvinoff, Barnet
MacDonald, Malcolm
Maier, Beatrice

May, Phineas
Morse, Joan
Neter, Hans
Oppenheimer, Max
Patai, Saul
Schild, Warner
Schwab, Henry
Summerfeld, Eva

ORGANISATIONS, SOCIETIES, INSTITUTIONS

Two deserve special mention. Hapag-Lloyd, successors to the Hamburg-American Line, regretted that they could not be more helpful. At headquarters in Hamburg we were told, the "St. Louis documents are missing; we presume that during World War II things got lost." The files in Hapag's New York office were confiscated in 1941 by the F.B.I., and subsequently destroyed.

The F.B.I., too, was friendly, but they regretted their job was "to collect information, not dispense it."

On the other hand, persons named below in parentheses were particularly co-operative.

Alliance Israelite Universelle, Paris
American Friends Service Committee, Inc., Philadelphia
American Jewish Committee, Paris (Zachariah Shuster); New York (Morton Yarmon); Blaustein Library (Harry Alderman)
American Jewish Congress, New York
American Jewish Joint Distribution Committee, Inc., New York (Herbert Katzki, Rose Klepfisz)
American Joint Distribution Committee, Geneva and Paris
Association Consistoriale Israelite de Paris
Association of Jewish Refugees in Great Britain, London (W. Rosenstock)
AUFBAU, New York
Berliner Allgemeine, Duesseldorf (Lilli Marx)
British Broadcasting Corporation, London
British Museum, London and Colindale
Bund des Antifashisten VVN, Frankfurt
Central British Fund for Jewish Relief and Habilitation (Joan Stiebel)
Central Zionist Archives, Jerusalem
Centre de Documentation Israel et le Moyen Orient, Paris
Centre de Documentation Juive Contemporaine, Paris
Centre de Recherches et Etudes Historiques de World War II, Brussels (M. Bok)
Columbia University, Lehman Papers, New York (William Liebmann)
Comite d'Action Sociale Israelite de Paris
Consistoire Central Israelite de France et d'Algerie, Paris (Marice Moch)
Department of the Navy, Naval History Division, Washington, D.C. (Mrs. Lloyd Allard)
Dokumentationszentrum, Vienna (Simon Wiesenthal)
Embassy of Belgium, London
Embassy of Cuba, London
Embassy of France, London
Embassy of Israel, London and Washington
Embassy of the Netherlands, London
Embassy of the United Kingdom, Washington

Embassy of the United States, London
Embassy of West Germany, London
Federal Bureau of Investigation, Washington
Franklin D. Roosevelt Library, Hyde Park, New York
General Register and Record Office of Shipping and Seamen, Cardiff
Hapag-Lloyd A.G., Hamburg
Hebrew University, Institute of Contemporary Jewry, Jerusalem
Herzfeld and Rubin, New York
Institute for Advanced Studies in Contemporary History, Weiner Library, London (Mrs. G. Johnson)
Institute of Jewish Affairs, London
Jabotinsky Institute in Israel, Tel Aviv
Jedioth Chadoshot, Haifa
Jerusalern Post
Jewish Agency, Jerusalem
Jewish Chronicle, The, London (William Frankel)
Jewish Historical Society of England, London
Jewish Observer and Middle East Review, London
Jewish Refugees Committee, London
Jews' College Library, London
Jews Temporary Shelter, London
Joods Historisch Museum, Amsterdam
Leo Baeck Institute, London (Arnold Howell); New York (Fred Grubel); and Jerusalem
Library du Centre National des Hautes Etudes Juives, Brussels (M. Reicher)
Library of Congress, National Archives, Washington (State Department Bureau of Public Affairs Historical Office, Security Room, Modern Military Section, John Taylor)
Lloyd's Intelligence Unit, Historical Research Section, London (T. M. Dinan)
Lloyd's Register of Shipping, London
Maariv, Tel Aviv
Ministerie Van Buitenlandse Zaken', S-Gravenhage
Ministry for Foreign Affairs, Information Division, Jerusalem
Ministry of Defence, Admiralty Historical Branch, London
National Maritime Museum, London
New York Public Library, Jewish Division and Refugee Section
New York Times, The
Office of Alien Property, Department of Justice, Washington
Paris-Match
Public Records Office, London
Rijksinstituut voor Oorlogsdocumentatie, Amsterdam (L. de Jong)
Royal Institute of International Affairs, London
Service for Foreign Born, National Council of Jewish Women, New York
Stern, New York (Yvonne Luter); Hamburg (Heidi Repp-Gwlo)
United HIAS Service, New York
United Restitution Organisation, New York
United States Committee for Refugees, New York
United States Secret Service, Washington
University of Southampton
Weizmann Archives, Rehovot (Julian Meltzer)
World Jewish Congress, London
Yad Vashem Remembrance Authority, Jerusalem
YIVO Institute for Jewish Research, New York (Zosa Szajkowski)

BIBLIOGRAPHY

BOOKS:

This list is of a general nature, most of the books referring to refugees and allied matters; few refer directly or in detail to the voyage of the St.Louis.

Batista, Fulgencio, The Growth and Decline of the Cuban Republic, Devin-Adair, New York, 1964.
Bemis, Samuel Flagg, Diplomatic History of the United States, Jonathan Cape, London, 1937.
Bennet, Marion T., American Immigration Policies, Public Affairs Press, Washington, 1963.
Bentwich, Norman, They Found Refuge, Cresset Press, London, 1956.
Bermant, Chaim, The Cousinhood, Eyre and Spottiswoode, London, 1971.
Birley, Robert, Speeches and Documents in American History, Oxford University Press, London, 1942.
Black Book The, Jewish Black Book Committee, New York, 1946.
Bowle, John, Viscount Samuel, Gollancz, London, 1957.
Bullock, Alan, Hitler, Bantam, New York, 1961.
Bums, James M., Roosevelt, Harcourt, Brace and World, New York, 1956.
Cecil, Lamar, Albert Ballin, Princeton University Press, 1967.
Chandler, Edgar H.S., The High Tower of Refuge, Odhams Press, London, 1959.
Chester, Edmund A., A Sergeant Named Batista, Henry Holt & Co., New York, 1954.
Dilks, David, Sir Alexander Cadogan, Cassell, London, 1971.
Elon, Amos, The Israelis, Holt, Rinehart and Winston, New York, 1971.
Encyclopaedia Judaica, Keter Publishing House Ltd., Jerusalem, 1971.
Epstein, Isidore, Judaism, Penguin, London, 1968,.
Feingold, Henry L., The Politics of Rescue, Rutgers University Press, New Brunswick, New Jersey, 1970.
Friedman, Philip, Guide to Jewish History under Nazi Impact. YIVO Institute, New York, 1960.
Graetz, H., History of the Jews, David Nutt, London, 1891.
Grossman, Kurt R., Emigration—Geschichte der Hitler—Fluchtlinge 1933-1945, Europaische Verlagsanstalt, Frankfurt am Main, 1969.
Gunther, John, Roosevelt in Retrospect, Harper & Bros., New York, 1950.
Haas, Jacob de, The Encyclopaedia of Jewish Knowledge, W. and G. Foyle, Ltd., London, 1934.
Habe, Hans, The Mission, Harrap & Co., London, 1967.
Hausner, Gideon, Justice in Jerusalem, Nelson, London, 1967.
Heimatlos auf Hoher See, Beckerdruck, Berlin, 1949.
Herlin, Hans, Kein gelobtes Land, Nannen Verlag, Hamburg, 1961.
Herzl, Theodor (S. d'Avigdor, trans.) The Jewish State, H. Pordes, London, 1967.r
Hilberg, Raul, The Destruction of the European Jews, Quadrangle Books, Chicago, 1967.
Hirschmann, Ira, Life Line to a Promised Land, Vanguard Press, New York, 1946.
Hodgson, Stuart, Lord Halifax, Christophers, London, 1941.
Levin, Nora, The Holocaust, Thos. Y. Crowell Co., New York, 1968.
Long, Breckinridge, The War Diary of Breckinridge Long, University of Nebraska Press, Lincoln, 1966.
Morse, Arthur, While Six Million Died, Random House, New York, 1968.
Paneth, Philip, Eichmann—Technician of Death, Robert Speller & Sons, New York, 1960.
Pearlman, Moshe, The Capture and Trial of Adolph Eichmann, Simon and Schuster, New York, 1963.
Phillips, R. H., Cuba: Island of Paradox, McDowell Obolensky, New York, 1959.
Pool, David de Sola, Why I Am a Jew, Thomas Nelson & Sons, Edinburgh, 1957.
Presser, J. (Arnold Pomerans, trans.), Ashes in the Wind, Souvenir Press, London, 1968.
Proudfoot, Malcolm J., European Refugees, Faber and Faber, London, 1956.

Reitlinger, Gerald, The Final Solution, Vallentine Mitchell, London, 1968.

Ritter, Gerhard (R. T. Clark, trans.), The German Resistance, Geo. Allen and Unwin, London, 1958.

Robinson, Jacob, And the Crooked Shall Be Made Straight, Macmillan, New York, 1965

Roosevelt, Eleanor, This I Remember, Harper & Bros., New York, 1949.

Roosevelt, Franklin, The Public Papers and Addresses of Franklin D. Roosevelt, Random House, New York, 1950.

Russell, Lord, The Trial of Adolph Eichmann, Heinemann, London, 1962.

Sapir, Boris, The Jewish Community of Cuba, ITSP Press, New York, 1948.

Schröder, Gustav, Fernweh und Heimweh, Rutten and Loenig Verlag, Potsdam, 1943.

Sharf, Andrew, The British Press and Jews under Nazi Rule, Oxford University Press, London, 1964.

Shirer, William L., The Rise and Fall of the Third Reich, Secker and Warburg, London, 1960.

Simpson, John Hope, The Refugee Problem, Oxford University Press, London, 1939.

Stein, Leonard, The Balfour Declaration, Vallentine Mitchell, London, 1961.

Sykes, Christopher, Cross Roads to Israel, London, 1965.

Tartakower, Arieh, and Grossmann, Kurt, The Jewish Refugee, Institute of Jewish Affairs, New York, 1944.

Thomas, Hugh, Cuba, Eyre and Spottiswoode, London, 1971.

Uris, Leon, Exodus, Corgi, London, 1971.

Visas to Freedom: The History of HIAS, World Publishing Co., New York, 1956.

Weisgal, Meyer, So Far, Weidenfeld and Nicolson, London, 1971.

White, Lyman Cromwell, 300,000 New Americans, Harper and Bros., New York, 1956.

Wischnitzer, Mark, To Dwell in Safety, Jewish Pub. Society of America, Philadelphia, 1948.

Wise, Stephen S., Challenging Years, Putnam, New York, 1949.

Wyman, David S., Paper Walls, University of Massachusetts Press, 1969.

PERIODICALS, PAPERS, DIARIES, FILES, ETC.

This list is not comprehensive, and does not include any of the hundreds of magazines and newspapers consulted, published in America, Great Britain, Belgium, Holland, France, Germany and Cuba, some of which are mentioned specifically in the text. Reports in the British and American press were the most accurate, in particular the London and New York Times; those in the Jewish and German were almost always highly suspect; the Cuban papers were, as ever, inaccurate but entertaining.

Brochure, S.S. St. Louis. Hamburg-Amerika Linie, Hamburg, 1937.

Periodical, Contemporary Jewish Record, vol. II, no. 4, July-August, American Jewish Committee, New York, 1939.

Periodical, Central Council for Jewish Refugees, Report, London 1939.

Yearbook, American Jewish, vol. 41, pp. 387-88, Jewish Pub. Society of America, Philadelphia, 1939.

Yearbook, Willing's Press Guide, London, 1939.

Files, President Roosevelt's Official and Personal, Franklin D. Roosevelt Library, Hyde Park, N.Y. Also Morgenthau Diaries, and Files of War Refugee Board.

Files, Official and Personal Papers of James Grover McDonald, Chairman President's Advisory Committee on Political Refugees, 1938-45, Columbia University, New York.

Files, Official and Personal Papers of Herbert H., governor of New York, 1933-42, Columbia University, New York.

Files, American Jewish Joint Distribution Committee, St. Louis, New York City.

Files, YIVO, 1939, New York City.

Files, American Jewish Committee, 1939, New York City.

Files, Diplomatic Records, Group 59, no. 837.55J, National Archives, Washington.

Also Modern Military Records, Group 165

Files, Naval History, Group C-10-e, Register 22889, and Group C-lOe, Register 20764-A, Operational Archives, Washington.

Files, Foreign Office Despatches, most under file FO 371/24101, Public Record Office, London.

Pamphlet, "Paper Concerning the Treatment of German Nationals in Germany 1938-1939," His Majesty's Stationery Office, CMD 6120, 1939.

Letters, Heinz Grunstein, 1939.

Letter, Charlotte Sachs, 1939.

Letter, Herman Schliessor, 1939.

Letter, Gertrude Meijer, 1939.

Letter, Oscar Schwartz, 1939.

Letter, Hans Cramer, 1939.

Diary, Rose Bergmann, 1939.

Diary, Otto Bergmann, 1939.

Diary, Aaron Pozner, 1939.

Diary, Carl Lenneberg, 1939.

Diary, Werner Feig, 1939.

Report, St. Louis passenger committee, 1939.

Notices, posted on St. Louis, 1939.

Telegrams, to and from St. Louis, 1939.

Letter, Gustav Schröder, 1950.

Bulletin, Wiener Library, vol. IX, nos. 3-4, May-August, Refugee Internment in Britain 1939-1940, by H. Jaeger, London, 1955.

Yearbook, Leo Baeck Institute, no. 1, pp. 373-90. "A survey of Jewish Emigration from Germany," by W. Rosenstock, London, 1956.

Periodical, Yad Vashem Studies, no. 1, pp. 125-52. "The Rescue of Latin American States," by Nathan Eck, Jerusalem, 1957.

Diary, Anne Frank (B. M. Mooyaart, trans.), Vallentine Mitchell, London, 1958.

Periodical, Yad Vashem Studies, vol. II, pp. 205-18. "The Role of the Gestapo in Obstructing and Promoting Jewish Emigration" by Arthur Prinz, Jerusalem, 1958.

Bulletin, AJR Information, vol. XIX, no. 7, July, Association of Jewish Refugees, London, 1964.

Periodical, Mainstream, vol. XII, no. 3, March, Theodor Herzl Foundation, New York, 1966.

Periodical, Jewish Quarterly, vol. 14, no. 4 (52), Winter Jewish Literary Publications, London, 1967.

Booklet, "Short History of the Hamburg-Amerika Linie," Hamburg, 1968.

Atlas, Jewish History, Martin Gilbert, Weidenfeld and Nicolson, London, 1969.

Periodical, American Jewish Historical Quarterly, vol. 61, no. 2, pp. 144-56. "The St. Louis Tragedy" by Irwin Gellman, December 1971.

Yearbook, Leo Baeck Institute, no. 16, pp. 63-95. "The Immigration and Acculturation of the German Jew in the United States of America," by H. A. Strauss, London, 1971.

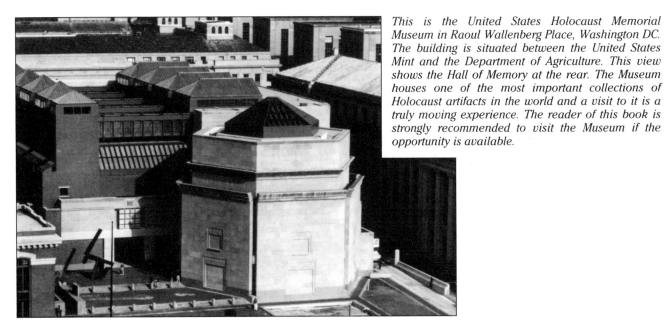

This is the United States Holocaust Memorial Museum in Raoul Wallenberg Place, Washington DC. The building is situated between the United States Mint and the Department of Agriculture. This view shows the Hall of Memory at the rear. The Museum houses one of the most important collections of Holocaust artifacts in the world and a visit to it is a truly moving experience. The reader of this book is strongly recommended to visit the Museum if the opportunity is available.

This miniature Torah is a truly memorable piece of family history. When Heinrich Glücksmann was arrested on Kristallnacht, he had it with him. We will never know how, but it was still with him as he left Buchenwald in December 1938. The Torah then travelled with him on the "St Louis", out and back, into Britain as he was admitted through Southampton, then on to the Isle of Man and Warth Mill internment camps. He carried it with him throughout his service with the British Army and on into civilian life. It stands as a symbol of one man's endurance and today is one of the proudest possessions of "Heini's"son, Edgar.